Lecture Notes in Computer Science　8966

Commenced Publication in 1973
Founding and Former Series Editors:
Gerhard Goos, Juris Hartmanis, and Jan van Leeuwen

Editorial Board

More information about this series at http://www.springer.com/series/7407

Stephen A. Jarvis · Steven A. Wright
Simon D. Hammond (Eds.)

High Performance Computing Systems

Performance Modeling, Benchmarking, and Simulation

5th International Workshop, PMBS 2014
New Orleans, LA, USA, November 16, 2014
Revised Selected Papers

 Springer

Editors
Stephen A. Jarvis
University of Warwick
Coventry
UK

Simon D. Hammond
Sandia National Laboratories CSRI
Albuquerque, New Mexico
USA

Steven A. Wright
University of Warwick
Coventry
UK

ISSN 0302-9743   ISSN 1611-3349 (electronic)
Lecture Notes in Computer Science
ISBN 978-3-319-17247-7   ISBN 978-3-319-17248-4 (eBook)
DOI 10.1007/978-3-319-17248-4

Library of Congress Control Number: 2015935420

Springer Cham Heidelberg New York Dordrecht London

Printed on acid-free paper

Springer International Publishing AG Switzerland is part of Springer Science+Business Media
(www.springer.com)

Preface

This volume contains the 14 papers that were presented at the 5th International Workshop on Performance Modeling, Benchmarking, and Simulation of High Performance Computing Systems (PMBS 2014), which was held as part of the 26th ACM/IEEE International Conference for High Performance Computing, Networking, Storage, and Analysis (SC 2014) at the Ernest N. Morial Convention Centre in New Orleans during November 16–21, 2014.

The SC conference series is the premier international forum for high-performance computing, networking, storage, and analysis. The conference is unique in that it hosts a wide range of international participants from academia, national laboratories, and industry; this year's conference attracted over 10,000 attendees and featured over 350 exhibitors in the industry's largest HPC technology fair.

This year's conference was themed *HPC Matters*, recognizing the immense impact that high-performance computing has on our lives. Specifically, SC 2014 was focused not only on the very visible way in which HPC is changing the world around us, but also on how HPC is improving every aspect of our lives in the most unexpected ways.

SC offers a vibrant technical program, which includes technical papers, tutorials in advanced areas, Birds of a Feather sessions (BoFs), panel debates, a doctoral showcase, and a number of technical workshops in specialist areas (of which PMBS is one).

The focus of the PMBS 2014 workshop was comparing high-performance computing systems through performance modeling, benchmarking, or the use of tools such as simulators. We were particularly interested in receiving research papers which reported the ability to measure and make tradeoffs in hardware/software co-design to improve sustained application performance. We were also keen to capture the assessment of future systems, for example, through work that ensured continued application scalability through peta- and exa-scale systems.

The aim of the PMBS 2014 workshop was to bring together researchers from industry, national laboratories, and academia, who were concerned with the qualitative and quantitative evaluation and modeling of high-performance computing systems. Authors were invited to submit novel research in all areas of performance modeling, benchmarking, and simulation, and we welcomed research that combined novel theory and practice. We also expressed an interest in submissions that included analysis of power consumption and reliability, and were receptive to performance modeling research that made use of analytical methods as well as those based on tracing tools and simulators.

Technical submissions were encouraged in areas including: performance modeling and analysis of applications and high-performance computing systems; novel techniques and tools for performance evaluation and prediction; advanced simulation techniques and tools; micro-benchmarking, application benchmarking, and tracing; performance-driven code optimization and scalability analysis; verification and validation of performance models; benchmarking and performance analysis of novel hardware; performance concerns in software/hardware co-design; tuning and auto-tuning of HPC applications and algorithms; benchmark suites and proxy apps; performance visualization; real-world case studies; studies of novel hardware such as Intel Xeon Phi coprocessor technology, NVIDIA Kepler GPUs, and AMD Fusion APU.

PMBS 2014

We received an excellent number of submissions for this year's workshop. As a result of this we were able to be very selective in those papers that were chosen; 14 full papers were accepted from a total of 53 submissions (26%). The resulting papers show worldwide programs of research committed to understanding application and architecture performance to enable peta-scale computational science.

Contributors to the workshop included Argonne National Laboratory, the Barcelona Supercomputing Center, IBM, Inria, Jülich Supercomputing Centre, Lawrence Berkeley National Laboratory, Lawrence Livermore National Laboratory, NVIDIA, Sandia National Laboratories, Technische Universität Dresden, the University of Illinois, the University of Oxford, and the University of Stuttgart, among many others.

Several of the papers are concerned with *Performance Benchmarking and Optimization*, see Section A. The paper by Hormozd Gahvari et al. explores the use of a Cray XC30 system using a Dragonfly interconnect topology for running an Algebraic Multigrid solver application. Andrew V. Adinetz et al. present initial benchmarking results for IBM's new POWER8 architecture. The paper by Guido Juckeland et al. outlines a new SPEC benchmark suite specifically designed for accelerator architectures. Everett Phillips and Massimiliano Fatica outline the development of a CUDA implementation of the HPCG benchmark – a benchmark that is growing in popularity due to LINPACK's well-documented shortcomings. Gihan Mudalige et al. present the porting of the CloverLeaf hydrodynamics application, from Sandia National Laboratories' Mantevo proxy app suite, to the OPS high-level abstraction framework being developed at the University of Oxford.

Section B of the proceedings collates papers concerned with *Performance Analysis and Prediction*. Waleed Alkohlani and colleagues utilize dynamic binary instrumentation in order to identify characteristics that affect an applications performance. Yu Jung Lo et al. build upon previous work with the Roofline model to develop a toolkit for auto-generating Roofline models, including extending these models to accelerator architectures. Raúl de la Cruz et al. document the development of a performance model for Intel's Xeon Phi coprocessor architecture with a particular focus on stencil computations. A performance model for the HPCG benchmark is presented by Vladimir Marjanović et al. showing a strong correlation between memory bandwidth and HPCG performance. Elmar Peise et al. build performance models for tensor contraction calculations. Their models allow the most efficient algorithm to be chosen ahead of runtime using the results from a set of micro-benchmarks to inform algorithm choice.

The final section of the proceedings, Section C, is concerned with *Power, Energy, and Checkpointing*. Anne Benoit et al. present a general-purpose model to handle both fail-stop and silent errors, utilizing this model to determine the optimal checkpoint and verification period under a variety of different execution scenarios. The work by Shane Snyder et al. explores the use of an infection-style group membership protocol for managing faults in HPC storage systems. Prasanna Balaprakash et al. build upon work presented at the previous PMBS workshop showing the tradeoffs that exist between performance and energy consumption when using multilevel checkpointing libraries. The final paper by Balaji Subramaniam and Wu-chun Feng deals with the energy consumption for distributed NoSQL data stores under load. Specifically, they analyze the use of three resource provisioning techniques, demonstrating a significant power saving when both power and performance are considered as part of the provisioning algorithm.

Acknowledgments

The PMBS 2014 workshop was extremely well attended and we thank the participants for the lively discussion and positive feedback received throughout the workshop. We hope to be able to repeat this success in future years.

The SC conference series is sponsored by the IEEE Computer Society and the ACM (Association for Computing Machinery). We are extremely grateful for the support we received from the SC 2014 Steering Committee, and in particular from Torsten Hoefler and Martin Swany, the SC 2014 Workshop Chairs.

The PMBS 2014 workshop was only possible thanks to significant input from AWE in the UK, and from Sandia National Laboratories and the Lawrence Livermore National Laboratory in the USA. We acknowledge the support of the AWE Technical Outreach Programme (project CDK0724) and the Royal Society Industry Fellowship scheme (IF090020).

We are also grateful to LNCS for their support, and to Alfred Hofmann and Anna Kramer for assisting with the production of this issue.

November 2014   Stephen A. Jarvis
                                                 Steven A. Wright
                                                 Simon D. Hammond

Organization

Program Committee

Workshop Chairs

Stephen A. Jarvis   University of Warwick, UK
Steven A. Wright   University of Warwick, UK
Simon D. Hammond   Sandia National Laboratories (NM), USA

Workshop Technical Program Committee

Pavan Balaji   Argonne National Laboratory, USA
Patrick Carribault   CEA, France
Todd Gamblin   Lawrence Livermore National Laboratory, USA
Jeff Hammond   Intel, USA
Andrew Jones   NAG Ltd, UK
Darren Kerbyson   Pacific Northwest National Laboratory, USA
Michael Klemm   Intel, Germany
David Lecomber   Allinea Software Ltd, UK
Branden J. Moore   Sandia National Laboratories, USA
John Pennycook   Intel, UK
Karthik Raman   Intel Corporation, USA
Rolf Riesen   IBM Research, Dublin, Ireland
Arun Rodrigues   Sandia National Laboratories (NM), USA
Ali Saidi   ARM Research and Development, USA
Matthew Street   Rolls-Royce plc, UK
Christian Trott   Sandia National Laboratories (NM), USA
Ash Vadgama   UK Atomic Weapons Establishment, UK
Meghan Wingate-McClelland   Samsung/Xyratex, USA
Yunquan Zhang   Chinese Academy of Sciences, China

Contents

Section C: Power, Energy and Checkpointing

Section A: Performance Benchmarking and Optimisation

Algebraic Multigrid on a Dragonfly Network: First Experiences on a Cray XC30

Hormozd Gahvari[1]([✉]), William Gropp[2], Kirk E. Jordan[3], Martin Schulz[1], and Ulrike Meier Yang[1]

[1] Lawrence Livermore National Laboratory, Livermore, CA 94551, USA
{gahvari1,schulzm,umyang}@llnl.gov
[2] University of Illinois at Urbana-Champaign, Urbana, IL 61801, USA
wgropp@illinois.edu
[3] IBM TJ Watson Research Center, Cambridge, MA 02142, USA
kjordan@us.ibm.com

Abstract. The Cray XC30 represents the first appearance of the dragonfly interconnect topology in a product from a major HPC vendor. The question of how well applications perform on such a machine naturally arises. We consider the performance of an algebraic multigrid solver on an XC30 and develop a performance model for its solve cycle. We use this model to both analyze its performance and guide data redistribution at runtime aimed at improving it by trading messages for increased computation. The performance modeling results demonstrate the ability of the dragonfly interconnect to avoid network contention, but speedups when using the redistribution scheme were enough to raise questions about the ability of the dragonfly topology to handle very communication-intensive applications.

1 Introduction

The network topology of an HPC system has a critical impact on the performance of parallel applications. In recent years, vendors have experimented with a wide range of topologies. A topology that has found wide interest is the dragonfly topology [18]. Introduced several years ago, it has seen its first major deployment in the Cray XC30. As more XC30s and other machines that make use of dragonfly interconnects are deployed, the question of application performance on these machines becomes paramount. How suited is the dragonfly topology for particular applications? What are its advantages and disadvantages? What are its future prospects as machines get even larger?

This paper examines one application, algebraic multigrid (AMG), on an XC30, to see how well it performs on this topology and get a first look at potential hazards it and other applications would face on a dragonfly machine. AMG is a popular solver for large, sparse linear systems of equations with many scientific and engineering applications. It is very attractive for HPC owing to ideal computational complexity, but faces challenges on emerging parallel machines [3,4] that served as motivation for a recent in-depth study [11] into its performance

© Springer International Publishing Switzerland 2015
S.A. Jarvis et al. (Eds.): PMBS 2014, LNCS 8966, pp. 3–23, 2015.
DOI: 10.1007/978-3-319-17248-4_1

and ways to improve it. We present results from that study on modeling the performance of the AMG solve cycle on an XC30 and using the performance model to improve its performance on that architecture.

Our specific contributions are as follows:

- We successfully extend a performance model that previously covered fat-tree and torus interconnects to a dragonfly interconnect.
- We use that model at runtime to guide data redistribution within the AMG solve cycle to improve its performance on a dragonfly machine.
- We point out an important hazard faced by the dragonfly interconnect in a real-world scenario.

The model predicts cycle times to accuracies mostly between 85 and 93 percent in our experiments, and covers both all-MPI and hybrid MPI/OpenMP programming models. The data redistribution involves having processes combine data, trading messages they would send amongst themselves for increased computation. Resulting speedups range from modest to over 2x overall, with the large speedups occurring during the communication-heavy setup phase of AMG or when solving a communication-intense linear elasticity problem. This occurs despite the model rating the XC30 interconnect as being effective overall at avoiding network contention, leading to questions about the ability of the dragonfly interconnect when tasked with handling a large number of messages.

2   Dragonfly Networks

The general principle behind dragonfly interconnects is to keep the minimum hop distance low like a fat-tree, while also providing high bandwidth between nodes and low network contention at less cost [18]. This is accomplished through a generalized two-level design. The core of the network is formed by a number of groups of routers, with each group connected by optical cables to every other group. The routers in each individual group have their own specific topology. This is diagrammed in Fig. 1.

2.1   Implementation on the Cray XC30

The dragonfly implementation on the XC30 is called the Aries interconnect [2]. In the Aries interconnect, the routers in each group are arranged as rows and columns of a rectangle, with all-to-all links across each row and column but not diagonally. There are 16 routers in the horizontal dimension and 6 in the vertical dimension, for a total of 96 routers per group. Four nodes are connected to each router, bringing the number of nodes per group to 384. This is illustrated in Fig. 2.

2.2   Target System

We ran our experiments on Eos, an XC30 at Oak Ridge National Laboratory. Eos consists of 744 compute nodes with two eight-core 2.6 GHz Intel Xeon E5-2670 processors per node. The hardware bandwidth between nodes is 16 GB/s.

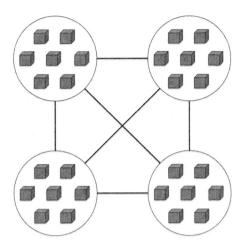

Fig. 1. Dragonfly network basics. Routers (boxes) are in groups (circled), with each group connected to every other group. The routers within groups can be connected in many different ways; no particular topology is shown here.

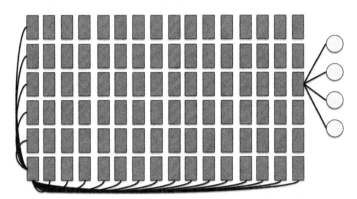

Fig. 2. Group topology in the Aries network, with 16 routers in the horizontal dimension and 6 in the vertical dimension. Each router is connected to every other router in its row and column, which is shown for the router in the lower left-hand corner. Four nodes are connected to each router, which is shown for one of the routers in the rightmost column.

All experiments save for those in Sect. 6.2 use the Intel compiler, version 13.1.3. The MPI implementation is Cray's native MPI. Eos also features simultaneous multithreading (SMT) in the form of Intel Hyper-Threading [19]. This allows for users to run their jobs on up to two times the number of physical cores. However, we do not consider it here, as we have yet to have developed a performance model for this form of SMT.

3 Algebraic Multigrid

The application we focus on in our study is algebraic multigrid (AMG). It is one of the multigrid solvers, which are best known for having a computational cost linear in the number of unknowns being solved. This is very attractive for HPC, where the goal is to solve large problems, and it is therefore of great interest to study the performance of multigrid methods on HPC platforms. Multigrid methods operate by performing some of the work on smaller "coarse grid" problems instead of concentrating it all on the original "fine grid" problem. On each grid, a smoother, typically a simple iterative method like Jacobi or Gauss-Seidel, is applied. Afterwards, a correction is typically solved for on the next coarsest grid, which except for the very coarsest grid involves solving another coarse grid problem. This correction is then applied to accelerate the solution process. The coarsest grid is often solved directly. This particular order of progression through grids, from finest to coarsest and back to finest, is called a V-cycle, which is the most basic multigrid cycle and the one we consider here.

AMG is a means of leveraging multigrid, which was originally developed to solve problems on structured grids, to solve problems with no explicit grid structure, where all that is known is a sparse linear system $A^{(0)}u^{(0)} = f^{(0)}$. This requires AMG to consist of two phases, setup and solve, which are illustrated in Fig. 3. The setup phase involves selecting the variables that will remain on each coarser grid and defining the restriction ($R^{(m)}$) and interpolation ($P^{(m)}$) operators that control the transfer of data between levels. There are a number of algorithms for doing this, and they can be quite complicated. For our experiments, we use the AMG code BoomerAMG [16] in the hypre software library [17] We use HMIS coarsening [7] with extended+i interpolation [6] truncated to at most 4 coefficients per row and aggressive coarsening with multipass interpolation [22] on the finest level. Each coarse grid operator $A^{(m+1)}$ is formed by computing the triple matrix product $R^{(m)}A^{(m)}P^{(m)}$. This operation, particularly for unstructured problems, leads to increasing matrix density on coarse grids, which in turn results in an increasing number of messages being sent among an increasing number of communication partners. These have resulted in substantial challenges to performance and scalability on some machines [3,4], even when using advanced coarsening and interpolation schemes like the ones we use in our experiments, and serve as added motivation for studying AMG on the XC30.

In the solve phase, the primary operations are the smoothing operator and matrix-vector multiplication to form r^m and perform restriction and interpolation. In our experiments, we use hybrid Gauss-Seidel as the smoother. Hybrid Gauss-Seidel uses the sequential Gauss-Seidel algorithm to compute local data within process boundaries, but uses Jacobi smoothing across process boundaries to preserve parallelism. Applying this smoother is a very similar operation to matrix-vector multiplication.

Sparse matrices in BoomerAMG are stored in the ParCSR data structure. A matrix A is partitioned by rows into matrices A_k, $k = 0, 1, \ldots, P - 1$, where P is the number of MPI processes. Each matrix A_k is stored locally as a pair

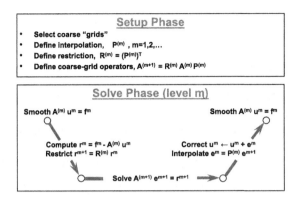

Fig. 3. Setup and solve phase of AMG.

of CSR (compressed sparse row) matrices D_k and O_k. D_k contains all entries of A_k with column indices that point to rows stored locally on process k, and O_k contains the remaining entries. Matrix-vector multiplication Ax or smoothing requires computing $A_k x = D_k x^D + O_k x^O$ on each process, where x^D is the portion of x stored locally and x^O is the portion that needs to be sent from other processes. More detail can be found in [9].

The ability to use a shared memory programming model is provided in BoomerAMG in the form of OpenMP parallelization within MPI processes. This is done using `parallel for` constructs at the loop level, which spawn a number of threads that can each execute a portion of the loop being parallelized. Static scheduling is used, which means the work is divided equally among the threads before the loop starts. The loops parallelized in this fashion are the ones that perform smoother application, matrix-vector multiplication, and the triple matrix product.

4   Performance Model

In previous work [12–14], we developed an accurate performance model for AMG and validated it on a wide range of platforms and network topologies, including Linux clusters, prior Cray machines, and IBM Blue Gene systems. We now expand the model to the dragonfly interconnect and contrast the results.

4.1   Model Specifics

Our model is based on the simple α-β model for interprocessor communication. The time to send a message consisting of n double precision floating-point values is given by

$$T_{\text{send}} = \alpha + n\beta,$$

where α is the communication startup time, and β is the per value send cost. We model computation time by multiplying the number of floating-point operations by a computation rate t_i. We allow this to vary with each level i in the multigrid hierarchy because the operations in an AMG cycle are either sparse matrix-vector multiplication or a smoother application, which is a similar operation. An in-depth study [10] found that the computation time for sparse matrix-vector multiplication varies with the size and density of the matrix, and the operators in an AMG hierarchy have varying sizes and densities. We do not consider the overlap of communication and computation, as there is very little room for this on the communication-intensive coarse grid problems on which our concerns our focused.

We treat the AMG cycle level-by-level. If there are L levels, numbered 0 to $L-1$, the total cycle time is given by

$$T_{\text{cycle}}^{AMG} = \sum_{i=0}^{L-1} T_{\text{cycle}}^i,$$

where $T^i{}_{\text{cycle}}$ is the amount of time spent at level i of the cycle. This is in turn broken down into component steps, diagrammed in Fig. 4, which we write as

$$T_{\text{cycle}}^i = T_{\text{smooth}}^i + T_{\text{restrict}}^i + T_{\text{interp}}^i.$$

Smoothing and residual formation, which are combined into $T^i{}_{\text{smooth}}$, are treated as matrix-vector multiplication with the solve operator. Interpolation is treated as matrix-vector multiplication with the interpolation operator. Restriction is treated as matrix-vector multiplication with the restriction operator, which for the purposes of our experiments is the transpose of the interpolation operator.

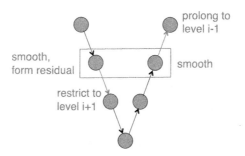

Fig. 4. Fundamental operations at each level of an AMG V-cycle.

To enable us to write expressions for each component operation, we define the following terms to cover different components of the operators that form the multigrid hierarchy:

- P – total number of processes.
- C_i – number of unknowns on grid level i.

- $s_i, \hat{s}_i$ – average number of nonzero entries per row in the level i solve and interpolation operators, respectively.
- $p_i, \hat{p}_i$ – maximum number of sends over all processes in the level i solve and interpolation operators, respectively.
- $n_i, \hat{n}_i$ – maximum number of elements sent over all processes in the level i solve and interpolation operators, respectively.

We assume one smoothing step before restriction and one smoothing step after interpolation, which is the default in BoomerAMG. The time spent smoothing on level i is given by

$$T^i_{\text{smooth}} = 6\frac{C_i}{P}s_it_i + 3(p_i\alpha + n_i\beta).$$

The time spent restricting from level i to level $i+1$ is given by

$$T^i_{\text{restrict}} = \begin{cases} 2\frac{C_{i+1}}{P}\hat{s}_it_i + \hat{p}_i\alpha + \hat{n}_i\beta & \text{if } i < L-1 \\ 0 & \text{if } i = L-1. \end{cases}$$

The time spent interpolating from level i to level $i-1$ is given by

$$T^i_{\text{interp}} = \begin{cases} 0 & \text{if } i = 0 \\ 2\frac{C_{i-1}}{P}\hat{s}_{i-1}t_i + \hat{p}_{i-1}\alpha + \hat{n}_{i-1}\beta & \text{if } i > 0. \end{cases}$$

To this baseline, we add terms and penalties to cover phenomena seen in practice that the α-β model alone does not cover. One such phenomenon is communication distance. While it is assumed that the hop count has a very small effect on communication time, we cannot assume this on coarse grid problems in AMG where many messages are being sent at once. The further a message has to travel, the more likely it is to run into delays from conflicts with other messages. To take this into account, we introduce a communication distance term γ that represents the delay per hop, changing the model by replacing α with

$$\alpha(h) = \alpha(h_m) + (h - h_m)\gamma,$$

where h is the number of hops a message travels, and h_m is the smallest possible number of hops a message can travel in the network.

Another issue is limited bandwidth, of which we consider two sources. One is the inability to make full use of the hardware. The peak hardware bandwidth is rarely achieved even under ideal conditions, let alone the non-ideal conditions under which applications usually run. The other source of limited bandwidth is network contention from messages sharing links. Let B_{max} be the peak aggregate per-node hardware bandwidth, and B be the measured bandwidth corresponding to β. Let m be the total number of messages being sent, and l be the number of network links available. Then we multiply β by the sum $\frac{B_{\text{max}}}{B} + \frac{m}{l}$ to take both of these factors into account. The limited hardware bandwidth penalty functions as a baseline, with link contention becoming the dominant factor when it is significant (it might not be significant in certain problems on which the fine grids do not feature much communication).

Multicore nodes are another potential source of difficulties. If the interconnect is not suited to handle message passing traffic from many cores at once, then there can be contention in accessing the interconnect and contention at each hop when routing messages. To capture these effects, we multiply either or both of the terms $\alpha(h_m)$ and γ described earlier by $\left\lceil t\frac{P_i}{P} \right\rceil$, where t is the number of MPI tasks per node, and P_i is the number of active processes on level i. Active processes mean ones that still have unknowns in their domains on coarse grids and thus have not "dropped out."

We treat hybrid MPI/OpenMP as follows. The message counts for MPI communication are assumed to change with the number of processes. What we modify explicitly is the computation term t_i. Let b_j be the available memory bandwidth per thread for j threads. We then multiply t_i by $\frac{b_1}{b_j}$. We do this to take into account limited memory bandwidth from threads contending to access memory shared by multiple cores. We expect a slowdown here versus the all-MPI case because there is no longer a definite partitioning of memory when using threads. Our original hybrid/OpenMP model also had a penalty to cover slowdowns from threads being migrated across cores that reside on different sockets [13]; we do not consider this here as it can be readily mitigated by pinning threads to specific cores.

4.2   Adaptation to Dragonfly Networks

The model as presented above is straightforward to adapt to dragonfly networks. It boils down to how to best determine the needed machine parameters. Most of them are readily determined from benchmark measurements, as was the case with other machines. α and β were measured using the latency-bandwidth benchmark in the HPC Challenge suite [8]. α was set to the best reported latency, and β was set to the value corresponding to the best reported bandwidth, which for a reported bandwidth of B bytes per second is $\frac{8}{B}$ for sending double precision floating point data. The t_i terms were measured by performing serial sparse matrix-vector multiplications using the operators for the test problem we used when validating the model; this is further described in Sect. 5.1. The values for b_j needed to evaluate the penalty for hybrid MPI/OpenMP were taken by using the STREAM Triad benchmark [20] and dividing by the number of threads being used.

We determined γ from the measured values of α and β. Starting with the formulation of α as a function of the number of hops h

$$\alpha(h) = \alpha(h_m) + \gamma(h - h_m),$$

we set $\alpha(h_m)$ to be the measured value of α. If D is the diameter of the network, the maximum latency possible is

$$\alpha(D) = \alpha(h_m) + \gamma(D - h_m).$$

We use the maximum latency reported by the same benchmark we used to measure α as a value for $\alpha(D)$. Then

$$\gamma = \frac{\alpha(D) - \alpha(h_m)}{D - h_m}.$$

For dragonfly interconnects, we set h_m to 2 (reflecting the case where two nodes connected to the same router are communicating). We charge the distance D to each message sent, analogous to the role the height of the tree played for fat-tree interconnects in [12,13]. Though pessimistic, this distance is charged to reflect the potential impact of routing delays. When counting the number of links available to a message for determining the link contention portion of the limited bandwidth penalty, we use the midpoint of the fewest possible (all the nodes in one group are filled before moving onto the next one) and most possible (each node is in a new group until all groups are in use), as there is no simple geometric formula like there is with a mesh or torus network.

To make the numbers specific to the Aries interconnect, we set D equal to 7; the maximum shortest path between two nodes involves traversing one link to get to the routers in that node's group, two links to find an available connection to reach the next group (not all routers in the Aries interconnect are connected to the optical network), one link to reach that group, two more links to traverse the routers, and then one last link to reach the target node. When counting links for the limited bandwidth penalty, we treat the optical links between groups as four links because they have four times the bandwidth. If there are N nodes in use, and G groups in the network, then the minimum possible number of available links is

$$N + 170 \left\lceil \frac{N}{384} \right\rceil + 4\min\left\{ \left\lfloor \frac{N}{384} \right\rfloor, \frac{G(G-1)}{2} \right\},$$

and the maximum possible number of available links is

$$N + 170\min\{N, G\} + 4\min\left\{ N - 1, \frac{G(G-1)}{2} \right\}.$$

In both expressions, the first term accounts for the number of links connecting nodes to routers. The second accounts for the number of router-to-router links in groups, which number $16 \cdot 5 + 6 \cdot 15 = 170$ per group. The third accounts for the number of optical links.

5 Model Validation

5.1 Experimental Setup

For each of our experiments on Eos, the Cray XC30 we are evaluating, we ran 10 AMG solve cycles and measured the amount of time spent in each level, dividing by 10 to get average times spent at each level. For our test problem, we used a

3D 7-point Laplace problem on a cube with $50 \times 50 \times 25$ points per core, as was done in past experiments used to validate this model on other machines [12–14]. The mapping of MPI tasks to nodes was the default block mapping, in which each node is filled with MPI tasks before moving onto the next one. We report results on 1024 and 8192 cores.

Machine parameters for Eos are given in Table 1. How we obtained the values for α, β, and γ was described in Sect. 4.2. We measured t_i by measuring the time for 10 sparse matrix-vector multiplies using the local portion of the solve operator A_i on each level in the MPI-only case and dividing the largest time over all the processes by the number of floating point operations. For $i \geq 3$, we used the value measured for t_2. Per-thread memory bandwidths for the hybrid MPI/OpenMP penalty are in Table 2.

Table 1. Measured machine parameters on Eos.

Parameter	α	β	γ	t_0	t_1	t_2
Value	0.238 μs	0.858 ns	0.416 μs	1.59 ns	0.806 ns	0.545 ns

Table 2. Per thread memory bandwidths on Eos.

No. Threads	1	2	4	8	16
Bandwidth (MB/s)	11106	5335.5	2755.0	1374.8	678.56

5.2   Results

To help us understand the XC30 interconnect, we compared the measured AMG cycle time at each level with what the performance model would predict, with the different penalties turned on and off. Results are plotted in Fig. 5 for the all-MPI case and in Fig. 6 for the hybrid MPI/OpenMP case. In each plot, the measured cycle time at each level is shown as a solid black line. Six different model scenarios are also shown as colored lines with markers, with the best fit solid and the others dotted:

1. Baseline model *(α-β Model)*.
2. Baseline model plus distance penalty *(α-β-γ Model)*.
3. Baseline model plus distance penalty and bandwidth penalty on β *(β Penalty)*.
4. Baseline model plus distance penalty, bandwidth penalty on β, and multicore penalty on α *(α,β Penalties)*.
5. Baseline model plus distance penalty, bandwidth penalty on β, and multicore penalty on γ *(β,γ Penalties)*.
6. Baseline model plus distance penalty, bandwidth penalty on β, and multicore penalties on α and γ *(α,β,γ Penalties)*.

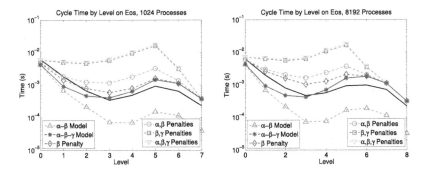

Fig. 5. Measured and modeled AMG cycle time by level on Eos using 1024 (left) and 8192 (right) cores, running all-MPI.

We did not allow the best fit to be a model with more penalties than the best fit for a configuration with more MPI tasks per node. We enforced this constraint because the penalties listed above deal specifically with issues resulting from there being many messages in the network, so it would not make sense for there to be a greater number of penalties when there are fewer MPI tasks per node. All levels are plotted except for the coarsest level. It is not shown because it was solved directly using Gaussian Elimination instead of smoothing.

In all cases, the best fit model was the baseline model plus only the distance penalty. We chose this over the model which also had the bandwidth penalty because the latter was overly pessimistic on 8192 cores in the all-MPI case but not so for 1024 cores. Given that using 8192 cores on Eos involves using 69 % of the machine while using 1024 cores on Eos involves using only 9 % of it, including limited bandwidth from link contention would, if it were a big factor, more accurately capture the performance when using more of the machine. Overall cycle time prediction accuracies are in Table 3. They are almost all at least 85 %, and in some cases above 90 %.

From these results, it is clear that the Aries interconnect does a good job avoiding contention, which is one of the goals of the dragonfly topology [18]. In fact, it is better at doing so in terms of penalty scenarios than any other interconnect on which the performance model has been tested [12–14]. There is also not much slowdown in cycle time when going from 1024 to 8192 cores. However, even with these key positives, there is still a lot of room for improvement. In spite of the lack of contention penalties, the baseline α-β model predicted much better performance than what was actually observed. The γ term was actually larger than the α term; the only other machines on which we observed this were a pair of fat-tree machines on which performance on coarse grids and scalability were very poor [12]. Hybrid MPI/OpenMP performance was also disappointing, highlighted by more rapid deterioration in the available memory bandwidth per thread than was seen in other machines on which the hybrid model was tested [11].

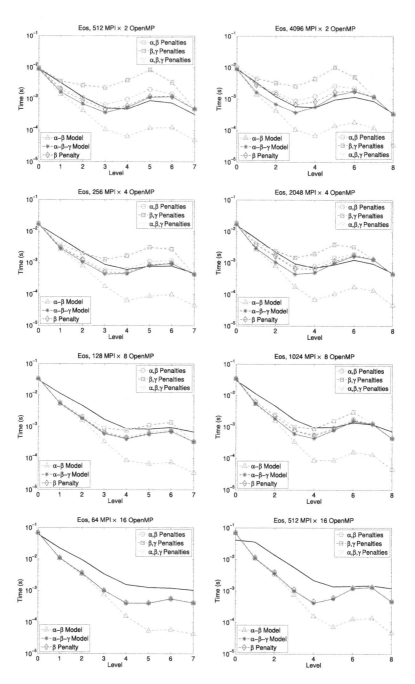

Fig. 6. Measured and modeled AMG cycle time by level on Eos using 1024 (left column) and 8192 (right column) cores, running hybrid MPI/OpenMP. The plot titles show the total number of MPI tasks and the number of OpenMP threads per MPI task.

Table 3. Measured and modeled AMG cycle times and cycle time prediction accuracies on Eos, organized by on-node MPI × OpenMP mix.

Mix	1024 Cores			8192 Cores		
	Modeled	Measured	Accuracy	Modeled	Measured	Accuracy
16×1	9.75 ms	11.3 ms	86.0 %	11.7 ms	13.0 ms	90.4 %
8×2	14.9 ms	16.3 ms	91.3 %	16.8 ms	18.1 ms	92.8 %
4×4	24.2 ms	27.6 ms	87.4 %	26.5 ms	29.7 ms	89.2 %
2×8	44.2 ms	51.8 ms	85.3 %	46.7 ms	53.9 ms	86.6 %
1×16	86.4 ms	104 ms	83.4 %	88.4 ms	104 ms	85.9 %

6   Model-Guided Performance Improvements

We have observed that, even with low network contention, there is still much room for improvement in the performance of AMG on Eos. We will now turn to a systematic means of improving the performance, driven by the performance model, that will also enable us to gain further insight into the machine.

6.1   Approach

We build on earlier work [15] that used a performance model to drive data redistribution in AMG. This work tested a method which reduced the number of messages sent between processes on coarse grids by having certain groups of processes combine their data and redundantly store it amongst themselves. The method was driven by applying the performance model we described in Sect. 4 during the setup phase before performing each coarsening step to make a decision on whether to redistribute or not. Once redistribution was performed, the remaining levels of the setup phase, and the corresponding level and all coarser ones in the solve phase, were performed using the redistributed operators. Processes would then only communicate with only a handful of other processes, rather than potentially hundreds of them, resulting in speedups often exceeding 2x on an Opteron cluster on which performance and scalability problems had been observed in the past. We use a similar approach with some differences; we will explain as we describe our approach and make note of the differences as they come up.

What we specifically need from the performance model are two quantities, which we call T^i_{switch} and T^i_{noswitch}. The former represents the time spent at level i in the AMG cycle if we perform redistribution, and the latter represents the time spent at that level if we do not. We compute these at each level $i > 0$, and perform redistribution on the first level for which $T^i_{\text{switch}} < T^i_{\text{noswitch}}$. We assume the network parameters α, β, and γ are available to us, along with the particular combination of penalties that is the best match to the overall performance on the machine. The other information we need is problem dependent. Much of it, however, is already available to us. The needed communication and computation counts for the solve operator can be obtained from the ParCSR data structure. The interpolation operator is not available; forming it would require actually performing coarsening, and we want to decide on redistribution before doing that, so we instead approximate both restriction and interpolation with matrix-vector multiplication using the solve operator. This enables us to write an expression for T^i_{noswitch} in terms of the baseline model:

$$T^i_{\text{noswitch}} = 10\frac{C_i}{P}s_it_i + 5(p_i\alpha + n_i\beta)$$

We still need a value for t_i, which we measure on all active processes like we described in Sect. 5.1. However, instead of stopping after measuring t_2, we stop when the measured value for t_i is greater than the measured value for t_{i-1}. This happens when processes are close to running out of data. Then their t_i measurements are measuring primarily loop overhead instead of computation. t_i is expected to decrease as i increases because the time per floating-point operation has been observed to decrease with the trend of decreasing matrix dimension and increasing matrix density [10] that is seen when progressing from fine to coarse in AMG. Once we stop measuring, we set $t_i = t_{i-1}$ and $t_j = t_{i-1}$ for all levels $j > i$. A question arises of what to do in the hybrid MPI/OpenMP case, which was not covered in [15]. What we do here is use the same measurement scheme we just described, which measures t_i within MPI processes. The measured value will implicitly take the further division of labor into account.

We now turn to computing T^i_{switch}. An expression for this requires both an expression for collective communication used to perform the data redistribution itself and an expression for matrix-vector multiplication with the redistributed solve operator. Reference [15] used an all-gather operation to distribute data redundantly among processes that combined data. We instead use nonredundant data redistribution, where groups of processes combine their data but only one process stores the combined data. The reason for this is that the use of fully redundant redistribution creates many new MPI communicators, and at scale there would be enough to run into a memory-based or implementation-based upper limit on the number of new communicators [5]. Performing nonredundant redistribution in the solve cycle involves two gather operations to combine data from the solution vector and the right-hand side, and one scatter operation when it is time to transfer the result from the levels treated using the redistributed operators to the finer grids that do not use them.

Assuming that C groups of processes combine their data over a binary tree, we get a total of $\lceil \log_2 \frac{P_i}{C} \rceil$ sends for each collective operation. The gather operations involve sends of approximately size $\frac{C_i}{2C}, \frac{C_i}{4C}, \frac{C_i}{8C}, \ldots$ to combine the data, which we charge as the geometric sum $\frac{C_i}{C}\left(\frac{1}{1-\frac{1}{2}} - 1\right) = \frac{C_i}{C}$ units of data sent. The scatter operation is assumed to send approximately $\frac{C_i}{C}\lceil \log_2 \frac{P_i}{C} \rceil$ units of data per send. In terms of the baseline model, the time spent in collective operations is then

$$T^i_{\text{collective}} = 3\left\lceil \log_2 \frac{P_i}{C} \right\rceil \alpha + \frac{C_i}{C}\left(2 + \left\lceil \log_2 \frac{P_i}{C} \right\rceil\right)\beta.$$

The work in [15] sought to keep data movement on-node through a combination of a cyclic mapping of MPI tasks to nodes and having groups of $\frac{P}{C}$ adjacent MPI ranks combine their data. The machine it considered, however, exhibited much better on-node MPI performance than off-node MPI performance [4]. Running on a newer machine, and lacking an on-node performance model, we do not consider localizing data movement. We instead form an MPI communicator out of the processes that still have data and form groups consisting of $\frac{P_i}{C}$ adjacent MPI ranks. If C does not evenly divide P_i, then the first $P_i \mod C$ groups have $\lceil \frac{P_i}{C} \rceil$ processes, and the rest have $\lfloor \frac{P_i}{C} \rfloor$ processes.

We now derive an expression for the amount of time matrix-vector multiplication with the redistributed operator would take. We assume equal division of the gathered data, and equal division of the amount of data sent per message among the total number of sends in the nonredistributed operator. We also assume the number of groups of processes that combine data is less than the largest number of messages a process would send before redistribution, i.e., we are capping the number of communication partners a process could have at $C - 1 < p_i$, and we assume this number of communication partners for each process. The cost for matrix-vector multiplication using the redistributed operator then becomes, in terms of the baseline model,

$$T^i_{\text{new\_matvec}} = 2\frac{C_i}{C} s_i t_i + (C - 1)\left(\alpha + \frac{n_i}{p_i}\beta\right).$$

Treating the operations at level i in the AMG solve cycle as five matrix-vector multiplications with the solve operator, as we did for the case with no redistribution, gives us the expression

$$T^i_{\text{switch}} = 5T^i_{\text{new\_matvec}} + T^i_{\text{collective}}$$

for the predicted time at level i when performing redistribution.

We note here that redistribution, by increasing the amount of data per process, will likely result in a different value for t_i that would ideally be used when computing $T^i_{\text{new\_matvec}}$. Measuring this value, however, could only be done after redistribution is performed. To avoid incurring this expense, we instead, as we search for the number of groups of processes C to form, restrict the lower end of the search space so that the locally stored data in the redistributed operator on each process participating in redistribution does not increase too much in size. Without this constraint, the minimum possible value for C is 1, which corresponds to all of the involved processes combining their data onto just one process. The size of the local data is determined to be one of three possibilities, which were used in [10] to classify sparse matrix-vector multiplication problems:

- Small: the matrix and the source vector fit in cache
- Medium: the source vector fits in cache, but the matrix does not
- Large: the source vector does not fit in cache.

We specifically exclude values of C that result in the problem category being at least halfway towards one of the larger ones. Crossing the boundaries from one size classification to another typically results in substantial changes in observed performance, and degradation when moving into a larger problem category sometimes occurs well before the boundary is crossed [10]. For categorization, the cache size is determined by dividing the size of the shared on-node cache by the number of MPI processes per node, as our t_i measurement occurs within MPI processes. The value of C resulting in the lowest value for T^i_{noswitch} is what is used when making a decision on whether or not to redistribute. When searching for this value, we searched over the powers of two less than p_i to save time in the setup phase; a more thorough search is an item for future work.

We employ one other safeguard against overeager redistribution. We do not redistribute if doing so is expected to have a big impact on the overall cycle time. To accomplish this, we keep track of a running sum of the time at each level in the solve cycle as predicted by the model, summing up T^i_{noswitch} for the current level and all finer ones. If there is a projected gain from switching, but that gain is projected to be less than 5 %, then we do not switch. This was not done in [15], but the experiments in that work were performed on an older machine on which coarse grid performance dominated overall runtime when no redistribution was performed. On a newer machine, we want to be more careful, and would rather miss a speedup than risk slowing the cycle down while chasing a small gain.

6.2   Redistribution Experiments

We tested model-guided data redistribution on Eos on two different problems, a 3D 7-point Laplacian and a linear elasticity problem on a 3D cantilever beam with an 8:1 aspect ratio. The 3D Laplacian was run with $30 \times 30 \times 30$ points per core on 512, 4096, and 8000 cores to match one of the test problems from [15]. The linear elasticity problem, which was generated by the MFEM software library [1], was run on 1024 and 8192 cores. Weak scaling in MFEM is accomplished by additional refinement of the base mesh, which resulted in a problem with 6350 points per core on 1024 cores and 6246 points per core on 8192 cores. The elasticity problem is governed by the equation

$$-\text{div}(\sigma(\mathbf{u})) = \mathbf{0},$$

where

$$\sigma(\mathbf{u}) = \lambda \text{div}(\mathbf{u})I + \mu(\nabla \mathbf{u} + \mathbf{u}\nabla).$$

The beam has two material components discretized using linear tetrahedral finite elements. $\lambda = \mu = 50$ on the first component, and $\lambda = \mu = 1$ on the second. $\mathbf{u}$ is a vector-valued function $\mathbf{u}(x, y, z)$ with a component in each of the three dimensions. The boundary conditions are $\mathbf{u} = \mathbf{0}$ on the boundary of the first component, which is fixed to a wall, $\sigma(\mathbf{u}) \cdot \mathbf{n} = \mathbf{0}$ elsewhere on the boundary of the first component, and $\sigma(\mathbf{u}) \cdot \mathbf{n} = \mathbf{f}$ on the boundary of the second component. The force $\mathbf{f}$ is a vector pointing in the downward direction with magnitude 0.01. The beam is diagrammed in Fig. 7.

We ran 10 trials of solving each problem to a tolerance of 10^{-8} using conjugate gradient preconditioned by AMG, recording both the setup and solve phase

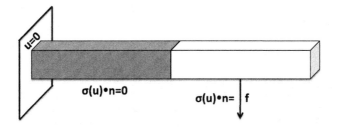

Fig. 7. 3D cantilever beam for the linear elasticity problem. The first component (left) is attached to the wall. The downward force **f** is pulling on the second component (right).

times. Like with the model validation experiments, we used the default block mapping of MPI tasks to nodes. We had to switch compilers to the PGI compiler, version 13.7-0, because the default Intel compiler failed to compile MFEM. When making the switching decision, we used the best fit performance model from Sect. 5.2, the baseline model plus the distance penalty term γ.

For the Laplace problem, we ran three different on-node mixes of MPI and OpenMP: 16×1, 8×2, and 4×4. We ran the elasticity problem using exclusively MPI, owing to difficulties compiling MFEM with OpenMP enabled, as hybrid MPI/OpenMP support in MFEM is currently experimental [1]. We did not use aggressive coarsening for the linear elasticity problem due to much poorer convergence when using it, following the default behavior of the linear elasticity solver in MFEM. Results for the Laplace problem are in Fig. 8, and results for the elasticity problem are in Table 4.

Table 4. Results on Eos for the Linear Elasticity problem.

	1024 Cores			8192 Cores		
	Setup	Solve	Total	Setup	Solve	Total
No redistribution	0.78 s	1.06 s	1.84 s	6.72 s	2.64 s	9.36 s
With redistribution	0.75 s	0.82 s	1.58 s	2.99 s	1.55 s	4.54 s
Speedup	1.04	1.29	1.16	2.25	1.93	2.06

The Laplace results reveal some interesting behavior. In the case of the solve phase, the best performance was using exclusively MPI, and there were mostly modest gains from data redistribution. This is not surprising when considering that the best fit from the performance modeling experiments was the model with no penalties to the baseline beyond the introduction of the distance term, a very favorable contention scenario. The setup phase, however, was a different story. Here, performance improved with the introduction of OpenMP, and the more MPI-rich configurations showed substantial speedups from redistribution

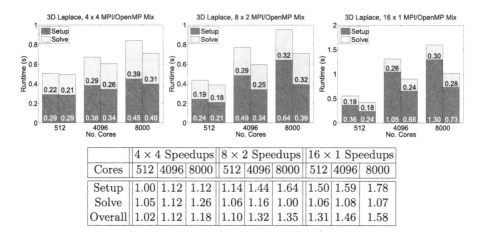

	4 × 4 Speedups			8 × 2 Speedups			16 × 1 Speedups		
Cores	512	4096	8000	512	4096	8000	512	4096	8000
Setup	1.00	1.12	1.12	1.14	1.44	1.64	1.50	1.59	1.78
Solve	1.05	1.12	1.26	1.06	1.16	1.00	1.06	1.08	1.07
Overall	1.02	1.12	1.18	1.10	1.32	1.35	1.31	1.46	1.58

Fig. 8. Results and corresponding speedups when using model-guided data redistribution for the 3D 7-point Laplace problem on Eos. The bars on the left in each graph show timings when doing no redistribution, while the bars on the right show timings when doing redistribution.

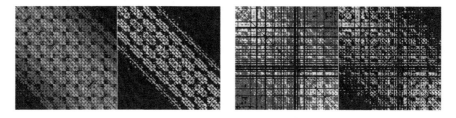

Fig. 9. Communication patterns on levels 4 (left) and 5 (right) for the 3D Laplace problem from the performance model validation experiments, with the setup phase on the left and the solve phase on the right.

at scale. This is a significant discrepancy in performance between the two phases; we will comment further in the next section.

Moving onto the linear elasticity problem, we see a modest speedup for the run on 1024 cores, but a large one for the run on 8192 cores. There was no big discrepancy between setup and solve phase speedup either. We should note that this problem had coarse grids with much larger stencils than the Laplace problem, with the largest coarse grid stencil for the elasticity problem averaging just under 500 nonzero entries per row compared to just under 100 for the Laplace problem. This means more messages are being sent over the interconnect, and we are seeing a big performance gain from reducing the number of messages even with an interconnect that was not showing much in the way of contention problems when we were validating the model. We will discuss this further in our concluding remarks.

7   Conclusions

To better understand the HPC potential of the dragonfly interconnect, we studied the performance of algebraic multigrid on a Cray XC30, developing a performance model and using it to analyze the performance of the AMG solve cycle. We made further use of the same performance model to guide data redistribution to improve performance. Substantial improvements in the setup phase for a 3D Laplace problem and in both phases for a linear elasticity problem showed that even an interconnect that rated very strongly in terms of penalties added on top of a basic α-β model does not automatically mean that there are no issues with interprocessor communication that could be improved upon.

One trait of note that was mentioned before is that the γ term in the performance model is larger than the α term, which was observed on two older fat-tree machines that suffered from poor coarse grid performance that hurt overall scalability. Though Eos features a much better interconnect, the presence of this property is still noteworthy, and suggests that communication between different router groups could suffer from substantial delays. That data redistribution has its biggest effect on runs using the majority of the machine hints at this.

What really stood out were the difference between the solve and setup phase speedups when using data redistribution for the 3D Laplace problem and the large speedup when solving the linear elasticity problem on 8192 cores. We mentioned earlier that the linear elasticity problem features much larger stencil sizes on coarse grids and thus dramatically increased interprocessor communication compared to the Laplace problem. The setup phase of AMG also features increased communication, substantially more than the solve phase. Figure 9 shows the communication patterns on the two most communication-intensive levels in the hierarchy from the 3D Laplace problem from the performance model validation experiments, levels 4 and 5, run in an all-MPI programming model on 128 cores on a multicore Opteron cluster that was analyzed in [12]. The plots were obtained using the performance analysis tool TAU [21]. On both levels, there was a lot more communication in the setup phase, with it being almost all-to-all on level 5.

So while the XC30 interconnect rated favorably in terms of contention penalties when we were testing our performance model, we saw that there were still large benefits to reducing the number of messages sent when that number was very large, whether it was through data redistribution, using a hybrid programming model, or a combination of both. In contrast, these benefits were found to be more modest for the same test problems on an IBM Blue Gene/Q, where reported overall speedups from data redistribution peaked at 17 % for the Laplace problem and 39 % for the linear elasticity problem, even though its interconnect did not rate as well in terms of the network contention penalties in our performance model [11]. Future work will involve examining the communication behavior and its effects on performance in more detail, including the construction of a performance model for the setup phase of AMG, to help pinpoint the major bottlenecks and see if there is a threshold at which network contention becomes a serious problem and if so, map it.

What we have seen so far on the Cray XC30, though, hints that the dragonfly topology will have problems with communication-heavy applications. Though the topology allows for wide variety in the specifics of the individual groups of routers that comprise the overall network, there is still the unifying feature of the all-to-all connections between the groups. Experiments in which we tasked the interconnect with handling a large number of messages led to performance degradation, especially when using the majority of the machine, that was readily improved when messages were traded for computation. These results point to a risk of slowdowns when communicating between groups of routers that will need to be addressed to make dragonfly interconnects effective at scale.

Acknowledgements. This work was supported in part by the Office of Advanced Scientific Computing Research, Office of Science, U.S. Department of Energy awards DE-SC0004131 and DE-FG02-13ER26138/DE-SC0010049, and performed in part under the auspices of the U.S. Department of Energy by Lawrence Livermore National Laboratory under contract DE-AC52-07NA27344 (LLNL-CONF-659475). It used resources of the Oak Ridge Leadership Computing Facility at the Oak Ridge National Laboratory, which is supported by the Office of Science of the U.S. Department of Energy under Contract No. DE-AC05-00OR22725. Neither Contractor, DOE, or the U.S. Government, nor any person action on their behalf: (a) makes any warranty or representation, express or implied, with respect to the information contained in this document; or (b) assumes any liabilities with respect to the use of, or damages resulting from the use of any information contained in this document.

References

1. MFEM: Finite Element Discretization Library. https://code.google.com/p/mfem
2. Alverson, B., Froese, E., Kaplan, L., Roweth, D.: Cray XC® Series Network (2012). http://www.cray.com/Assets/PDF/products/xc/CrayXC30Networking.pdf
3. Baker, A.H., Gamblin, T., Schulz, M., Yang, U.M.: Challenges of scaling algebraic multigrid across modern multicore architectures. In: 25th IEEE Parallel and Distributed Processing Symposium, Anchorage, AK, May 2011
4. Baker, A.H., Schulz, M., Yang, U.M.: On the performance of an algebraic multigrid solver on multicore clusters. In: Palma, J.M.L.M., Daydé, M., Marques, O., Lopes, J.C. (eds.) VECPAR 2010. LNCS, vol. 6449, pp. 102–115. Springer, Heidelberg (2011)
5. Balaji, P., Buntinas, D., Goodell, D., Gropp, W., Kumar, S., Lusk, E., Thakur, R., Träff, J.L.: MPI on a million processors. In: Ropo, M., Westerholm, J., Dongarra, J. (eds.) EuroPVM/MPI. LNCS, vol. 5759, pp. 20–30. Springer, Heidelberg (2009)
6. De Sterck, H., Falgout, R.D., Nolting, J.W., Yang, U.M.: Distance-two interpolation for parallel algebraic multigrid. Numer. Linear Algebra Appl. **15**, 115–139 (2008)
7. De Sterck, H., Yang, U.M., Heys, J.J.: Reducing complexity in parallel algebraic multigrid preconditioners. SIAM J. Matrix Anal. Appl. **27**, 1019–1039 (2006)
8. Dongarra, J., Luszczek, P.: Introduction to the HPCChallenge Benchmark Suite. Technical report ICL-UT-05-01, University of Tennessee, Knoxville, March 2005

9. Falgout, R.D., Jones, J.E., Yang, U.M.: Pursuing scalability for hypre's conceptual interfaces. ACM Trans. Math. Softw. **31**, 326–350 (2005)
10. Gahvari, H.: Benchmarking Sparse Matrix-Vector Multiply. Master's thesis, University of California, Berkeley, December 2006
11. Gahvari, H.: Improving the Performance and Scalability of Algebraic Multigrid Solvers through Applied Performance Modeling. Ph.D. thesis, University of Illinois at Urbana-Champaign (2014)
12. Gahvari, H., Baker, A.H., Schulz, M., Yang, U.M., Jordan, K.E., Gropp, W.: Modeling the performance of an algebraic multigrid cycle on HPC platforms. In: 25th ACM International Conference on Supercomputing, Tucson, AZ, June 2011
13. Gahvari, H., Gropp, W., Jordan, K.E., Schulz, M., Yang, U.M.: Modeling the performance of an algebraic multigrid cycle on HPC platforms using hybrid MPI/OpenMP. In: 41st International Conference on Parallel Processing, Pittsburgh, PA, September 2012
14. Gahvari, H., Gropp, W., Jordan, K.E., Schulz, M., Yang, U.M.: Performance modeling of algebraic multigrid on blue Gene/Q: lessons learned. In: 3rd In-ternational Workshop on Performance Modeling, Benchmarking and Simulation of High Performance Computer Systems, Salt Lake City, UT, November 2012
15. Gahvari, H., Gropp, W., Jordan, K.E., Schulz, M., Yang, U.M.: Systematic reduction of data movement in algebraic multigrid solvers. In: 5th Workshop on Large-Scale Parallel Processing, Cambridge, MA, May 2013
16. Henson, V.E., Yang, U.M.: BoomerAMG: a parallel algebraic multigrid solver and preconditioner. Appl. Numer. Math. **41**, 155–177 (2002)
17. hypre: High performance preconditioners. http://www.llnl.gov/CASC/hypre/
18. Kim, J., Dally, W.J., Scott, S., Abts, D.: Technology-driven, highly-scalable dragonfly topology. In: 35th International Symposium on Computer Architecture, Beijing, China, June 2008
19. Marr, D.T., Binns, F., Hill, D.L., Hinton, G., Koufaty, D.A., Miller, J.A., Upton, M.: Hyper-threading technology architecture and microarchitecture. Intel Technol. J. **6**, 4–15 (2002)
20. McCalpin, J.D.: Sustainable Memory Bandwidth in Current High Performance Computers. Technical report, Advanced Systems Division, Silicon Graphics Inc. (1995)
21. Shende, S.S., Malony, A.D.: The TAU parallel performance system. Int. J. High Perform. Comput. Appl. **20**, 287–311 (2006)
22. Yang, U.M.: On long-range interpolation operators for aggressive coarsening. Numer. Linear Algebra Appl. **17**, 453–472 (2010)

Performance Evaluation of Scientific Applications on POWER8

Andrew V. Adinetz[1], Paul F. Baumeister[1(✉)], Hans Böttiger[3],
Thorsten Hater[1], Thilo Maurer[3], Dirk Pleiter[1], Wolfram Schenck[4],
and Sebastiano Fabio Schifano[2]

[1] Jülich Supercomputing Centre, Forschungszentrum Jülich, 52425 Jülich, Germany
p.baumeister@fz-juelich.de
[2] Dipartimento di Matematica e Informatica, Università di Ferrara and INFN,
Ferrara, Italy
[3] IBM Deutschland Research and Development GmbH, 71032 Böblingen, Germany
[4] SimLab Neuroscience, Institute for Advanced Simulation and JARA,
Forschungszentrum Jülich, 52425 Jülich, Germany

Abstract. With POWER8 a new generation of POWER processors
became available. This architecture features a moderate number of cores,
each of which expose a high amount of instruction-level as well as thread-
level parallelism. The high-performance processing capabilities are integrated with a rich memory hierarchy providing high bandwidth through
a large set of memory chips. For a set of applications with significantly
different performance signatures we explore efficient use of this processor
architecture.

1 Introduction

With power consumption limiting the performance of scalar processors there
is a growing trend in high-performance computing (HPC) towards low clock
frequencies but extremely parallel computing devices to achieve high floating-
point compute performance. A remarkable increase in the number of systems
exploiting accelerators like GPGPUs and Xeon Phi for leading Top500 systems
can be observed. The POWER server processors, while providing increasing on-
chip parallelism, continue to be optimized for high single-thread performance. In
June 2014 the most recent generation of POWER processors, namely POWER8,
became available in a pre-release program. In this paper we investigate the
performance of this processor for a set of micro-benchmarks as well as mini-
applications based on real-life scientific HPC applications.

A description of the processor architecture with up to 12 cores be found in
[1,2]. POWER8 complies with version 2.07 of the Power ISA like its predecessor,
but features changes to the underlying micro-architecture. For an early evaluation of the architecture we used a single SMP server with two dual-chip-modules
(DCM) and a total of twenty cores. Each core can be clocked at up to 4.2 GHz
and is capable of running up to eight hardware threads per core in simultaneous
multi-threading (SMT) mode. Per core there are two floating point pipelines

© Springer International Publishing Switzerland 2015
S.A. Jarvis et al. (Eds.): PMBS 2014, LNCS 8966, pp. 24–45, 2015.
DOI: 10.1007/978-3-319-17248-4_2

capable of executing single and double precision scalar instruction or vector instructions on 128 bit registers. Alternatively, this VSX unit can operate on fixed point vectors. Further, two fixed point pipelines are present. All arithmetic functional units can execute fused-multiply-add instructions and variants thereof. The interface to the memory system consists of two load/store units and two dedicated load units. All of these may execute simple fixed point computations. The dispatch unit is capable of out-of-order execution.

The cache hierarchy consists of three levels. L1 and L2 are core private and inclusive. L1 is split between data and instructions with a capacity of 64 KiB and 32 KiB, respectively. The 512 KiB L2 cache is unified. The L2 caches are connected via a cache coherency protocol and can move data between caches. The store engine is located in L2, with L1 being write-through. L3 consists of 8 MiB of embedded DRAM (eDRAM) per core and functions as a victim cache for the local L2 and remote L3 caches. The pre-fetch engine pulls data into L3 directly and into L1 over the normal demand load path.

One of the differentiating features of the POWER8 architecture is the inclusion of external memory interface chips with an integrated cache, the Centaur chip. Its additional cache level of 16 MiB eDRAM is some times referred to as the fourth level cache (L4). Each link connecting processor and memory buffer offers an 8 GB/s to 9.6 GB/s write and 16 GB/s to 19.2 GB/s read bandwidth. With up to 8 links the aggregate peak bi-section bandwidth per socket is 192 to 230.4 GB/s. The dual-socket system evaluated in this paper featured an aggregated read bandwidth of 256 GB/s and 128 GB/s for write access.

We used a pre-release version of Red Hat Enterprise Linux 7.0 which features support for the POWER8 architecture. In this paper we only report on results obtained using the GCC compiler version 4.8.2 which includes POWER8 support and offers access to vector intrinsics.

As SMP domains grow in size and heterogeneity, the placement of memory allocations becomes more important. The test system comprises four NUMA domains, as each socket consists of a dual-chip-module. The standard tool `numactl` was used for pinning allocations.

With this paper we make the following contributions:

- Performance evaluation of different aspects of the POWER8 through micro-benchmarks.
- Performance characterization on POWER8 for different scientific applications.
- Identification of a set of events relevant for analyzing performance of such applications.

2   Related Work

Recently various papers have been published exploring the POWER7 architecture and investigating its performance. Very few papers have been published about the new POWER8 processor.

The approach taken in [3] is close to our's in the sense that the performance of relevant scientific applications was analysed on a POWER7-IH system. In this paper a system comprising 8 nodes and a total of 256 POWER7 cores was used. Focussing on scale-up capabilities of POWER7, analysis of data transport performance, like memory-to-processor or processor-to-processor, was given more attention than evaluation of the micro-architecture which is the focus of this paper.

The performance evaluation presented in [4] takes a more architectural approach by analysing the performance benefits of specific features of the POWER7 processor like different SMT modes, support of different clock speeds and the use of (at that time new) VSX instructions. For this purpose synthetic benchmarks are used. Detailed information on the POWER7 performance measurement capabilities is given.

First papers on POWER8 [1,2] mainly focus on chip design, applied technologies and I/O capabilities.

3   Methodology

3.1   Hardware Counters

The POWER8 processor allows for monitoring of up to six hardware events in a single set. These events can be chosen out of more than a thousand defined counters. We identify those that map to the functional units at the disposal of the core:

Unit	Counter
Vector scalar units	`VSU{0,1}_FIN`
Fixed point units	`FXU{0,1}_FIN`
Branch unit	`BRU_FIN`

The common prefix `PM_` has been suppressed for brevity in all counter names. We use PAPI version 5.3.2 to access the counter values via the interface to platform specific hardware counters [5]. In Fig. 1 we summarize our analysis of the memory architecture for the propagation of load requests. As to our knowledge, all counters are specific to the core executing the read request. However, some information is missing, like how to compute data movements from L2 to L3 and from L1 to L2.

3.2   Performance Metrics

In [6] a set of performance metrics was defined in order to characterize application behavior on the BG/Q architecture. We use these metrics as a basis for our work on the POWER8 architecture. However, we focus on those relevant to the core micro-architecture, mainly instruction counts and their interplay with the available functional units. Further we address the data movement between the CPU and memory, as well as chip-internal traffic. We give a summary in Table 1.

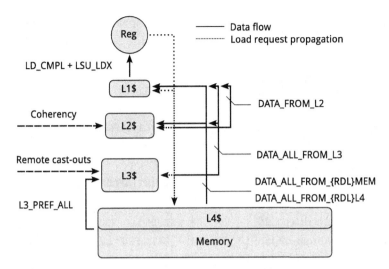

Fig. 1. Memory hierarchy for load request propagation and prefetch resolution. All values have to be scaled by the width of a cache line of 128 B, except the traffic between register file and L1 where the factor is the register width of 8 B.

3.3   Porting and Tuning

All applications and micro-benchmarks were ported to the POWER8 architecture. We give results for the optimal performance we were able to attain. Details for tuning applications can be found in the relevant sections, but we give some general methods here.

OpenMP: Thread placement – the mapping of threads to CPU cores – is a critical factor for the performance of concurrent applications beyond modest numbers of threads. We use the GNU OpenMP runtime control variables to control the layout. The best results are achieved by using a round-robin allocation with stride $s = min(8, \frac{160}{T})$ for T threads.

NUMA: The Linux tool `numactl` was used to tune memory allocation, where the interleaving of the four NUMA domains shows the best results.

4   Micro-benchmark Results

We investigated the baseline of available performance in terms of instruction throughput, memory bandwidth and multi-threading overhead by a series of micro-benchmarks.

4.1   Instruction Throughput and Latency

We use an in-house tool to measure the latency and saturated throughput of various assembly instructions. The basic approach is to time a tight loop of assembly

Table 1. Performance metrics for characterizing applications on POWER8.

Name	Description	Formula
t_{wc}	Wallclock time	CYC*
N_x	Instructions	INST_CMPL
N_{FX}	Fixed point instructions	FXU{01}_FIN + LSU_FX_FIN
N_{FP}	Floating point instructions	$\sum_n$ VSU{01}_nFLOP
N_{LS}	Load/Store instructions	LD_CMPL + ST_FIN
N_{BR}	Branch instructions	BRU_FIN
N_{fp-op}	FLOPs	$\sum_n$ VSU{01}nFLOP
$Reg{\leftarrow}L1\$$	Data read from L1	$8 \cdot$ (LD_CMPL + LSU_LDX)B
$Reg{\rightarrow}L2\$$	Data written L2†	$8 \cdot$ (ST_CMPL + VSU{01}_SQ)B
$L1\${\leftarrow}L2\$$	Data from L2 into L1$^+$	$128 \cdot$ DATA_FROM_L2B
$L1\${\leftarrow}L3\$$	Data from L3 into L1	$128 \cdot$ DATA_ALL_FROM_L3B
$L1\${\leftarrow}Mem$	Data from memory into L1	$128 \cdot$ (DATA_ALL_FROM_{LDR}MEM+ DATA_ALL_FROM_{LDR}L4)B
$L3\${\leftarrow}Mem$	Data from memory into L3	$128 \cdot$ (L3_PREF_ALL)B
$L3\${\rightarrow}Mem$	Data into memory from L3	$128 \cdot$ (L3_CO_ALL)B
N_{mem}	Total data from/to memory	$L1\${\leftarrow}Mem + L3\${\leftarrow}Mem + L3\${\rightarrow}Mem$

* Only incremented while thread is active.
† L1 is store-through.
$^+$ L1 and L2 have the same prefetch states, so no prefetch is excluded.

instructions, which is then repeatedly executed to achieve stable results. Using independent instructions allows for estimating the maximum throughput, while the introduction of dependencies will yield the minimal latency between instructions. Results for a selection of assembly instructions are given in Table 2.

4.2   Memory Sub-system (STREAM)

We first investigated the behavior of the memory sub-system under an artificial load designed to exercise the memory bandwidth. We used version 5.9 of the STREAM benchmark [7], which we tuned for the POWER8 architecture. STREAM consists of four micro-benchmarks on the vectors **a**, **b**, **c** and a scalar

$$\text{copy } \mathbf{c} \leftarrow \mathbf{a} \qquad \text{scale } \mathbf{b} \leftarrow s \cdot \mathbf{c}$$
$$\text{sum } \mathbf{a} \leftarrow \mathbf{b} + \mathbf{c} \quad \text{triad } \mathbf{a} \leftarrow s \cdot \mathbf{b} + \mathbf{c}$$

The GCC compiler fails to recognize the opportunity to vectorize the *copy* benchmark. The necessary vectorization was done by hand using VSX intrinsics. To achieve better parallel performance, *core binding* and *NUMA placement* were investigated, see Sect. 3.

First, we turn to the raw bandwidth between CPU and main memory. The working set size was chosen to be 512 MiB per array in order to avoid cache

Table 2. Latency and maximum throughput for examples of fixed point, simple and complex floating point and memory access instructions.

Instruction	Type	Latency	Throughput
add	Fixed	8	1
ld	Memory	–	1
st	Memory	–	1
ld+st	Memory	–	$1/7$
xsmuldp	$64\,b$ Floating	6	1
xsdivdp	$64\,b$ Floating	33	$1/29$

effects. As the STREAM benchmarks are highly regular, the efficiency of the pre-fetching mechanism has a large impact on the results. To obtain statistically sound results, we repeated the measurements 1000 times. We give the optimal results as the median values for all four benchmarks in Fig. 2 as a function of the number of threads. We find sustainable bandwidths for *triad* of just over $320\,GB/s$, corresponding to roughly $84.6\,\%$ of the maximum sustained bandwidth. The achievable bandwidth for *copy* and *scale* is lower than for *sum* and *triad*. The later use two load and one store streams which fits the balance of the memory links exactly. The peak performance is achieved with 40 threads, at which point every LSU is busy. For this case, the inset in Fig. 2 shows the distribution of the results over 1000 runs of the benchmark. We notice a clearly peaked distribution at the median and a quite long tail towards smaller values.

Next, we investigate the impact of the different cache levels. Due to the prefetch mechanism, we expect only the first and third level to have impact on the STREAM benchmarks. Cache lines recognized as part of a prefetch stream are fetched into L1 and L2 up to six cache lines ahead of the stream. These requests traverse the cache hierarchy like demand loads. The last level cache L3 is populated by the prefetcher directly from the memory up to 16 lines ahead of the stream. STREAM is perfectly regular, so we expect no significant impact of the L2 on the memory bandwidths. In the steady state of the prefetch engine, every load request must hit in L1 as it is large enough to hold three streams for eight threads per core. Prefetch requests themselves miss L2, as it has the same data prefetched, and hit L3 as it is ahead of the L1 prefetch. Every line is only traversed once. We monitor hardware counters to understand the impact of the prefetcher and cache hierarchy, and recorded the counter values for different array lengths. The data for the *copy* benchmark is presented in Fig. 3. Despite the effort of rotating the arrays to avoid such behavior, for small n, when the majority of the working set fits in L2, it supplies the full data to the core. For larger n, the traffic from L2 into L1 drops to a constant, due to remnants of the working set in L2. The last level cache satisfies almost all requests, including prefetches, beyond the size of L2. A constant amount of data is fetched directly from memory into L1, most likely before prefetch streams are established.

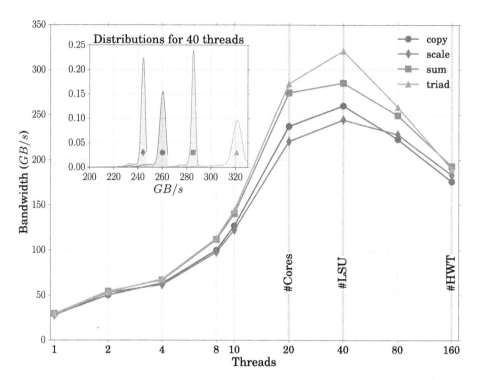

Fig. 2. Median bandwidths for the STREAM benchmarks over number of threads. We mark the thread counts where every core is occupied by single thread (#Core), by two threads (#LSU) and the SMT capacity is fully used (#HWT). Beyond using every LSU on all cores, the achievable bandwidth drops off sharply. **Inset:** Probability density estimates for the bandwidths at 40 threads over 1000 repetitions of the experiment. Note the clear peak at the median value and the relatively long tail towards smaller values, most probably indicating other system activity at the time of the iteration

The traffic volumes between the register file and the L1 cache fit the prediction of $8 \cdot nB$ perfectly, as does the store volume (not shown). The accumulated transfers into L1, from L2, L3 and memory, sum up to the same values within the margin of error. We find a clear effect of cache sizes as the data set grows too large for each level. The impact of the second level cache at small sizes is explained by the fact that at this point the full working set fit into L2. Although the design of the benchmark tries to avoid caching effects by rotating the assignments, this does not fully work for small sizes n.

4.3 OpenMP Overheads

The POWER8 system is relying on thread-level parallelism for optimal performance. A total of 20 threads are needed to occupy all cores with a single thread (ST mode). Further gains may be achieved by using multiple threads

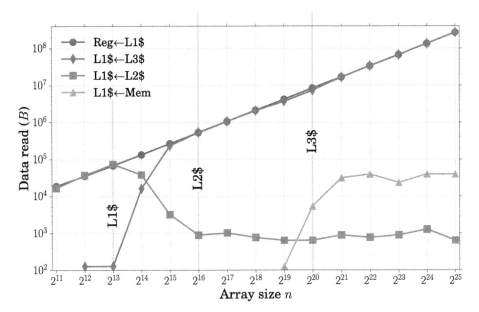

Fig. 3. Memory traffic as derived by monitoring hardware counters over the number of double precision array elements for STREAM *copy*. Counters were summarized into traffic volumes according to Sect. 3.1 and scaled into units of bytes. The predicted value of $8 \cdot nB$ perfectly matches the line for $Reg \leftarrow L1\$$.

on a single core in simultaneous multi-threading mode (SMT). This has the benefit of issuing more instructions per cycle, thus utilizing voids in the execution pipelines. However, as more threads are executing on the same hardware, the overheads for managing these threads, synchronization and bookkeeping grow. Since almost all applications and micro-benchmarks in this study are parallelized using OpenMP, we can estimate an upper bound for the number of threads to be used productively.

We use the OpenMP micro-benchmark suite (version 3.X) from EPCC to quantify these overheads [8]. The *overhead* $\tau(n)$ at n threads is here defined as the difference in execution time between expected and measured timings. We execute independent workloads, essentially empty loops, for a given number of iterations and time the execution $t(n)$ with n threads

$$\tau(n) = t(n) - \frac{t_0}{n}$$

where t_0 is the timing of serial execution of the same workload. The whole measurement is repeated to achieve a representative result.

The central component is the GNU OpenMP runtime shipped with GCC 4.8.2 and its interaction with the test-system. Relevant environment variables for distributing threads over cores and tuning thread migration and waiting policy are tuned for performance as described in Sect. 3.3.

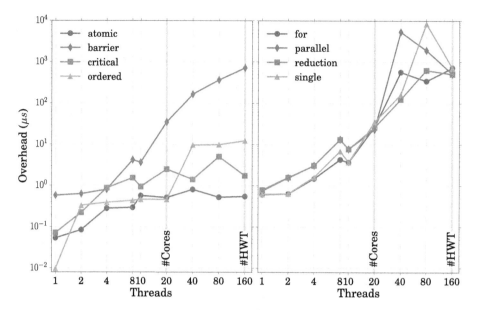

Fig. 4. Overheads for OpenMP threading as measured by the EPCC suite v3.X. The baseline cost setting up worksharing constructs and synchronization is well below one micro-second. **Left:** Explicit synchronization constructs. The most expensive statement to use is `barrier`, consuming up to 0.75 ms on 160 threads. **Right:** Implicit synchronization by closing a parallel region and the overhead of various worksharing constructs. Apart from a few outliers, we observe overheads of 0.6 μs to 0.7 ms.

Figure 4 summarizes our findings for the impact of various explicit and implicit synchronization constructs. These are the relevant sources of overhead for the further workloads in this report. The large overhead at the maximum number of 160 threads of around a millisecond suggests that using this level of concurrency will generally not be beneficial for worksharing. Regarding explicit synchronization, using `atomic` sections is to be preferred over the alternatives.

5   Application Performance Results

We present results on the analysis of three scientific applications on the POWER8 architecture: Lattice Boltzmann, MAFIA and NEST. The applications cover a wide scientific field: fluid dynamics (LB), data analysis (MAFIA) and neuronal networks (NEST). Furthermore, their performance profiles are diverse and gives good coverage of the architectural features.

5.1   Lattice Boltzmann Performance Results

The Lattice Boltzmann (LB) method is widely used in computational fluid dynamics, to numerically solve the equation of motion of flows in two and

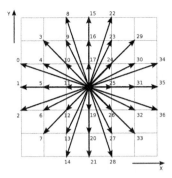

Fig. 5. The 37 element stencil for the `propagate` function.

three dimensions. While conceptually less efficient than spectral methods, LB approaches are able to handle complex and irregular geometries as well as complex and multi-phase flows. From a computational point of view, LB methods are "easy" to implement and a large degree of parallelism is exposed.

LB methods (see, e.g., [9] for an introduction) are discrete in position and momentum spaces; they are based on the synthetic dynamics of *populations* located at the sites of a discrete lattice. At each time step, populations are *propagated* from lattice-site to lattice-site and then incoming populations *collide* among one another, that is, they mix and their values change accordingly.

LB models in x dimensions with y populations are labeled as $DxQy$. Here, we consider the $D2Q37$ a state-of-the-art bi-dimensional model with 37 populations per site, see Fig. 5, that correctly reproduces the thermo-hydrodynamical equations of motion of a fluid in two dimensions and automatically enforces the equation of state for an ideal gas ($p = \rho T$) [10,11].

From a computational point of view the most relevant steps performed by a LB simulations are the computation of the `propagate` and `collide` functions:

1. `propagate` moves populations across lattice sites according to a stencil extent pattern of 7×7 excluding corners; it collects at each site all populations that will interact at the next phase: `collide`. Implementation-wise, `propagate` moves blocks of memory locations allocated at sparse memory addresses, corresponding to populations of neighbor cells.
2. `collide` performs all the mathematical steps associated to the computation of the collisional function, and computes the population values at each lattice site at the new time step. Input data for this phase are the populations gathered by the previous `propagate` phase.

We stress again that the D2Q37 LB method correctly and consistently describes the thermo-hydrodynamical equations of motion as well as the equation of state of a perfect gas; the price to pay is that, from a computational point of view, its implementation is more complex than simpler LB models. This translates into severe requirements in terms of memory bandwidth and floating-point throughput.

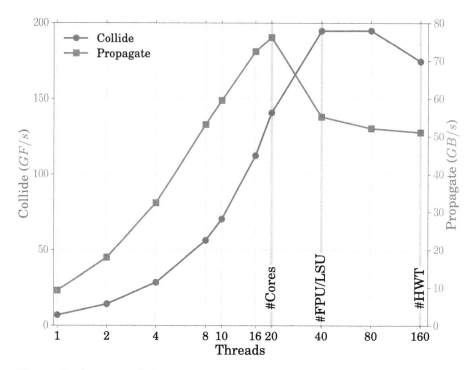

Fig. 6. Performance of the *D2Q37* kernels over the number of threads used. The efficiency of `collide` is given in GF/s and `propagate` measured in GB/s.

Indeed, `propagate` implies accessing 37 neighbor cells to gather all populations; this step is mainly memory-bound and takes approximately 10 % of the total run-time. The `collide` requires approximately 7600 double-precision floating point operations per lattice point, some of which can be optimized away by the compiler, see later sub-section. `collide` exhibits a significant arithmetic intensity and is the dominating part of the overall computation, taking roughly 90 % of the total run-time. All tests have been performed on a lattice of 3200 × 2000 sites, corresponding to 1.76 GiB of data per lattice. Input/output, diagnostics and computation of boundary conditions are not accounted for in this benchmark.

The D2Q37 model is highly adaptable and has been implemented on a wide range of parallel machines like BG/Q [12] as well as on a cluster of nodes based on commodity CPUs [13], GPGPUs [14] and Xeon-Phi [15]. It has been extensively used for large scale simulations of convective turbulence (see e.g., [16,17]). These implementations have been extensively tuned for the hardware in question, which is beyond scope of this study.

The `collide`-operation consists of three phases, first computing the moments of the distribution function, then resolving the collision effects in terms of these moments and those of the equilibrium distribution and finally transforming the result back. All transformations are linear. The GCC compiler generates optimized code with 4550 instructions. The main optimization is unrolling of each of the three loops over 37 into one single iteration and 18 iterations with vectorized load and FP instructions. All results for the hardware counter analysis are given per lattice site, corresponding to 37 elements of 64 b floating point data. For a break-down of the instruction mix and pipeline filling refer to Table 3. We find that the required 6200 floating point operations are performed in 2100 instructions, which are mostly vectorized fused-multiply-add instructions. Address calculation and loop variables contribute roughly 860 fixed-point instructions. There are just above 1500 load instructions plus close to 100 store instructions, in addition to the input data of $37 \cdot 8$ B we have to read some constants, but the bulk of this overhead stems from spilling the working set to L1. The actual amount of data read from memory is 459 B, roughly 50 % more than the 37 populations. The additional traffic may be explained by the coefficients for the polynomial expansions and the data that is prefetched but cast-out of L3 before it is used and re-read later. This is supported by the fact that almost all incoming memory traffic is due to pre-fetches (457 B). The function stores $37 \cdot 8$ B = 296 B, which is the updated site data, into memory. The full operation take 3000 cycles per site.

A thread scaling analysis of `collide` in Fig. 6 shows that the peak performance of 194 GF/s is reached with 80 threads on 20 cores, i.e. 9.7 GF/s per core in SMT4 mode, closely followed by 9.65 GF/s in SMT2 mode. It is interesting to see that further oversubscription of the core (160 threads, SMT8) reduces the performance by 11 % compared to the maximum. The performance of a single thread per core is reported as 7 GF/s. The POWER8 core architecture is optimized for both single threaded execution (ST) as well as SMT threading; it adapts the way instruction dispatch works accordingly. This explains the subtle differences in the interplay of functional units that can be observed in the two modes. The peak performance is about 74 % higher than running on a single thread per core (ST mode). This gain stems from better filling of the instruction pipelines.

`Propagate` performs a swap on 37 memory locations per lattice site and is, therefore, limited by the effective random access memory bandwidth. Benchmarking with thread numbers between 1 and 160 shows that the shortest runtime of `propagate` is reached at 20 threads, i.e. one thread per core (ST mode).

The structure of memory access leads to a factor 3 to 4 lower bandwidth compared to values for the sustained bandwidth obtained with the STREAM benchmark Sect. 4.2. Here, we can see that the throughput of instructions is highest in ST mode and, similar to the performance of the `collide`-kernel, degrades the more threads we use per core. The lower part of the scaling analysis – 1 to 20 threads – shows the effect of shared resources. The original version of the code exhibited less than optimal performance due to misuse of the cache hierarchy. The loop over the lattice was optimized by using cache blocking, giving a gain of 20 % in bandwidth. Again, Table 3 shows a detailed breakdown of the instruction mix and pipeline filling. No floating point operations are performed, although the VSU pipelines report significant filling, since store instructions are executed in both LSU and VSU. We find exactly 37 load and store instructions, one per population. These result in 296 B of write traffic and 1837 B are read from memory. This is roughly six times more than we would naively expect.

Table 3. Left: Characteristics of LBM seen by the instruction pipelines; measured on a single thread. Given are the relative fractions dispatched to the pipelines and the throughput relative to the maximum for different numbers of threads per core. **Right:** Instruction counts and general metrics for the LBM application.

			Throughput			
Function	**Unit**	**Fraction**	ST	SMT2	SMT4	SMT8
`collide`	**LSU**	0.35	0.28	0.42	0.43	0.38
	VSU	0.50	0.41	0.57	0.57	0.51
	FXU	0.14	0.11	0.13	0.12	0.11
`propagate`	**LSU**	0.45	0.04	0.04	0.05	0.04
	VSU	0.41	0.04	0.06	0.12	0.05
	FXU	0.11	0.01	0.02	0.05	0.03

Metric	`collide`	`propagate`
t_{wc}	3007	214
N_x	4933	87
N_{FX}	857	12
N_{FP}	2122	–
N_{BR}	80	2
N_{LS}	1641	74
N_{mem}	755	2141
N_{fp-op}	6197	–

Again, almost every incoming byte is due to pre-fetching (1537 B), indicating that streams may be established, but never fully utilized. Further, due to the nature of the stencil the read accesses are not continuous, potentially resulting partially consumed cache lines. Addressing and loop computations result in 12 fixed point computations per site. Processing a single site requires 214 cycles.

In summary, LBM is split into two parts, both of which have completely different performance requirements. The computationally expensive `collide` operation, which is largely vectorized by the compiler, reaches about 29 % of the peak floating point performance. It further benefits from the higher pipeline filling by using up to four threads per core. On the other hand `propagate` which is purely memory bound can capitalize roughly 20 % of the aggregated read-/write bandwidth. However, the maximum *achievable bandwidth* is 256 GB/s as the requirements of `propagate` are symmetric in read and write. Of this figure, we can exploit close to 30 %, the remaining gap is mainly a result of the non-continuous access pattern.

The overall performance is summarized in Fig. 6, the maximum achieved for 40 threads or two per core, which is due to the unequal shares of both phases on the total runtime. We find close to ideal scaling up to twenty threads and significant gains from using two threads per core, beyond that, performance stagnates (SMT4) and finally degrades (SMT8). This is expected as the application utilizes the available pipelines efficiently at SMT2. Gains from filling potential voids in the pipelines are offset by threading overheads as described in Sect. 4.3. We are investigating the reduced bandwidth at more than one thread per core.

5.2 MAFIA Performance Results

MAFIA is a subspace clustering application [18] which implements the algorithm of the same name [19]. For the purpose of this report, we concentrate on the CPU version implemented using OpenMP. MAFIA algorithm builds *dense units (DUs)* starting from lower dimensionalities and progressing to higher ones, until no new

DUs can be built. For each dimensionality, it generates *candidate DUs (CDUs)* from DUs of lower dimensionality. The CDU is accepted as a DU if the number of contained points lies above a certain threshold. The cardinality computation, **pcount**, is the most computationally intensive kernel of the algorithm. The generated DUs are then merged into clusters, which are the final output.

In MAFIA, each CDU is represented as a cartesian product of *windows*, one window per dimension of the CDU. Each window, in turn, is represented by a set of contained points, implemented as a bit array. Thus, the number of points inside a CDU can be computed as the number of bits set in intersection (bitwise AND) of all windows. The loop over words of the bit array was strip-mined, so that auto-vectorization by the compiler is possible.

Reference [18] presents performance estimates as well as an empirical analysis of MAFIA. Assume that the algorithm runs on n points in d dimensions, and the dataset contains a single hidden cluster of dimensionality k. Then the total number of logical bit AND operations in **pcount** kernel for the entire program run is given by the equation

$$N_{bitops} = n \cdot k \cdot 2^{k-1}. \tag{1}$$

As the number of windows is several orders of magnitude smaller than the number of points ($\mathcal{O}(10)$ versus $\mathcal{O}(10^6)$), it can be assumed that the array of window indices is cached, and only bit arrays need to be transferred from memory. Thus, Eq. 1 also gives the number of bits transferred from memory by the **pcount** kernel.

We started by analyzing the scaling behavior of MAFIA with different OpenMP thread placements, by altering the stride s with which the threads are spread out across cores. The **pcount** kernel was parallelized across CDUs, with only a single thread executing the point count loop for each CDU. Scalability results for the **pcount** kernel for a dataset with $n = 10^7$ points of dimensionality $d = 20$ and a cluster of dimensionality $k = 14$ are presented in Fig. 7. The scalability is quite good, with a speedup of up to 25 achieved with 80 threads and threads allocated round-robin to every second core, see Sect. 3.

We then proceeded to analyzing counter values. The MAFIA application was run with 20, 40, 80 and 160 threads with the same point and cluster dimensionalities as above ($k = 14$, $d = 20$). The number of points, n, varied on a logarithmic scale between $1 \cdot 10^6$ to $64 \cdot 10^6$. Counter values are given as averages across three runs.

Next, we analyze vector instruction throughput. As MAFIA **pcount** contains only integer vector instructions, counters for floating-point vector instructions are of no interest here. For each of the three counters, we assume that its value can be modeled by the equation

$$c(n) = (c_0 2^k + c_1 k 2^{k-1}) \cdot \frac{n}{128} \tag{2}$$

where the coefficients c_0 and c_1 are both in terms of operations performed on a single vector. The term with c_1 is derived from Eq. 1, and corresponds to the

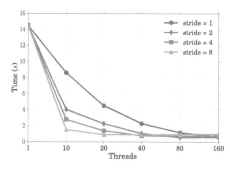

Fig. 7. MAFIA OpenMP scaling

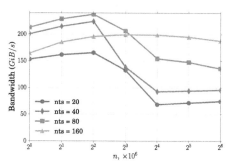

Fig. 8. Theoretical memory bandwidth for MAFIA

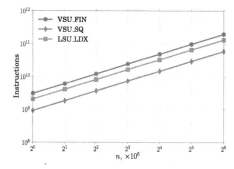

Fig. 9. Predicted and measured values for vector instruction counters for 20 threads

Table 4. Coefficients for vector counters, both expected based on the code and actual extracted from the assembly

Counter	Assembly		Expected	
	c_0	c_1	c_0	c_1
VSU_SQ	0.125	1.0	0	0
VSU_FIN	2.5	3.0	1	1
LSU_LDX	1	2.125	0	1

loop over windows, where the number of iterations varies with CDU dimensionality. The term with c_0 corresponds to the rest of the iteration of the loop over words, where the number of instructions executed does not depend on CDU dimensionality.

For prediction purposes, we derived values for c_0 and c_1 from the assembly code generated by the compiler. Their values for different counters are listed in Table 4. The innermost loop was unrolled by the compiler, therefore some coefficients have a fractional part. Figure 9 compares predictions with the actual measured values. The predictions are almost perfect, with less than 0.001 % difference. Numbers for other thread counts are very similar and are omitted for brevity.

It is also worth comparing coefficients extracted from assembly to the minimum values expected by looking at the original code; both are listed in Table 4.

– One store instruction is executed per vector instead of none expected. This indicates that the storage for words resulting from logical AND operation is in L1 rather than registers.

- Similarly, there are 2.125 load instructions instead of one expected. One of those is needed to load the array holding result of logical AND to registers (from cache), and 0.125 is due to imperfect alignment of bit arrays in main memory.
- Three vector instructions are generated instead of one expected. One is due to vector store counted as a vector instruction, and the second is a permutation instruction, again to compensate for mis-alignment of the bit arrays in memory.

The values obtained from the assembly differ from minimum values expected from the original code, which indicates optimization potential. Compiler optimization is one of the way to address that, and we are planning to look into that.

We then proceeded with analyzing the memory traffic. Figure 8 plots a semi-empirical memory bandwidth, i.e. the estimate of memory traffic divided by measured running time. For a given number of points, more bandwidth actually indicates *lower running times*, as the theoretical memory traffic does not depend on the number of threads. Figure 10 plots the ratio of traffic between main memory and various levels of caches to the theoretical value, derived from Eq. 1.

With 20 threads, L1/L2 caches and L3 cache partition of a single core are used by a single thread only, which gives the most predictable plot. Indeed, the amount of data flowing into L1 cache is very close to the theoretical prediction. L1 is mostly filled from L3, and data flow from L2 is almost non-existent. Up to

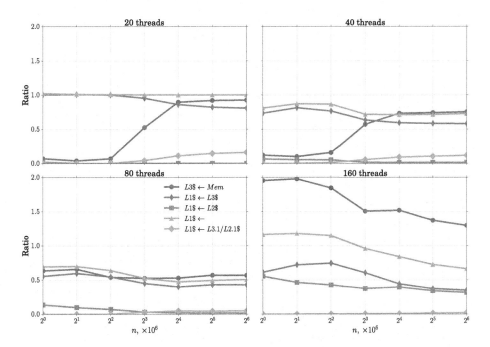

Fig. 10. Memory traffic ratio for various thread counts. Ratio for $L1\$ \leftarrow Mem$ is very close to zero and therefore not shown.

and including $4 \cdot 10^6$ points, the aggregated size of the bit arrays fits into L3; only after that is data fetched from main memory. Even then, it is mostly prefetched into L3, from where it goes further up. Because of that, there is almost no need to fetch the data from main memory directly into L1.

The plots for 40 and 80 threads show the same qualitative behavior, although effects of cache sharing play a role. On the positive side, the same cache lines can be used by multiple threads; as a result, the amount of data loaded into L1 is actually *less* than the theoretical prediction, down to 50 % for 80 threads. On the negative side, as the amount of cache of all levels per thread is lower, there is less space to store data on-chip. As a result, for 80 threads, data should be fetched from memory for all dataset sizes. However, this does not seem to affect performance, as the 80-thread version is actually the fastest for the cases when the data size fits into L3 cache. It may be that though the L3 prefetcher kicks in, it does not provide the data further referenced by the algorithm. For 20 to 80 threads, there is also a small but not insignificant amount of data retrieved from cache partitions of other cores.

The plot for 160 threads differs qualitatively from the others. First of all, there is significant over-prefetching of data from the main memory. We assume that due to too many threads contending for prefetcher resources, prefetch streams get tried but do not reach steady state. Also, a much larger fraction of data is sourced from L2. Again, we assume that due to over-subscription of over-prefetching into L1, many of the prefetched L1 cache lines get cast out into L2 even before they get accessed. This agrees with other counters, which indicate that lines from L2 and L3 come due to explicit accesses and not due to prefeches. Nevertheless, overall use of hardware with 160 threads is relatively good, as for more than $8 \cdot 10^6$ points this is where the maximum performance is achieved.

To summarize, MAFIA's **pcount** loop is rather regular, and we can get a good understanding of it. Vector instruction counters are perfectly understood in terms of algorithmic properties and instructions in the assembler code. Memory behavior is also understandable, particularly for lower number of threads $nts \le 40$, where effects of L3 cache size are clearly visible. With larger number of threads, however, our understanding is limited, and it is here where the highest performance is achieved. We thus assume that the application is latency-limited, as neither instruction throughput nor memory bandwidth limit its performance.

5.3 NEST Performance Results

NEST (NEural Simulation Tool) is an application from the field of computational neurobiology [20]. It models brain tissue as a graph of neurons interconnected by synapses. Neurons exchange spikes along the synapse connections. On an abstract level, NEST can be understood as a discrete event simulator on a distributed sparse graph. It is built as an interpreter of a domain specific modeling language on top of a C++ simulation core. Most simulations include stochastic connections and sources of spikes, which makes static analysis and load balancing unfeasible.

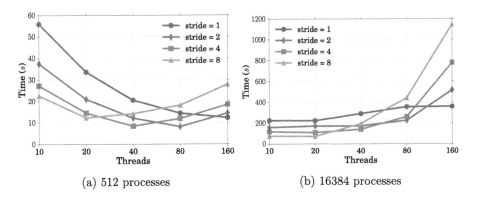

(a) 512 processes   (b) 16384 processes

Fig. 11. NEST scaling behavior with OpenMP

The performance profile of NEST leans towards fixed point operations due to the necessary graph operations and dynamic dispatch of events. Memory capacity is a major bottleneck for large-scale simulations with NEST, so optimizations tend to favor size over speed. Despite the obvious need for good fixed point performance, a small but non-negligible fraction of floating point operations is needed to update the neuron models.

For our experiments, we used *dry run* mode of NEST. This enables simulating performance characteristics of a NEST run on many thousands of nodes by running on a single system. The parameters of a run are the simulated number of MPI processes, M, and the number of threads running on a single node, T. Typically, NEST run parameters also include n, the number of neurons owned by a single process, which is fixed at $n = 9375$, and therefore omitted, in our experiments. The total number of neurons is proportional to M. Each active thread is called a *virtual process (VP)* and the total number of VPs is given by $M \cdot T$. For our experiments, we simulate random balanced networks with nM neurons and both static and adaptive synapses [21].

We started with analyzing performance of NEST simulation loop with different OpenMP settings. We performed experiments with 10, 20, 40, 80 and 160 threads strided by 1, 2, 4 and 8 over the cores under 3 values of M. Results for $M = 512$ and $M = 16384$ processes are depicted in Fig. 11; results for $M = 4096$ (not shown) exhibit the same behavior.

NEST exhibits non-trivial scaling behavior. Some parts, such as *neuron update* or *synapse processing*, scale well, while others, such as *spike buffer processing*, do not scale, as all threads should go through the entire spike buffer. Moreover, with larger number of processes, and as a consequence, of neurons, the relative weight of spike buffer processing increases. Therefore, while with $M = 512$ having more threads per core improves performance to some extent, with $M = 16384$, more threads always means worse performance. For each T, the optimal stride is given by $min(160/T, 8)$, which we use for further experiments.

We then proceeded to analyzing hardware performance counters for NEST. Understanding how resource contention affects running times of various parts of

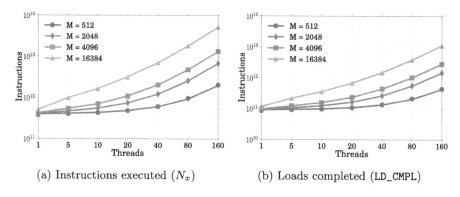

(a) Instructions executed (N_x)   (b) Loads completed (LD_CMPL)

Fig. 12. Modeling values of NEST "work-related" counters

NEST is still a work in progress. We therefore restrict ourselves to counters which can be characterized as *amount of work performed*, such as the number of instructions or loads executed. We analyzed only the *spike delivery* phase, as for a large number of processors, it takes more than 90 % of simulation time. We performed experiments with $T = 1, 5, 10, 20, 40, 80, 160$ and $M = 512, 2048, 4096, 16384$. The work done in spike delivery phase can be broken into contributions from processing the following items:

– **synapses**, which is constant for fixed n;
– **spikes in the buffer**, proportional to $M \cdot T$, as the number of spikes is proportional to M, and this work has to be done by each thread;
– **markers in the buffer**, proportional to $M \cdot T^2$, as the number of markers is equal to the number of virtual processes and the work is done in each thread;

Note that the code for all components is intermixed, so it is impossible to accurately measure each of them without introducing significant measurement bias. The total amount of work done can be written as the sum of all components

$$C = c_0 + c_1 \cdot MT + c_2 \cdot MT^2. \tag{3}$$

The coefficients of the Eq. 3 has been derived by fitting it into experimental data using least squares method. Figure 12 plots values for both total instructions (N_x) and loads executed. The points represent the measured values, and the lines represent the fitted values. The fits are very close, with the deviation being less than 5.5 % (mostly less than 3.3 %) for instructions and less than 7.5 % (most less than 3.7 %) for loads. Note that Eq. 3 also holds for other work-related counters, which include: floating point loads and stores, vector instructions, both the total and actual arithmetic operations.

To summarize, though our understanding of NEST performance characteristics is far from complete, some points are clear. Specifically, spike delivery takes most of the time for simulations with large number of MPI processes M. We also understand the number of instructions executed by spike delivery, and it is clear that it contains parts that do not scale with either the number of processes M or threads T. And while scalability with T could be improved by parallelizing the loop processing spikes in the buffer, improving scalability with M requires more fundamental changes in NEST architecture, specifically the way spikes are exchanged between processes.

6   Summary and Conclusions

We presented the characterization of three different scientific codes on a new server-class processor, the POWER8. Further, results of micro-benchmarks were collected as a first impression of the performance characteristics.

The LBM and MAFIA applications benefit from the available instruction-level parallelism and vectorization capabilities. Although parts of LBM depend strongly on the memory bandwidth, the available capacity can only be exploited to a fraction, due to the access pattern. NEST is an irregular application limited by memory accesses, and could, in theory, benefit from SMT. However, in order to achieve this, its scalability should be improved first.

On the basis of the performance we were able to achieve in our tests, POWER8 is a candidate for the host CPU in GPU-accelerated systems. The focus on integer performance, out-of-order execution and memory bandwidth complement the floating-point optimized profile of the accelerator. Exploring this direction is planned for the near future.

With up to 160 threads in total or eight per core, overheads from thread management, especially by the OpenMP runtime, become an important factor. This is even more critical, as the SMT facilities are means to optimize pipeline filling and therefore require lightweight threading. However, the gains from these large numbers of threads per core are expected to be significant only if the pipelines are not sufficiently saturated to begin with. The applications we tested did not suffer from this problem, so speed-ups were not expected. We were not able to obtain results with an OpenMP runtime optimized for POWER8 in the time frame of the preview. This too, is planned for the near future.

References

1. Friedrich, J., Le, H., Starke, W., Stuechli, J., Sinharoy, B., Fluhr, E., Dreps, D., Zyuban, V., Still, G., Gonzalez, C., Hogenmiller, D., Malgioglio, F., Nett, R., Puri, R., Restle, P., Shan, D., Deniz, Z., Wendel, D., Ziegler, M., Victor, D.: The POWER8 processor: designed for big data, analytics, and cloud environments. In: IEEE International Conference on IC Design Technology (ICICDT) (2014)
2. Fluhr, E., Friedrich, J., Dreps, D., Zyuban, V., Still, G., Gonzalez, C., Hall, A., Hogenmiller, D., Malgioglio, F., Nett, R., Paredes, J., Pille, J., Plass, D., Puri, R., Restle, P., Shan, D., Stawiasz, K., Deniz, Z., Wendel, D., Ziegler, M.: POWER8: a 12-core server-class processor in 22 nm SOI with 7.6 Tb/s off-chip bandwidth. In: Solid-State Circuits Conference Digest of Technical Papers (ISSCC), IEEE International (2014)

3. Barker, K.J., Hoisie, A., Kerbyson, D.J.: An early performance analysis of POWER7-IH HPC systems. In: Proceedings of 2011 International Conference for High Performance Computing, Networking, Storage and Analysis. SC 2011. ACM, New York (2011)
4. Srinivas, M., Sinharoy, B., Eickemeyer, R., Raghavan, R., Kunkel, S., Chen, T., Maron, W., Flemming, D., Blanchard, A., Seshadri, P., Kellington, J., Mericas, A., Petruski, A.E., Indukuru, V.R., Reyes, S.: IBM POWER7 performance modeling, verification, and evaluation. IBM J. Res. Dev. **55**(3), 4:1–4:19 (2011)
5. Browne, S., Dongarra, J., Garner, N., London, K., Mucci, P.: A Scalable Cross-platform Infrastructure for Application Performance Tuning Using Hardware Counters (2000)
6. Baumeister, P.F., Boettiger, H., Hater, T., Knobloch, M., Maurer, T., Nobile, A., Pleiter, D., Vandenbergen, N.: Characterizing performance of applications on blue gene/q. In: Bader, M., Bode, A., Bungartz, H.J., Gerndt, M., Joubert, G.R., Peters, F.J. (eds.) Parallel Computing: Accelerating Computational Science and Engineering. Advances in Parallel Computing, pp. 113–122. IOS Press, Amsterdam (2013)
7. McCalpin, J.D.: STREAM: Sustainable Memory Bandwidth in High Performance Computers. Technical report, University of Virginia (1991–2007)
8. Bull, J.M., O'Neill, D.: A microbenchmark suite for OpenMP 2.0. SIGARCH Comput. Archit. News **29**(5), 41–48 (2001)
9. Succi, S.: The Lattice-Boltzmann Equation. Oxford University Press, Oxford (2001)
10. Sbragaglia, M., Benzi, R., Biferale, L., Chen, H., Shan, X., Succi, S.: Lattice Boltzmann method with self-consistent thermo-hydrodynamic equilibria. J. Fluid Mech. **628**, 299–309 (2009)
11. Scagliarini, A., Biferale, L., Sbragaglia, M., Sugiyama, K., Toschi, F.: Lattice Boltzmann methods for thermal flows: continuum limit and applications to compressible rayleigh-taylor systems. Phys. Fluids **22**(5), 055–101 (2010)
12. Pivanti, M., Mantovani, F., Schifano, S., Tripiccione, R., Zenesini, L.: An optimized lattice boltzmann code for bluegene/q. In: Wyrzykowski, R., Dongarra, J., Karczewski, K., Wasniewski, J. (eds.) Parallel Processing and Applied Mathematics. LNCS, vol. 8385, pp. 385–394. Springer, Heidelberg (2014)
13. Biferale, L., Mantovani, F., Pivanti, M., Pozzati, F., Sbragaglia, M., Scagliarini, A., Schifano, S.F., Toschi, F., Tripiccione, R.: Optimization of multi-phase compressible Lattice Boltzmann codes on massively parallel multi-core systems. In: Proceedings of the International Conference on Computational Science, ICCS 2011, vol. 4. Procedia Computer Science (2011)
14. Kraus, J., Pivanti, M., Schifano, S.F., Tripiccione, R., Zanella, M.: Benchmarking GPUs with a parallel Lattice-Boltzmann code. In: 25th International Symposium on Computer Architecture and High Performance Computing (SBAC-PAD), IEEE (2013)
15. Crimi, G., Mantovani, F., Pivanti, M., Schifano, S.F., Tripiccione, R.: Early experience on porting and running a Lattice Boltzmann code on the Xeon-Phi co-processor. Procedia Comput. Sci. **18**, 551–560 (2013)
16. Biferale, L., Mantovani, F., Sbragaglia, M., Scagliarini, A., Toschi, F., Tripiccione, R.: Second-order closure in stratified turbulence: simulations and modeling of bulk and entrainment regions. Phys. Rev. E **84**(1), 016–305 (2011)
17. Biferale, L., Mantovani, F., Sbragaglia, M., Scagliarini, A., Toschi, F., Tripiccione, R.: Reactive rayleigh-taylor systems: front propagation and non-stationarity. EPL (Europhys. Lett.) **94**(5), 54004 (2011)

18. Adinetz, A., Kraus, J., Meinke, J., Pleiter, D.: GPUMAFIA: Efficient subspace clustering with MAFIA on GPUs. In: Wolf, F., Mohr, B., Mey, D.A. (eds.) Euro-Par 2013 Parallel Processing. LNCS, vol. 8097, pp. 838–849. Springer, Heidelberg (2013)
19. Nagesh, H., Goil, S., Choudhary, A., Kumar, V.: Parallel algorithms for clustering high-dimensional large-scale datasets. In: Grossman, R.L., Kamath, C., Kegelmeyer, P., Namburu, R.R. (eds.) Data Mining for Scientific and Engineering Applications, pp. 335–336. Springer, New York (2001)
20. Gewaltig, M.O., Diesmann, M.: NEST (NEural Simulation Tool). Scholarpedia **2**(4), 1430 (2007)
21. Morrison, A., Aertsen, A., Diesmann, M.: Spike-timing-dependent plasticity in balanced random networks. Neural comput. **19**(6), 1437–1467 (2007)

SPEC ACCEL: A Standard Application Suite for Measuring Hardware Accelerator Performance

Guido Juckeland[1,2]([✉]), William Brantley[1,3], Sunita Chandrasekaran[1,4],
Barbara Chapman[1,4], Shuai Che[1,3], Mathew Colgrove[1,5], Huiyu Feng[1,6],
Alexander Grund[1,2], Robert Henschel[1,7], Wen-Mei W. Hwu[1,8], Huian Li[1,7],
Matthias S. Müller[1,9], Wolfgang E. Nagel[1,2], Maxim Perminov[1,10],
Pavel Shelepugin[1,10], Kevin Skadron[1,11], John Stratton[1,8,12],
Alexey Titov[1,3], Ke Wang[1,11], Matthijs van Waveren[1,13],
Brian Whitney[1,14], Sandra Wienke[1,9], Rengan Xu[1,4],
and Kalyan Kumaran[1,15]

[1] SPEC High Performance Group, Gainesville, USA
info@spec.org
http://www.spec.org/hpg
[2] Center for Information Services and High Performance Computing (ZIH),
Technische Universität Dresden, 01062 Dresden, Germany
guido.juckeland@tu-dresden.de
[3] Advanced Micro Devices, Inc., Sunnyvale, CA, USA
[4] University of Houston, Houston, TX, USA
[5] NVIDIA, Santa Clara, CA, USA
[6] Silicon Graphics International Corp., Milpitas, CA, USA
[7] Indiana University, Bloomington, IN, USA
[8] University of Illinois (UIUC), Champaign, IL, USA
[9] RWTH Aachen University, Aachen, Germany
[10] Intel, Nizhny Novgorod, Russia
[11] University of Virginia, Charlottesville, VA, USA
[12] Colgate University, Hamilton, NY, USA
[13] Compilaflows, Toulouse, France
[14] Oracle, Redwood Shores, CA, USA
[15] Argonne National Laboratory, Lemont, IL, USA

Abstract. Hybrid nodes with hardware accelerators are becoming very common in systems today. Users often find it difficult to characterize and understand the performance advantage of such accelerators for their applications. The SPEC High Performance Group (HPG) has developed a set of performance metrics to evaluate the performance and power consumption of accelerators for various science applications. The new benchmark comprises two suites of applications written in OpenCL and OpenACC and measures the performance of accelerators with respect to a reference platform. The first set of published results demonstrate the viability and relevance of the new metrics in comparing accelerator performance. This paper discusses the benchmark suites and selected published results in great detail.

© Springer International Publishing Switzerland 2015
S.A. Jarvis et al. (Eds.): PMBS 2014, LNCS 8966, pp. 46–67, 2015.
DOI: 10.1007/978-3-319-17248-4_3

Keywords: SPEC · SPEC ACCEL · OpenCL · OpenACC · Energy measurements

1   Introduction

The Standard Performance Evaluation Cooperation (SPEC) stands as a successful example of collaboration among vendors and researchers in creating benchmarks that lead to fair comparison and reproducible results. SPEC's High Performance Group (HPG) has been active for over 20 years – since its initial benchmark derived from David Kuck's Perfect Suite – in creating industry standard benchmarks that highlight and compare various aspects of high performance computing systems. The group's members are leading high performance computing (HPC) vendors, national laboratories, and universities from all around the world.

SPEC HPG has been developing and maintaining application based benchmarks and performance metrics supporting a variety of programming models and stressing various hardware features. This includes inter-node parallelism (covered by SPEC MPI2007), intra-node parallelism (covered by SPEC OMP2012), and offloading computation to a hardware accelerator (covered by SPEC ACCEL in this paper). SPEC MPI2007 offers a suite of 18 applications running on up to 2,048 message passing interface (MPI) ranks [22]. Its goal is to evaluate MPI-parallel, floating point, compute intensive performance of clusters and multi-processor systems. SPEC OMP2012 offers a suite of 14 applications based on scientific and engineering application codes using the OpenMP 3.1 standard [21]. The benchmark also includes an optional metric for measuring energy consumption.

The advent of hardware accelerators as a standard component in high performance computers led SPEC HPG to investigate performance characterization in this additional layer of parallelism. Keeping with the group's guidelines, a performance evaluation must be based on an open programming model so that multiple hardware and software environments can be evaluated. As a result, the popular but vendor specific programming model—CUDA—was not investigated. Instead OpenCL, as a low level, and OpenACC, as a high level, hardware accelerator programming models have been chosen to provide two independent subsuites within SPEC ACCEL[1]. In a similar manner, the group has carefully brought together applications from various computational and scientific domains that stress the accelerator with very different demands. The runtime and energy consumption of the application is monitored during multiple runs and results are presented in the typical SPEC manner. The peer review process for every published result ensures the validity and reproducibility of a SPEC ACCEL run.

This paper first presents previous work in Sect. 2, then introduces the measurement methodology in Sect. 3. The selected applications for each of the two subsuites/programming model are discussed in Sect. 4. Section 5 shows how energy

---

[1] Since OpenMP 4.0 offloading is still limited to one hardware platform and one compiler it has at the moment vendor specific characteristics. OpenACC on the other hand offers three different compilers and also four (via the CAPS compilers, two via the PGI compilers) hardware platforms.

measurements can enrich the performance data. Section 6 demonstrates how the first published results underline the usefulness of the benchmark in comparing both hardware and software environment for accelerators.

2 Related Work

There has been work done in creating benchmarks for measuring hardware accelerator performance, but all of them are academic in nature and none of them share SPEC's philosophy when it comes to design for standard benchmarks. SPEC strongly believes in same source code for all, a detailed set of run and reporting rules for compliant results, and a peer review process for all results before publication on the SPEC website. This enables fair comparison of results.

With respect to OpenCL benchmarking, both the Parboil [27] and Rodinia [4,5] have been very popular academic benchmarks with more than 1,000 citations between them in research papers. The Parboil and Rodinia developers approached SPEC to standardize the benchmark, to develop a set of run and reporting rules that enable fair performance metrics, and to build a result repository, since the groups could not provide that themselves. SPEC HPG worked with both groups of developers to ensure that the benchmarks taken into the OpenCL suite are running on all available platforms. A number of improvements suggested by SPEC HPG has made it into recent releases of Parboil and Rodinia.

SHOC [7] is a benchmark suite that evolved in the academic circles and includes both the OpenCL and CUDA implementations. As another approach for OpenCL, the SHOC benchmark measures low level hardware performance features rather than general application run time performance. It is, therefore, not suitable for the SPEC approach, but has its relevance on comparing very specific small scale algorithms on various platforms.

On the OpenACC side, the Edinburgh Parallel Computing Centre (EPCC) has developed a benchmark suite [14] comprising a set of low-level operations designed to test raw performance of compilers and hardware and a set of kernels found in scientific codes. The SPEC ACCEL OpenACC suite, on the other hand, is comprised of full scientific applications rather than kernels.

3 Design and Principles of SPEC ACCEL

3.1 Benchmark Philosophy and General Design

The goal of SPEC ACCEL is to measure the performance of compute intensive applications using hardware acceleration. It is designed to compare different accelerator platforms, but also different devices within a platform. A platform consists of all the hardware and software components necessary to execute SPEC ACCEL: the accelerator, the host system including its CPU, the interconnect or bus used for the data transfers between host and accelerator, the support libraries and drivers, and the compiler.

SPEC ACCEL uses vendor independent programming standards to target the accelerators. In its current implementation, OpenCL and OpenACC are supported. Both standards apply the offload model for the accelerated computation. The offload model consists of a CPU (host) which runs the main program, copies the data needed by the accelerated computation to and from discrete memory on the accelerator, and launches the accelerated routines.

The SPEC ACCEL benchmark is provided within the SPEC harness that is also used for other SPEC benchmarks like SPEC CPU2006, SPEC OMP2012, and SPEC MPI2007. With the help of a user supplied config file, the benchmark codes are automatically compiled, the total execution times measured, the results verified for correctness, and a report generated. Optionally, a power measurement is also included to allow the comparison of both time-to-solution and energy-to-solution [16].

The generated performance reports may be submitted to SPEC for publication. The SPEC HPG committee reviews SPEC ACCEL results for consistency, adherence to the run rules, and whether enough details have been supplied for others to reproduce the results. If the committee accepts the results, they are published together with the config file on the SPEC website.

3.2   Run Rules

The run rules cover the procedure for the building and running the benchmark and disclosing the benchmark results. They closely follow the established SPEC run rules but need to take into account the peculiarities of systems with hardware accelerators. This section explains where the run rules from SPEC ACCEL extend or deviate from the common rule set of SPEC. The goal is that users of accelerator systems can compare objectively the accelerators of different vendors on the SPEC web site.

The SPEC ACCEL benchmark suite supports base, peak, and power metrics. The performance metrics are the geometric mean of the run time ratios of the system under test with the run time of the reference machine. The reference system is a SGI C3108-TY11 (a dual socket Intel Xeon E5620 system with 24 GB of main memory) using an NVIDIA Tesla C2070 with error checking and correcting (ECC) enabled as the accelerator. The system runs SLES11 SP2 as the operating system and uses the built-in GNU compilers for the OpenCL suite and the PGI compilers version 13.9 for the OpenACC suite. The reference measurements also include energy metrics recorded from a ZES Zimmer LMG450 power analyzer. All benchmarks in the two suites were targeted to run for at least 100 s on the reference machine in order to provide a useful time for measurements, even for future hardware with significantly higher performance.

A set of tools is supplied to build and run the benchmarks. These SPEC tools must be used to generate publishable results. This helps ensure reproducibility of results by requiring that all individual benchmarks in the suite are run in the same way and that a configuration is available that defines the optimizations used.

The optimizations used are expected to be applicable beyond the SPEC benchmarks, and it is expected that system or compiler vendors would endorse the general use of these optimizations by customers who seek to achieve good application performance. The system components, including software, must be generally available within 90 days of publication; there needs to be a certain level of maturity and general applicability in the methods.

For the base metric, the same compiler must be used for all applications of a given language within a benchmark suite. Except for portability flags, all flags or options that affect the transformation process from SPEC-supplied source to the completed executable must be the same for all modules of a given language. For the peak metric, each module may be compiled with a different compiler and a different set of flags or options. For the OpenCL suite, it is also allowed to change the work distribution on the accelerator by using a different work group size per benchmark.

As used in these run rules, the term run-time dynamic optimization (RDO) refers broadly to any method by which a system adapts an executing program for improved performance based upon observation of its behavior as it runs. Run time dynamic optimization is allowed, subject to the provisions that the techniques must be generally available, documented, and supported.

Results are published on the SPEC web site. A published result must contain enough information to enable others to replicate the result. The information to document an accelerator includes the model name, name of hardware vendor, name and type of the accelerator, description of the connection to the host system, whether ECC is enabled or not, and the device driver names and versions.

4   Description of the Applications

The applications comprising the SPEC ACCEL benchmark fall into two categories depending on the programming model: OpenCL or OpenACC. They cover a wide range of scientific domains and also have very different performance characteristics as shown in Tables 1 and 2. The SPEC ACCEL suite is written to comply with OpenCL 1.1 [15] and OpenACC 1.0 [1]. This section introduces both suites of the SPEC ACCEL benchmark.

4.1   SPEC ACCEL OCL Suite

In order to fit into the design principles for SPEC ACCEL (see Sect. 3), the original benchmarks taken into the OpenCL suite were in part heavily modified. Some benchmarks were dropped when they could not be modified to meet the SPEC HPG requirements. The Parboil Benchmark Suite [27] is the origin of the first nine OpenCL applications of SPEC ACCEL, the other ten applications are taken from the Rodinia Benchmark Suite [4,5]. A number of benchmarks received larger data sets than they originally had, so that their runtime increased to the required 100 s on the reference machine. All benchmarks were tested on all hard- and software platforms available to the HPG members. This resulted in numerous bug fixes both in the benchmarks but also in OpenCL runtime environments, thus, showcasing how this benchmark suite can be used as a validation suite for OpenCL hardware and software as well.

The selected applications span a wide area of science ranging from astronomy, bioinformatics, computer science, electrical engineering, mathematics, mechanical engineering, medicine and physics. They are also selected to cover different usage modes for hardware accelerators. Benchmarks like *101.tpacf* and *121.lavamd* use one or two long running kernels. Other benchmarks like *123.nw* use almost 350,000 very short kernel launches in order to see how well the accelerator ecosystem can handle such extreme cases. The same is true for the number of data transfers between the host and device and the amount of data being transferred. While most benchmarks follow the usual offloading scheme of limiting the amount of transfers, *116.histo*, *117.bfs*, and *127.srad* use well over 10,000 data transfers, in case of *127.srad* also of very small size. The accelerator utilization (which is the amount of time the accelerator is occupied), as well as the time for data transfers, also offers a broad spectrum of load situations. However, most applications try to utilize the accelerator fully, while only a few like *116.histo*, *120.kmeans*, or *127.srad* primarily stress the host-device transfers. *114.mriq* is a special case since it shows both a high device utilization, but also high data transfer time. In this case, the data transfers are launched asynchronously, but the NVIDIA OpenCL runtime forces them to synchronize, thus, completing the transfer only after the previously launched kernel has completed.

The computational algorithms employed by the applications of the benchmark suite also vary widely:

101.tpacf computes the two-point angular correlation function of a collection of observed and randomly generated astronomical bodies. It compares pairs of angular coordinates, computes their angular distance, and computes a histogram of those distances. The histogram is privatized, with multiple copies in each work group, reducing bandwidth and atomic operation demand on the global memory system.

103.stencil implements an iterative Jacobi solver of the heat equation on a 3-D structured grid. The implementation uses double buffering to eliminate timing effects on numerical output values for a fixed number of iterations. On the reference machine, each iteration completes quickly enough so that platform overheads for kernel launches and other operations has an impact on the total performance.

104.lbm is related to the SPEC CPU2006 benchmark of the same name, and implements the Lattice-Boltzmann Method for fluid dynamics simulation [23]. This particular implementation supports immobile solid obstacles to fluid flow in a lid-driven closed cavity. Individual iterations have a long enough runtime that kernel execution performance is the most relevant factor for the total application performance.

110.fft implements a 1-D, Radix-2 Fast Fourier Transform. The kernel source included could be configured to support other radices, but for consistency, the benchmark only supports Radix-2.

Table 1. OpenCL application key facts. Profiling data taken from VampirTrace OpenCL tracing when running on NVIDA Tesla K20 using NVIDIA OpenCL.

Application	Lines of code	Language	Area
101.tpacf	520	C++	Astrophysics
103.stencil	308	C++	Thermodynamics
104.lbm	853	C++	Fluid dynamics
110.fft	642	C	Signal processing
112.spmv	1,108	C++	Sparse linear algebra
114.mriq	569	C	Medicine
116.histo	1,174	C	Silicon wafer verification
117.bfs	452	C	Electronic design automation, graph traversals
118.cutcp	1,192	C	Molecular dynamics
120.kmeans	2,243	C++	Dense linear algebra, data mining
121.lavamd	773	C	N-body, molecular dynamics
122.cfd	1,677	C++	Unstructured grid, fluid dynamics
123.nw	468	C++	Dynamic programming, bioinformatics
124.hotspot	407	C	Structured grid, physics simulation
125.lud	656	C++	Dense linear algebra, linear algebra
126.ge	1,497	C++	Dense linear algebra, linear algebra
127.srad	1,499	C	Structured grid, image processing
128.heartwall	4,671	C	Structured grid, medical imaging
140.bplustree	2,870	C	Graph traversal, search

Application	Kernel invocations	Accelerator utilization	MiBytes transferred	Number of transfers	Transfer time
101.tpacf	1	98.7%	56.2	3	0.02%
103.stencil	20,000	97.0%	294	3	0.10%
104.lbm	5,000	95.3%	331	3	0.15%
110.fft	12,800	97.9%	200	1	0.07%
112.spmv	50,000	88.3%	161	8	0.04%
114.mriq	197	94.2%	61.3	206	96.0%
116.histo	48,000	0.29%	186,755	37,041	95.8%
117.bfs	40,977	73.2%	17,636	84,349	20.8%
118.cutcp	3,250	94.3%	72.6	5	0.07%
120.kmeans	1,617	4.74%	6,296	3,233	60.0%
121.lavamd	2	94.8%	2,650	5	0.94%
122.cfd	72,217	81.9%	12.5	8	0.49%
123.nw	347,088	70.4%	512	2	0.51%
124.hotspot	30,000	85.8%	16.0	1	0.01%
125.lud	17,988	97.2%	6,836	7	1.43%
126.ge	11,262	97.9%	484	6	0.19%
127.srad	39,002	23.2%	112	13,006	97.1%
128.heartwall	100	99.0%	186	109	0.05%
140.bplustree	3,200	98.6%	68.7	18	0.14%

112.spmv implements a sparse-matrix, dense-vector multiplication. The input sparse matrix file format is given in coordinate (COO) format, which is internally translated into a transposed jagged diagonal storage (JDS) format before multiplication. The benchmark reflects classes of applications where the sparse matrix remains constant, but is iteratively multiplied into a variety of vectors, allowing the cost of the data format conversion to be amortized over a large number of operations.

114.mriq computes the Q matrix used in non-Cartesian magnetic resonance image reconstruction algorithms [26]. It is used to compensate for artifacts caused by the sampling trajectory on the actual samples recorded. The first kernel preprocesses one of the input sets, and is negligible in the total runtime. The second kernel accumulates contributions from each sample point to each cell in a 3-D regular grid, using a large number of trigonometric operations. The combination of the multiplicative algorithm complexity and the more complex mathematical operations cause this second kernel to dominate the runtime.

116.histo implements a saturating histogram, which is a very large, two-dimensional matrix of char-type bins with a maximum value of 255. The benchmark is customized to a certain class of input, exemplary of a silicon wafer verification application, which follows a nearly Gaussian distribution, roughly centered in the output histogram. The benchmark executes kernels in four phases. It first runs a small kernel on a subset of the input to estimate the centroid of the output distribution. Second, it decomposes the histogram indexes of the input into separate row and column indexes. Work-groups in the third kernel privatize a portion of the histogram locally, and scan the input for items that fall within that region. Finally, the results from all the privatized histograms are combined into the complete results. Each kernel runs very quickly, and the benchmark executes iteratively, representing the streaming analysis application in which it would be deployed. The relatively small runtime for each individual kernel increase the relative impact of kernel launch and device communication overheads in the platform.

117.bfs implements a single-source shortest-path search through a graph using a breadth-first search [20]. The application performs multiple simultaneous searches on the same graph to estimate the average distance between each node in the graph and all other nodes, based on a sampled subset of sources.

118.cutcp computes a cutoff-limited Coulomb potential field for a set of charges distributed in a volume [10]. The application is set to use a cutoff distance of 12 Å, and builds a spatial data structure of the input charges to reduce the number of distance tests that must be performed for each output cell. The field calculation is performed iteratively, reflecting the computational pattern of a typical analysis of the time-averaged field values.

120.kmeans [3] implements the well-known clustering algorithm of datamining - K-means. In *120.kmeans*, a data object is comprised of several features. By dividing a set of data objects into K clusters, k-means represents all the data objects by the mean values or centroids of their respective clusters. In each iteration, the algorithm associates each data object with its nearest center, based on some chosen distance metric. The new centroids are calculated by taking the mean of all the data objects within each cluster respectively. As a data intensive application, *120.kmeans* transposes the data matrix before doing clustering for better coalesced memory access. However, this benchmark still stresses the memory bandwidth when many single instruction multiple data (SIMD) compute units access global memory simultaneously.

121.lavamd [29] implements an algorithm of molecular dynamic simulation in 3D space. The code calculates particle potential and relocation due to mutual forces between particles within a large 3D space. This space is divided into cubes, or large boxes, that are allocated to individual cluster nodes. The large box at each node is further divided into cubes, called boxes. 26 neighbor boxes surround each box (the home box). Home boxes at the boundaries of the particle space have fewer neighbors. Cutoff-radius strategy is applied enforcing short-range interaction between particles, which stress communication between neighboring work-item groups. *121.lavamd* requires the communication of boundary elements of each box with it neighbor boxes. On a typical GPU, the inter-work-group communication can only be done via synchronized global-memory-access. This benchmark stresses both memory latency and synchronization.

122.cfd [6] is an unstructured-grid, finite-volume solver for the 3D Euler equations for compressible flow. The Runge-Kutta method is used to solve a differential equation. Effective GPU memory bandwidth is improved by reducing total global memory access and overlapping computation, as well as using an appropriate numbering scheme and data layout. Each time step depends on the results of the previous time step and each time step needs a kernel finalization (an implicit synchronization) and re-launch. This benchmark stresses memory bandwidth and has many kernel launches.

123.nw [3] is a nonlinear global optimization method for DNA sequence alignments - Needleman-Wunsch. The potential pairs of sequences are organized in a 2D matrix. In the first step, the algorithm fills the matrix from top left to bottom right, step-by-step. The optimum alignment is the pathway through the array with maximum score, where the score is the value of the maximum weighted path ending at that cell. Thus, the value of each data element depends on the values of its northwest-, north-, and west-adjacent elements. The first step is parallelized on the GPU. Data blocks in each diagonal strip can be processed in parallel with serial dependency across strips. Blocks are mapped to local memory for data locality. In the second step, the maximum path is traced backward to deduce the optimal alignment. When computation is going on, the workload of each step increases at first and then decreases. At some steps, the computation workload is not enough to fill up all the computation units. In certain phases, the throughput is constrained by *123.nw*'s limited parallelism.

124.hotspot [3,13] is a widely used tool to estimate processor temperature based on an architectural floor plan and simulated power measurements. This benchmark solves a differential equation boundary-value problem on a 2D structured grid by using a finite difference method. Each output cell in the computational grid represents the average temperature value of the corresponding area of the chip.

125.lud [5] implements the well-known LU decomposition for a non-singular matrix. The block-wise operation provides enough parallelism for a GPU-like SIMD device. The degree of block-level parallelism reduces as execution proceeds. *125.lud* utilizes the local memory improve data reuse and coalesced memory access. This benchmark stresses floating point computation units and the compute units' local memory.

126.ge solves linear equations using a row-by-row Gaussian elimination. The algorithm requires synchronization between row-wise iterations, but the values calculated in each iteration can be computed in parallel. This benchmark stresses fine-grained global communication and synchronization with many kernel launches.

127.srad [3,28] implements the speckle reducing anisotropic diffusion (SRAD) method, which is a diffusion method for ultrasonic and radar imaging applications based on partial differential equations (PDEs). It is used to remove locally correlated noise, known as speckles, without destroying important image features. SRAD consists of several pieces of work: image extraction, continuous iterations over the image (preparation, reduction, statistics, computation, and image compression). Each stage requires global synchronization across all the workgroups (kernel calls) before proceeding to the next stage. This benchmark also presents a lot of global memory accesses. This benchmark stresses floating point units, global memory access, and global synchronization.

128.heartwall [28] tracks the movement of a mouse heart over a sequence of ultrasound images to record response to the stimulus. In order to reconstruct approximated full shapes of heart walls, the program generates ellipses that are superimposed over the image and sampled to mark points on the heart walls (Hough search). In its final stage (heart wall tracking presented in Ref. [5]), the program tracks movement of surfaces by detecting the movement of image areas under sample points as the shapes of the heart walls change throughout the sequence of images. The tracking kernel continues dealing with consecutive image frames. This benchmark stress floating point units and memory bandwidth.

140.bplustree [9] traverses B+ trees in parallel, avoiding the overhead of selecting the entire table to transform into row-column format and leveraging the logarithmic nature of tree searches. This benchmark utilizes braided parallelism, running independent queries in each work group concurrently, to avoid the need of global synchronization. It involves irregular memory access and therefore stresses memory bandwidth and latency.

4.2 SPEC ACCEL ACC Suite

The OpenACC suite consists of 15 applications. Some applications are direct ports from the OpenCL suite, others have been ported from the SPEC OMP2012 suite. A number of numerical aerodynamic simulation (NAS) parallel benchmarks as well as a few novel applications are included as well.

Similar to the OpenCL suite, the OpenACC suite of the SPEC ACCEL benchmarks also tries to stress the hardware accelerator ecosystem in various ways. The applications vary between few (*314.omriq*) or lots of accelerator

Table 2. OpenACC application key facts. Profiling data taken from PGI OpenACC runtime using an NVIDIA Tesla K40 and the CUDA 5.5 backend

Application	Lines of code	Language	Area
303.ostencil	796	C	Thermodynamics
304.olbm	923	C	Computational fluid Dynamics, Lattice Boltzmann method
314.omriq	693	C	Medicine
350.md	2,479	Fortran	Molecular dynamics
351.palm	48,583	Fortran	Large-eddy simulation, atmospheric turbulence
352.ep	480	C	Random number generation
353.clvrleaf	6,477	C, Fortran	Explicit hydrodynamics
354.cg	638	C	Conjugate gradient
355.seismic	750	Fortran	Seismic wave modeling
356.sp	2,693	Fortran	Scalar Penta-diagonal solver
357.csp	2,364	C	Scalar Penta-diagonal solver
359.miniGhost	6,334	C, Fortran	Finite difference
360.ilbdc	1,065	Fortran	Fluid Mechanics
363.swim	249	Fortran	Weather: shallow water modeling
370.bt	5,524	C	Block tridiagonal solver for 3D PDE

Application	Kernel invocations	# of regions	Accel. usage	MiBytes transferred	# of transfers	Transfer time
303.ostencil	20,000	20,000	92.2%	392	28	0.07%
304.olbm	5,000	5,000	96.2%	16,562	1,053	0.72%
314.omriq	2	2	99.1%	112	12	0.00%
350.md	607	607	97.3%	1,019	2,428	0.01%
351.palm	50,185	46,584	35.4%	102,438	26,377	5.02%
352.ep	1,760	1,760	97.0%	0.027	2,345	0.00%
353.clvrleaf	256,021	203,821	94.4%	3,445	9,678	0.21%
354.cg	13,234	13,234	80.4%	1,173	10,781	0.08%
355.seismic	10,402	3,201	92.8%	6,142	4,431	0.66%
356.sp	27,691	27,691	95.1%	657	46	0.04%
357.csp	26,087	26,087	95.4%	657	46	0.04%
359.miniGhost	72,040	64,040	73.1%	1,622	112,124	1.14%
360.ilbdc	5,000	5,000	88.7%	1,925	121	0.42%
363.swim	90,999	26,000	44.2%	198,563	26,000	40.0%
370.bt	8,051	8,051	95.3%	206	15	0.02%

regions (*353.clvrleaf*), as well as one (most of the applications) or multiple kernel invocation per accelerator region (*363.swim*). In the same manner, the amount and number of data transfers between the host and device differ. At the moment a large amount of data transfers also results in a poorer accelerator utilization. This can, however, change for future OpenACC implementations that better overlap computation and transfer.

The included applications cover a wide area of scientific domains and computational schemes:

303.ostencil is an iterative Jacobi solver of the heat equation on a 3-D structured grid, which can also be used as a building block for more advanced multigrid PDE solvers. This code it ported from the serial version of 103.stencil from Parboil. While the accelerated loop is a fairly simple stencil operation, the code shares the same workload as 103.stencil and offers a way to directly compare an OpenCL and OpenACC implementation of the same code.

304.olbm, like 104.lbm, is ported from the SPEC CPU2006 benchmark and uses the Lattice Boltzmann Method (LBM) to simulate incompressible fluids in 3D. The accelerated portion of the code is a more complex 19-point stencil which stresses the accelerator's global memory and potential cache infrastructure.

314.omriq simulates magnetic resonance imaging (MRI) image reconstruction by converting sampled radio responses into magnetic field gradients. This is a port of the serial version of 114.mriq also from Parboil and uses the same workload. The accelerated loop is fairly small but includes an inner loop reduction, use of `cos` and `sin` functions, and due to the use of an array of structs, some memory accesses are not coalesced. Non-coalesced memory accesses are generally not well suited for accelerators, but are often found in complex applications.

350.md was written at Indiana University to perform molecular dynamics simulations of dense nuclear matter such as those occurring in Type II supernovas, the outer layers of neutron stars, and white dwarf stars [12]. While an earlier version of this code appears in the SPEC OMP2012 benchmark suite, this version has been updated to better utilize the massive parallelization available with accelerators.

351.palm is a large-eddy simulation (LES) model for atmospheric and oceanic flows from Leibniz University of Hannover [25]. It solves prognostic equations for velocity (Navier-Stokes equation), temperature (first law of thermodynamics), and humidity (transport equation for scalar). 351.palm is the largest and most complex of the codes in SPEC ACCEL and best represents how large scale applications can utilize accelerators. The source code includes a host implementation of the Temperton fast Fourier transform (FFT) routines which dominates the compute time spent on the host. However, for the peak metric, an optimized host or accelerated Fastest Fourier Transform in the West (FFTW) library may be used.

352.ep is from the University of Houston and is a port of the embarrassing parallel (EP) benchmark from the NAS Parallel Benchmark (NPB) suite [2]. The port required the use of a blocking algorithm since the entire problem size could not fit within the 2 GB memory limit set in SPEC ACCEL. The benchmark also tests the use of reductions. [17–19]

353.clvleaf is the CloverLeaf [11] mini-application which is used to solve the compressible Euler equations on a Cartesian grid, using an explicit, second-order method.

354.cg is NPB's conjugate gradient (CG) OpenMP benchmark ported to OpenACC by the University of Houston. This benchmark uses the inverse power method to find an estimate of the largest eigenvalue of a symmetric positive definite sparse matrix with a random pattern of nonzeros. The code required few changes from the OpenMP version. [17,18].

355.seismic is ported from University of Pau's SEISMIC_CPML perfectly matched layer (PML) Collino 3D isotropic solver [8], a 3D classical split PML program for an isotropic medium using a second-order, finite-difference spatial operator, for comparison. The code was originally ported to OpenACC for use in tutorials, but due to the minimal number of OpenACC directives used, highlights a compiler's ability to schedule loops and perform reduction operations.

356.sp and *357.csp* are both derived from NPB's singal processing (SP) benchmark, using different languages. Although they do both solve the same problem using the same data set, the SPEC HPG committee thought having both would give a good comparison of using OpenACC with Fortran versus C. The SP benchmark solves a synthetic system of partial differential equations using a penta-diagonal matrix.

359.miniGhost is a finite difference mini-application from Sandia National Laboratory [24] used to test a broad range of stencil algorithms on accelerators. The code also performs inter-process boundary (halo, ghost) exchange and global summation of grid values.

360.ilbdc is an OpenACC port from SPEC OMP2012 [21] and is geared to the collision-propagation routine of an advanced 3-D lattice Boltzmann flow solver using a two-relaxation-time (TRT-type) collision operator for the D3Q19 model. The code uses a similar algorithm to 304.lbm although written in Fortran and uses a minimal number of OpenACC directives.

363.swim is also ported from SPEC OMP2012 and is a finite-difference approximation of the shallow-water equations. Because the data is printed after each time step, the benchmark highlights the cost of moving data between the accelerator and the host which also includes the data movement between the hosts application user memory space and the accelerator driver memory space.

370.bt is NPB's BT benchmark ported to OpenACC. Like SP, it solves a synthetic system of partial differential equations, but instead uses a block tridiagonal matrix.

5   Energy Awareness

Computer systems using hardware accelerators are seen as one method for more energy efficient data processing. The SPEC ACCEL benchmark suites take that into account by providing the same power measurement capabilities as the previously released SPEComp2012 suite. As a result, the energy consumption can be recorded during a measurement run as well. Recording energy consumption is not mandatory but encouraged.

Energy measurement is enabled by changing the `power` setting in the configuration file for the measurement run to `yes` and setting up power and temperature measurement daemons (PTDaemon). The SPEC runtime system then connects to these daemons and continuously samples the energy consumption of the whole system under test every second and the air intake temperature every five seconds. The SPEC ACCEL run rules define how the energy measurement needs to be set up. The power analyzers need to be calibrated in the last 12 months to ensure the energy measurement accuracy. The temperature is measured to prevent reducing the energy consumption by running the system under test at unusually low temperatures – a valid run needs to be carried out with at least 20 °C air intake temperature. The PTDaemon can connect to a variety of power meters and temperature probes and offers range checking, uncertainty calculation, and multi-channel measurements. The SPEC runtime system ensures that at least 99 % of all power samples are reported as valid samples by the PTDaemon. Otherwise, it will abort the run or mark it as invalid.

When the SPEC ACCEL benchmark is run with energy measurement enabled, it will generate two additional metrics per suite:

$$\texttt{SPECaccel\_\{acc|ocl\}\_energy\_\{base|peak\}}.$$

Similar to the standard metrics, the energy metrics compare the energy consumption of the system under test to the energy consumption of the reference system. A higher number indicates a lower energy consumption or better energy efficiency. Energy for this metric means power consumption integrated over time, hence an energy metric of 2 indicates that the system under test consumed half the energy (measured in Joules) than the reference system on the benchmark. As a result, the SPEC ACCEL energy metrics can be used for an energy-to-solution comparison. While the standard SPEC ACCEL metrics provide a measurement for time-to-solution, they may be used in combination to determine the reason why a system under test consumes more or less energy than the reference system. A SPEC_ocl_base rating of 2 and a SPEC_ocl_energy_base rating of 2 indicate that the system under test ran the benchmarks twice as fast as the reference system, but on average consumed the same amount of power. A SPEC_ocl_base rating of 1 and a SPEC_ocl_energy_base rating of 2 indicate that the system under test ran the benchmark in the same time as the reference system, but used on average half the power. In total, both systems consumed half the energy than the reference system, thus, running the benchmark induces only half the energy costs.

The report for a benchmark run lists the consumed energy, the maximum power usage, the average power usage, and the energy ratio for each individual benchmark. The idle power consumption can be taken from the log-file of the benchmark run. Figure 1 shows that the maximum and average power consumption varies quite a lot between benchmarks. The power measurement can be used to indirectly deduce the behavior of the various benchmarks:

– A benchmark with low maximum and average power consumption is mainly data transfer bound since both the host and the device are idle during the transfers.
– A benchmark with a high maximum and average power is largely device bound. There can be both compute or memory access activity on the device.

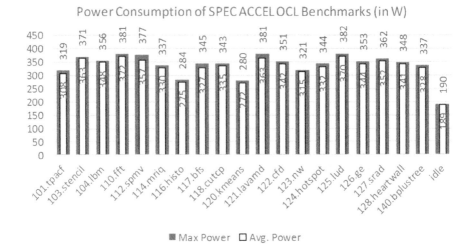

(a) OpenCL benchmarks

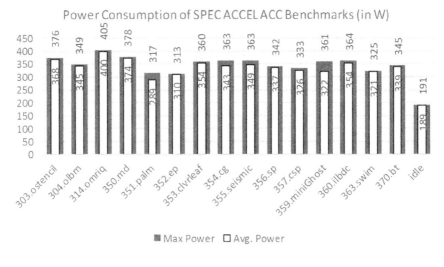

(b) OpenACC benchmarks

Fig. 1. Maximum and average power consumption for all benchmarks as well as idle power consumption when running both SPEC ACCEL suites on the reference system

– A benchmark with a significantly higher maximum than average power consumption has both: phases with lots of data transfers, but also device bound phases resulting in a high variation in power consumption.

6   Discussion of First Results

A run of SPEC ACCEL produces a number of output files in the `result` sub-directory. It writes a logfile of the benchmark run – in case of any errors also a more detailed debug log – as well as text and raw output for each data set (test, train, or ref) it was run on. The runtime and energy consumption of the benchmarks, when executed on the reference machine serve as the basis for normalization. If your SPEC rate is larger than 1, this indicates that your system performs better at running the workload of the selected benchmark suite than the reference system. As a result, the single metric enables a first method of comparing hardware platforms and software environments. The text output for the ref data set also allows a benchmark-by-benchmark comparison with the published results, as shown in Table 3. In this result, it can be seen that not all benchmarks benefit equally from the more modern accelerator. 120.kmeans, for example, only shows an 11 % performance increase while 114.mriq runs over three times as fast. In a similar manner, one can see that this hardware platform is more energy efficient than the reference system and requires less than half the energy to run the suite (as indicated by the SPECaccel_ocl_energy_base value).

The SPEC tool `rawformat` can produce reports from a measurement run that are comparable to the results officially published on the SPEC website. It shows the results from all runs of the ref data set, so that run-to-run variation can be examined as well. The SPEC tools also run tests to determine the hardware and software configuration to aid the gathering of all performance relevant data about the setup of the system under test.

In order to share your results with others on the SPEC website, a reportable run must be done. This will invoke the benchmark suite with the test and train data set once, and the ref data set at least three times. The `rawformat` tool checks for missing system setup information in the result file. One very common issue is a lack of compiler flag description. SPEC requires an xml-based description of all used compiler commands and compiler flags. A result that has been submitted for publication is peer reviewed by HPG members in order to ensure compliance of the benchmark result with the run rules. The review process also ensures that the result contains all information necessary to reproduce the measurement. All published results have passed multiple stages of checking, verification, and cross-checking, thus, serving as a sustainable source for performance data.

A published result is split into multiple sections[2]:

- The header lists the hardware vendor, the used accelerator, and the system name, along with results in all four metrics of the benchmark. It also lists who ran the benchmark, when it was carried out, and when the used hardware and software components are available.
- It is followed by a diagram that shows the distribution of the individual benchmarks. The distribution provides insight into which applications perform well

---

[2] The reference result for the OpenCL suite is available at http://spec.org/accel/results/res2014q1/accel-20140228-00006.html and for the OpenACC suite at http://spec.org/accel/results/res2014q1/accel-20140228-00005.html.

Table 3. SPEC ACCEL OpenCL results for an ASUS P9X79 Motherboard with an Intel Core i7-3930K and an NVIDIA Tesla K40c (ECC enabled) using base optimizations.

Benchmarks	Ref. time	Run time	Ratio	Energy	Max power	Average power	Energy ratio
101.tpacf	107	67.7	1.58	15.3	241	225	2.14
103.stencil	125	61.6	2.03	17.5	296	284	2.59
104.lbm	112	43.4	2.58	12.2	289	280	3.16
110.fft	111	76.0	1.46	22.9	316	302	1.79
112.spmv	147	79.0	1.86	21.8	293	276	2.41
114.mriq	109	33.2	3.28	8.49	271	256	4.25
116.histo	114	80.8	1.41	16.0	216	198	1.95
117.bfs	117	59.2	1.98	14.7	266	248	2.59
118.cutcp	99	34.4	2.88	9.01	273	262	3.68
120.kmeans	100	90.1	1.11	18.0	211	199	1.50
121.lavamd	109	60.2	1.81	17.3	307	288	2.28
122.cfd	126	73.3	1.72	19.1	273	260	2.26
123.nw	115	69.8	1.65	16.0	237	229	2.26
124.hotspot	114	38.7	2.95	10.9	303	281	3.48
125.lud	119	80.9	1.47	22.8	295	282	1.93
126.ge	155	54.1	2.86	14.3	280	265	3.74
127.srad	114	60.7	1.88	16.9	292	278	2.36
128.heartwall	106	88.0	1.20	21.7	255	247	1.66
140.bplustree	108	70.0	1.54	17.3	257	247	2.05
SPECaccel_ocl_energy_base							2.43
SPECaccel_ocl_base			1.87				

or not so well on the system under test. The bars also have ticks for all runs of the ref data set so that run-to-run variation is also easily visible.

- The system description section lists the host and accelerator's hardware properties along with the software set up.
- With energy measurement enabled, the next section shows the properties of its setup including power supply, power analyzer used, and the temperature probe.
- The result table(s) lists the execution time and the ratio for each iteration of every benchmark, as well as the energy measurement results (if energy measurement is enabled).
- The notes section shows the output from the SPEC sysinfo tool and any custom notes by the submitter of the result.

Table 4. SPEC ACCEL OpenACC results for an ASUS P9X79 Motherboard with an Intel Core i7-3930K and an NVIDIA Tesla K40c (ECC enabled) running at various GPU clock frequencies using base optimizations

Benchmarks	745 MHz		810 MHz			
	Ratio	ERatio	Ratio	Speedup	ERatio	ESaving
303.ostencil	2.60	3.09	2.96	13%	3.27	5%
304.olbm	1.99	2.61	2.20	9%	2.74	5%
314.omriq	2.37	2.96	2.57	8%	2.99	1%
350.md	2.31	2.97	2.59	11%	3.05	3%
351.palm	1.88	2.50	1.97	5%	2.57	2%
352.ep	1.36	1.80	1.49	9%	1.91	5%
353.clvrleaf	2.65	3.37	2.94	10%	3.48	3%
354.cg	2.50	3.24	2.74	9%	3.40	5%
355.seismic	2.38	3.20	2.64	10%	3.37	5%
356.sp	2.04	2.65	2.26	10%	2.78	5%
357.csp	1.65	2.16	1.82	10%	2.28	5%
359.miniGhost	2.17	2.82	2.69	19%	3.25	13%
360.ilbdc	3.11	4.10	3.64	14%	4.45	8%
363.swim	2.31	3.14	2.50	7%	3.25	4%
370.bt	2.50	3.35	2.81	11%	3.58	7%
Overall	**2.21**	**2.88**	**2.47**	**10%**	**3.03**	**4%**

Benchmarks	745 MHz		875 MHz			
	Ratio	ERatio	Ratio	Speedup	ERatio	ESaving
303.ostencil	2.60	3.09	3.17	18%	3.16	2%
304.olbm	1.99	2.61	2.35	15%	2.78	6%
314.omriq	2.37	2.96	2.70	12%	2.91	-2%
350.md	2.31	2.97	2.78	17%	2.97	0%
351.palm	1.88	2.50	2.01	7%	2.54	2%
352.ep	1.36	1.80	1.61	16%	1.96	8%
353.clvrleaf	2.65	3.37	3.07	14%	3.44	2%
354.cg	2.50	3.24	2.84	12%	3.37	4%
355.seismic	2.38	3.20	2.79	15%	3.38	5%
356.sp	2.04	2.65	2.35	13%	2.74	3%
357.csp	1.65	2.16	1.89	13%	2.25	4%
359.miniGhost	2.17	2.82	2.80	22%	3.21	12%
360.ilbdc	3.11	4.10	3.77	18%	4.37	6%
363.swim	2.31	3.14	2.60	11%	3.25	3%
370.bt	2.50	3.35	2.95	15%	3.56	6%
Overall	**2.21**	**2.88**	**2.59**	**14%**	**3.01**	**4%**

- The compiler section lists the compiler(s) and compiler flags used for every individual application in the suite. It also provides a link to the previously mentioned flags file explaining the compiler settings in more detail.

Among the initially submitted results from the SPEC ACCEL OpenACC suite is an experiment on how different GPU clock frequency affects application per-

Table 5. SPEC ACCEL OpenACC results for an ASUS P9X79 Motherboard with an Intel Core i7-3930K and an NVIDIA Tesla K40c using base optimizations with ECC enabled and disabled

Benchmarks	ECC enabled		ECC disabled			
	Ratio	ERatio	Ratio	Speedup	ERatio	ESaving
303.ostencil	2.60	3.09	2.67	2.7%	3.19	3.2%
304.olbm	1.99	2.61	4.37	120%	5.62	115%
314.omriq	2.37	2.96	2.86	20.7%	3.45	16.6%
350.md	2.31	2.97	2.35	1.7%	3.00	1.0%
351.palm	1.88	2.50	1.96	4.3%	2.62	4.8%
352.ep	1.36	1.80	1.37	0.7%	1.81	0.6%
353.clvrleaf	2.65	3.37	2.98	12.5%	3.72	10.4%
354.cg	2.50	3.24	2.60	4.0%	3.43	5.9%
355.seismic	2.38	3.20	2.55	7.1%	3.43	7.2%
356.sp	2.04	2.65	2.45	20.1%	3.19	20.4%
357.csp	1.65	2.16	1.91	15.8%	2.51	16.2%
359.miniGhost	2.17	2.82	2.84	30.9%	3.62	28.4%
360.ilbdc	3.11	4.10	4.09	31.5%	5.21	27.1%
363.swim	2.31	3.14	2.46	6.5%	3.35	6.7%
370.bt	2.50	3.35	2.80	12.0%	3.79	13.1%
Overall	**2.21**	**2.88**	**2.59**	**22.7%**	**3.35**	**16.3%**

formance. The experiment uses the GPU Boost capabilities of the NVIDIA K40c GPU where the clock speed can be increased from the default 745 MHz to 810 and 875 MHz. The results are shown in Table 4. All benchmarks benefit from the increased GPU clock rate and none consume more energy to run the applications. Since the energy savings are less than the performance gain, the system actually draws more power, but over a shorter period of time. Increasing the GPU's clock speed also helps with memory bandwidth efficiency, hence, some benchmarks see improvements greater than the clock boost. Other benchmarks see less performance since they either have a high percentage of time spent on the host (351.palm, 354.cg) or have higher memory transfer rate between the host and device (363.swim). As a result of this study, a site such as Oak Ridge or or National Center for Supercomputing Applications (NCSA) could decide to increase the GPU clock rate by default since a broad range of applications benefit from it (reduced runtime) without extra costs (same or less energy consumption).

Another widely discussed question that can be answered with the currently published results is the impact of ECC on accelerator performance. Table 5 shows the results for the SPEC ACCEL OpenACC benchmarks with ECC turned on and off. As expected, performance improvements, due to the increased memory bandwidth when ECC is disabled, actually vary by a very large amount for the applications used. On average, disabling ECC yields a performance increase of 22.7 %, and the energy consumption also slightly improves due to the reduced computing times. Whether this nominal performance increase is worth the risk of wrong results is a different discussion. Within the SPEC harness, the result verification routine ensures that the applications generate the expected results.

7 Summary and Future Work

SPEC HPG set out to develop a performance measurement environment based on the SPEC principles for hardware accelerators. As a result, two application suites – one with OpenCL and one with OpenACC applications – have been released with SPEC ACCEL. They deliver performance and energy consumption metrics that enable comparing hardware devices and software environments. The goals set by HPG for the development of these application suites are met. The metrics reflect the impact of different hardware and hardware settings, but also show how different software environments (e.g., compilers, runtimes) affect application performance. The mix of selected applications also demonstrates that not all applications react in a similar manner to such a change. The suites can also serve as a yardstick for determining the best hardware and software for solving particular scientific problems. Furthermore, the suites have already been used by compiler and runtime vendors as a mean for verification of the developed software stacks.

SPEC ACCEL is set apart from other accelerator benchmarks for hardware accelerators since it is simple to run, yet has a performance evaluation process that uses real world applications under a strict measurement environment and a peer review process for published results. Furthermore, the energy consumption metric enables comparison between results not only by runtime of the applications, but also energy consumed.

HPG plans to extend SPEC ACCEL with a third suite covering OpenMP 4.0 target directives in the near future. The OpenACC applications will be ported to support OpenMP 4.0 target directive so that devices that are currently not supported by OpenACC may be compared to devices that are. Beyond that effort, SPEC HPG is investigating future updates to the various suites to support more current versions of OpenCL and OpenACC.

Acknowledgments. The authors thank Cloyce Spradling for his work on the SPEC harness as well as the SPEC POWER group for their work on enabling the integration of power measurements into other SPEC suites.

SPEC®, SPEC ACCEL™, SPEC CPU™, SPEC MPI®, and SPEC OMP® are registered trademarks of the Standard Performance Evaluation Corporation (SPEC). AMD is a trademarks of Advanced Micro Devices, Inc. OpenCL is a trademark of Apple, Inc. used by permission by Khronos. Other names used in this presentation are for identification purposes only and may be trademarks of their respective owners.

Contributions by the University of Houston were supported in part by NVIDIA and Department of Energy under Award Agreement No. DE-FC02-12ER26099.

References

1. The OpenACC Application Programming Interface, November 2011. http://www.openacc.org/sites/default/files/OpenACC.1.0_0.pdf, version 1.0
2. Bailey, D., Barszcz, E., Barton, J., Browning, D., Carter, R., Dagum, L., Fatoohi, R., Fineberg, S., Lasinski, T., Schreiber, R., Simon, H., Venkatakrishnan, V., Weeratunga, S.: The NAS parallel benchmarks. Technical report RNR-94-2007, NASA (1994). http://www.nas.nasa.gov/assets/pdf/techreports/1994/rnr-94-007.pdf
3. Che, S., Boyer, M., Meng, J., Tarjan, D., Sheaffer, J.W., Skadron, K.: A performance study of general-purpose applications on graphics processors using CUDA. J. Parallel Distrib. Comput. **68**(10), 1370–1380 (2008). http://dx.doi.org/10.1016/j.jpdc.2008.05.014
4. Che, S., Boyer, M., Meng, J., Tarjan, D., Sheaffer, W.J., Lee, S.H., Skadron, K.: Rodinia: a benchmark suite for heterogeneous computing. In: Proceedings of the IEEE International Symposium on Workload Characterization (IISWC), pp. 44–54, October 2009
5. Che, S., Sheaffer, W.J., Boyer, M., Szafaryn, L.G., Wang, L., Skadron, K.: A characterization of the rodinia benchmark suite with comparison to contemporary CMP workloads. In: Proceedings of the IEEE International Symposium on Workload Characterization (IISWC), December 2010
6. Corrigan, A., Camelli, F., Lohner, R., Wallin, J.: Running unstructured grid CFD solvers on modern graphics hardware. In: Proceedings of the 19th AIAA Computational Fluid Dynamics Conference, June 2009
7. Danalis, A., Marin, G., McCurdy, C., Meredith, J.S., Roth, P.C., Spafford, K., Tipparaju, V., Vetter, J.S.: The scalable heterogeneous computing (SHOC) benchmark suite. In: Proceedings of the 3rd Workshop on General-Purpose Computation on Graphics Processing Units, GPGPU 2010, pp. 63–74. ACM, New York (2010). http://doi.acm.org/10.1145/1735688.1735702
8. Komatitsch, D., Martin, R.: University of Pau: SEISMIC_CPML. http://geodynamics.org/cig/software/seismic_cpml/
9. Fix, J., Wilkes, A., Skadron, K.: Accelerating braided B+ tree searches on a GPU with CUDA. In: Proceedings of the 2nd Workshop on Applications for Multi and Many Core Processors: Analysis, Implementation, and Performance (A4MMC), in Conjunction with ISCA, June 2011
10. Hardy, D.J., Stone, J.E., Vandivort, K.L., Gohara, D., Rodrigues, C., Schulten, K.: Fast molecular electrostatics algorithms on GPUs. In: GPU Computing Gems (2010)
11. Herdman, J., Gaudin, W., McIntosh-Smith, S., Boulton, M., Beckingsale, D., Mallinson, A., Jarvis, S.: Accelerating hydrocodes with OpenACC, OpeCL and CUDA. In: 2012 SC Companion: High Performance Computing, Networking, Storage and Analysis (SCC), pp. 465–471, November 2012
12. Horowitz, C.J., Berry, D.K., Brown, E.F.: Phase separation in the crust of accreting neutron stars. Phys. Rev. E **75**, 066101 (2007). http://link.aps.org/doi/10.1103/PhysRevE.75.066101
13. Huang, W., Ghosh, S., Velusamy, S., Sankaranarayanan, K., Skadron, K., Stan, M.: HotSpot: a compact thermal modeling methodology for early-stage VLSI design. IEEE Trans. Very Large Scale Integr. (VLSI) Syst. **14**(5), 501–513 (2006)
14. Johnson, N.: EPCC OpenACC benchmark suite. https://www.epcc.ed.ac.uk/research/computing/performance-characterisation-and-benchmarking/epcc-openacc-benchmark-suite

15. Khronos Group: OpenCL 1.1 API and C Language Specification, June 2011. https://www.khronos.org/registry/cl/specs/opencl-1.1.pdf, revision 44

16. Lange, K.D.: Identifying shades of green: the SPECpower benchmarks. Computer **42**, 95–97 (2009)

17. Lee, S., Eigenmann, R.: OpenMPC: extended OpenMP programming and tuning for GPUs. In: Proceedings of the 2010 ACM/IEEE International Conference for High Performance Computing, Networking, Storage and Analysis, pp. 1–11. IEEE Computer Society (2010)

18. Lee, S., Min, S.J., Eigenmann, R.: OpenMP to GPGPU: a compiler framework for automatic translation and optimization. ACM Sigplan Not. **44**(4), 101–110 (2009)

19. Lee, S., Vetter, J.S.: Early evaluation of directive-based gpu programming models for productive exascale computing. In: Proceedings of the International Conference on High Performance Computing, Networking, Storage and Analysis, p. 23. IEEE Computer Society Press (2012)

20. Luo, L., Wong, M., Hwu, W.W.: An effective GPU implementation of breadth-first search. In: Proceedings of the 47th Design Automation Conference, pp. 52–55, June 2010

21. Müller, M.S., et al.: SPEC OMP2012 — an application benchmark suite for parallel systems using OpenMP. In: Chapman, B.M., Massaioli, F., Müller, M.S., Rorro, M. (eds.) IWOMP 2012. LNCS, vol. 7312, pp. 223–236. Springer, Heidelberg (2012). http://dx.doi.org/10.1007/978-3-642-30961-8_17

22. Müller, M.S., van Waveren, M., Lieberman, R., Whitney, B., Saito, H., Kumaran, K., Baron, J., Brantley, W.C., Parrott, C., Elken, T., Feng, H., Ponder, C.: SPEC MPI2007 - an application benchmark suite for parallel systems using MPI. Concurr. Comput. Pract. Exper. **22**(2), 191–205 (2010). http://dx.doi.org/10.1002/cpe.v22:2

23. Qian, Y.H., D'Humieres, D., Lallemand, P.: Lattice BGK models for navier-stokes equation. Europhys. Lett. **17**, 479–484 (1992)

24. Barrett, R.F., Vaughan, C.T., Heroux, M.A.: MiniGhost: A miniapp for exploring boundary exchange strategies using stencil computations in scientific parallel computing, Version 1.0. Techical report (2012)

25. Raasch, S.: Leibniz University of Hannover: PALM. http://palm.muk.uni-hannover.de/

26. Stone, S.S., Haldar, J.P., Tsao, S.C., Hwu, W.W., Liang, Z., Sutton, B.P.: Accelerating advanced MRI reconstructions on GPUs. In: International Conference on Computing Frontiers, pp. 261–272 (2008)

27. Stratton, J.A., Rodrigues, C., Sung, I.J., Obeid, N., Chang, L., Liu, G., Hwu, W.W.: Parboil: a revised benchmark suite for scientific and commercial throughput computing. Technical report IMPACT-12-01. University of Illinois at Urbana-Champaign, Urbana, March 2012

28. Szafaryn, L.G., Skadron, K., Saucerman, J.J.: Experiences accelerating MATLAB systems biology applications. In: Proceedings of the Workshop on Biomedicine in Computing: Systems, Architectures, and Circuits (BiC) 2009, in Conjunction with the 36th IEEE/ACM International Symposium on Computer Architecture (ISCA), June 2009

29. Szafaryn, L.G., Gamblin, T., de Supinski, B.R., Skadron, K.: Trellis: portability across architectures with a high-level framework. J. Parallel Distrib. Comput. **73**(10), 1400–1413 (2013)

A CUDA Implementation of the High Performance Conjugate Gradient Benchmark

Everett Phillips$^{(\boxtimes)}$ and Massimiliano Fatica

NVIDIA Corporation, Santa Clara, CA 95050, USA
ephillips@nvidia.com

Abstract. The High Performance Conjugate Gradient (HPCG) benchmark has been recently proposed as a complement to the High Performance Linpack (HPL) benchmark currently used to rank supercomputers in the Top500 list. This new benchmark solves a large sparse linear system using a multigrid preconditioned conjugate gradient (PCG) algorithm. The PCG algorithm contains the computational and communication patterns prevalent in the numerical solution of partial differential equations and is designed to better represent modern application workloads which rely more heavily on memory system and network performance than HPL. GPU accelerated supercomputers have proved to be very effective, especially with regard to power efficiency, for accelerating compute intensive applications like HPL. This paper will present the details of a CUDA implementation of HPCG, and the results obtained at full scale on the largest GPU supercomputers available: the Cray XK7 at ORNL and the Cray XC30 at CSCS. The results indicate that GPU accelerated supercomputers are also very effective for this type of workload.

1 Introduction

After twenty years of the High Performance Linpack (HPL) benchmark, it is now time to complement this benchmark with a new one that can stress different components in a supercomputer. HPL solves a dense linear system using Gaussian Elimination with partial pivoting, and its performance is directly correlated with dense matrix-matrix multiplication. While there are applications with similar workload (material science codes like DCA++ or WL-LSMS, both winners of the Gordon Bell awards), the vast majority of applications cannot be recast in terms of dense linear algebra and their performance poorly correlates with the performance of HPL.

In 2013, Dongarra and Heroux [1] proposed a new benchmark designed to better represent modern application workloads that rely more heavily on memory system and network performance than HPL. The new benchmark, HPCG, solves a large sparse linear system using an iterative method. It is an evolution of one of the Mantevo Project applications from Sandia [12]. The Mantevo Project was an effort to provide open-source software packages for the analysis, prediction and improvement of high performance computing applications. This is not the first time that a new benchmark has been proposed to replace or augment the

© Springer International Publishing Switzerland 2015
S.A. Jarvis et al. (Eds.): PMBS 2014, LNCS 8966, pp. 68–84, 2015.
DOI: 10.1007/978-3-319-17248-4_4

Top 500 list. The HPCC benchmark suite [2] and the Graph 500 benchmark [4] are two well known proposals, but up to now the uptake has been limited. Graph 500 after 4 years is still listing only 160 systems.

This paper presents a CUDA implementation of HPCG and the results on large supercomputers. Although we use CUDA, the algorithms and methods are applicable in general on highly parallel processors. The paper is organized as follows: after a short introduction to CUDA, we describe the algorithmic details of HPCG. A description of the CUDA implementation and optimization is then given, followed by a section on results and comparison with available data.

2   GPU Computing and CUDA

The use of GPUs in high performance computing, sometimes referred to as *GPU computing*, is becoming very popular due to the high computational power and high memory bandwidth of these devices coupled with the availability of high level programming languages.

CUDA is an entire computing platform for C/C++/Fortran on the GPU. Using high-level languages, GPU-accelerated applications run the sequential part of their workload on the CPU - which is optimized for single-threaded performance - while accelerating parallel processing on the GPU.

CUDA follows the data-parallel model of computation. Typically each thread executes the same operation on different elements of the data in parallel. Threads are organized into a 1D, 2D or 3D grid of thread-blocks. Each block can be 1D, 2D or 3D in shape, and can consist of up to 1024 threads on current hardware. Threads within a thread block can cooperate via lightweight synchronization primitives and a high-speed on-chip shared memory cache.

Kernel invocations in CUDA are asynchronous, so it is possible to run CPU and GPU in parallel. Data movement can also be overlapped with computations and GPU can DMA directly from page-locked host memory. There are also a large number of libraries, from linear algebra to random number generation. Two libraries that are particularly relevant to this benchmark are CUBLAS [8] and CUSPARSE [9], that implement linear algebra operations on dense or sparse matrices. In the benchmark, we also used Thrust [10], a C++ template library for CUDA based on the Standard Template Library (STL), to sort and find unique values.

3   HPCG

The new HPCG benchmark is based on an additive Schwarz Preconditioned Conjugate Gradient (PCG) algorithm [3].

The benchmark has 8 distinct phases:

1. Problem and Preconditioner setups
2. Optimization phase

3. Validation testing
4. Reference sparse Matrix-vector multiply and Gauss-Seidel kernel timings
5. Reference PCG timing and residual reduction
6. Optimized PCG setup
7. Optimized PCG timing and analysis
8. Report results

During the initial setup, data structures are allocated and the sparse matrix is generated. The sparse linear system used in HPCG is based on a simple elliptic partial differential equation discretized with a 27-point stencil on a regular 3D grid. Each processor is responsible for a subset of matrix rows corresponding to a local domain of size $N_x \times N_y \times N_z$, chosen by the user in the hpcg.dat input file. The number of processors is automatically detected at runtime, and decomposed into $P_x \times P_y \times P_z$, where $P = P_x P_y P_z$ is the total number of processors. This creates a global domain $G_x \times G_y \times G_z$, where $G_x = P_x N_x$, $G_y = P_y N_y$, and $G_z = P_z N_z$. Although the matrix has a simple structure, it is only intended to facilitate the problem setup and validation of the solution, and may not be taken advantage of to optimize the solver.

Between the initial setup and validation, the benchmark calls a user-defined optimization routine, which allows for analysis of the matrix, reordering of the matrix rows, and transformation of data structures, in order to expose parallelism and improve performance of the SYMGS smoother. This generally requires reordering matrix rows using graph coloring for performance on highly parallel processors such as GPUs. However, this introduces a slowdown in the rate of convergence, which in turn increases the number of iterations required to reach the solution. The time for these additional iterations, as well as the time for the optimization routine, is counted against the final performance result.

Next, the benchmark calls the reference PCG solver for 50 iterations and stores the final residual. The optimized PCG is then executed for one cycle to find out how many iterations are needed to match the reference residual. Once the number of iterations is known, the code computes the number of PCG sets required to fill the entire execution time. The benchmark can complete in a matter of minutes, but official results submitted to Top500 require a minimum of one hour duration.

3.1   The PCG Algorithm

The PCG algorithm solves a linear system $Ax = b$ given an initial guess x_0 with the following iterations:

We can identify these basic operations:

A. Vector inner products $\alpha := y^T z$. Each MPI process computes its local inner product and then calls a collective reduction to get the final value.
B. Vector updates $w = \alpha y + \beta z$. These are local updates, where performance is limited by the memory system.

Algorithm 1. Preconditioned Conjugate Gradient [1]

1: $k = 0$
2: Compute the residual $r_0 = b - Ax_0$
3: **while** $(\|r_k\| < \epsilon)$ **do**
4:     $z_k = M^{-1} r_k$
5:     $k = k + 1$
6:     **if** $k = 1$ **then**
7:         $p_1 = z_0$
8:     **else**
9:         $\beta_k = r_{k-1}^T z_{k-1} / r_{k-2}^T z_{k-2}$
10:        $p_k = z_{k-1} + \beta_k p_{k-1}$
11:    **end if**
12:    $\alpha_k = r_{k-1}^T z_{k-1} / p_k^T A p_k$
13:    $x_k = x_{k-1} + \alpha_k p_k$
14:    $r_k = r_{k-1} - \alpha_k A p_k$
15: **end while**
16: $x = x_k$

C. Application of the preconditioner $w := M^{-1}y$, where M^{-1} is an approximation to A^{-1}. The preconditioner is an iterative multigrid solver using a symmetric Gauss-Seidel smoother (SYMGS). Application of SYMGS at each grid
level involves neighborhood communication, followed by local computation
of a forward sweep (update local elements in row order) and backward sweep
(update local elements in reverse row order) of Gauss-Seidel. The ordering
constraint makes the SYMGS routine difficult to parallelize, and is the main
challenge of the benchmark.

D. Matrix-vector products Ay. This operation requires neighborhood communication to collect the remote values of y owned by neighbor processors, followed
by multiplication of the local matrix rows with the input vector. The pattern
of data access is similar to a sweep of SYMGS, however the rows may be
trivially processed in parallel since there are no data dependencies between
rows (the output vector is distinct from the input vector).

All of these are BLAS1 (vector-vector) or BLAS2 (sparse matrix-vector) operations. We are not able to use BLAS3 operations, such as DGEMM, as we were
able to do for HPL. An important point is that the benchmark is not about
computing a highly accurate solution to this problem, but is only intended to
measure performance of the algorithm.

3.2   Preconditioner

The problem is solved using a domain decomposition where each subdomain is
locally preconditioned. The preconditioner in initial version (v1.x) was based
on a symmetric Gauss-Seidel sweep. The latest version (v2.x) is based on a
multigrid preconditioner where the pre and post smoothers are also a symmetric
Gauss-Seidel sweep.

Gauss-Seidel Preconditioner. Since the PCG method could be used only on a symmetric positive definite matrix, the preconditioner must also be symmetric and positive definite. The matrix M is computed from lower triangular (L), diagonal (D) and upper triangular (U) parts of A:

$$M_{SGS} = (D + L)D^{-1}(D + U)$$

It is easy to verify that this matrix is symmetric and positive definite using the identity $(D+U)^T = (D+L)$. The application of the preconditioner requires the solution of upper and lower triangular systems.

Multigrid Preconditioner. The latest version of the benchmark is using a multigrid preconditioner instead of the simple iterative Gauss-Seidel. An iterative solver like Gauss-Seidel is very effective in damping the high frequency components of the error, but is not very effective on the low frequency ones. The idea of the multigrid is to represent the error from the initial grid on a coarser grid where the low frequency components of the original grid become high frequency components on the coarser one [14]. The multigrid V-cycle includes the following steps:

A. Perform a number of Gauss-Seidel iterations to smooth the high frequencies and compute the residual $r^H = Ax^H - b$, where the superscript H denotes the grid spacing.
B. Transfer the residual r^H on a coarser grid of space $2H$. This operation is often called *restriction*, and R the restriction matrix.

$$r^{2H} = Rr^H$$

C. Perform a number of Gauss-Seidel iterations to smooth the error on the coarser grid residual equation

$$Ae^{2H} = r^{2H}$$

D. Transfer the correction e^{2H} back on the fine grid of space H. This operation is often called *prolongation*, and P the prolongation matrix.

$$e^H = Pe^{2H}$$

The process can be extended to multiple levels. The HPCG benchmark is using a V-cycle strategy with 3 coarser levels and performs a single pre- and post- smoother Gauss-Seidel at each level.

3.3   Selecting Node Count

HPCG detects the number of MPI tasks at runtime and tries to build a 3D decomposition. Clearly if the number of tasks, N, is a prime, the only possible 3D decomposition is $N \times 1 \times 1$ (or a permutation). While this is a valid configuration, it is highly unlikely that a real code would run with such a configuration.

We always try to select a 3D configuration that is as balanced as possible. Since the jobs on large supercomputers go through a batching system and the number of available nodes may vary due to down nodes, it is useful to know the best node count in a certain range. We have extracted the routine internally used by HPCG and made a standalone program that we use to analyze the possible decompositions. A simple criterion is to sort N1, N2, N3 and compute the product of the ratios N_max/N_min and N_mid/N_min. The closer to the unity this product is, the more balanced the decomposition is.

4   CUDA Implementation

The GPU porting strategy is primarily focused on the parallelization of the Symmetric Gauss-Seidel smoother (SYMGS), which accounts for approximately two thirds of the benchmark Flops. This function is difficult to parallelize due to the data dependencies imposed by the ordering of the matrix rows. Although it is possible to use analysis of the matrix structure to build a dependency graph which exposes parallelism, we find it is more effective to reorder the rows using graph coloring.

Our implementation begins with a baseline using CUDA libraries, and progresses into our final version in the following steps:

A. CUSPARSE (CSR)
B. CUSPARSE + color ordering (CSR)
C. Custom Kernels + color ordering (CSR)
D. Custom Kernels + color ordering (ELL)

4.1   Baseline CUSPARSE

Starting with CUSPARSE has the benefit of keeping the coding effort low, and hiding the complexity of parallelizing the Symmetric-Gauss-Siedel smoother. It also allows us to easily validate the results against the reference solution, and perform experiments with matrix reordering.

With CUSPARSE, we are required to use a compatible matrix data format, which is based on compressed sparse row (CSR). The matrix elements and column index arrays must be stored in contiguous memory in row major order. An additional requirement is a row_start index array which gives the position of the starting element of each row. By contrast, the matrix format in HPCG uses arrays of row pointers, with a separate memory allocation for the elements and column indices for each row. There is also an array which gives the number of nonzero elements per row.

Additionally, the CUSPARSE triangular solver routine requires elements within each row to be sorted such that elements with column index smaller than the diagonal appear before the diagonal, and elements with column index larger than the diagonal appear after the diagonal. The default matrix format in HPCG violates this assumption in rows that are on the boundary of the local domain. In these rows the halo elements (those received from a neighbor processor) have column indices larger than the number of rows, but may appear before the diagonal because the order is inherited from the natural ordering of the global matrix.

Next, we describe the implementation of the SYMGS smoother, using the CUSPARSE and CUBLAS library routines. The main computational kernel, the sparse triangular solve, requires information about the structure of the matrix in order to expose parallelism. Thus, a pre-processing step is required to analyze the matrix structure using `cusparseDcsrsv_analysis` before any calls to `cusparseDcsrsv_solve` can be made. The analysis function essentially builds a task dependency graph that is later used when the solver is called. We must perform the analysis for both the upper and lower triangular portions of the matrix. This analysis phase maps nicely to the optimization phase of the benchmark, and the time spent here is recorded in the optimization timing.

The following lists the library calls that are made to perform SYMGS:

```
r  <-- rhs      cublasDcopy
r  <-- r - A*x  cusparseDcsrmv (SPMV)
y  <-- L*y=r    cusparseDcsrsv_solve
y  <-- y*D      cublasDaxpy
dx <-- U*dx=y   cusparseDcsrsv_solve
x  <-- x+dx     cublasDaxpy
```

This sequence is not as efficient as the reference algorithm which combines the SPMV, vector updates, and triangular solves, reducing the number of steps and the number of times data must be accessed from memory. The WAXPBY is another example of a function which looses efficiency when implemented with library calls, in general it requires three calls: `cublasDcopy`, `cublasDscale`, and `cublasDaxpy`. Other routines are more straightforward using the libraries, Dot-Product is simply a call to `cublasDdot`, SPMV is a single call to `cusparseDcsrmv`.

The only CUDA kernels we wrote for this version, are for the routines which have irregular access patterns to gather or scatter values based on an index array. This occurs when gathering elements from the local domain that must be sent to neighbor processors, and also when performing restriction and prolongation operators (the coarse grid elements each read or write to a fine grid element given by the `f2c` index array).

4.2   Reordering with Graph Coloring

The matrix can be re-ordered based on a multi-coloring where every row is assigned a color that is not shared with any rows to which it has a connection. Parallel algorithms have been developed to solve this problem [19,20]. The basic idea is to assign a random value to each row, and then designate a color to rows whose values are local maxima when comparing their random values with connected uncolored rows. The process is repeated, adding a new color in each step. Although this can be done completely in parallel, several iterations are required before all rows are assigned a color, and the number of colors is typically sub optimal (larger than the minimum number of colors which would be computed using a serial greedy algorithm).

We adopt several improvements proposed by Cohen et al. [21]. Namely, we replace the random number generation with an on-the-fly hash of the row index, and each row redundantly computes the hash of all neighbors. This trades off additional computation in order to avoid storing the hash values and reduces memory bandwidth requirements. We also compute two independent sets of colors in each step, one for local maxima, and another for local minima. The following code illustrates the basic coloring algorithm where `minmax_hash_step` assigns two colors in each iteration, where A_col is the matrix column index array, and colors is a vector of integers representing the color of each row:

```
while( colored < rows ){
minmax_hash_step<<<>>>(A_col, colors...);
colored += thrust::count(colors, ...);
}
```

We improve the coloring quality in cases where the number of colors is too large, by performing a re-coloring. We loop over each original color, from greatest to smallest, and every row of that color attempts to reassign itself a lower color not shared with any neighbors. Since all rows of the same color are independent, we can safely update their colors in parallel. The process could be repeated to further reduce the color count, but the benefits are reduced with each pass. The following code snippet shows a single re-coloring pass:

```
if( max_color > target ){
for( color=max_color; color>0; color-- )
 recolor_step<<<>>>(A_col, colors...);
}
```

After the coloring is completed, we use the color information to create a permutation vector, which is used to reorder the rows in the matrix according to their colors. The permutation vector is initialized with the natural order, and then sorted by key, using colors as the key. The following code snippet shows the creation of the perm vector using the THRUST `sort_by_key` routine:

```
thrust::sort_by_key(colors, colors+rows, perm);
```

4.3   Custom Kernels CSR Version

Next, we replace the CUSPARSE calls with our own routines. This allows us to adopt a more flexible matrix format which simplifies the reordering of the matrix, and removes the need for sorting of the row elements with respect to the diagonal. Using the reordered matrix, we can perform the SYMGS sweeps using the same algorithm as the reference. The following code shows the SYMGS kernel:

```
__global__ void smooth(double* A_vals, ...
{
int row_index = threadIdx.x ...
```

```
if( row_index < last_row ){
 double sum = rhs[row_index];
 for( i=start_index; i<end_index; i+=stride ){
  if(A_col[i] != -1 )
  if(A_col[i] != row_index ){
   sum += -A_vals[i] * x[A_col[i]];
  }else{
   diag = A_vals[i];
  }
 }
 x[row_index] = sum/diag;
}
}
```

The smoother is applied to one color at a time for both the forward and backward sweeps. The following is the CPU code which calls the smoother kernels:

```
for( color=0; color<num_colors; color++ )
smooth<<<>>>(A_vals, A_col, rhs, x,...);

for( color=num_colors; color>=0; color-- )
smooth<<<>>>(A_vals, A_col, rhs, x,...);
```

4.4   Optimized Version

From our experience in the CUDA porting of the Himeno benchmark on clusters with GPUs [17], optimizing memory bandwidth utilization is a key design element to achieve good performance on codes with low compute intensity (the ratio between floating point operations and memory accesses). In this case most of the data access is to the matrix, so we are able to improve the performance by storing the matrix in the ELLPACK format. This allows matrix elements to be accessed in a coalesced access pattern.

In addition to the optimized matrix storage format, we also performed several other optimizations, listed here:

A. SYMGS: removing redundant communications and work
B. SPMV: overlapping communications with computations
C. CG: overlapping MPI_Allreduce with vector update
D. SYMGS + SPMV: using LDG load instructions

SYMGS: Removing Redundant Work. The SYMGS routine is called for the pre-smoother and post-smoother of the multi-grid V-cycle. The initial value of the solution at each level is set to zero, which allows us to avoid some of the communications and computations that occur during the first application of the smoother at each level. The SYMGS smoother routine begins by calling exchange_halo, which communicates boundary elements of the local matrix with neighbor processors. Since we know the values are all zeros, we can skip this communication step. We may also avoid processing the zero elements of the initial solution vector by restricting the forward sweep to matrix elements below the diagonal. We use a special smoother kernel for this case that checks if the column index is lower than the row index by adding `if(A_col[i] < row_index)` in the kernel code. We also note that in the CUSPARSE implementation, the zero values could allow one to skip the SPMV used to construct the residual (since the right hand side will be equal to the residual in this case), and the vector update in the last step of SYMGS where the computed delta is added to the initial solution.

SPMV: Overlapping Communications with Computations. The SPMV routine also begins with a call to `exchange_halo`, which updates the portion of the solution that is owned by other processors. However, these points, referred to as the halo points, are only required for the computation of the rows that are along the boundary of the local domain. Thus, we can safely split the computation into two phases, first computing the points which do not require the boundary, called interior, and next computing those which do require the boundary, called exterior. In this way we can overlap the computation of the interior with the halo communications.

The communications involve copying of the boundary data from GPU to CPU, MPI send/recv with neighbor processes, and copy results back to the GPU. We overlap the CPU to GPU communication by using cuda streams, with the copies placed into a different stream than the computation kernels.

While it is possible to use the same matrix structure for both interior and exterior computations, the efficiency of the exterior is greatly reduced because there is little locality in the access of the boundary matrix entries. It is more efficient to use a separate data structure, which only contains the boundary rows of the matrix, to process the boundary elements. For this purpose we also construct a boundary row index array which gives the row index of all boundary rows.

The fastest way to compute the boundary index array is to start with a copy of the already existing `elementsToSend` index array, and simply apply `thrust::sort` and `thrust::unique` functions. Then the boundary index array can be used to copy rows from the original matrix into the much smaller boundary matrix. The overhead of these operations are included in the optimization phase timing, and represent only a small fraction of the total optimization time.

CG: Overlapping MPI_Allreduce with Vector Update. In the CG algorithm, the solution vector x is never required as an input to any of the steps. So we may delay the vector update of the solution in order to overlap the update time with the next dot product `MPI_Allreduce()` time. This scheme allows one of the three dot products in the CG solver to overlap with computations.

LDG: Read-Only Cache Load Instructions. The Kepler class of GPUs have a read-only data cache, which is well suited for reading data with spatial locality or with irregular access patterns. In previous GPU generations, a programmer would have to bind memory to texture objects and load data with special texture instructions to achieve this. However, on Kepler, the GPU cores can access any data with a new compute instruction called LDG. These special load instructions may be generated by the compiler provided it can detect that the data is read-only and no aliasing is occurring. This can be achieved by marking all the pointer arguments to a kernel with __restrict keywords. Unfortunately, this method will not always produce the best use of the memory system. For example, in the SYMGS kernels, the matrix is read-only, but the X vector is both read and written. Thus, when using __restrict, the compiler will use LDG for the matrix data, and regular loads for the solution vector. Ironically, the Matrix data is better suited to regular loads, since there is no data reuse and the access pattern is coalesced, while the irregular access of the solution vector is better suited to the read-only cache. By omiting the __restrict keywords, and using the __ldg( ) intrinsic for the load of X, we are able to increase performance by an additional 4 %.

5   Results

In this section, we present results for single node and for clusters. The single node experiments allow us to have a better understanding of the relationship between HPCG performance and processor floating point and memory bandwidth capabilities.

5.1   Comparison of Different Versions

Before looking at the single node results on different hardware, we compare the effects of the optimizations applied in the four implementations discussed in the previous section. Figure 1 shows the timing of the four versions of the code on a K20X GPU with ECC enabled. As we can see the matrix reordering has the most relevant effect, since it exposes more parallelism in the SYMGS routine.

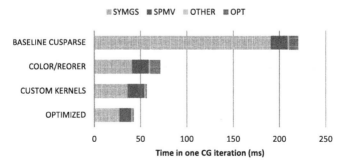

Fig. 1. Time comparison between the initial CUSPARSE implementation and the other custom versions, with 128^3 domain, on K20X with ECC enabled

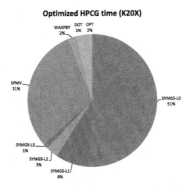

Fig. 2. Time distribution for optimized version with 128^3 domain, on K20X with ECC enabled

Table 1. Specs of the GPUs and CPU used in the benchmark, with clocks in MHz.

Processor	CC	# SM	# Cores SP/DP	Core clock	GFLOPS DP/SP	Memory clock	Memory bus width	Memory bandwidth	DP flops per byte
Tegra K1	3.2	1	192/8	852	13.6/327	924	64 bit	14.7 GB/s	0.93
Tesla K10	3.0	8	1536/64	745	95/2289	2500	256 bit	160 GB/s	0.59
Tesla K20X	3.5	14	2688/896	732	1312/3935	2600	384 bit	250 GB/s	5.28
Tesla K40	3.5	15	2880/960	745	1430/4291	3000	384 bit	288 GB/s	4.96
Xeon E5-2697	N/A	N/A	12	2700	259/518	1866	256 bit	60 GB/s	4.32

Figure 2 shows a detailed timing breakdown for the optimized version on a single GPU. The SYMGS kernel on all the multigrid levels takes up 55 % of the time, followed by the SPMV kernel with 26 %.

5.2   Single Node Results

Next, we compare the performance on different classes of Kepler GPUs ranging from the smallest CUDA-capable GK20A found in the Tegra K1 mobile processor, to the highest performing Tesla K40. The Tesla K20X and K40 are both Kepler based, but they differ in the number of Symmetric Multiprocessors (SM), the amount of memory (6 GB for the K20X vs 12 GB for the K40) and the core/memory clocks (detailed specs are in Table 1). The K40 can also boost the core clock to 875 MHz, which also results in a better memory throughput.

The Compute intensity, or flops/bytes ratio, is a useful metric for determining whether an application will be bandwidth or floating point limited. In this case, the workload is dominated by Matrix-Vector operations, where the compute intensity may be estimated as $2 * nonzerosperrow Flops/(16 + 12 * nonzerosperrow)Bytes = 54/340 = 0.158$. This is much lower than the $flop/byte$ ratios for the hardware given in Table 1. Therefore, we can expect performance to be limited much more by memory bandwidth than floating point throughput capabilities.

Fig. 3 shows the scaling of HPCG performance across the GPUs used in our study. Figure 4 demonstrates the efficiency of our implementation by compar-

HPCG GFLOP/s COMPARISON

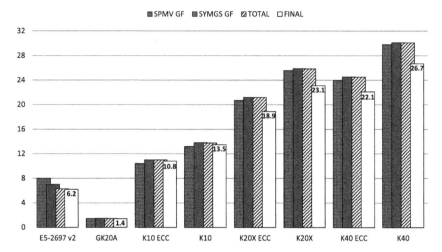

Fig. 3. Comparison of HPCG flop rate on single GPUs and Xeon E5-2697-v2 12-core CPU

HPCG BANDWIDTH COMPARISON

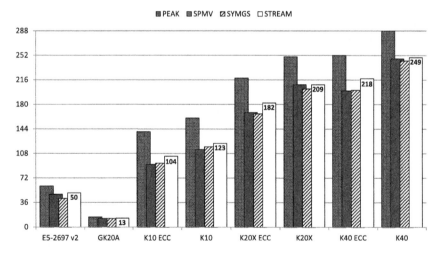

Fig. 4. Comparison of HPCG flop rate and bandwidth on single GPUs and Xeon E5-2697-v2 12-core CPU

ing the performance of the SYMGS and SPMV routines with the STREAM banchmark [16]. We also include the same metrics for an optimized CPU implementation developed by Park and Smelyanskiy [18]. As we can see in Fig. 5, there is an excellent correlation between the HPCG score and the STREAM benchmark result.

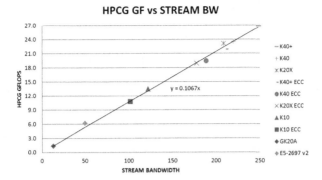

Fig. 5. Correlation between STREAM and HPCG benchmark results on single GPUs and E5-2697-v2 12-core CPU

5.3 Multi Node Results

The cluster runs were performed on the Titan system at the Oak Ridge National Laboratory (ORNL) and on the Piz Daint system at the Swiss National Supercomputing Centre (CSCS). They are both Cray systems, but while Titan is a Cray XK7 based on AMD Opteron and a Gemini network, Piz Daint is a new Cray XC30 with Intel Xeon and the new Aries network. Titan has 18,688 nodes, each with a 16-core AMD Opteron processor, 32 GB of system memory and a 6 GB NVIDIA K20X GPU. The network uses the Gemini routing and communications ASICs and a 3D torus network topology. Piz Daint has 5,272 nodes, each with an Intel Xeon E5 processor, 32 GB of system memory and a 6 GB NVIDIA K20X GPU. The network uses the new Aries routing and communications ASICs and a dragonfly network topology.

Table 2 shows the performance of the optimized version on a wide range of nodes, up to the full size machine on Titan and Piz-Daint. The raw number is the total performance number, before the reduction due to the increased iteration count caused by the multi-coloring.

Table 2. HPCG supercomputer results in GFlops: local grid size $256 \times 256 \times 128$

Nodes	Titan raw	Titan final	Titan Eff.	Piz-Daint raw	Piz-Daint final	Piz-Daint Eff.
1	21.23	20.77	100.0	21.25	20.79	100.0
8	168.3	161.4	99.1	168.8	161.9	99.3
64	1321	1221	97.2	1341	1239	98.6
512	10414	9448	95.8	10719	9904	98.5
2048				42777	38806	98.3
3200	62239	56473	91.6			
5265				109089	98972	97.5
8192	158779	144071	91.3			
18648	355189	322299	89.7			

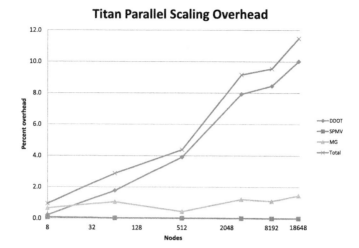

Fig. 6. Scaling overhead on Titan.

Table 3. HPCG supercomputer results comparison

HPCG rank	System	HPCG GFLOPS	Iterations	#Procs	Processor type	HPCG Per Proc	Bandwidth Per Proc	Efficiency FLOP/BYTE
1	Tianhe-2	580,109	57	46,080	Xeon-Phi-31S1P	12.59 GF	320 GB/s	0.039
2	K	426,972	51	82,944	Sparc64-viiifx	5.15 GF	64 GB/s	0.080
3	Titan	322,321	55	18,648	Tesla-K20X+ECC	17.28 GF	250 GB/s	0.069
5	Piz-Daint	98,979	55	5,208	Tesla-K20X+ECC	19.01 GF	250 GB/s	0.076
8	HPC2	49,145	54	2,610	Tesla-K20X+ECC	18.83 GF	250 GB/s	0.075
	HPC2	60,642	54	2,600	Tesla-K20X	23.32 GF	250 GB/s	0.093

At full scale, Piz-Daint is reaching 0.098 PF, compared to the 6.2 PF during HPL. Since we are running very close to peak bandwidth and the code has no problem scaling up to the full machine, there is not much space left for large improvements. Even with no coloring overhead, the full machine will deliver only 0.1 PF. Same conclusion holds for Titan, the achieved HPCG performance of 0.322 PF is far away from the sustained 17.59 PF during HPL.

In Fig. 6, we analyze the communication time on the Titan runs. The dot products require `all_reduce` communications, that scale as the logarithm of the node count. The other communications are instead with neighbors and remain constant with the number of nodes. The ones in the SPMV phase are completely overlapped with computations, in the current version the ones in the multigrid phase are not but the overlapping will be implemented in an upcoming version.

5.4   Comparisons

The first official HPCG ranking was published at the International Supercomputing Conference in June 2014 and included 15 supercomputers. All the GPU supercomputers on the list ran the optimized version described in this paper.

Table 3 summarizes the results of several of the top systems: Thiane-2 is based on Xeon Phi processors (currently number one in the Top500 list), K is a CPU-only system based on Sparc64 Processors. Instead of looking at the peak flops of these machines, we evaluate the efficiency based on the ratio of the HPCG result to the memory bandwidth of the processors.

The efficiency of the GPU implementation is comparable to the one of K and the performance per processor is noticeably higher.

6   Conclusion and Future Plans

The results in the paper show that GPU accelerated clusters perform very well in the new HPCG benchmark. Our results are the fastest per processor ever reported. GPUs, with their excellent floating point performance and high memory bandwidth, are very well-suited to tackle workloads dominated by floating point, like HPL, as well as those dominated by memory bandwidth, like HPCG.

The current implementation is all on the GPUs, but since the CPUs could give a significant contribution, we are investigating a hybrid scheme where both CPU and GPU are used together.

Acknowledgments. This research used resources of the Oak Ridge Leadership Computing Facility at the Oak Ridge National Laboratory, which is supported by the Office of Science of the U.S. Department of Energy under Contract No. DE-AC05-00OR22725. We wish to thank Buddy Bland, Jack Wells and Don Maxwell of Oak Ridge National Laboratory for their support. This work was also supported by a grant from the Swiss National Supercomputing Centre (CSCS) under project ID g33. We also want to acknowledged the support from Gilles Fourestey and Thomas Schulthess at CSCS. We wish to thank Lung Scheng Chien and Jonathan Cohen at NVIDIA for relevant discussions.

References

1. Dongarra, J., Heroux, M.A.: Toward a New Metric for Ranking High Performance Computing Systems. Sandia report SAND2013-4744 (2013)
2. Dongarra, J., Luszczek, P.: Introduction to the HPC challenge benchmark Suite, ICL Technical report, ICL-UT-05-01, (Also appears as CS Dept. Tech report UT-CS-05-544) (2005)
3. Heroux, M.A., Dongarra, J., Luszczek, P: HPCG Technical specification, Sandia report SAND2013-8752 (2013)
4. Graph 500. http://www.graph500.org
5. Green 500. http://www.green500.org
6. CUDA Toolkit. http://developer.nvidia.com/cuda-toolkit
7. CUDA Fortran. http://www.pgroup.com/resources/cudafortran.htm
8. CUBLAS Library. http://docs.nvidia.com/cuda/cublas
9. CUSPARSE Library. http://docs.nvidia.com/cuda/cusparse
10. THRUST Library. http://docs.nvidia.com/cuda/thrust
11. http://devblogs.nvidia.com/parallelforall/cuda-pro-tip-generate-custom-application-profile-timelines-nvtx/

12. Barrett, R.F., Heroux, M.A., Lin, P.T., Vaughan, C.T., Williams, A.B.: Poster: mini-applications: vehicles for co-design. In: Proceedings of the 2011 Companion on High Performance Computing Networking, Storage and Analysis Companion (SC 2011 Companion), pp. 1–2. ACM, New York (2011)
13. Golub, G.H., Van Loan, C.F.: Matrix Computations, 3rd edn. John Hopkins University Press, USA (1996)
14. Briggs, W.L., Henson, V.E., McCormick, S.F.: A Multigrid Tutorial. SIAM, USA (2000)
15. Green 500: Energy efficient HPC System workloads power measurement methodology (2013)
16. McCalpin, J.D.: Memory bandwidth and machine balance in current high performance computers. In: IEEE Computer Society Technical Committee on Computer Architecture (TCCA) Newsletter, December 1995
17. Phillips, E.H., Fatica, M.: Implementing the Himeno benchmark with CUDA on GPU clusters. In: IEEE International Symposium on Parallel & Distributed Processing IPDPS, pp. 1–10 (2010)
18. Park, J., Smelyanskiy, M.: Optimizing Gauss-Seidel Smoother in HPCG. In: ASCR HPCG Workshop, Bethesda MD, 25 March 2014
19. Luby, M.: A simple parallel algorithm for the maximal independent set problem. SIAM J. Comput. 15(4), 1036–1053 (1986)
20. Jones, M.T., Plassmann, P.E.: A parallel graph coloring heuristic. SIAM J. Sci. Comput. 14, 654–669 (1992)
21. Cohen, J., Castonguay, P.: Efficient graph matching and coloring on the GPU. In: GPU Technology Conference, San Jose CA, 14–17 May 2012. http://ondemand.gpu techconf.com/gtc/2012/presentations/S0332-Efficient-Graph-Matching-and-Coloring-on-GPUs.pdf

Performance Analysis of a High-Level Abstractions-Based Hydrocode on Future Computing Systems

G.R. Mudalige[1]([⊠]), I.Z. Reguly[1], M.B. Giles[1], A.C. Mallinson[3],
W.P. Gaudin[2], and J.A. Herdman[2]

[1] Oxford e-Research Centre, University of Oxford,
7, Keble Road Oxford, Oxford OX1 3QG, UK
{gihan.mudalige,istvan.reguly}@oerc.ox.ac.uk,
mike.giles@maths.ox.ac.uk
[2] High Performance Computing, UK AWE plc., Aldermaston, UK
{Wayne.Gaudin,Andy.Herdman}@awe.co.uk
[3] Department of Computer Science, University of Warwick,
Coventry, UK
acm@dcs.warwick.ac.uk

Abstract. In this paper we present research on applying a domain specific high-level abstractions (HLA) development strategy with the aim to "future-proof" a key class of high performance computing (HPC) applications that simulate hydrodynamics computations at AWE plc. We build on an existing high-level abstraction framework, OPS, that is being developed for the solution of multi-block structured mesh-based applications at the University of Oxford. OPS uses an "active library" approach where a single application code written using the OPS API can be transformed into different highly optimized parallel implementations which can then be linked against the appropriate parallel library enabling execution on different back-end hardware platforms. The target application in this work is the CloverLeaf mini-app from Sandia National Laboratory's Mantevo suite of codes that consists of algorithms of interest from hydrodynamics workloads. Specifically, we present (1) the lessons learnt in re-engineering an industrial representative hydro-dynamics application to utilize the OPS high-level framework and subsequent code generation to obtain a range of parallel implementations, and (2) the performance of the auto-generated OPS versions of CloverLeaf compared to that of the performance of the hand-coded original CloverLeaf implementations on a range of platforms. Benchmarked systems include Intel multi-core CPUs and NVIDIA GPUs, the Archer (Cray XC30) CPU cluster and the Titan (Cray XK7) GPU cluster with different parallelizations (OpenMP, OpenACC, CUDA, OpenCL and MPI). Our results show that the development of parallel HPC applications using a high-level framework such as OPS is no more time consuming nor difficult than writing a one-off parallel program targeting only a single parallel implementation. However the OPS strategy pays off with a highly maintainable single application source, through which multiple parallelizations can be realized, without compromising performance portability on a range of parallel systems.

© Springer International Publishing Switzerland 2015
S.A. Jarvis et al. (Eds.): PMBS 2014, LNCS 8966, pp. 85–104, 2015.
DOI: 10.1007/978-3-319-17248-4_5

1   Introduction

High performance computing (HPC) is currently in a period of enormous change. For many years, increased performance was achieved through higher clock frequencies, but that trend was brought to an abrupt halt by the corresponding increase in energy consumption. The clear direction now is towards improved performance through increasing parallelism, even reducing the clock frequency a little to improve the energy efficiency, which is becoming a key concern. However, there is no clear consensus yet on the best architecture for HPC. On the one hand there are many-core accelerators such as GPUs and the new Intel Xeon Phi, usually with 16–64 functional units, each of which can be viewed as a vector processor with many elements (cores) performing the same operation at the same time but with different data. On the other hand, we have mainstream Intel/AMD CPUs with very large caches and a more modest number of functional units (cores) each with their own vector components (e.g. AVX units), or the IBM BlueGene systems which are based on a large network of relatively small but energy-efficient CPUs. In the future, we may also have interesting energy-efficient designs from ARM [9] and other companies [19] which have achieved great energy efficiency for mobile and embedded applications, and are now targeting HPC which increasingly shares similar goals.

In the light of these developments, an application developer faces a tough problem. Optimizing their application for execution on a particular platform requires an increasing amount of platform-specific knowledge, and possibly a major re-write to reduce data communications. At the same time, there is considerable uncertainty about which platform to target; it is not clear which architectural approach is likely to "win" in the long-term, and it is not even clear in the short-term which platform is best for any given application.

Currently the common approach for utilizing novel hardware, or different many-core accelerators is to manually port the legacy application, in many cases by converting key compute kernels to utilize the accelerators. In some cases a major ground-up rewrite is required, for example if you need to reduce data communications to efficiently utilize the new hardware. The conversion process is highly error-prone and takes significant amounts of developer effort to program, validate and optimize. It is unreasonable for domain scientists to be engaged in such optimization work that will require them to port the application for each new generation of systems. Thus "future proofing" HPC applications for their continued performance and portability on a diverse range of hardware and future emerging systems is of critical importance.

One such approach, is the use of domain specific high-level abstractions (HLAs), such as domain specific languages (DSLs) and active libraries [13, 31]. The key idea is to provide the application developer with a set of domain specific constructs to declare the problem to be computed, without specifying its implementation [18]. It is then the task of a lower implementation level to apply automated techniques for translating the specification into different implementations for different hardware and software platforms. The use of such a development strategy has previously been shown to have significant benefits both for developer productivity and gaining near-optimal performance [14,28]. However, currently these still remain as experimental research projects and have not yet been adopted by a wider HPC community. Partly the reason is a lack of DSLs or high-level frameworks that are actively used for creating production level applications. On the other hand, previous work has only developed such frameworks for a few application domains.

The research in this paper is thus motivated by the need to explore further the utility of high-level abstraction frameworks for future proofing parallel scientific simulation applications from a range of application domains. Here we focus on a hydro-dynamics application, belonging to an important class of codes which form a key part of the HPC workload at many organizations such as the AWE. We make use of a previously developed mini-application called Clover-Leaf [8], which implements algorithms of interest related to this workload. This research explores the performance of CloverLeaf after re-engineering the application based on a domain specific HLA framework. CloverLeaf is open source software and forms part of Sandia National Laboratory's Mantevo project [5]. With the use of an unrestricted application as a proxy, our aim is to demonstrate to a wider HPC audience the performance portability resulting from an HLA based development and how this strategy might help in addressing various scientific simulation challenges on future emerging systems.

The CloverLeaf mini-application has been previously manually ported [16,17,20] to execute on many parallel platforms. These include parallelizations based on single-instruction-multiple-data (SIMD, e.g. SSE and AVX) and shared memory multi-threading for multi-core CPUs (e.g. OpenMP), single instruction multiple thread (SIMT, e.g. CUDA, OpenCL and OpenACC) for GPUs and the Intel's Xeon Phi and distributed memory parallelization (e.g. MPI) for clusters of CPUs/GPUs. Recently the code was re-written [10] with a domain specific high-level abstraction framework, called OPS which resulted in a single high-level application source. Automated code generation techniques of OPS were then used to generate a range of parallel implementations. In this paper we compare the performance of the resulting parallelizations to that of the original hand-tuned CloverLeaf applications. Unlike previous work, the availability of highly optimized, manually hand-tuned parallel versions gives us a unique opportunity to compare and contrast the high-level development process both in terms of developer productivity and performance portability. Our research demonstrates, through performance analysis and benchmarking on a range of hardware and software systems, the benefits of the HLA approach giving significant insights into high-level methods for "future proofing" HPC applications. The main contributions of this paper are twofold:

1. We present lessons learnt in re-engineering an industrially representative hydro-dynamics application to utilize the OPS high-level framework and subsequent code generation to obtain a range of parallel implementations. Through OPS we generate code targeting OpenMP thread level multi-core parallelism, single-instruction multiple-thread (SIMT) many-core parallelism using CUDA, OpenCL and OpenACC and distributed memory parallelism with MPI.

2. The performance of the OPS versions of CloverLeaf is compared to that of the performance of the original CloverLeaf implementations on a range of platforms. These include the latest Intel multi-core CPUs (Sandy Bridge), NVIDIA GPUs (Kepler K20c), a Cray XC30 distributed memory cluster (Archer [7]) and a large Cray XK7 GPU cluster (Titan [11]). Key performance bottlenecks are analyzed and further optimizations are discussed.

The rest of this paper is organized as follows: in Sect. 2 we briefly present the OPS abstraction, its API, design and code generation process; in Sect. 3, a benchmarking and performance analysis of the of the application is carried out comparing the OPS based CloverLeaf with the original hand-tuned version; Sect. 4 will briefly detail related work in this area and compare them to our contributions in this paper. Finally Sect. 5 notes future work and conclusions.

2   OPS

Previous work at the University of Oxford developed a high-level abstraction framework called OP2 [6] targeting the domain of unstructured mesh based applications. With OP2 we demonstrated that both developer productivity as well as near-optimal performance could be achieved on a wide range of parallel hardware. Research published as a result of this work includes a number of performance analysis studies on standard CFD benchmark applications [23] as well as a full industrial-scale application from the production work-load at Rolls-Royce plc. [28].

OPS (Oxford Parallel Library for Structured-mesh solvers) follows much of the design of OP2, but targets the domain of multi-block structured applications. Multi-block structured mesh applications can be viewed as an unstructured collection of structured mesh blocks. As CloverLeaf is a single block-structured mesh code, it only required OPS's single block API to re-engineer the application. The structured mesh domain is distinct from the unstructured mesh applications domain due to the implicit connectivity between neighboring mesh elements (such as vertices, cells) in structured meshes/grids. The key idea is that operations involve looping over a "rectangular" multi-dimensional set of grid points using one or more "stencils" to access data.

OPS is designed to appear as a classical software library with a domain specific API. It then uses source-to-source translation techniques to parse the API calls and generate different parallel implementations. These can then be linked against the appropriate parallel library enabling execution on different back-end hardware platforms. The aim is to generate highly optimized platform specific code and link with equally efficient back-end libraries utilizing the best low-level features of a target architecture. The next section briefly illustrates the OPS API using examples from CloverLeaf.

2.1   The OPS API

The CloverLeaf mini-app involves the solution of the compressible Euler equations, which form a system of four partial differential equations. The equations are statements of the conservation of energy, density and momentum and are solved using a finite volume method on a structured staggered grid. The cell centers hold internal energy and density while nodes hold velocities. The solution involves an explicit Lagrangian step using a predictor/corrector method to update the hydrodynamics, followed by an advective remap that uses a second order Van Leer upwinding scheme. The advective remap step returns the grid to its original position. The original application [8] is written in Fortran and operates on a 2D structured mesh. It is of fixed size in both x and y dimensions.

OPS separates the specification of such a problem into four distinct parts: (1) structured blocks, (2) data defined on blocks, (3) stencils defining how data is accessed and (4) operations over blocks. Thus the first aspect of declaring such a single-block structured mesh application with OPS is to define the size of the regular mesh over which the computations will be carried out. In OPS vernacular this is called an ops_block. OPS declares a block with the ops_decl_block API call by indicating the dimension of the block (2D in this case) and assigning it a name for identification and runtime checks (see Fig. 1).

```
1  /* Declare a single structured block */
2  ops_block cgrd = ops_decl_block(2, "clover grid");
3
4  int size[2]  = {x_cells+5, y_cells+5};
5  double* dat = NULL;
6
7  /* Declare data on block */
8  ops_dat density0, energy0, ..., pressure, volume;
9
10 density0=ops_decl_dat(cgrd,1,size,dat,"double","density0");
11 energy0 =ops_decl_dat(cgrd,1,size,dat,"double","energy0");
12 ......
13 pressure=ops_decl_dat(cgrd,1,size,dat,"double","pressure");
14 volume  =ops_decl_dat(cgrd,1,size,dat,"double","volume");
```

Fig. 1. OPS API example for declaring blocks, data and stencils

CloverLeaf works on a number of data arrays (or fields) which are defined on the 2D structured mesh (e.g. density, energy, x and y velocity of particles). OPS allows users to declare these using the ops_decl_dat API call; the density0, energy0, ... pressure and volume are ops_dats that are declared through this API. A key idea is that once a field's data is declared via ops_decl_dat the ownership of the data is transfered from the user to OPS, where it is free to rearrange the memory layout as is optimal for the final parallelization and execution hardware. In contrast, each of the original CloverLeaf implementations explicitly involve the allocation and management of memory specific to each parallel implementation at the application source level. In this example a NULL pointer of type double is passed as an argument. CloverLeaf initializes these values later, as part of the application itself. When a NULL array is supplied, OPS will internally allocate the required amount of memory based on the type of the data array and its size. On the other hand an array containing the relevant initial data can be used in declaring an ops_dat. In the future we will provide the ability to read in data from HDF5 files directly using a ops_decl_dat_hdf5 API call. Note above in an ops_decl_dat call, a single double precision value per grid element is declared. A vector of a number of values per grid element could also be declared (e.g. a vector with three doubles per grid point to store x, y and z velocities).

All the numerically intensive computations in the structured mesh application can be described as operations over the block. Within an application code, this corresponds to loops over a given block, accessing data through a stencil, performing some calculations, then writing back (again through the stencils) to the data arrays. A loop from the advec_cell routine in CloverLeaf's reference implementation [8] is detailed in Fig. 2, operating over each grid point in the structured mesh. Note that here the data arrays are all declared as Fortran allocatable 2D arrays. The loop operates in column major order.

```
1 DO k=y_min-2,y_max+2
2   DO j=x_min-2,x_max+2
3     pre_vol(j,k)=volume(j,k)+
4                 (vol_flux_x(j+1,k)-vol_flux_x(j,k)+
5                  vol_flux_y(j,k+1)-vol_flux_y(j,k))
6     post_vol(j,k)=pre_vol(j,k)-
7                 (vol_flux_x(j+1,k)-vol_flux_x(j,k))
8   ENDDO
9 ENDDO
```

Fig. 2. Original loop from advec_cell kernel

An application developer declares this loop using the OPS API as illustrated in Fig. 3 (lines 31–37), together with the "elemental" kernel function (lines 2–14). The elemental function is called a "user kernel" in OPS to indicate that it represents a computation specified by the user (i.e. the domain scientist) to apply to each element (i.e. grid point). User kernels are usually placed in a separate header file, which gets included in the file declaring the ops_par_loop. By "outlining" the user kernel in this fashion, OPS can factor out the declaration of the problem from its parallel implementation. The macros OPS_ACC0, OPS_ACC1, OPS_ACC2 etc. will be resolved to the relevant array index to access the data stored in density0, energy0, pressure etc.[1] The explicit declaration of the stencil (lines 19–28) additionally will allow for error checking of the user code. In this case we use three

---

[1] A similar approach is used in the C kernel implementations of the original CloverLeaf application.

```
1  /*user kernel*/
2  inline void advec_cell_kernel1_xdir (
3      double *pre_vol, double *post_vol,
4      const double *volume,
5      const double *vol_flux_x,
6      const double *vol_flux_y){
7
8  pre_vol[OPS_ACC0(0,0)] = volume[OPS_ACC2(0,0)] +
9    (vol_flux_x[OPS_ACC3(1,0)]- vol_flux_x[OPS_ACC3(0,0)]+
10    vol_flux_y[OPS_ACC4(0,1)]- vol_flux_y[OPS_ACC4(0,0)]);
11
12 post_vol[OPS_ACC1(0,0)] = pre_vol[OPS_ACC0(0,0)] -
13    (vol_flux_x[OPS_ACC3(1,0)]- vol_flux_x[OPS_ACC3(0,0)]);
14 }
15 //mesh execution range
16 int rangexy[] = {x_min-2,x_max+2,y_min-2,y_max+2};
17
18 //declare stencils
19 ops_stencil S2D_00, S2D_00_P10, S2D_00_OP1;
20 /*single point stencil*/
21 int s2D_00[] = {0,0};
22 S2D_00 = ops_decl_stencil( 2, 1, s2D_00, "00");
23
24 /*2 point stencils*/
25 int s2D_00_P10[] = {0,0, 1,0};
26 S2D_00_P10 = ops_decl_stencil(2,1,s2D_00_P10,"0,0,:1,0");
27 int s2D_00_OP1[] = {0,0, 0,1};
28 S2D_00_OP1 = ops_decl_stencil(2,1,s2D_00_OP1,"0,0,:0,1");
29
30 /*parallel loop declaration*/
31 ops_par_loop(advec_cell_kernel1_xdir,
32    "advec_cell_kernel1_xdir", clover_grid, 2, rangexy,
33    ops_arg_dat(work_array1,S2D_00,"double",OPS_WRITE),
34    ops_arg_dat(work_array2,S2D_00,"double",OPS_WRITE),
35    ops_arg_dat(volume,S2D_00,"double",OPS_READ),
36    ops_arg_dat(vol_flux_x,S2D_00_P10,"double",OPS_READ),
37    ops_arg_dat(vol_flux_y,S2D_00_OP1,"double",OPS_READ));
```

Fig. 3. Loop from advec_cell converted to use the OPS API

stencils, one consisting of a single point referring to the current element, the second accessing the $(1,0)$ stencil and the third accessing the $(0,1)$ stencil. More complicated stencils can be declared giving the relative position from the current $(0,0)$ element. The ops_par_loop declares the structured block to be iterated over, its dimension, the iteration range and the ops_dats involved in the computation. OPS_READ indicates that density0 will be read only. The actual parallel implementation of the loop is specific to the parallelization strategy involved. OPS is free to implement this with any optimizations necessary to obtain maximum performance. The ops_arg_dat(..) in Fig. 3 indicates an argument to the parallel loop that refers to an ops_dat. A similar function ops_arg_gbl() enables users to indicate global reductions.

2.2   Porting CloverLeaf to OPS

The original CloverLeaf 2D application written in Fortran 90 was converted to the OPS API by manually extracting the user kernels, outlining them in header files and converting the application to the OPS's C/C++ API. All effort was taken to keep the naming conventions of routines and files as similar to the original as possible. After conversion, the OPS CloverLeaf version consists of 80 ops_par_loops spread across 16 files with about 7000 lines of code. This application can be code generated to obtain a range of parallel implementations. In comparison each of the original CloverLeaf implementations are self contained separate parallel implementations, one for each of MPI+CUDA, MPI+OpenMP etc. The original CloverLeaf reference implementation (i.e. the MPI+OpenMP parallelization) consists of about 7000 lines of source code. The OPS back-end library (implemented in C and C++) which currently supports parallelizing with OpenMP, CUDA, OpenACC, OpenCL and MPI including common support functions for all these parallelizations and other utility functions, plus the code generation tools, in total consists of about 15000 lines of source code. However, the important fact to note here is that the back-end libraries and code generation tools are generic to be applicable to any application developed with the OPS API, not just CloverLeaf.

Once converted to the OPS API, an application can be validated as a single threaded implementation, simply by including the header file ops_seq.h and linking with OPS's sequential back-end library. The header file and the library implement API calls for a single threaded CPU and can be compiled and linked using conventional (platform specific) compilers (e.g. gcc, icc) and executed as a serial application.

The serial developer version allows for the application's scientific results to be inspected before code generation takes place. It also validates the OPS API calls and provides feedback on any errors, such as differences between declared stencils and the corresponding user kernels or differences between data types. All such feedback is intended to reduce the complexity of programming and ease debugging. There is opportunity at this stage to add further checks and tests to increase developer productivity, for example report cases where the iteration range of a loop written by a developer attempts to access elements beyond the number of grid points in any dimension of an ops_dat. Including the developer header file and linking with OPS's distributed memory (MPI) back-end libraries can also be used to obtain a low performance MPI parallelization of the application for testing purposes. The full CloverLeaf developer version can be found under the OPS git-hub repository [10].

The manual conversion of the original application to the OPS API required no more effort than what is typically required by a developer proficient in a given

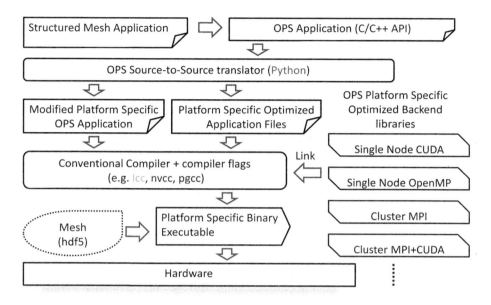

Fig. 4. OPS code generation and build process

parallel computing model (OpenMP, CUDA etc.) for directly porting to a different parallel implementation. However once converted, the use of OPS to generate different parallelizations of the application was trivial. Therefore we believe that the conversion is an acceptable one-off cost for legacy applications attempting to utilize the benefits of high level frameworks such as DSLs or Active Libraries. As we will show in this paper, the advantages of such frameworks far outweigh the costs, by significantly improving the maintainability of the application source, while making it possible to also gain near optimal performance and performance portability across a wide range of hardware.

Once the application developer is satisfied with the validity of the results produced by the sequential application, parallel code can be generated. The build process to obtain a parallel executable as illustrated in Fig. 4 follows that of OP2's code generation process [23]. The API calls in the application are parsed by the OPS source-to-source translator which will produce a modified main program and back-end specific code. These are then compiled using a conventional compiler (e.g. gcc, icc, nvcc) and linked against platform specific OPS back-end libraries to generate the final executable. As mentioned before, there is the option to read in the mesh data at runtime. The source-to-source code translator is written in Python and only needs to recognize OPS API calls; it does not need to parse the rest of the code. We have deliberately chosen to use Python and a simple source-to-source translation strategy to significantly simplify the complexity of the code generation tools and to ensure that the software technologies on which it is based have long-term support. The use of Python makes the code generator easily modifiable allowing for it to even be maintained internally within an organization.

Furthermore, the code generated through OPS is itself human readable which helps with maintenance and development of new optimizations.

OPS currently supports parallel code generation for execution on (1) single threaded vectorized CPUs, (2) multi-threaded CPUs/SMPs using OpenMP, (3) NVIDIA GPUs using CUDA and OpenACC, (4) OpenCL devices such as AMD GPUs, the Intel XeonPhi, etc. (5) distributed memory clusters of single threaded CPUs using MPI (6) a cluster of multi-threaded CPUs using MPI and OpenMP and (7) a cluster of GPUs using MPI and CUDA. A more complete discussion of the code generation and optimizations for the multi-core CPU, NVIDIA GPU and MPI parallelizations is given in [10]. In the next section we delve directly into the performance of each of these generated versions.

3 Performance

In this section, we present quantitative results exploring the performance portability and scaling of CloverLeaf developed with OPS and compare it to the performance of the various original implementations. Tables 1 and 2 provide details of the hardware and software specifications of the benchmark systems. The first two systems, Broomway and K20 are single node systems which we use to benchmark the multi-threaded CPU and GPU performance respectively. The third system is the UK national supercomputing resource – Archer [7] which we use to benchmark OPS's distributed memory performance. The final system is Titan [11], the large scale K20x GPU based Cray XK7 system at ORNL. To be consistent with the

Table 1. Single node benchmark systems

System	Broomway	K20
Node architecture	2 × 8-core Intel Xeon E5-2680 2.70 GHz (Sandy bridge)	NVIDIA Tesla K20c
Memory per node	64 GB	5 GB/GPU (ECC off)
OS	Red Hat Enterprise Linux 6	Red Hat Enterprise Linux 6.4
Compilers and flags	Intel CC 14.0.0 Intel MPI 4.1.3 -O3 IEEE_FLAGS[a]	CUDA 6.0 IEEE_FLAGS[a] -gencode arch=compute_35, code=sm_35 -O3 NVIDIA OpenCL PGI compiler 14.2 (for OpenACC)

[a]On Intel compilers, IEEE_FLAGS=-ipo -fp-model strict -fp-model source -prec-div -prec-sqrt

Table 2. Distributed memory benchmark systems

System	Archer	Titan
Node architecture	2 × 12-core Intel Xeon E5-2697 2.70 GHz (Ivy Bridge)	16-core AMD Opteron 6274 + NVIDIA K20X
Memory per node	64 GB	32 GB + 6 GB/GPU (ECC on)
Interconnect	Cray Aries	Cray Gemini
OS	CLE	CLE
Compilers and flags	Cray C Compilers 8.2.1 cray-mpich/6.1.1 -O3 -Kieee	Cray C Compilers 8.2.2 -cray-mpich/6.3.0 -O3 -hgnu -O3 -arch=sm_35 PGI Compiler 13.10-0

compiler flags recommended for gaining accurate results from the original Clover-Leaf application, we enforce IEEE floating-point mathematics compliance on each compiler and benchmark[2]

On the single node systems we present the total runtime of the hydro loop of CloverLeaf for the 960×960 (`clover_bm.in`) and 3840×3840 (`clover_bm16_short.in`) mesh input decks. Figures 5 and 6 present times taken by the main hydro iteration loop to solve these problems. The MPI and OpenMP results are from the dual socket Intel CPUs on Broomway while the CUDA and OpenACC results are from the NVIDIA K20c GPU. We also ran the OpenCL version of the application on both the CPU and GPU. To reduce the NUMA effects on performance, both the original and OPS OpenMP versions were executed with the `KMP_AFINITY` environmental variable set to `compact`. We found that this gave the best performance on this two socket CPU node. Additionally, the MPI processes were bound to a specific core using the `numactl` command at runtime, again to reduce NUMA issues on the two socket CPU node.

We see that on the Intel CPU node for both problems with the exception of the OpenMP only parallelization, the OPS version executes within 10 % of the original implementation's runtime. The OPS's OpenMP parallelization gives better performance. We believe that this is due to OPS explicitly partitioning the iteration space and allocating them to be computed by the available OpenMP threads. In the original version allocating work to threads is handled automatically by OpenMP. The best runtime for the 960×960 mesh is achieved using OPS's pure MPI version, which is about 3 % faster than the best runtime achieved with the original MPI version. The OpenCL runtime on the CPUs are about 30 % worse than the OpenMP versions, however OPS matches the runtime of the original CloverLeaf OpenCL version. The poor OpenCL performance on the CPU may be due to NUMA effects

---

[2] On Intel compilers, IEEE_FLAGS=-ipo -fp-model strict -fp-model source -prec-div -prec-sqrt.

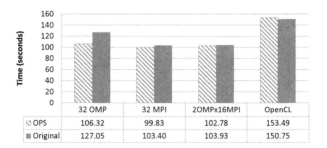

(a) Broomway (Intel Xeon E5-2680 CPU)

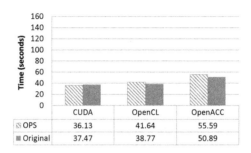

(b) K20 (NVIDIA Tesla K20c)

Fig. 5. CloverLeaf performance - 960 × 960 mesh (≈2955 iterations)

as the OpenCL runtime does not yet have facilities for explicitly placing and binding threads to cores. A further reason could be poorer vectorization from OpenCL compared to vectorization achieved with SIMD pragmas using the Intel compiler. On the NVIDIA K20c GPU with CUDA, OpenCL and OpenACC all application versions perform approximately the same. The CUDA version gives a speedup of 3× over the best runtime on the two socket Intel CPU node.

The code generated with OPS additionally consists of profiling instrumentation for capturing `ops_par_loop` execution times and achieved bandwidths. This information, together with details of approximate number of double precision floating-point operations executed per `ops_par_loop` (gathered through a profiler) enables us to compute the achieved floating-point operation rates and memory bandwidths. Table 3 details this achieved performance per single node on the CPU and GPU systems for each of the related parallelizations. Only the results for the most time consuming routines are given in the table. As a comparison we note the achieved DGEMM (double precision generic matrix-matrix multiply [15]) floating point operation rate on both the CPU and GPU, the STREAM [22] memory bandwidth achieved on the CPU node, and the resulting bandwidth from NVIDIA's bandwidthTest [2] benchmark. The peak achievable performance (Number of Cores × Average frequency × Operations per cycle for Intel CPUs and for NVIDIA K20c GPU [3]), for each platform is also presented.

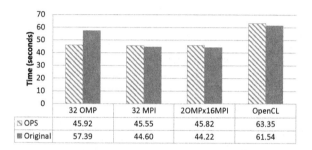

(a) Broomway (Intel Xeon E5-2680 CPU)

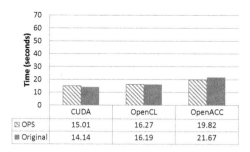

(b) K20 (NVIDIA Tesla K20c)

Fig. 6. CloverLeaf performance - 3840 × 3840 mesh (≈87 iterations)

On the two socket Intel CPU node, Broomway, we see that some loops achieve over 80 % of the STREAM memory bandwidth (with MPI). However, only a small fraction out of the 304 GFlops/s DGEMM floating-point operation rate is achieved. On the K20c GPU, the achieved fraction of peak bandwidth is even higher, with loops in `flux_calc` obtaining 155.27 GB/s (with CUDA), which is over 90 % of the bandwidth achieved with the bandwidthTest benchmark. Again, the achieved floating-point rate is significantly smaller compared to the GPU's theoretical and practical peak rates. Thus we can say that the CloverLeaf application is much more bandwidth limited, than compute limited. OpenCL parallelization on the CPU performs considerably less well than MPI and OpenMP. However on the K20c GPU, OpenCL was as good as the CUDA implementation.

Next, we benchmark the scaling performance of the distributed memory parallelization, on two large-scale clusters. The first is on Archer, a Cray XC30, on which we benchmark CloverLeaf's pure MPI performance. Figure 7 details the results from this system for both strong scaling and weak scaling on up to 1024 nodes (12,288 cores). The strong scaling mesh consists of 15360^2 (≈230 million) grid points, while for weak scaling a mesh size of 3840^2 is assigned per socket of a node (i.e. for the 2 socket Archer node a mesh of 2×3840^2 is assigned per node). We see that again, OPS CloverLeaf version's runtime at increasing scale

Table 3. Single node performance - 960×960 mesh (≈ 2955 iterations)

Loop	Broomway CPU Node ($2 \times$ Intel Xeon E5-2680) $Peak_{Flops} = 345.6 GFlops/s$, $Peak_{BW} = 102.4 GB/s$ $DGEMM_{Flops} = 304 GFlops/s$, $STREAM_{BW} = 78 GB/s$					
	32 OpenMP		32 MPI		OpenCL	
	GFlops/s	GB/s	GFlops/s	GB/s	GFlops/s	GB/s
viscosity	81.79	23.72	86.48	20.14	81.86	23.66
accelerate	25.67	43.45	30.42	50.81	21.45	36.17
pdv	48.92	53.55	42.46	47.28	38.59	42.10
ideal_gas	43.92	50.19	57.79	63.29	25.52	29.06
flux_calc	9.44	50.33	12.19	64.27	5.18	27.52
advec_mom	17.04	46.69	21.39	63.79	10.44	28.51
advec_cell	25.70	44.02	30.04	54.88	18.52	31.61

Loop	K20 GPU (NVIDIA K20c) $Peak_{Flops} = 1.17 TF/s$, $Peak_{BW} = 208 GB/sec$ $DGEMM_{Flops} = 625 GFlops/s$, $BWTest_{BW} = 165 GB/s$					
	CUDA		OpenCL		OpenACC	
	GFlops/s	GB/s	GFlops/s	GB/s	GFlops/s	GB/s
viscosity	248.55	72.08	250.26	72.57	176.35	51.16
accelerate	90.84	153.75	69.37	117.41	39.36	66.64
pdv	126.78	138.80	122.20	133.78	131.52	103.08
ideal_gas	127.43	145.64	125.71	143.67	52.85	122.82
flux_calc	29.11	155.27	23.66	126.18	25.10	133.93
advec_mom	47.08	129.01	42.52	116.54	39.43	108.10
advec_cell	76.09	130.33	74.53	127.66	64.70	110.85

matches that of the original MPI version to within less than 10 %. This is true for both configurations. A closer look at the compute time vs communications time reveals that for both strong and weak scaling the time spent in communications, including message set up costs and time to communicate messages is less than 10 % of the total run time for any execution on Archer. Profiling the number of MPI messages sent/received in both OPS and original Cloverleaf versions reveals that OPS performs $4\times$ more MPI messages than the original version. This is due to the finer granularity of each ops_par_loop, each of which only sends MPI messages for data sets belonging to it. In contrast the original version only does halo exchanges in the update_halo routine, aggregating all the MPI messages that need to be sent/received for all subsequent loops. In other words, OPS communicates messages as and when required (i.e. on demand) which only enables a much smaller number of halos to be aggregated.

Figure 8 presents the benchmarking results from Titan. One node in Titan contains one NVIDIA K20x GPU, thus we have allocated one MPI process per node when executing the MPI+CUDA parallelizations. The figure also plots the run times gained on this system with the MPI only parallelization. In this case, we have allocated 8 MPI processes per node, the reason being that on Titan,

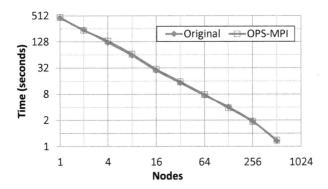

(a) Strong Scaling 15360×15360 mesh - Runtime

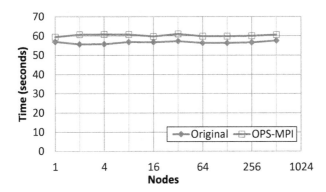

(b) Weak Scaling 2×3840×3840 mesh per node - Runtime

Fig. 7. CloverLeaf scaling performance on Archer (≈87 iterations)

there is only one AMD Interlagos CPU consisting of 16 cores, where two cores share one floating point operation unit (FPU). For the weak scaling runs the mesh size allocated per Titan node is 3840 × 3840 as there is only one CPU socket per node on Titan.

The OPS MPI+CUDA results again match the original CloverLeaf application's hand tuned MPI+CUDA version and demonstrates that the HLA approach to OPS's development has not resulted in any performance degradation. However, comparing OPS's MPI only version to that of the original, OPS loses about 30 % performance at 8 K nodes. We believe that the reason is due to OPS's on-demand MPI messaging strategy which at the very large scale results in significantly larger number of messages. The latency of these messages dominates the runtime due to the very low amount of compute performed on each MPI process. Currently we are exploring further message aggregation strategies for improving performance of OPS to resolve this issue.

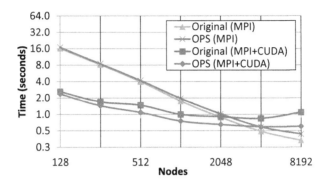

(a) Strong Scaling 15360×15360 mesh - Runtime

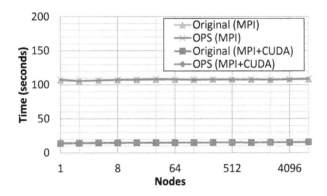

(b) Weak Scaling 3840×3840 mesh per node-Runtime

Fig. 8. CloverLeaf scaling performance on Titan (≈87 iterations) - 1 MPI process per node for MPI+CUDA, 8 MPI processes per node for pure MPI

The MPI only version strong-scales better than the MPI+CUDA version, where beyond 2 K nodes on Titan, MPI+CUDA does not give any additional speedups. We believe that this is almost certainly due to the cost of the PCIe latencies dominating the computation of the small problems at the higher node sizes. Even using NVIDIA's GPU direct, which can be utilized with OPS for MPI+CUDA applications did not give any notable benefits. The MPI-only versions do not suffer from this issue. However MPI+CUDA achieves a higher speedup (up to 8×) at very low node counts, which then subsequently diminishes at scale. With weak scaling this 8× speedup is maintained at increasing scale. Additionally, at the higher node scales, the same performance loss experienced with OPS when strong-scaling does not occur with weak-scaling. We believe that in this case, the amount of computation carried out per MPI process is large enough to hide the MPI message latencies.

4   Related Work

Several similar research projects have shown the significant benefits of utilizing high-level frameworks such as domain specific languages (DSLs) or active libraries. These include Firedrake [1], FENiCS [25] and Liszt [14], OP2 [6] for unstructured mesh applications and Paraiso [24], Ypnos [26], Pochoir [30] and SBLOCK [12] for explicit stencil based applications (structured mesh applications).

Ypnos [26] is a functional, declarative domain specific language, embedded in Haskell and extends it for parallel structured grid programming. The language introduces a number of domain specific abstract structures, such as *grids* (representing the discrete space over which computations are carried out), *grid patterns* (stencils) etc. in to Haskell, allowing different back-end implementations, such as C with MPI or CUDA. Similarly, Paraiso [24] is a domain-specific language embedded in Haskell, for the automated tuning of explicit solvers of partial differential equations (PDEs) on GPUs, and multi-core CPUs. It uses algebraic concepts such as tensors, hydrodynamic properties, interpolation methods and other building blocks in describing the PDE solving algorithms. In contrast SBLOCK [12] uses extensive automatic source code generation very much similar to the approach taken by OP2 and OPS, and expresses computations as kernels applied to elements of a set.

Pochoir [30] is a compiler and runtime system for implementing stencil computations on multi-core processors. The main aim of the project is to generate cache efficient multi-threaded CPU code for structured mesh (i.e. stencil) computations. The OPS project also aims to implement cache efficient, "tiling" algorithms through lazy-execution techniques in the future. The work presented in this paper is created from static source-to-source translation techniques to investigate the performance of the resulting code that we believe will be improved via tiling.

Liszt [14] from Stanford University implements a domain specific language (embedded in Scala [4]) for the solution of unstructured mesh based partial differential equations (PDEs). A Liszt application is translated to an intermediate representation which is then compiled by the Liszt compiler to generate native code for multiple platforms. The aim, as with OP2, is to exploit information about the structure of data and the nature of the algorithms in the code and to apply aggressive and platform specific optimizations. Performance results from a range of systems (a single GPU, a multi-core CPU, and an MPI based cluster) executing a number of applications written using Liszt have been presented in [14].

The FEniCS [25] project defines a high-level language, UFL, for the specification of finite element algorithms. The FEniCS abstraction allows the user to express the problem in terms of differential equations, leaving the details of the implementation to a lower level library. Although well established finite element methods could be supported by such a declarative abstraction, it lacks the flexibility offered by frameworks such as OP2 for developing new applications/algorithms. Currently, a runtime code generation, compilation and execution framework that is based on Python, called PyOP2 [27], and a larger framework that supports finite element application development called Firedrake [1,21] is being developed at Imperial College London.

Another related project of note is Delite [29] a compiler framework and runtime for developing parallel embedded domain-specific languages (DSLs) where the aim is to enable the rapid construction DSLs for a given domain.

5   Conclusions

In this paper, we explored the performance of a Hydrodynamics mini-app called CloverLeaf, after re-engineering it to use the OPS domain specific high-level abstractions framework. OPS provides an API for developing multi-block structured mesh applications and uses code generation techniques to translate an application to a range of parallel implementations.

The OPS based CloverLeaf's performance was compared to that of the various original hand-tuned versions on a number of single-node multi-core/many-core platforms and distributed memory cluster systems. OPS based CloverLeaf's performance on single node systems matched the original versions to within 10 % for most parallelizations and sometimes out-performed it by up to about 20 %. The achieved memory bandwidth on single node systems showed that the OPS implementations achieve over 80 % of the practical peak bandwidth of each system for some parallel loops. However only a small fraction of the peak floating-point rates are reached on all single node systems. This points to the fact that CloverLeaf is much more constrained by bandwidth than the compute capability of a system. Distributed memory parallelizations on both the Archer (Cray XC30) and Titan (Cray XK7) systems showed excellent scalability, matching that of the original application on both strong- and weak-scaling configurations. However we found that OPS's MPI implementation exchanges about 4× more shorter messages than that of the original. Further MPI message aggregation strategies for OPS are currently being explored to improve strong-scaling performance.

Nevertheless, our experience clearly shows that the development of parallel HPC applications through the careful factorization of a parallel program's functionality and implementation, using a high-level framework such as OPS, is no more time consuming nor difficult than writing a one-off parallel program targeting only a single parallel implementation. However the OPS strategy pays off with a highly maintainable single application source without compromising performance portability on parallel systems on which it will be executed. It also lays the groundwork for providing support for execution on future parallel systems. We believe such an approach will be an essential paradigm shift for utilizing the ever-increasing complexity of novel hardware and software technologies.

Acknowledgements. This research is funded by the UK AWE plc. under project "High-level Abstractions for Performance, Portability and Continuity of Scientific Software on Future Computing Systems".

The OPS project is funded by the UK Engineering and Physical Sciences Research Council projects EP/K038494/1,EP/K038486/1, EP/K038451/1 and EP/K038567/1 on "Future-proof massively-parallel execution of multi-block applications"and EP/ J010553/1 "Software for Emerging Architectures" (ASEArch) project. This paper used the Archer UK National Supercomputing Service from time allocated through UK Engineering and Physical Sciences Research Council projects EP/I006079/1, EP/I00677X/1 on "Multi-layered Abstractions for PDEs".

This research used resources of the Oak Ridge Leadership Computing Facility at the Oak Ridge National Laboratory, which is supported by the Office of Science of the U.S. Department of Energy under Contract No. DE-AC05-00OR22725.

Cloverleaf development is supported by the UK Atomic Weapons Establishment under grants CDK0660 (The Production of Predictive Models for Future Computing Requirements) and CDK0724 (AWE Technical Outreach Programe) and also the Royal Society through their Industry Fellowship Scheme (IF090020/AM).

We are thankful to Endre László at PPKE Hungary for his contributions to OPS, David Beckingsale at the University of Warwick and Michael Boulton at the University of Bristol for their insights into the original CloverLeaf application and its implementation.

References

1. The Firedrake Project. http://www.firedrakeproject.org/
2. Nvidia CUDA Toolkit Documentation. http://docs.nvidia.com/cuda/cuda-samples/#bandwidth-test
3. Nvidia Tesla Kepler Family Datasheet. http://www.nvidia.com/content/tesla/pdf/NVIDIA-Tesla-Kepler-Family-Datasheet.pdf
4. The SCALA Programming Language, http://www.scala-lang.org/
5. The Mantevo Project (2012). http://mantevo.org/
6. OP2 for Many-Core Platforms (2013). http://www.oerc.ox.ac.uk/research/op2
7. Archer - UK national high performance computing facility (2014). http://www.archer.ac.uk/
8. AWE cloverleaf (2014). http://warwick-pcav.github.io/CloverLeaf/
9. The montblanc project (2014). http://www.montblanc-project.eu/
10. OPS for Many-Core Platforms (2014). http://www.oerc.ox.ac.uk/projects/ops
11. Titan Cray XK7 (2014). https://www.olcf.ornl.gov/titan/
12. Brandvik, T., Pullan, G.: SBLOCK: a framework for efficient stencil-based PDE solvers on multi-core platforms. In: Proceedings of the 2010 10th IEEE International Conference on Computer and Information Technology, CIT 2010, pp. 1181–1188. IEEE Computer Society, Washington, DC (2010)
13. Czarnecki, K., Glück, R., Vandevoorde, D., Veldhuizen, T.L.: Generative programming and active libraries. In: Jazayeri, M., Musser, D.R., Loos, R.G.K. (eds.) Dagstuhl Seminar 1998. LNCS, vol. 1766, pp. 25–39. Springer, Heidelberg (2000)
14. DeVito, Z., Joubert, N., Palacios, F., Oakley, S., Medina, M., Barrientos, M., Elsen, E., Ham, F., Aiken, A., Duraisamy, K., Darve, E., Alonso, J., Hanrahan, P.: Liszt: a domain specific language for building portable mesh-based PDE solvers. In: Proceedings of 2011 International Conference for High Performance Computing, Networking, Storage and Analysis, SC 2011, pp. 9:1–9:12. ACM, New York (2011)
15. Dongarra, J.J., Du Croz, J., Hammarling, S., Duff, I.S.: A set of level 3 basic linear algebra subprograms. ACM Trans. Math. Softw. **16**(1), 1–17 (1990). http://doi.acm.org/10.1145/77626.79170
16. Gaudin, W., Mallinson, A., Perks, O., Herdman, J., Beckingsale, D., Levesque, J., Jarvis, S.: Optimising hydrodynamics applications for the cray XC30 with the application tool suite. In: The Cray User Group 2014, Lugano, Switzerland, 4–8 May 2014

17. Herdman, J.A., Gaudin, W.P., McIntosh-Smith, S., Boulton, M., Beckingsale, D.A., Mallinson, A., Jarvis, S.: Accelerating hydrocodes with OpenACC, OpenCL and CUDA. In: High Performance Computing, Networking, Storage and Analysis (SCC), 2012 SC Companion, pp. 465–471, November 2012
18. Howes, L.W., Lokhmotov, A., Donaldson, A.F., Kelly, P.H.J.: Deriving efficient data movement from decoupled access/execute specifications. In: Seznec, A., Emer, J., O'Boyle, M., Martonosi, M., Ungerer, T. (eds.) HiPEAC 2009. LNCS, vol. 5409, pp. 168–182. Springer, Heidelberg (2009)
19. Lindtjorn, O., Clapp, R., Pell, O., Fu, H., Flynn, M., Fu, H.: Beyond traditional microprocessors for geoscience high-performance computing applications. IEEE Micro **31**(2), 41–49 (2011)
20. Mallinson, A., Beckingsale, D., Gaudin, W., Herdman, J., Jarvis, S.: Towards portable performance for explicit hydrodynamics codes. In: International Workshop on OpenCL (IWOCL 2013), Atlanta, USA, May 2013
21. Markall, G.R., Slemmer, A., Ham, D.A., Kelly, P.H.J., Cantwell, C.D., Sherwin, S.J.: Finite element assembly strategies on multi- and many-core architectures. Int. J. Numer. Meth. Fluids **71**, 80–97 (2013). http://dx.doi.org/10.1002/fld.3648
22. McCalpin, J.D.: Memory bandwidth and machine balance in current high performance computers. In: IEEE Computer Society Technical Committee on Computer Architecture (TCCA) Newsletter, pp. 19–25, December 1995
23. Mudalige, G.R., Giles, M.B., Thiyagalingam, J., Reguly, I.Z., Bertolli, C., Kelly, P.H.J., Trefethen, A.E.: Design and initial performance of a high-level unstructured mesh framework on heterogeneous parallel systems. Parallel Comput. **39**(11), 669–692 (2013)
24. Muranushi, T.: Paraiso: an automated tuning framework for explicit solvers of partial differential equations. Comput. Sci. Discov. **5**(1), 015003 (2012)
25. Ølgaard, K.B., Logg, A., Wells, G.N.: Automated Code Generation for Discontinuous Galerkin Methods. CoRR abs/1104.0628 (2011)
26. Orchard, D.A., Bolingbroke, M., Mycroft, A.: Ypnos: declarative, parallel structured grid programming. In: Proceedings of the 5th ACM SIGPLAN Workshop on Declarative Aspects of Multicore Programming, DAMP 2010, pp. 15–24. ACM, New York (2010)
27. Rathgeber, F., Markall, G.R., Mitchell, L., Loriant, M., Ham, D.A., Bertolli, C., Kelly, P.H.J.: PyOP2: a high-level framework for performance-portable simulations on unstructured meshes. In: High Performance Computing, Networking, Storage and Analysis (SCC), 2012 SC Companion, pp. 1116–1123 (2012)
28. Reguly, I.Z., Mudalige, G.R., Bertolli, C., Giles, M.B., Betts, A., Kelly, P.H.J., Radford, D.: Acceleration of a full-scale industrial CFD application with OP2. ACM Trans. Parallel Comput. (2013, under review). http://arxiv-web3.library.cornell.edu/abs/1403.7209
29. Sujeeth, A.K., Brown, K.J., Lee, H., Rompf, T., Chafi, H., Odersky, M., Olukotun, K.: Delite: a compiler architecture for performance-oriented embedded domain-specific languages. ACM Trans. Embed. Comput. Syst. (TECS) **13**(4s), 134 (2014)
30. Tang, Y., Chowdhury, R.A., Kuszmaul, B.C., Luk, C.K., Leiserson, C.E.: The pochoir stencil compiler. In: Proceedings of the Twenty-Third Annual ACM Symposium on Parallelism in Algorithms and Architectures, SPAA 2011, pp. 117–128. ACM, New York (2011)
31. Veldhuizen, T.L., Gannon, D.: Active libraries: rethinking the roles of compilers and libraries. In: Proceedings of the SIAM Workshop on Object Oriented Methods for Inter-operable Scientific and Engineering Computing (OO 1998). SIAM Press (1998)

Section B: Performance Analysis and Prediction

Insight into Application Performance Using Application-Dependent Characteristics

Waleed Alkohlani[1]([⊠]), Jeanine Cook[2], and Nafiul Siddique[1]

[1] Klipsch School of Electrical and Computer Engineering,
New Mexico State University, Las Cruces, USA
{wkohlani,nafiul}@nmsu.edu
[2] Sandia National Laboratories, Albuquerque, USA
jeacook@sandia.gov

Abstract. Carefully crafted performance characterization can provide significant insight into application performance and can be beneficial to computer designers, compiler and application developers, and end users. To achieve all the benefits of performance characterization, the characterization must incorporate a comprehensive set of characteristics that affect performance and can be measured with minimal perturbation from the underlying micro-architecture. To this end, we advocate the use of *application-dependent* characteristics that allow general conclusions to be drawn about the application itself rather than its observed performance on a specific architecture. In our prior work [7], we introduced a set of application-dependent characteristics and showed that they are consistent across architectures. In this work, we present an efficient characterization methodology that incorporates a more comprehensive set of application-dependent characteristics. We also explain in detail how these characteristics can be used to reason about and gain insight into application performance. Finally, we report characterization results on SPEC MPI2007 and Mantevo benchmarks. To our knowledge, this is the first work to present application-dependent characterization results for SPEC MPI2007 and some of the new Mantevo benchmarks.

1 Introduction

If carefully crafted, application performance characterization can provide valuable insight into performance and significant benefits to a wide range of users from hardware designers to application developers and end users. Architecture designers can use application performance characterization to quickly define an optimal initial baseline architecture for a given application or workload. Performance characterization also helps reveal code optimization opportunities for application developers and aids end-users in selecting the platform(s) that result in optimal performance. Furthermore, application benchmark developers use characterization to choose benchmarks that are representative of a particular domain and/or to compare benchmarks and determine their (dis)similarity. Finally, performance characterization can be used to provide insight into why an application performs the way it does on a particular architecture.

© Springer International Publishing Switzerland 2015
S.A. Jarvis et al. (Eds.): PMBS 2014, LNCS 8966, pp. 107–128, 2015.
DOI: 10.1007/978-3-319-17248-4_6

To achieve these and other benefits of performance characterization, the characterization must incorporate a comprehensive set of characteristics that affect performance and the measurements must be done in a micro-architecture-independent fashion. By using a comprehensive set of important performance characteristics, a more complete picture of application performance can be drawn. Therefore, in this work, we present and advocate the use of application-dependent (i.e., micro-architecture-independent) characteristics that allow general conclusions to be drawn about the application itself rather than its observed performance on a specific architecture. In other words, because they are the characteristics of the application that realize the observed performance, application-dependent characteristics help us understand the *fundamental cause* of the observed performance on a specific architecture.

In our prior work [7], we introduced a set of application-dependent characteristics and showed that they are consistent across architectures. In this work, we present an efficient characterization methodology that incorporates a more comprehensive set of application-dependent characteristics including spatial and temporal locality, memory usage and memory footprint, branch predictability, instruction mix, as well as characteristics related to ILP (instruction-level parallelism). To allow these characteristics to be measured quickly and in a micro-architecture independent manner, we define all characteristics such that they are easily obtainable using dynamic binary instrumentation (DBI). By using *only* DBI, our methodology does not depend on slow (possibly inaccurate) simulators and is, therefore, faster.

Although the idea of micro-architecture-independent characteristics has been explored in prior studies, the methodology and metrics presented in this paper are defined and used differently as illustrated below and in Sect. 5. Further, the set of measured characteristics (metrics) defined is more comprehensive than prior studies [12–14, 20] and includes new metrics.

Workload characterization has been primarily used to understand the behavior of applications on specific platforms and to understand the similarity of benchmarks within or across benchmark suites. In this work, we define a characterization method that can be applied in a wider context. In particular, we show how to use the results of application-dependent characterization to

- reason about and gain insight into application performance
- intuitively understand how performance characteristics map to machine characteristics
- aid in benchmark comparison and/or selection.

Additional contributions of this work include (1) a comprehensive set of application-dependent metrics that includes new performance metrics, and (2) detailed performance characterization data for benchmarks that have not been characterized before as well as others that have only been lightly studied.

2   Methodology and Characteristics

In this section, we present our application-dependent performance characteristics and metrics and show how they can be used to gain insight into application performance. Our aim is to define a minimum number of characteristics that maximally capture an application's unique and diverse behavior. We also briefly describe how to use characterization results to compare applications or to select benchmarks for a particular study. The application-dependent characteristics are classified into *general* and *memory* characteristics as described below.

2.1   General Characteristics

Dynamic Instruction Mix

The dynamic instruction mix provides information about the types and ratios of instructions executed by an application and can be used to gain a high-level understanding of what the application needs in terms of the type of execution units. To support CISC (e.g., x86) instructions that perform multiple operations, we decompose each instruction into its single operations (ops) such as *add*, *load*, or *store* ops. All the operations performed by a program are then grouped into the following five categories: (1) Loads, (2) Stores, (3) FP Ops, (4) Int Ops, and (5) Branches. These categories are chosen to correspond to the different execution units that may be implemented in a micro-architecture. Additionally, for each category, we capture a frequency distribution of the distance separating two same-type ops measured in number of instructions. Such a distribution helps us understand how particular execution units are stressed. For example, having multiple FP execution units can improve performance if FP ops occur in bursts (i.e., one after another). The distance distributions contain 513 distances or bins that start from zero to a maximum distance of 511, with the last entry representing distances larger than or equal to 512. Figure 1a shows an example distribution of the distances between load ops for the *104.milc* benchmark. The figure shows that load op pairs that follow each other (i.e., distance of 1) represent approximately 18 % of the total loads in the benchmark.

Instruction Dependence

We characterize the dependence between instructions using the register dependence distance, which is the distance measured in number of dynamic instructions between the instruction writing or producing a specific register and the instruction reading or consuming it. For each application, we capture a frequency distribution of register dependence distances. This characteristic is indicative of the amount of ILP (Instruction-Level Parallelism) inherently present in the application and indicates whether the application can utilize increased processor issue width, more in-flight instructions (i.e., larger window), or more execution units. For example, if an application exhibits tight register dependence distances, the opportunities to execute multiple instructions in parallel become limited, which in turn leads to decreased performance. In contrast, an application with long dependence distances will perform better on wide-issue processors. Figure 1b shows the register dependence distance distribution for the *CloverLeaf* benchmark. The figure shows that *CloverLeaf* has tight dependence distances; a register is written and then read by the same instruction (i.e., distance of 0) 32 % of the time while a register is written and read by the next instruction (i.e., distance of 1) about 20 % of the time.

Conditional Branch Predictability

Conditional branch predictability is measured for a given application using a metric called *branch transition rate* [11]. Branch transition rate measures how often a branch switches direction between taken and not taken during execution. Branches are easily predictable if they do not change direction often or if they switch direction most of the time. Branches that have a transition rate of around 50 % are the most difficult to predict. We classify branches into 11 groups (0–10) based on their transition rates: 0–5 %, 5–10 %, 10–15 %, 15–20 %, 20–30 %, 30–70 %, 70–80 %, 80–85 %, 85–90 %, 90–95 %, and 95–100 %. Class 0 corresponds to the percentage of branches that transition 0–5 % of the time; class 1 corresponds to the percentage of branches that transition 5–10 % of the time and so on.

An application that has mostly class 0 or class 10 branches requires only a simple branch predictor and will likely experience a low misprediction rate. In contrast, an application characterized by primarily class 5 branches requires a more sophisticated predictor and will more likely have a higher misprediction rate. Figure 1c shows the percentage of branches in each branch transition rate class for the *miniMD* and *104.milc* benchmarks. *MiniMD* has a high percentage of hard-to-predict branches (Classes 4 and 5) while *104.milc* has mostly easy-to-predict branches (Class 0). Therefore, *miniMD* is likely to have a higher branch misprediction rate than *104.milc* (see Sect. 4).

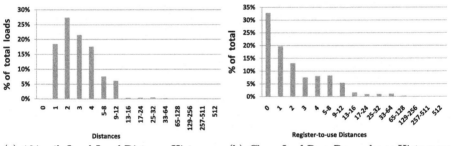

(a) *104.milc* Load-Load Distance Histogram   (b) *CloverLeaf* Reg. Dependence Histogram

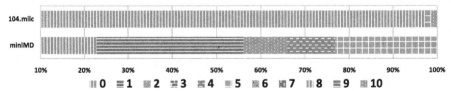

(c) % of Branches in Each Branch Transition Class for *miniMD* and *104.milc*

Fig. 1. Example general characteristics

Computational Intensity

Computational intensity is the ratio of floating-point operations to memory accesses and is a commonly used characteristic for floating-point scientific applications. Computational intensity is an indirect measure of *data movement*.

Because moving a piece of data is typically much slower than doing an operation on it, application and algorithm developers strive to achieve higher computational intensities. Reducing data movement also reduces energy.

Average Instruction Size

The average size (in bytes) of instructions executed by an application can aid in understanding how an application utilizes a given fetch width and whether a wider fetch width is needed. This is particularly useful for CISC (e.g., x86) instructions that vary in size, affecting both the fetch and decode stages of a processor pipeline. To achieve optimal performance, the block of bytes (code) fetched on every cycle must at a minimum contain a number of instructions equal to the processor width (i.e., dispatch and commit width). We measure a distribution of instruction sizes from which we calculate the average size.

Average Basic Block Size

A basic block is a single-entry, single-exit sequence of code. Measured in number of instructions, basic block sizes are indicative of the amount of ILP available to exploit which, in turn, informs fetch width and is correlated to branch frequency. Since taken branches typically cause what is called a *fetch bubble* in a processor pipeline, an application with small basic blocks (i.e., high rate of branches) may experience frequent fetch bubbles and thus experience a decreased fetch rate. We measure a frequency distribution of the dynamic basic block sizes and calculate the average.

2.2   Memory Characteristics

Due to the dominance of the memory system in affecting performance, understanding the inherent memory characteristics of an application is key to understanding its performance. To this end, we define a comprehensive set of memory characteristics and metrics as described below.

Data Working Set Size

The working set size determines the memory size required for an application and it is defined as the total number of unique memory bytes touched by the application during its execution. The working set size (or *data intensiveness*) helps us understand the memory demands of an application and has been found to be the biggest differentiator between real applications and benchmarks [18].

Timeline of Memory Usage

This performance metric captures the size of new memory used by an application as its execution progresses in time. Starting from the beginning of execution and for every interval of one billion instructions, we track and record the total number of new and unique memory bytes touched by the application. Besides knowing the periods of execution at which the application accesses new memory, the memory usage timeline may be used to identify phases of execution. It has been shown in [15] that the working set captured for execution intervals can be an effective phase detection method.

Figure 2 shows an example timeline for the *HPCCG* benchmark. The y-axis shows the size of new memory used as a percentage of the benchmark's total working set size, and the x-axis represents execution progress. As illustrated in the figure, the entire working set size of the *HPCCG* benchmark is accessed within the first 4 % of execution; 58 %, 36 %, and 6 % of the working set size is accessed in the first, second, and forth percent of execution, respectively. This also suggests that after 4 % of execution elapses, *HPCCG* goes into a *single* execution phase for the remainder of execution. Note that it may well be that an application initializes all of its data structures (i.e. accesses all its memory) at the beginning of execution. In such a case, the memory usage timeline can not provide useful information about execution phases (see Sect. 6).

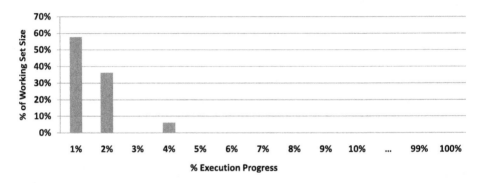

Fig. 2. Memory usage timeline for *HPCCG*

Average Requested Memory Size

This metric measures the average number of bytes read/written per memory operation, indicating the average data size used by the application. This can be useful when used with computational intensity to determine, on average, the amount of data being moved per floating-point operation. Note that depending on their types, memory instructions can read/write a widely varying number of memory bytes. Therefore, knowing the number of memory operations must be complemented by knowing the number of bytes those operations read or write.

Temporal and Spatial Locality

To mitigate the high latency of accessing memory, modern micro-architectures feature small and fast cache memories that hold frequently-accessed data closer to the processor. All caches work by exploiting the *locality of reference* exhibited (to varying extents) by all applications. There are two types of locality: *temporal locality* which is the reuse over time of a data item from memory, and *spatial locality* which is the use of data items in memory near other recently used items. By carefully analyzing an application's temporal and spatial locality, not only can we understand how effectively the application utilizes a given cache organization, but we can also reason about the optimal cache configuration for the application. Our approach to achieving this goal starts by capturing a frequency distribution of the application's memory-reuse distances.

A memory-reuse distance (MRD) is defined as the distance measured in number of *unique* memory blocks accessed between two accesses to the same block. In all of our experiments, the maximum tracked MRD is 32 MB, which corresponds to a cache size of 32 MB. Using 16-byte, 32-byte, 64-byte, and 128-byte memory block sizes, we capture one MRD distribution for each block size. Note that these block sizes correspond to four potential cache line sizes. Since higher levels of cache typically store either data or instructions while lower levels of cache store both, we capture separate MRD distributions for data references, instruction references, and unified (both data and instruction) references.

We now illustrate how MRD distributions are used to characterize an application's spatial and temporal locality. Note that the conclusions drawn from the examples below are only a small sample of the conclusions that can be drawn from the data. Figure 3a shows a portion of the unified MRD distribution for the *HPCCG* benchmark. The x-axis represents the distance in number of unique 64-byte block accesses between two accesses to the same 64-byte block, and the y-axis represents the percentage of the total memory references.

The goal of characterizing an application's spatial locality is to help us understand how effectively and quickly the application consumes the data available to it in a cache block. To achieve this and at the same time visualize spatial locality, we plot the points from the MRD distribution that correspond to short memory-reuse distances; zero through 64 (Fig. 3b). In other words, we determine the percentage of memory references that reuse data from the same block (line) after n accesses to other blocks, where $n = \{0, 1, 2, 4, 8, 16, 32, 64\}$. Other studies [12–14, 20] capture spatial locality only for a distance of zero by considering only successive references. We believe that using a window of n references intuitively provides more accurate spatial locality information but is computationally more complex.

As shown in Fig. 3b, about 42 % of the references in *HPCCG* immediately reuse the same line (i.e., distance of 0), and around 34 % of references reuse the same line after one access to a different line (i.e., distance of 1). Figure 3d illustrates how *HPCCG*'s spatial locality changes over different block sizes. Within the maximum distance of 64 line accesses, 91 %, 96 %, 98 %, and 99 % of references are spatially local using 16-, 32-, 64-, and 128-byte blocks, respectively. Note that in an n-way set-associative cache, there is a possibility that the intermediate block accesses are to the same set (see discussion below), which may cause a block to be evicted by the time it is referenced again. Thus, it may be more accurate to look at spatial locality for short distances (e.g., 2, 4, and 8) that correspond to the cache associativity of interest. For example, Fig. 3d shows that the percentage of references spatially local within a distance of 2 is 70 %, 89 %, and 93 % for block sizes of 16, 32, and 64 bytes, respectively. As also seen in Fig. 3d, *HPCCG*'s spatial locality improves only slightly by increasing the block size from 64 to 128 bytes. From this, we can conclude that the optimal cache line size for exploiting *HPCCG*'s spatial locality is 64 bytes.

To visualize temporal locality, the distances on the x-axis of the MRD distribution are grouped into bins that correspond to potential cache sizes. The first

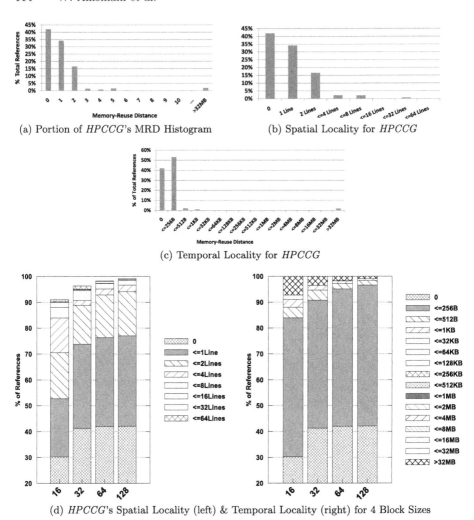

(a) Portion of *HPCCG*'s MRD Histogram

(b) Spatial Locality for *HPCCG*

(c) Temporal Locality for *HPCCG*

(d) *HPCCG*'s Spatial Locality (left) & Temporal Locality (right) for 4 Block Sizes

Fig. 3. Temporal and spatial locality examples

four distance bins are set to 0, 4, 8, and 64 *times* the line size. The rest of the bins go from 32 KB up to 32 MB, doubling each time. Figure 3c shows the temporal locality plot for *HPCCG* based on 64-byte blocks and unified references.

The figure shows that 95 %, 97 %, and 98 % of references are temporal within the distances of 256 B, 512 B, and 1 KB, respectively. This implies that a 1 KB cache is large enough to keep 98 % of references temporally local within the cache. Figure 3d shows how *HPCCG*'s temporal locality changes over different cache line sizes. For example, the percentage of references that are temporal within 1 KB is 91 %, 96 %, 98 %, and 99 % for 16-, 32-, 64-, and 128-byte blocks, respectively.

The above temporal and spatial locality analysis assumes that the target cache is fully associative. However, in an n-way set associative cache, the block accesses that occur between two accesses to the same block can be to the same set, which may cause a block to be evicted by the time it is re-accessed. For caches with a high degree of associativity, which are typical of lower-level caches and closely approximate fully-associative caches, our above analysis is valid and is confirmed using actual measurements (see Sect. 4). However, for low associative caches, it is important to look at the access patterns of cache sets. To this end, we capture a frequency distribution of the set-reuse distances, where a set-reuse distance (SRD) is the number of sets accessed between two accesses to the same set. To capture the SRD distribution, assumptions must be made about the size of the cache, the size of a cache line, and the number of ways in a cache set. In all our experiments, the cache size is assumed to be 32 MB. We use four cache line sizes (16, 32, 64, and 128 bytes) and four associativities (2, 4, 8, and 16 ways). One SRD distribution is captured for every unique combination of line sizes and number of ways.

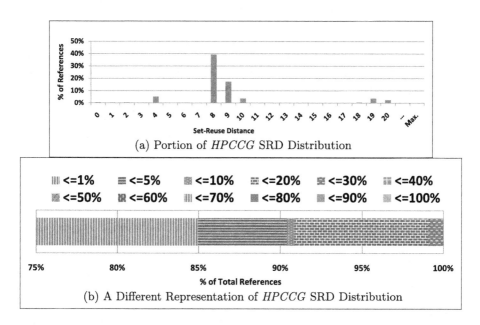

(a) Portion of *HPCCG* SRD Distribution

(b) A Different Representation of *HPCCG* SRD Distribution

Fig. 4. Set-reuse distances for *HPCCG*

Figure 4a shows a portion of the SRD distribution for *HPCCG*. In capturing this distribution, the 32 MB cache is assumed to be 8-way set associative with 64-byte lines. As shown in Fig. 4a, about 40 % of references re-access the same set after accessing eight other sets (i.e., distance of 8). It can also be seen that around 67 % of references have a set-reuse distance of less than or equal to 10. This suggests that a set is frequently re-accessed within a short period of time. This may lead to more conflict misses provided that a low-associative cache is used and that the MRD distribution shows a high ratio of references with long MRDs compared to SRDs. That is, *different* blocks within a set are frequently accessed within a short period of time, which increases the likelihood of conflict misses. In Fig. 4b, we group the set-reuse distances into bins that represent distances as a percentage of the total sets in the 32 MB cache. As illustrated in the figure, around 85 %, 90 %, and 99 % of total references re-access the same set after 1 %, 5 %, and 20 %, respectively, of sets are accessed.

2.3   Selection and Comparison of Benchmarks

In addition to gaining insight into performance and reasoning about hardware resources optimal for performance, the application-dependent characteristics described above can also be used to select an appropriate set of benchmarks for a particular study or to determine the (dis)similarity among benchmarks. For example, if one is interested in studying branch behavior or evaluating branch predictors, they need to choose benchmarks with diverse branch predictability characteristics. On the other hand, if evaluating memory system configurations or studying memory behavior is of interest, the benchmarks with the most diverse memory characteristics should be considered.

To compare benchmarks, the metrics used to measure the application-dependent characteristics for each benchmark can be grouped into a vector that can be called *the performance vector*. For example, the percentage of each of the five categories in the instruction mix and the percentage of references in each bin of the memory-reuse distance distribution can be included in the performance vector. The performance vectors of different benchmarks can then be normalized and compared using a simple distance measure.

3   Experimental Setup

In this section, we briefly describe the platforms and tools used to capture the application-dependent characteristics described in Sect. 2 as well as the benchmarks used in this study.

Platforms

All of our experiments are conducted on a Dell cluster that includes eight nodes, each of which runs the Scientific Linux (version 6.3) operating system [4] and has 48 GB of available RAM. Each node contains two six-core Intel Xeon X5670 processors that are clocked at 2.93 GHz. While all the cores share a 12 MB 16-way L3 cache, each core has a 32 KB 4-way L1 instruction cache, a 32 KB 8-way L1 data cache, and 256 KB 8-way L2 unified cache. A cache line is 64 bytes in all the levels of cache. Each of the Intel Xeon X5670 processor cores implements the Westmere-EP micro-architecture which features: (1) a 4-way superscalar out-of-order execution pipeline, (2) a 128-entry re-order buffer, and (3) three integer, three floating-point, and four address generation units.

Tools

We capture the application-dependent characteristics described in Sect. 2 using dynamic binary instrumentation (DBI) tools that we developed in-house using Pin [17]. The slowdown caused by DBI depends on the type of analysis performed and the number of dynamic instructions instrumented. However, DBI is still orders of magnitude faster than simulation and there exist techniques such as sampling to effectively speed up the execution of instrumented binaries.

Capturing the memory-reuse and set-reuse distance distributions (see Sect. 2) is nontrivial and can cause extreme slowdowns. To capture these reuse distances, a FIFO(First-In-First-Out) queue is typically used to hold memory references and for every new reference encountered during execution, the queue is searched for a prior occurrence of the reference to determine a reuse distance. We implement three optimization methods to speed up our DBI tool. First, we limit the size of the FIFO queue by restricting the maximum reuse distance to 32 MB which is sufficient to study the behavior of most modern caches. Second, we implement the FIFO queue using a balanced binary tree to achieve much faster search and update times. Finally, rather than instrumenting the entire benchmark binary, we use representative sampling [9,10] to select a limited number of representative samples. Then, the instrumentation is applied only to the selected samples. For each benchmark, up to ten 100-million-instruction samples are identified using the PinPoints methodology [19] which is based on the well-known SimPoint tool [24]. In [7], we show that the reuse distributions measured with and without sampling are statistically similar at 95 % confidence.

Using our optimized tools and for all the benchmarks listed in Table 1, it took approximately two weeks to capture all the characterization data on the 8-node platform described above. Finally, the PapiEx [3] tool is used to obtain counts from the on-chip hardware performance counters

Table 1. List of benchmarks used

Suite	Benchmark	Lang.	Application domain
SPEC MPI2007	104.milc	C	Quantum chromodynamics
	107.leslie3d	Fortran	Computational fluid dynamics
	113.GemsFDTD	Fortran	Computational electromagnetics
	132.zeusmp2	C/Fortran	Computational fluid dynamics
	137.lu	Fortran	Computational fluid dynamics
Mantevo MiniApps	miniFE	C++	Unstructured Implicit Finite Element
	HPCCG	C + +	Unstructured implicit finite element
	miniMD	C + +	Molecular dynamics
	miniXyce	C + +	Circuit simulation
	CloverLeaf	C/Fortran	Hydrodynamics

Benchmarks

Table 1 shows a list of all the benchmarks used in this study. Although all are parallel benchmarks, we execute them serially for the purposes of this work. All benchmarks are built using compilers from the Gnu Compiler Collection(GCC) [1] and are drawn from the following benchmark suites:

1. **SPEC MPI2007** (version 1.1) is a benchmark suite from System Performance Evaluation Corporation (SPEC) containing thirteen MPI-parallel,

floating point, compute intensive benchmarks [5]. We select five benchmarks
(Table 1) that are the only benchmarks that can be executed serially.
2. **Mantevo MiniApps**, developed at Sandia National Laboratories, are small
   self-contained proxies of real scientific applications used in the lab [2]. At the
   time of doing this study, version 1.0 of the Mantevo suite contained seven
   MiniApps. Of these seven MiniApps, we use five (Table 1) and exclude two
   (*miniGhost* and *CoMD*) that we could not successfully run with our tools.
   The problem sizes of the selected MiniApps are manually configured such
   that the number of instructions they execute is similar to that of the SPEC
   MPI2007 benchmarks (i.e., few trillion instructions per benchmark).

4   Results

In this section, we present measured application-dependent characteristics for all
the studied benchmarks. We also show performance data from on-chip counters
on the platform described in Sect. 3. We select and show only the counts that
help in interpreting the application-dependent characterization data.

Instruction Mix and ILP Characteristics

Figure 5a shows the instruction mix for each of the studied benchmarks. On
average, SPEC benchmarks execute more floating-point instructions (55 % vs
32 %), more loads (28 % vs 24 %), and slightly more stores (7 % vs 5 %) than
Mantevo benchmarks. On the other hand, Mantevo benchmarks execute more
integer operations (30 % vs 8 %) and more branch instructions (9 % vs 2 %).
However, unlike SPEC benchmarks, Mantevo benchmarks exhibit more diversity
in their instruction mixes. For example, *CloverLeaf* and *miniMD* have high
ratios of floating-point operations, *miniXyce* has the highest ratio of integer
operations, and both *HPCCG* and *miniFE* have a more even distribution of
integer and floating-point operations. In general, all the SPEC benchmarks will
likely benefit from more floating-point execution resources while the Mantevo
benchmarks will benefit from a mix of more floating-point, integer, and branch
execution resources. Although both benchmark suites have relatively similar
ratios of memory instructions, understanding their optimal memory resources
requires the understanding of their memory access patterns and other memory
characteristics that are presented later in this section.

Figure 5c shows the average register dependence distance as well as the average
distance between a load or a floating-point instruction to their consumer instruction. On average, Mantevo benchmarks have shorter register dependence distances
(4.1 vs 5.6), shorter FP-to-use distances (4.5 vs 5.4), and much shorter load-to-
use distances (4.4 vs 11.1). Also, on average, Mantevo benchmarks have smaller
basic blocks than SPEC benchmarks (11 vs 33 instructions). From the above,
we can conclude that SPEC benchmarks, on average, exhibit more inherent ILP
(instruction-level parallelism) than Mantevo benchmarks. The long distances between load operations and their consumers in SPEC benchmarks suggests that
small memory latencies may be effectively hidden through out-of-order execution.

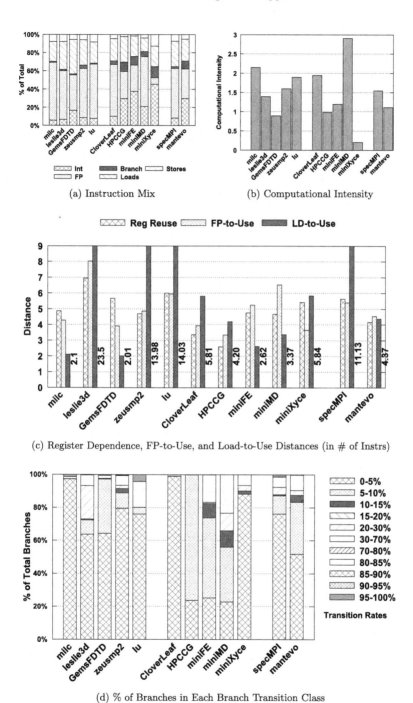

(a) Instruction Mix

(b) Computational Intensity

(c) Register Dependence, FP-to-Use, and Load-to-Use Distances (in # of Instrs)

(d) % of Branches in Each Branch Transition Class

Fig. 5. Select general characteristics of SPEC MPI2007 & Mantevo Mini Apps

On the other hand, depending on their memory access patterns and the likelihood of experiencing cache misses, benchmarks with short load-to-use distances may require code optimization to hide memory access latencies.

Branch Predictability

Figure 5d shows the benchmarks' branch predictability using their branch transition rates (Sect. 2). For each benchmark, the figure shows the percentage of branches in each transition rate class. As described in Sect. 2, branches with high or low transition rates are more easily predictable than branches with around 50 % transition rates. Almost all benchmarks have predominantly easy-to-predict branches and thus their measured branch misprediction rates are less than 1 % as seen in Fig. 9b. However, *miniMD* has the most diverse branch predictability and the highest ratio of hard-to-predict branches. Therefore, it experiences the highest branch misprediction rate (11.4 %), which can be a serious performance bottleneck given that 5.5 % of all instructions in *miniMD* are branches.

Computational Intensity

Figure 5b shows the computational intensity of all the studied benchmarks. As can be concluded from their instruction mix, SPEC benchmarks, on average, have higher computational intensities than Mantevo benchmarks. However, the Mantevo benchmarks show more diversity in computational intensity with *miniMD* being the most computationally intensive of all benchmarks and *miniXyce* the least. Note that with the exception of *milc*, memory instructions in all benchmarks read or write 8 bytes of data on average (Fig. 6b).

Data Working Set Size and Usage

Figure 6a shows the data working set size (data intensiveness) for all studied benchmarks. On average, Mantevo benchmarks have much larger working set sizes than SPEC benchmarks (4.5 GB vs 0.7 GB). As noted in Sect. 3, all benchmarks are configured such that they execute a similar number of instructions. With a working set size of 2 GB, *GemsFDTD* is the only SPEC benchmark that accesses more than 1 GB of data. The benchmark *HPCCG* has the largest working set size (11 GB) and *miniXyce* has the smallest (73 MB). Since cache performance is largely dependent on temporal and spatial locality characteristics as well as the cache configuration, having larger working sets does not necessarily lead to worse cache performance. This is supported by the actual cache miss measurements shown in Fig. 9c. These measurements show that some benchmarks (e.g., *miniXyce*) with small working sets experience more cache misses than benchmarks with much larger working sets.

Figure 6c shows the amount of new memory accessed with respect to execution progress. With the exception of *milc* and *miniFE*, all benchmarks access their entire working sets within the first 1 to 5 percent of execution. *miniFE* accesses around 93 % of its working set within the first 3 % of execution while *milc*'s memory usage is more distributed between 1 % and 60 % of execution. This suggests that *milc* has more diverse execution phases than the other benchmarks. However, as discussed in Sect. 2, our memory usage timeline may not accurately

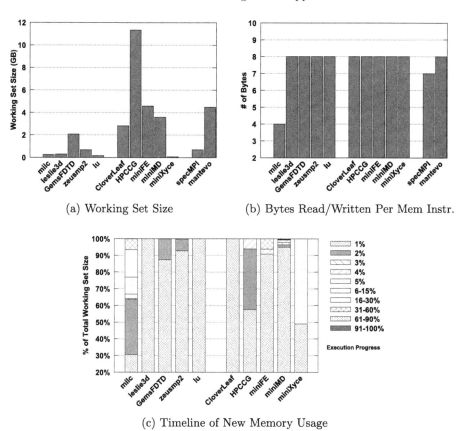

(a) Working Set Size

(b) Bytes Read/Written Per Mem Instr.

(c) Timeline of New Memory Usage

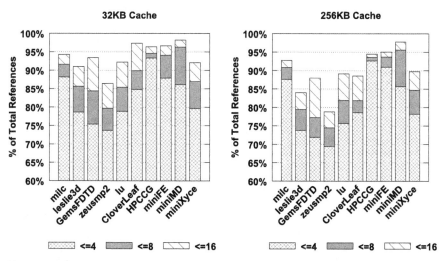

(d) Set-Reuse Distances Based on 32KB (left) and 256KB (right) Caches (64-byte lines, 8-way associativity)

Fig. 6. Select memory characteristics of SPEC MPI2007 & Mantevo mini apps

reflect execution phase behavior since benchmarks may start their execution by initializing their entire used memory. This issue will be addressed in future work.

Spatial and Temporal Locality

Spatial and temporal locality plots are presented in Figs. 7 and 8, respectively. For four different block (cache line) sizes, these plots show only the locality of data references. We describe below the locality characteristics of individual benchmarks and relate our conclusions to the actual cache miss measurements shown in Fig. 9c; cache details are in Sect. 3. To help relate conclusions to actual measurements, we capture and show in Fig. 6d the percentage of 64-byte references that have short set-reuse distances on two cache configurations that correspond to the actual 8-way 32 KB L1 and the 8-way 256 KB L2 caches implemented in the Westmere architecture (see Sect. 3 and Sect. 2).

Shown in Fig. 7, the spatial locality (i.e., the percentage of accesses reusing the same block within a small number of other accesses) of *milc* as well as of most of the other benchmarks, increases with increasing block sizes. For 16-, 32-, 64-, and 128-byte blocks, the percentage of references reusing the same block within a distance of 8 is 73 %, 83 %, 90 %, and 91 %, respectively. However, *milc*'s spatial locality increases only slightly by going from 64-byte to 128-byte blocks. As illustrated in Fig. 8, *milc* also exhibits a high degree of temporal locality with over 95 % of its 64-byte memory accesses being temporal within 4KB (64 × 64). Similar to its spatial locality, *milc*'s temporal locality does not significantly improve by using blocks larger than 64 bytes.

Figure 9c shows that *milc* experiences fewer L1 and L2 misses compared to the other SPEC benchmarks. This is due to its better temporal locality and better spatial locality within a distance of 8 (i.e., the L1/L2 cache associativity). However, *milc* encounters L1 and L2 misses despite its excellent temporal locality. This can be attributed to conflict misses caused by a high percentage of references re-accessing the same cache set within short distances (Fig. 6d).

Compared to *milc*, *leslie3d*, *GemsFDTD*, and *zeusmp2* exhibit less spatial locality with only 60 %, 50 %, and 50 %, respectively, of their 64-byte references being spatially local within a distance of 8 (Fig. 7). Also, of *GemsFDTD*'s, *zeusmp2*'s, and *leslie3d*'s 64-byte accesses, only 60 %, 50 %, and 50 %, respectively, are temporal within 4 KB (Fig. 8). This explains why these benchmarks experience more L1 and more L2 (except *zeusmp2*) cache misses than *milc* (Fig. 9c). The fewer L2 cache misses of *zeusmp2* can be attributed to fewer conflict misses since a lower ratio of its memory accesses reuse a recently-accessed set (Fig. 6d).

With 64-byte blocks, only about 70 % of *CloverLeaf*'s references exhibit spatial locality within a distance of 8 (Fig. 7). On the other hand, around 80 % of the memory references in *HPCCG*, *miniFE*, *miniMD*, and *miniXyce* are spatially local within a distance of 8. With the exception of *miniXyce*'s temporal locality, the spatial and temporal locality of all Mantevo benchmarks improves only slightly by increasing the block size from 64 to 128 bytes. Figure 8 shows Mantevo benchmarks have varying temporal locality for long MRDs but also high ratios of references that are temporal within short MRDs(i.e., small caches).

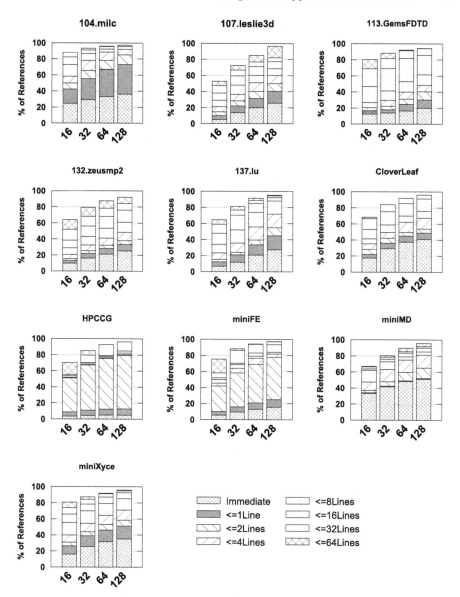

Fig. 7. Spatial locality

Because it exhibits less spatial and temporal locality compared to the other Mantevo benchmarks, *CloverLeaf* experiences more L1 cache misses (Fig. 9c). It also encounters more L2 cache misses than the other Mantevo benchmarks except *miniXyce*. As seen in Fig. 6d, both *CloverLeaf* and *miniXyce* have lower ratios of references with short set-reuse distances, which further indicates lower locality. *MiniXyce* has more L2 and L3 cache misses than all the other Mantevo

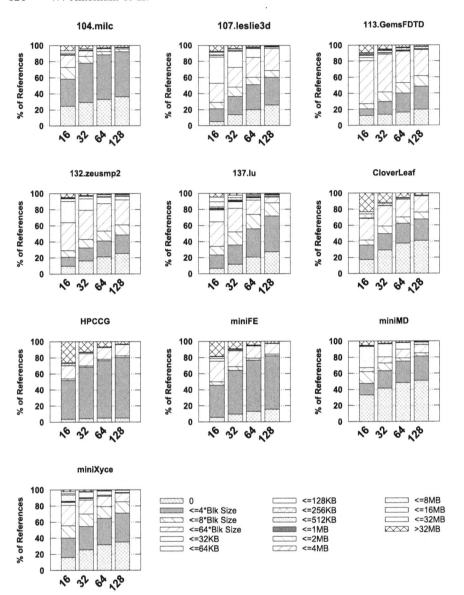

Fig. 8. Temporal locality

benchmarks because around 10 % of its references are not temporal within 256 KB or 12MB (i.e., L2 and L3 cache sizes). This also explains why most of its L2 cache misses are not satisfied in the L3 cache. On the other hand, *miniMD* has the lowest number of L1 and L2 cache misses because it exhibits the best temporal locality within 32 KB (99 % of references) and the highest ratio of references immediately reusing the same cache line.

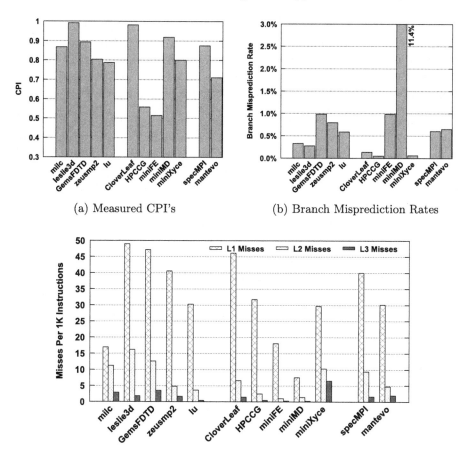

(a) Measured CPI's   (b) Branch Misprediction Rates

Fig. 9. Performance measurements from the intel platform (Sect. 3)

Discussion of Performance Measurements

Figure 9 presents the CPI, branch misprediction rates, and cache misses measured on the Intel platform described in Sect. 3. On average, Mantevo benchmarks perform better than SPEC benchmarks (0.71 vs 0.87 CPI). The relatively low performance of SPEC benchmarks could largely be attributed to their higher cache miss rates and higher ratio of floating-point operations. However, there is substantially more variance in the CPI's of the Mantevo benchmarks. This is consistent with the fact that Mantevo benchmarks exhibit more varying application-dependent characteristics as shown earlier in this section.

Of the SPEC benchmarks, *leslie3d* shows the worst performance (highest CPI). We believe this is due to its relatively larger number of L1 and L2 cache misses. On the other hand, although *milc* has a low L1 cache miss rate, it exhibits a relatively high CPI. This may be attributed to its short load-to-use distances (Fig. 5c) with which cache access latencies can not be effectively hidden.

Of the Mantevo benchmarks, *CloverLeaf* has the highest CPI which can be attributed to its relatively high L1, L2, and L3 cache miss rates. Also, with

CloverLeaf's tight register dependence distances, cache miss penalties can not be hidden. In contrast, *miniMD* shows a relatively high CPI although it has the lowest number of cache misses. This may be largely attributed to its high branch misprediction rate. *MiniXyce*'s CPI is also high and can be attributed to its relatively high L1, L2, and L3 miss rates. It also has the smallest basic blocks (5 instructions on average) and large instruction sizes (4 bytes on average) which can limit the number of instructions fetched by the processor per cycle (see Sect. 2). Finally, both *HPCCG* and *miniFE* encounter the lowest number of L2 and L3 cache misses. Because these two benchmarks exhibit relatively good ILP (long register dependence and load-to-use distances), their L1 cache miss penalties can be effectively hidden, which may explain their low measured CPI.

5   Related Work

Most prior characterization approaches use **hardware-dependent** performance metrics such as CPI or cache miss rates obtained from hardware performance counters or simulation [6,8,16,23]. The goal is to measure and understand application performance on a specific platform. Other approaches use similar hardware-dependent metrics to study benchmark similarities to find representative subsets of benchmark suites [21,22]. Besides the pitfalls of hardware-dependent characterization mentioned in [12,13], conclusions drawn from these studies only apply to the specific micro-architecture used. However, using **micro-architecture-independent** metrics as presented in this work, allows us to reason about application behavior on different machines, even those that do not exist yet.

Other studies use microarchitecture-independent characteristics such as instruction mix and memory footprint to study program similarities [12–14,20]. The primary objective of these studies is to reduce the number of benchmarks used in design space exploration and to discover programs with similar or unique program behavior within a benchmark suite. Besides being applied in a wider context, our methodology includes a more diverse set of characteristics and metrics. Also, the metrics we use are either new or *different* in that similar metrics are *defined* differently and, therefore, capture different behavior. For example, we capture branch predictability and consider larger windows for capturing ILP characteristics. Furthermore, we track a much larger number of memory references and provide a more precise definition of temporal and spatial locality to help in correlating with actual cache measurements.

6   Conclusions and Future Work

This work presents an architecture-independent methodology for characterizing application performance that is based on binary instrumentation and incorporates a diverse set of application-dependent characteristics. We report results on SPEC MPI2007 and Mantevo benchmarks. We show that SPEC benchmarks are more computationally intensive while Mantevo benchmarks have much larger memory demands. Also, Mantevo benchmarks exhibit more diverse behavior in all dimensions than SPEC benchmarks. To our knowledge, this work is the first to present architecture-independent characterization results for SPEC MPI2007 and some Mantevo benchmarks.

In future work, we plan to enhance our approach to capture the working set size such that it can accurately be used for detecting execution phases. We also plan to extend the methodology to characterize more aspects of performance that are important in multi-threaded and parallel applications such as synchronization and data movement.

References

1. The gnu compiler collection. http://gcc.gnu.org
2. The mantevo project. http://mantevo.org/
3. PapiEx. http://icl.cs.utk.edu/mucci/papiex/
4. Scientific Linux. http://www.scientificlinux.org/
5. SPEC MPI2007 benchmark suite. http://www.spec.org/mpi2007/
6. Bird, S., Phansalkar, A., John, L.K., Mercas, A., Idukuru, R.: Performance characterization of SPEC CPU benchmarks on Intel's core microarchitecture based processor. In: SPEC Benchmark Workshop (2007)
7. Alkohlani, W., Cook, J.: Towards performance predictive application-dependent workload characterization. In: Proceedings of the 2012 SC Companion: High Performance Computing, Networking Storage and Analysis, SCC 2012, pp. 426–436. IEEE Computer Society, Washington, DC (2012). http://dx.doi.org/10.1109/SC.Companion.2012.62
8. Conte, T.M., Wen-mei, W., Hwu, W.: Benchmark characterization. Computer **24**, 48–56 (1991)
9. Hamerly, G., Perelman, E., Calder, B.: How to use simpoint to pick simulation points. SIGMETRICS Perform. Eval. Rev. **31**(4), 25–30 (2004)
10. Hamerly, G., Perelman, E., Lau, J., Calder, B.: Simpoint 3.0: faster and more flexible program analysis. J. Instr. Level Parallelism **7**, 1–28 (2005)
11. Haungs, M., Sallee, P., Farrens, M.: Branch transition rate: a new metric for improved branch classification analysis. In: Proceedings of the HPCA, pp. 241–250 (2000)
12. Hoste, K., Eeckhout, L.: Comparing benchmarks using key microarchitecture-independent characteristics. In: 2006 IEEE International Symposium on Workload Characterization, pp. 83–92, October 2006
13. Hoste, K., Eeckhout, L.: Microarchitecture-independent workload characterization. IEEE Micro **27**(3), 63–72 (2007)
14. Joshi, A., Phansalkar, A., Eeckhout, L., John, L.K.: Measuring benchmark similarity using inherent program characteristics. IEEE Trans. Comput. **55**(6), 769–782 (2006). http://dx.doi.org/10.1109/TC.2006.85
15. Lau, J., Schoemackers, S., Calder, B.: Structures for phase classification. In: Proceedings of the 2004 IEEE International Symposium on Performance Analysis of Systems and Software, ISPASS 2004, pp. 57–67. IEEE Computer Society, Washington, DC (2004). http://dl.acm.org/citation.cfm?id=1153925.1154588
16. Li, S., Qiao, L., Tang, Z., Cheng, B., Gao, X.: Performance characterization of SPEC CPU2006 benchmarks on intel and amd platform. In: First International Workshop on Education Technology and Computer Science, ETCS 2009, vol. 2, pp. 116–121 (2009)

17. Luk, C.K., Cohn, R., Muth, R., Patil, H., Klauser, A., Lowney, G., Wallace, S., Reddi, V.J., Hazelwood, K.: Pin: building customized program analysis tools with dynamic instrumentation. In: Proceedings of the 2005 ACM SIGPLAN conference on Programming language design and implementation, PLDI 2005, pp. 190–200. ACM, New York (2005). http://doi.acm.org/10.1145/1065010.1065034

18. Murphy, R.C., Kogge, P.M.: On the memory access patterns of supercomputer applications: Benchmark selection and its implications. IEEE Trans. Comput. **56**(7), 937–945 (2007). http://dx.doi.org/10.1109/TC.2007.1039

19. Patil, H., Cohn, R., Charney, M., Kapoor, R., Sun, A., Karunanidhi, A.: Pinpointing representative portions of large intelitaniumprograms with dynamic instrumentation. In: Proceedings of the 37th Annual IEEE/ACM International Symposium on Microarchitecture, MICRO 37, pp. 81–92. IEEE Computer Society, Washington, DC (2004). http://dx.doi.org/10.1109/MICRO.2004.28

20. Phansalkar, A., Joshi, A., Eeckhout, L., John, L.: Measuring program similarity: Experiments with spec cpu benchmark suites. In: IEEE International Symposium on Performance Analysis of Systems and Software, ISPASS 2005, pp. 10–20, March 2005

21. Phansalkar, A., Joshi, A., John, L.K.: Analysis of redundancy and application balance in the. SPEC CPU2006 benchmark suite. In: Proceedings of the 34th annual international symposium on Computer architecture, ISCA 2007, pp. 412–423. ACM, New York (2007)

22. Phansalkar, A., Joshi, A., John, L.K.: Subsetting the SPEC CPU2006 benchmark suite. SIGARCH Comput. Archit. News **35**(1), 69–76 (2007). http://doi.acm.org/10.1145/1241601.1241616

23. Poovey, J.A., Levy, M., Gal-On, S., Conte, T.: A benchmark characterization of the EEMBC benchmark suite. IEEE Micro. **PP**(99), 1–1 (2009). doi:10.1109/MM.2009.50

24. Sherwood, T., Perelman, E., Hamerly, G., Calder, B.: Automatically characterizing large scale program behavior. In: ASPLOS-X: Proceedings of the 10th international conference on Architectural support for programming languages and operating systems, pp. 45–57. ACM, New York, NY (2002)

Roofline Model Toolkit: A Practical Tool for Architectural and Program Analysis

Yu Jung Lo$^{(\boxtimes)}$, Samuel Williams, Brian Van Straalen, Terry J. Ligocki, Matthew J. Cordery, Nicholas J. Wright, Mary W. Hall, and Leonid Oliker

Lawerence Berkeley National Laboratory, University of Utah,
Salt Lake City, USA
{yujunglo,mhall}@cs.utah.edu,
{swwilliams,bvstraalen,tjligocki,mjcordery,njwright,loliker}@lbl.gov

Abstract. We present preliminary results of the Roofline Toolkit for multicore, manycore, and accelerated architectures. This paper focuses on the processor architecture characterization engine, a collection of portable instrumented micro benchmarks implemented with Message Passing Interface (MPI), and OpenMP used to express thread-level parallelism. These benchmarks are specialized to quantify the behavior of different architectural features. Compared to previous work on performance characterization, these microbenchmarks focus on capturing the performance of each level of the memory hierarchy, along with thread-level parallelism, instruction-level parallelism and explicit SIMD parallelism, measured in the context of the compilers and run-time environments. We also measure sustained PCIe throughput with four GPU memory managed mechanisms. By combining results from the architecture characterization with the Roofline model based solely on architectural specifications, this work offers insights for performance prediction of current and future architectures and their software systems. To that end, we instrument three applications and plot their resultant performance on the corresponding Roofline model when run on a Blue Gene/Q architecture.

Keywords: Roofline · Memory bandwidth · CUDA unified memory

1 Introduction

The growing complexity of high-performance computing architectures makes it difficult for users to achieve sustained application performance across different architectures. Worse, quantifying the theoretical performance and the resultant gap between theoretical and observed performance is becoming increasingly difficult. As such, performance models and tools that facilitate this process are crucial. Such performance models need not be complicated, but should be practical and intuitive. A model should provide upper and lower bounds on performance for a given computation on a particular target architecture and be suggestive of where optimization would be profitable. Additionally, the model should provide an indication of the fundamental bottlenecks and inherent challenges associated with improving a specific kernel's performance on the target architecture.

© Springer International Publishing Switzerland 2015
S.A. Jarvis et al. (Eds.): PMBS 2014, LNCS 8966, pp. 129–148, 2015.
DOI: 10.1007/978-3-319-17248-4_7

An exemplar of such modeling capability is Roofline Model [2,19,20]. The Roofline model combines arithmetic intensity, memory performance, and floating-point performance together into a two-dimensional graph using bound and bottleneck analysis. In the conventional use, the x-axis is arithmetic intensity (flops per byte) and y-axis is performance in GFlop/s. The model thus defines an envelope in which one may attain performance. To date, this "textbook" Roofline model requires a human to manually analyze an architecture and any application kernels in order to populate the roofline. We wish to automate that process.

This paper will present our initial approach that constructs the Roofline model using an automated characterization engine. Moreover, we extend the Roofline formalism to address the emerging challenges associated with accelerated architectures. To that end, we constructed three benchmarks designed to drive empirical Roofline-based analysis. The first two represent the conventional memory hierarchy bandwidth and floating-point computation aspects of the Roofline. The third benchmark is a novel and visually intuitive approach to analyzing the importance of locality on accelerated architectures like GPUs. It quantifies the performance relationship between explicitly and implicitly managed spatial and temporal locality on a GPU. We evaluate these benchmarks on four platforms — Edison (Intel Xeon CPU), Mira (IBM Blue Gene/Q), Babbage (coprocessor only, Intel MIC Knights Corner), and Titan (GPU only, Nvidia Tesla K20x), and use the resultant empirical Rooflines to analyze three HPC benchmarks — HPGMG-FV, GTC, and miniDFT.

2   Related Work

Today, data movement often dominates computation. Typically, this data movement is between DRAM and the cache hierarchy and is often structured streaming (array) accesses. As such, the STREAM benchmark has become the de-facto solution for benchmarking the ultimate DRAM bandwidth of a multicore processor [18]. STREAM is OpenMP threaded and will perform a series of benchmarks designed to quantify the memory subsystem's performance as a function of common array operations. Unfortunately, all these operations write to the destination array without reading it. As such, the hidden data movement necessitated by a write-allocate operation effectively impedes the bandwidth. Today's instruction set architectures (ISA) often provide a means of bypassing this write allocate operation. Unfortunately, it is rare for a compiler to generate this operation appropriately on real applications. As such, we are motivated to augment stream with read-only (sum or dot product) or read-modify-write (increment) benchmarks in order to cleanly quantify this hidden data movement.

Modern microprocessors use hardware stream prefetchers to hide memory latency by speculatively loading cache lines. Unfortunately, the performance of these prefetchers is highly dependent on architecture and it has been observed that bandwidth is highly correlated with the number of elements accessed contiguously [15]. Short "stanzas" of memory access see substantially degraded performance. Stanza Triad was created to quantify this effect [9]. Unfortunately, it is not threaded and as such cannot identify when one has transitioned from a concurrency-limited regime to a throughput-limited regime when running on multicore processors.

When DRAM bandwidth is not the bottleneck to on-node application performance, then cache bandwidth often is. CacheBench (part of LLCbench) can be used to understand the capacities and bandwidths of the cache hierarchy [16]. Unfortunately, CacheBench is not threaded with OpenMP or parallelized with MPI. As such, it cannot measure contention at any level of the cache hierarchy (including DRAM like STREAM). Rather than taking this purely empirical approach, one can, with sufficient documentation, create an analytical model of the cache hierarchy using the Execution Cache Memory model [13].

Perhaps the most similar work to ours is encapsulated in the benchmarks used to drive the Energy Roofline Model [3]. In that work a series of experiments were constructed that varies arithmetic intensity in order to understand the architectural response in terms of both performance and power. When combined with a cache benchmark, one can infer the energy requirements for various computational and data movement operations. Whereas their goal was focused heavily on power and energy, we are focused on performance.

3 Experimental Setup

The diversity of existing and emerging hardware and programming models makes construction of generalized benchmarks particularly difficult. To demonstrate the utility of our automation strategy, we evaluate performance on four fundamentally different architectures — a conventional superscalar out-of-order Intel Xeon multicore processor (Edison), a low-power dual-issue in-order IBM Blue Gene/Q multicore processor (Mira), a high-performance in-order Intel Xeon Phi manycore processor (Babbage), and a high-performance NVIDIA Kepler K20x GPU accelerated system (Titan). These systems represent a basis of system architectures within the HPC community today. The next three sections provide some background on their processor architectures, programming model and compilation options, and execution on our selected platforms.

3.1 Architectural Platforms

Table 1 summarizes the key architectural characteristics of these platforms. Please note that the peak GFlop/s and bandwidths shown are theoretical.

Edison: is a MPP at NERSC [11]. Each node includes two 12-core Xeon E5 2695-V2 processors nominally clocked at 2.4 GHz (TurboBoost can increase this substantially). Each core is a superscalar, out-of-order, 2-way HyperThreaded core capable of performing two 4-way AVX SIMD instructions (add and multiply) per cycle in addition to loads and stores. Each core has a private 32 KB L1 data cache and a private 256 KB L2 cache. The 12 cores on a chip share a 30 MB L3 cache and a memory controller connected to four DDR3-1600 DIMMs. Extensive stream prefetchers are designed to saturate bandwidth at each level of the cache

Table 1. Architectural characteristics of four evaluation platforms. [a]One GPU per node. [b]CUDA cores. [c] without TurboBoost.

Platform	Edison	Mira	Babbage	Titan
MPU	Intel Xeon E5-2695v2	IBM BGQ	Xeon Phi KNC	Nvidia K20x
Clock rate (GHz)	2.4	1.6	1.053	0.732
Processors per node	2	1	1	1^a
Cores per processor	12	16	60	2688^b
Total threads	48	64	240	28672
Peak GFlops	460.8^c	204.8	1011	1310
L1 bandwidth (GB/s)	1843	819.2	4043	1310
DRAM pin bandwidth (GB/s)	102.6	42.66	352	232.46

hierarchy. Theoretically, the superscalar and out-of-order nature of this processor should reduce the need for optimized software and compiler optimization.

Mira: is an IBM Blue Gene/Q system installed at the Argonne National Lab [5]. Each node includes one 16-core BGQ SOC. Each of the 16 A2 cores is a 4-way SMT dual-issue in-order core capable of performing one ALU/Load/Store instruction and one four-way FMA per cycle. However, in order to attain this throughput rate, one must run at least two threads per core. Each core has a private 16 KB data cache and the 16 cores share a 32 MB L2 cache connected by a crossbar. Ideally, the SMT nature of this architecture should hide much of the effects of large instruction and cache latencies. However, the dual-issue nature of the processor can impede performance when integer instructions are a significant fraction of the dynamic instruction mix.

Babbage: is a Knights Corner (KNC) Manycore Integrated Core (MIC) test-bed at NERSC [1,6]. The KNC processor includes 60 dual-issue in-order 4-way HyperThreaded cores. Each core includes a 32 KB L1 data cache, a 512 KB L2 cache, and a 8-way vector unit. Although the L2 cache's are coherent, the ring NoC topology coupled with the coherency mechanism may impede performance. Unlike the aforementioned multicore processors, this manycore processor uses very high-speed GDDR memory which provides a theoretical pin bandwidth of over 350 GB/s. In order to proxy the future Knights Landing (KNL) MIC processor that will form the heart of the NERSC8 Supercomputer Cori [4], we conduct all experiments in "native" mode. As such, the host processor, the host memory, and the PCIe connection are not exercised.

Titan: is a Cray accelerated MPP system at the Oak Ridge National Lab. Each node includes a 16-core AMD Interlagos CPU processor and one NVIDIA K20x GPU [7]. Each GPU includes 14 streaming multiprocessors (SMX) each of which can schedule 256 32-thread warps and issue them four at a time to their 192 CUDA cores. Each SMX a 256 KB register file, a 64 KB SRAM that can be partitioned into L1 cache, and shared memory (scratchpad) segments. Each chip includes a 1.5 MB L2 cache shared among the SMX and is connected to high-speed GDDR5 memory with a pin bandwidth of 232 GB/s. Unfortunately, software on the production system Titan tends to lag behind NVIDIA releases. As such, we used a similar K20xm within the Dirac testbed at NERSC [10] in order to evaluate the CUDA unified virtual address and Unified (managed) Memory. For our purposes, the K20x and K20xm GPUs are identical.

3.2 Programming Model and Compilation

In this section, we provide the compiler flags that were on different platforms (Table 2). Nominally, all our codes are (MPI+)OpenMP or (MPI+)CUDA. Although for the most part compilation is straightforward, there are some variations across the three compilers.

First, Edison and Babbage both use the Intel C compiler. However, as MIC is run in native mode, it requires the "-mmic" option while Edison is compiled with "-xAVX". The Intel and IBM compilers enable OpenMP differently. On the Intel platforms, one uses "-openmp" while on XL/C, one uses "-qsmp=omp:noauto". To instruct the compilers there is no aliasing, we use the "-fno-fnalias" and "-qalias=ansi:allptrs" flags on the Intel and IBM compilers respectively. Finally, it should be noted that depending on the benchmark and platform, we either use CUDA 5 (Titan) or CUDA 6 (Dirac). The NVIDIA compiler requires one specify the "-arch=sm_35" flag to build the benchmark for the K20x series.

3.3 Benchmark Execution

Unlike simple desktop systems, the MPP supercomputers at NERSC, ALCF, and OLCF might launch jobs from one node and run them on another set of nodes. As such, the benchmark application launch routines vary somewhat from one platform to the next. Table 3 shows the relevant options used in our experiments.

On Edison, the Cray system at NERSC, one uses the aprun command to run programs on the compute nodes. To that end, we run the benchmark using two MPI tasks and bind each to one NUMA node with strict memory containment via the "-S 1 -ss -cc numa_node" options. On Mira, we evaluate both a fully threaded and a hybrid mode of 4 processes of 16 threads. We recommend "BG_THREADLAYOUT=1" to balance these threads within cores if the total

Table 2. Compilation flags for each platform

Platform	Compiler	Flags
Edison	Intel C	-O3 -xAVX -openmp -fno-alias -fno-fnalias
Mira	IBM XL/C	-O5 -qsimd=auto -qalias=ansi:allptrs -qsmp=omp:noauto
Babbage	Intel C	-O3 -mmic -fno-alias -fno-fnalias -liomp5
Titan	Nvidia CC	-O3 -arch=sm_35 -lcudart

Table 3. Execution mode for each platform

Platform	Application Execution command
Edison	aprun -n 2 -d 12 -N 2 -S 1 -ss -cc numa_node [benchmark]
Mira	qsub -n 1 –proccount 1 –mode c1 –env BG_SMP_FAST_WAKEUP=YES: BG_THREADLAYOUT=1: OMP_PROC_BIND=TRUE: OMP_NUM_THREADS=64: OMP_WAIT_POLICY=active [benchmark]
Babbage	mpirun.mic -n 1 -ppn 1 [benchmark]
Titan	aprun -n 1 [benchmark]

MPI process * OpenMP threads is smaller than 64. On Babbage, which uses the Intel MPI implementation, one uses the "-ppn" option to control the number of MPI tasks per card and the "-n" option to control the total number of MPI tasks. Unlike Edison where aprun controls affinity, one must use the "KMP_AFFINITY" environment variable on Babbage. We set it to "scatter" to distribute threads across the chip. On Titan, we once again use the aprun options. However, as we don't use the CPU cores, there was no need to control CPU thread affinity or NUMA bindings.

4   Memory and Cache Bandwidth

Today, bandwidth and data movement are perhaps the paramount aspect of performance on scientific applications. Unfortunately, as discussed in the related work, most existing benchmarks fail to proxy the contention, locality, or execution environment associated with real applications. To rectify this, we have created a Roofline bandwidth benchmark that uses a hybrid MPI+OpenMP model. Thus, programmers wishing to proxy a flat MPI code and run the Roofline benchmark in a flat MPI model. Those wishing to understand the performance on NUMA architectures can run in the hybrid mode.

4.1   Bandwidth Code

Like CacheBench, our Roofline bandwidth benchmark is designed to quantify the available bandwidth at each level of the memory hierarchy using a simple unit-stride streaming memory access pattern. However, unlike CacheBench, it includes the effects of contention arising form thread parallelism and finite NoC bandwidth. In that regime, it is similar to STREAM code [18] which uses the OpenMP work-share constructs to split loop iterations across multiple threads (Fig. 1). Rather than using the work-share construct, our Roofline bandwidth code creates a single parallel region and statically assigns threads to ranges of array indices. All initialization, synchronization, and computation takes place within this parallel region. The computation is expressed as the sum of a finite geometric series as it was hoped that no compiler could automatically eliminate

```
void STREAM(TYPE scalar){
  ssize_t j;
  #pragma omp parallel for
  for (j = 0; j <SIZE; j++)
    B[j] = scalar * A[j];
}

int main(){
  scalar = 3.0;
  for (k = 0; k < TIMES; k++)
  {
    // start timer here
    STREAM(scalar);
    // stop timer here
  }
}
```

```
void KERNEL(uint64_t size, uint64_t trials,
            double * __restrict__ A){
  double alpha = 0.5;
  uint64_t i, j;
  for (j = 0; j < trials; ++j) {
    for (i = 0; i < size; ++i) {
      A[i] = A[i] + alpha;
    }
    alpha = alpha * 0.5;
}}

int main(){
  ...
  #pragma omp parallel private(id)
  {
  uint64_t n, t;
  for (n = 16; n < SIZE; n *= 1.1) {
    for (t = 1; t < TRIALS; t *= 2) {
      // start timer here
      KERNEL(n, t, &A[nid]);
      // stop timer here
      #pragma omp barrier
      #pragma omp master
      {
        MPI_Barrier(MPI_COMM_WORLD);
      }
}}}}
```

Fig. 1. (left) STREAM facsimile. (right) Roofline bandwidth benchmark.

this nested loop. Essentially each term in the geometric series is a trial in the STREAM benchmark.

The benchmark may thus be used to quantify the capacity of each level of the memory hierarchy as well as the bandwidths between levels. Moreover, by adjusting the parameters, one can estimate the overhead for an MPI or OpenMP barrier. As the benchmark is MPI+OpenMP, one can explore these bandwidths and overheads across all scales.

4.2   Bandwidth Result

Figure 2 presents the results of our Roofline bandwidth benchmark running on our four platforms. On Edison, we run two processes per node, while all other machines run with a single process. Note, the x-axis represents the total working set summed across all threads. The blue line marks the theoretical bandwidth and capacities for each level of the memory hierarchy. On the CPU architectures, the red line presents resultant Roofline bandwidth.

We observe that on Edison, the hardware comes very close to the theoretical performance and transitions at the expected cache capacities. The smooth transitions in bandwidth at the cache capacities suggest the cache replacement policy may not be a true LRU or FIFO but a pseudo-variant. The notable exception is that Edison fails to come close to the DRAM pin bandwidth. This is not necessarily surprising as few machines have such high bandwidth and few machines

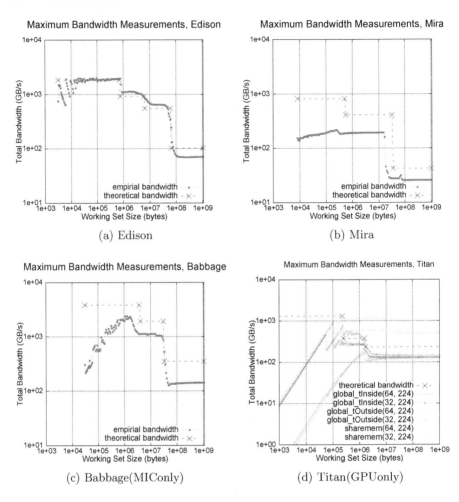

Fig. 2. Roofline bandwidth benchmark results on our four platforms. Please note the log-log scale. On the GPU, the syntax is Kernel(# threads per thread block, # of thread blocks per kernel).

ever attain the pin bandwidth. Moreover, the simple read-modify-write memory access pattern may be suboptimal for this architecture. Future work will explore alternate kernels that change the balance between reads and writes.

On Mira, performance was consistently below the theoretical bandwidth limits and the transitions seemed to indicate reduced effective cache capacities. The low L1 bandwidth was particularly surprising and may indicate the presence of a write-through or store-through L1 architecture. Further investigation is required.

On the highly-multithreaded MIC (Babbage), we found it was necessary to operate on working sets exceeding 1 MB (well over 4 KB per thread) in order to obtain good performance. As the architecture can load 64 bytes per cycle, it is not unreasonable to think 64 loads were necessary to amortize any loop overheads within the benchmark. For smaller working sets, performance was degraded indicating an underutilization of resources. Generally speaking, the benchmark correctly identified the L1 and L2 cache capacities, but the attained bandwidths were far less than the theoretical number. Low L2 bandwidth can be attributed to the lack of an L2 stream prefetcher like on Edison and Mira. If the compiler fails to insert software prefetches perfectly, memory latency will be exposed. Conversely, low DRAM bandwidth is a known issue on this machine and requires hardware solutions to rectify.

On Titan, using the GPU, we found it illustrative to run three slightly different kernels designed to quantify the effects of explicit and implicit reuse within the GPU's memory hierarchy. Both Kernel A ("global_tInside" legend on the Fig. 2(d)) and Kernel B ("global_tOnside") use global memory, but with the trials loop inside and outside, respectively. Kernel C ("sharemem') copies global memory data to shared memory, does trials loop inside the kernel, and copies back to global memory.

"Kernel B" is perhaps the most similar to the CPU implementations. The entire working set is parallelized across thread blocks and the summation (reuse) occurs at the CUDA kernel level. That is, there is one kernel call per iteration of the geometric sum. We explore performance as a function of the thread block size (32 or 64) with a constant 224 thread blocks. As on Babbage, we see substantial underutilization coupled with large CUDA kernel overheads at small working set sizes but performance eventually saturates at the DRAM limit, although this is well below the theoretical pin bandwidth. "Kernel A" restructures the summation loop to increase locality within a thread block and as such, exercises the L1 cache for the per thread-block working set (note, there are 7168 or 14336 threads in all). We see much better performance at the small scale (fewer CUDA kernel calls) and performance can hit the L1 and L2 limits before settling at the DRAM limit. Finally, "Kernel C" restructures the loop once again and exploits shared memory in a blocked manner. As such, it can reach the theoretical performance limit of about 1.3 TB/s for shared memory.

Overall, the trends in bandwidth performance on manycore and accelerators are a little disturbing. That is, the only way to get high performance is with massive parallelism on large working sets. For real applications, this observation will make it difficult to use accelerators or manycore processors to solve existing problems faster. Rather, one will be able to run larger problems in comparable time. Nevertheless, this benchmark can be used to help guide programmers as to when it will be viable to migrate to a manycore or accelerated architecture.

5 Floating-Point Compute Capability

Although many applications are limited by memory bandwidth, there are some that are still limited by on-chip computation and ultimately the in-core performance. When performance is on the cusp, proper exploitation of instruction-, data- , and thread-level parallelism can ensure the code is not artificially flop-limited. Unfortunately, there are relatively few benchmarks that accurately measure the importance of these facets of parallelism on modern manycore and accelerated architectures. To address this deficiency, we constructed a Roofline floating-point benchmark.

5.1   Reference Roofline Floating-Point Benchmark

We modified the Roofline bandwidth benchmark to implement a polynomial for each element. By varying the degree of the polynomial (a preprocessor macro), one can vary the number of flops per element. Doing so allows one to change the balance between loads/stores and floating-point operations from L1-limited to flop-limited. Figure 3 presents an example of this benchmark.

As one can see, the degree of parallelism per thread in this routine is O(nsize). An in-order processor would deliver performance limited by the floating-point latency rather than peak performance. A compiler could unroll this loop (at least by the floating-point latency) and express instruction-level parallelism and/or SIMDize the unrolled code to exploit data-level parallelism. Alternately, an out-of-order processor, with a sufficiently deep reorder buffer, could find the inherent instruction-level parallelism and attain high performance. Although, an out-of-order parallelism could reorder the instruction stream, it can never automatically SIMDize the instruction stream. As such, without compiler support for SIMD, it can never attain peak performance.

```
void KERNEL(uint64_t size, uint64_t trials, double * __restrict__ A){
  double alpha = 0.5;
  uint64_t i, j;
  for (j = 0; j < trials; ++j) {
    for ( i = 0; i < nsize; ++i) {
      double beta = 0.8;
      #if FLOPPERITER == 2
      beta = beta * A[i] + alpha;
      #elif FLOPPERITER == 4
      ...
      #endif
      A[i] = beta;
    }
    alpha = alpha * (1 - 1e-8);
  }
}
```

Fig. 3. Roofline floating-point benchmark

5.2   Performance as a Function of Implicit and Explicit Parallelism

On today's processors, thread- and data-level parallelism must be explicit in the code generated by a compiler. As auto-parallelizing and auto-vectorizing compilers are rarely infallible, these forms of parallelism must often be explicit in the source code as well. In order to quantify the disparity between the performance that can be obtained by the architecture on compiled code and the true performance capability of the architecture, we implemented three explicitly unrolled and SIMDized (via intrinsics) implementations of the Roofline floating-point benchmark — AVX, QPX, and AVX-512 versions. Figure 4 presents the performance of these implementations on Edison, Mira, and Babbage as a function of thread-level parallelism and unrolling (explicit instruction-level parallelism). Note, each implementation used a different number of flops per element (FPE).

We observe that Edison attains a little less than half the advertised peak with compiled C code. However, when using an optimized implementation, performance improves significantly and can actually exceed the nominal peak performance of 460 GFlop/s. The faster-than-light effect is due to the fact that TurboBoost is enabled on this machine. With a maximum frequency of 2.8 GHz with 12 cores, the true peak performance is about 537 GFlop/s — quite close to the observed performance. To verify this, we use the `aprun --p-state` option to peg the frequency at the advertised 2.4 GHz and performance is as expected. Although the machine is sensitive to instruction-level parallelism (unrolling), it generally does not require HyperThreading to attain good performance.

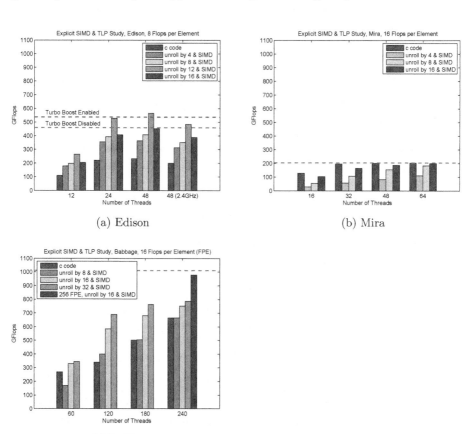

(a) Edison

(b) Mira

(c) Babbage

Fig. 4. Performance disparity between compiled code and optimized code in which thread-, instruction-, and data-level parallelism have been made explicit.

Running a similar set of experiments on Mira (BGQ), we see a very different outcome. First, compiled code delivers very good performance. This indicates that the XL/C compiler was able to effectively SIMDize and unroll the code sufficiently to hide the floating-point latency. Using explicitly unrolled code we observe that significant unrolling (2–4 SIMD instructions per thread) is required to reach peak performance. Unlike Edison, Mira clearly requires two threads to attain peak performance.

Finally, Babbage presents a mix of characteristics similar to both Edison and Mira. The compiler clearly fails to make full use of the architecture on even this simple kernel. With sufficient unrolling (4 SIMD instructions per thread), performance begins to saturate after two threads. Only with extremely high intensity (256 flops per element) does performance approach peak.

5.3   Performance as a Function of L1 Arithmetic Intensity

Even when one can maintain a working set in the L1, performance will be dependent on the dynamic instruction mix and the issue capability of the core. In this section, we leverage the Roofline Floating-Point benchmark to quantify performance as a function of L1 Arithmetic Intensity expressed as Flops per Element (FPE) — essentially the degree of the polynomial. For each architecture, we run both the reference C code quantifying the ability of the architecture as well as the best performing SIMDized and unrolled implementation. Figure 5 presents the resultant performance on each architecture. For reference, we include (in blue) a microarchitecture performance model that takes into account the issue rate of loads/stores compared to floating-point instructions given the mix demanded by the kernel.

Figure 5 demonstrates that Edison can quickly reach its peak performance and that performance tracks well with the theoretical model. Generally, speaking, at low FPE, performance is diminished due to the fact that the core can perform 8 flops per cycle, but can only sustain loading and storing 2 elements per cycle. Interestingly, the performance of the reference C code falls at high FPE. This is presumably a limit of the reorder buffer and the desire to continually find 5 independent floating-point instructions.

Mira's performance on both compiled and optimized code is shifted to the right. Generally, this suggests that additional instructions are consuming the same issue slots as loads or stores. On the dual issue A2 architecture, this could very well be integer or branch instructions. This effect was not present on Edison as it is a superscalar processor and can issue integer or branch instructions from ports other than those used for floating-point or load/store. With sufficient FPE, performance is pegged to peak.

Babbage shows a third behavior — asymptotically approaching peak performance. This behavior suggests that additional instructions (e.g. integer or branch) are consuming the same issue slot as floating-point instructions. As such, performance behaves like $FPE/(FPE+k)$ where k is the number of extra instructions impeding performance.

Finally, we constructed a similar CUDA C benchmark to run on the GPU. The theoretical bound is based on the assumption that each load/store unit can sustain loading 4 bytes per cycle (128 per SMX) from memory. We observe

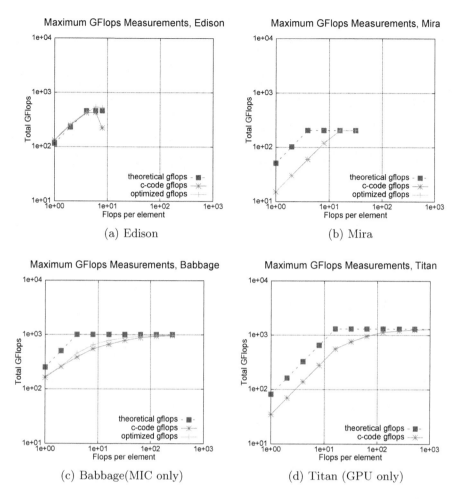

Fig. 5. Basic GFlops code and optimized SIMDized unrolling GFlops code compared to theoretical GFlops on four platforms.

that the GPU's performance seems to embody characteristics of both BGQ and MIC. That is, one lacks the issue bandwidth to fully drive the core and the SMX cannot sustain loading/storing 128 bytes per cycle from memory.

6   Beyond the Roofline — CUDA's Unified Memory

To date, accelerated architectures have been typically used as an accelerator with dedicated memory attached to a conventional system with a PCIe or similar bus. Not only does this dedicated memory have its own unique address space, but programmers were forced to explicitly copy data to and from device via a library interface. Doing so is not only unproductive, but also exposes the performance disparity between PCIe bandwidth and device bandwidth.

Recently, CUDA introduced two memory concepts — the Unified Virtual Address (UVA) space, and Unified Memory (i.e. managed memory) [8]. As the name suggests, UVA unifies the CPU and GPU address spaces and ensures (at the program level) that programs may transparently load and store memory without worrying about the locality of data (for correctness). As data remains pinned to host or device, there are strong NUMA effects. Unified (managed) memory extends this process by migrating data between the host and the device. As such, device memory can be viewed as a cache on the CPU memory. Ideally, this would address many of the productivity and performance challenges. In this section, we evaluate the performance of these approaches as a function of spatial and temporal locality.

6.1   CUDA Managed Memory Benchmark

Our initial approach to this benchmark was to create a benchmark that thrashes data back and forth between host and device. To that end, we reuse the Roofline bandwidth benchmark by having the GPU perform $k-1$ iterations of the summation and the CPU perform 1. As the net reuse k increases, we expect the cost of moving the data between host and device to be amortized.

Please note, this benchmark is not an unreasonable scenario in practice as many applications may package some data for the GPU, copy it to the device, operate on it a few times, then return it to the host. If written using Unified Memory, the data would thrash back and forth between host and device.

In this paper, we evaluate performance using four different approaches to controlling the locality of data on the device. First, we evaluate the conventional explicit copy (cudaMemCpy) approach using either a paged array or a page-locked array allocated on the host. Next, we evaluate the performance of zero copy memory. In this scenario, data is allocated and pinned on the host and it is the responsibility of the CUDA run time to map load and store requests to PCIe transfers. Finally, we evaluate the performance of the Unified (managed) Memory construct in which the CUDA run time may migrate data.

Figure 6 presents these implementations. As one can see, increased locality is affected via multiple CUDA kernel invocations. The macros "_CUDA_ZERO-COPY" and "_CUDA_UM" select the use of page-locked host with zero copy and unified memory management respectively. Page-locked host memory uses a normal malloc() function to allocate memory on host, and then uses cudaHost-Register() to register a device pointer on host memory address space. For unified memory, one uses cudaMallocManaged to allocate both host and device memory.

6.2   Results

As Titan does not support CUDA 6 yet, all of our experiments were run on a similar K20xm in the Dirac cluster[1].

---

[1] GPU driver version: 331.89; CUDA toolkit version: 6.0beta.

```
int main()
{
  // start timer here...
  for (uint64_t j = 0; j < trials; ++j) {
    #if defined(_CUDA_ZEROCPY) || defined(_CUDA_UM)
      cudaDeviceSynchronize();
    #else
      cudaMemcpy(d_buf, h_buf, SIZE, cudaMemcpyDefault);
    #endif
    for (uint64_t k = 0; k < reuse; ++k) {
      GPUKERNEL <<<blocks, threads>>> (n, d_buf, alpha);
      alpha = alpha * (1e-8);
    }
    #if defined(_CUDA_ZEROCPY) || defined(_CUDA_UM)
      cudaDeviceSynchronize();
    #else
      cudaMemcpy(h_buf, d_buf, SIZE, cudaMemcpyDefault);
    #endif
    CPUKERNEL(n, h_buf, alpha);
  }
  // stop timer here...
  double bytes = 2 * sizeof(double) * (double)n *(double)trials * (double)(reuse + 1);
}
```

Fig. 6. CUDA unified memory benchmark quantifies the ability of the run time to mange locality on the device

Figure 7 presents the resultant "effective bandwidth" for the four technologies as a function of working set size and temporal reuse. For small working set sizes, CUDA kernel launch time dominates and effective bandwidth is abysmal. This simply reinforces the conventional wisdom not to use the GPU for small operations. Comparing Fig. 7(a) and (b), we see that it is possible to approach the device bandwidth limit, but only for large working sets that are reused 50–100 times. Thus, offloading iterative solvers to the GPU is a viable option if one expects it to take hundreds of iterations to converge. Conversely, for large working sets with minimal reuse, we see that page-locked memory provides substantially better PCIe bandwidth.

As Zero Copy memory provides no caching benefit, we see no performance benefit in Fig. 7(c) from increased locality. Conversely, Fig. 7(d) presents the performance benefit from using Unified Memory to automate the management of data locality on the device. Broadly speaking, performance is qualitatively similar to the performance with explicitly managed locality. Unfortunately, the raw performance is substantially lower. For applications which could guarantee 1000-way reuse on the device, Unified memory would provide a productive and high performance solution. One can only hope that advances in hardware and runtime can bridge the performance gap at lower temporal locality.

Future work will extend this technology to track the development of any software cache coherency protocol NVIDIA implements. That is, there is no reason why both the CPU and GPU must both read-modify-write the array. Either could perform a read-only operation.

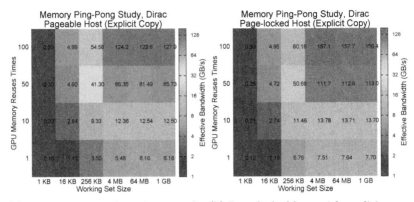

(a) Pageable host with explicit copy be-(b) Page-locked host with explicit copy
tween CPU and GPU   between CPU and GPU

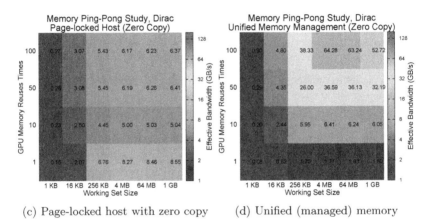

(c) Page-locked host with zero copy   (d) Unified (managed) memory

Fig. 7. Effective bandwidth as a function of GPU temporal locality (reuse) and working set size for four different GPU device memory management mechanisms.

7   Empirical Roofline Models and Their Use

Now that we have benchmarked the bandwidth and compute characteristics on each of our four platforms, we may construct empirical Roofline Models for each. Figure 8 shows the resultant models using both DRAM and L1 bandwidths as well as the theoretical or "textbook" Roofline for each platform. An ideal architecture is one that can fully exploit the technology on which it is built. We see that in general, Edison's empirical performance is very close to its theoretical limits. Conversely, on Mira and Babbage, we see substantial differences between theory and reality. The extreme multithreading paradigm allows the GPU to deliver a high fraction of its theoretical bandwidth when running on the device.

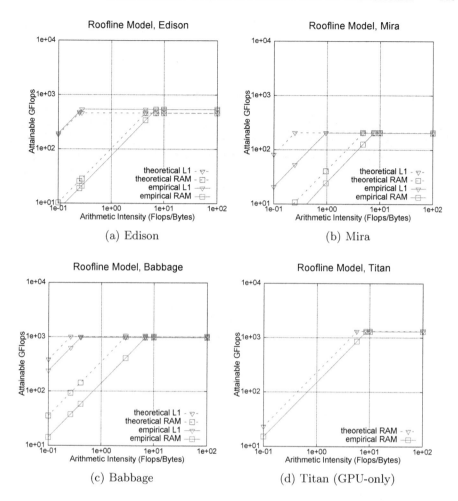

Fig. 8. Roofline model for four platforms.

7.1 Program Analysis

We use the resultant empirical Rooflines to analyze observed performance on three HPC benchmarks — the finite-volume High-Performance Geometric Multigrid (HPGMG-FV) benchmark [14], the Gyrokinetic Toroidal Code (GTC) [12], and miniDFT [17]. All benchmarks were run on Mira where the performance counters have been verified.

HPGMG-FV is a highly optimized multigrid benchmark that solves a variable coefficient Poisson's equation on a structured grid. Figure 9(a) shows that it has low compute intensity, but it delivers performance, whether flat MPI or OpenMP is DRAM, very close to its bandwidth limit.

GTC is a turbulent transport fusion simulation that uses the particle-in-cell (PIC) method. Its two dominant kernels are particle-to-grid interpolation (`chargei`) and grid-to-particle interpolation (`pushi`). Theoretically, these kernels are moderately compute intensive (`pushi` slightly more) but involve random access to a structured grid. Clearly, the performance of both routines is well below the roofline suggesting optimization could significantly improve it.

MiniDFT code uses plane-wave density functional theory (DFT) to compute the Kohn-Sham equations, part of the general-purpose Quantum Espresso (QE) code. This is a compute-intensive code, dominated by dense linear algebra and 3D FFT's (Fig. 9(b)). Although miniDFT uses matrix-matrix multiplications, the application performance is far less than peak DGEMM or ZGEMM performance. This is likely an artifact of the inherent performance differences between square multiplications and the block vector multiplications used in miniDFT. While flat MPI performance generally tracked the Roofline, the performance of the threaded code was orders of magnitude less than ideal perhaps due to limited parallelism in any one dimension. Further investigation is warranted.

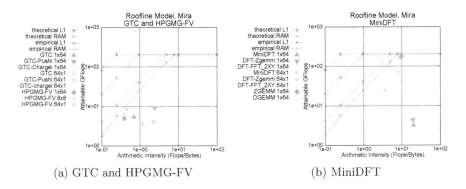

(a) GTC and HPGMG-FV   (b) MiniDFT

Fig. 9. GTC, HPGMG-FV, and MiniDFT results on Mira collected from BGQ performance counters. Legeneds denote "benchmark: number of MPI tasks x number of OpenMP threads."

8 Summary

In this paper, we have described a prototype architecture characterization engine for the Roofline Toolkit that quantifies the bandwidth and compute characteristics of multicore, manycore, and accelerated systems. We use the Toolkit to benchmark four leading HPC systems: Edison, Mira, Babbage, and Titan. The measurements demonstrate the ability of each architecture to attain peak bandwidth or performance and quantify its sensitivity to changes in parallelism or arithmetic intensity.

In order to quantify the benefits of the emerging software managed cache technologies in CUDA, we developed a benchmark that measures the performance of CUDA's Unified memory as a function of spatial and temporal locality. Although performance never reaches parity with explicitly managed locality, performance was far superior to the productive Zero Copy alternative.

Finally, we evaluated three complex HPC compputing benchmarks: HPGMG-FV, GTC, and miniDFT running on Mira (BGQ). Using the HPM performance counters, we plotted benchmark performance on an empirical Roofline model in order to quantitatively note which applications deliver and which underperform.

Future work will continue to generalize the Roofline toolkit as well as continued instrumentation, benchmarking, and analysis of HPC applications in order to explore performance and parallelism issues on emerging HPC platforms.

Acknowledgments. Authors from Lawrence Berkeley National Laboratory were supported by the U.S. Department of Energy's Advanced Scientific Computing Research Program under contract DE-AC02-05CH11231. This research used resources of the National Energy Research Scientific Computing Center, which is supported by the Office of Science of the U.S. Department of Energy under contract DE-AC02-05CH11231. This research used resources of the Argonne Leadership Computing Facility, which is supported by the Office of Science of the U.S. Department of Energy under contract DE-AC02-06CH11357. This research used resources of the Oak Ridge Leadership Facility at the Oak Ridge National Laboratory, which is supported by the Office of Science of the U.S. Department of Energy under Contract No. DE-AC05-00OR22725.

References

1. Babbage Testbed. https://www.nersc.gov/users/computational-systems/testbeds/babbage/
2. Bailey, D.H., Lucas, R.F., Williams, S.W.: Performance Tuning of Scientific Applications. CRC Press, New York (2011)
3. Choi, J.W., Bedard, D., Fowler, R., Vuduc, R.: A roofline model of energy. In: IEEE IPDPS, May 2013
4. Cori Cray XC30. https://www.nersc.gov/users/computational-systems/nersc-8-system-cori/
5. IBM Corporation: IBM system blue gene solution: Blue gene/q application development. IBM, June 2013
6. Intel Corporation: Intel xeon phi corprocessor system softeare developers guide. Intel, June 2012
7. Nvidia Corporation: Kepler gk 110: The fatest, most efficient hpc architecture ever built. Nvidia v1.0 (2012)
8. Nvidia Corporation: Cuda c programming guide. Nvidia PG-02819 v6.0, February 2014
9. Datta, K., Kamil, S., Williams, S., Oliker, L., Shalf, J., Katherine, Y.: Optimization and performance modeling of stencil computations on modern microprocessors. SIAM Rev. **51(1)**, 129–159 (2009)
10. Dirac Testbed. http://www.nersc.gov/users/computational-systems/testbeds/dirac/
11. Edison Cray XC30. http://www.nersc.gov/systems/edison-cray-xc30/
12. Gyrokinetic Toroidal Code Website. http://phoenix.ps.uci.edu/GTC/
13. Hager, G., Treibig, J., Habich, J., Wellein, G.: Exploring performance and power properties of modern multicore chips via simple machine models. CoRR abs/1208.2908 (2012)
14. HPGMG website. http://hpgmg.org

15. Kamil, S., Husbands, P., Oliker, L., Shalf, J., Yelick, K.: Impact of modern memory subsystems on cache optimizations for stencil computations. In: ACM MSP (2005)
16. LLCBench - Low Level Architectural Characterization Benchmark Suite. http://icl.cs.utk.edu/projects/llcbench/index.htm
17. QEforge website: MiniDFT. http://qe-forge.org/gf/project/minidft/
18. STREAM benchmark. http://www.cs.virginia.edu/stream/ref.html
19. Williams, S.: Auto-tuning performance on multicore computers. Ph.D. thesis, EECS Department, University of California, Berkeley, December 2008
20. Williams, S., Watterman, A., Patterson, D.: Roofline: an insightful visual performance model for floating-point programs and multicore architectures. Commun. ACM **52**(4), 65–76 (2009)

Modeling Stencil Computations on Modern HPC Architectures

Raúl de la Cruz[1][(✉)] and Mauricio Araya-Polo[2]

[1] CASE Department, Barcelona Supercomputing Center, Barcelona, Spain
delacruz@bsc.es
[2] Shell International Exploration and Production Inc., Houston, TX, USA
mauricio.araya@shell.com

Abstract. Stencil computations are widely used for solving Partial Differential Equations (PDEs) explicitly by Finite Difference schemes. The stencil solver alone -depending on the governing equation- can represent up to 90 % of the overall elapsed time, of which moving data back and forth from memory to CPU is a major concern. Therefore, the development and analysis of source code modifications that can effectively use the memory hierarchy of modern architectures is crucial. Performance models help expose bottlenecks and predict suitable tuning parameters in order to boost stencil performance on any given platform. To achieve that, the following two considerations need to be accurately modeled: first, modern architectures, such as Intel Xeon Phi, sport multi- or many-core processors with shared multi-level caches featuring one or several prefetching engines. Second, algorithmic optimizations, such as spatial blocking or Semi-stencil, have complex behaviors that follow the intricacy of the above described modern architectures. In this work, a previously published performance model is extended to effectively capture these architectural and algorithmic characteristics. The extended model results show an accuracy error ranging from 5–15 %.

Keywords: Stencil computation · FD · Modeling · HPC · Prefetching · Spatial blocking · Semi-stencil · Multi-core · Intel Xeon Phi

1 Introduction

Stencil computations are the core of many Scientific Computing applications. Geophysics [1], astrophysics [2], nuclear physics [20] or oceanography [8,13] are scientific fields where large computer simulations are frequently carried out. Their governing PDEs are usually solved by the Finite-Difference (FD) method, using stencil computations to explicitly calculate the differential operators which represent a large fraction of the total execution time.

In a stencil computation, each point of the computational domain accumulates the weighted contribution of certain neighboring points through every axis, thus solving the spatial differential operator. The more neighboring points are

© Springer International Publishing Switzerland 2015
S.A. Jarvis et al. (Eds.): PMBS 2014, LNCS 8966, pp. 149–171, 2015.
DOI: 10.1007/978-3-319-17248-4_8

used for this operation, the higher accuracy is obtained. Two inherent problems can be identified from the structure of the stencil computation [6]. First is the noncontiguous memory access pattern while accessing neighbors in the least-stride dimensions. Second is the low *Operational Intensity* (OI) of stencil computations, which leads to a poor data reuse of the values fetched to the CPU through the memory hierarchy. Therefore, optimizing stencil computations is crucial in order to reduce the application execution time.

The manual trial-and-error approach turns the process of optimizing codes lengthy and tedious. The large number of stencil optimization combinations, which might consume days of computing time, makes the process lengthy. Furthermore, the process is tedious due to the slightly different versions of code that must be implemented and assessed. To alleviate the cumbersome optimization process from user supervision, several auto-tuning frameworks [3, 10] have been developed to automatize the search by using heuristics to guide the parameter subspace. As an alternative, models that predict performance can be built without the requirement of any actual stencil computation execution. These models can be used in auto-tuning frameworks for compile- and run-time optimizations; making guided decisions about the best algorithmic parameters, thread execution configuration or even suggesting code modifications.

We propose a model that is highly time-cost effective compared to other approaches based on regression analysis. In regression-based analysis, users are required to conduct extensive and costly experiments in order to obtain the input data for regression. A wide range of hardware performance counters are gathered and machine learning algorithms used to determine correlations between architectural events and compiler optimizations. The more complex the model is, the more data is required to estimate the correlation coefficients. Furthermore, regression models lack of cache miss predictors and neither provide hints about algorithmic parameter candidates (e.g. spatial blocking). Albeit, regression analysis can be partially useful whether it is intended to give indications of possible performance bottlenecks and is combined with knowledge-based systems.

The performance characterization of a kernel code is not trivial and relies heavily on the ability to capture the algorithm's behavior in an accurate fashion, independently of the platform and the execution environment. In order to do so, the estimation of memory latencies is critical in memory-bound kernels. This is why predicting 3C (*compulsory, conflict* and *capacity*) misses accurately play an important role to effectively characterize the kernel performance.

In this paper, we extend our multi-level cache model for 3D stencil computations [5] by consolidating HPC support. Previous works have already proposed cache misses and execution time models for specific stencil optimizations. However, most of them have been designed for simplified architectures or low order stencil sizes (7-point), leaving aside many considerations of modern HPC architectures. Nowadays, multi- and many-core architectures with multi-level cache hierarchies, prefetching engines and SMT capabilities are common on HPC platforms but also disregarded or barely covered by previous works. The challenge is to cover all these features to effectively model stencil computation performance.

We have used a leading hardware architecture in our experiments, the popular Intel Xeon Phi 5100 series (SE10X model), also known as MIC. This architecture shows outstanding appeal for this work due to its support for all of the new features that our extended model intend to cover.

The remaining paper is organized as follows. Section 2 overviews briefly the related work. In Sect. 3, we elaborate on the basic fundamentals of our performance model, including some phenomena such as cache interference. Section 4 details the considerations to extrapolate the model to multi- and many-core architectures. Section 5 explains how the prefetching effect can be modeled. In Sect. 6, two stencil optimizations are discussed and added to the model. Section 7 presents the experimental results and evaluates their accuracy. Finally, Sect. 8 summarizes the findings of this work and concludes the paper.

2 Related Work

The modeling topic on stencil computations has been fairly studied in the recent years. A straightforward model was initially published by Kamil *et al.* [12], where they proposed cost models to capture the performance of 7-point stencils by taking into account three types of memory accesses (*first*, *intermediate* and *stream*) in a flat memory hierarchy. Then, a simple approach was devised by setting a lower bound ($2C_{stencil}$) with only compulsory misses and an upper bound ($4C_{stencil}$) with no cache reuse at all. Spatial blocking support was also added by modifying the number of cache-lines fetched using the three types of memory accesses due to the disruption of the prefetching effect. Regression analysis has also shown some appeal for modeling stencil computations [19]. They developed a set of formulas via regression analysis to model the overall performance on 7 and 27-point Jacobi and Gauss-Seidel computations. Their intent was not to predict absolute execution time but to extract meaningful insights that might help developers to effectively improve their codes. The time-skewing technique has been also modelized by Strzodka *et al.* [22]. They proposed a performance model for their cache accurate time skewing (CATS) algorithm, where the system and the cache bandwidths were estimated using regression analysis. The CATS performance model considered only two levels of memory hierarchy, and therefore it could be inaccurate on HPC architectures. Their aim was to find out which hardware improvements were required in single-core architectures to match the performance of future multi-core systems.

Likewise, performance modeling has been successfully deployed on numerical areas such as sparse matrix vector multiplications [18] and generic performance models for bandwidth-limited loop kernels [9,24].

3 Stencil Model

In this work, we use the model initially published at [5] as starting point. This performance model considers stencil computations as memory-bound, where the cost of computing the floating-point operations is assumed negligible due to the overlap with considerable memory transfers. This assumption is especially true for large domain problems where, apart from compulsory misses, capacity and conflict misses arise commonly leading to a low OI [6]. Some concepts of the initial model are improved and extended to fulfill the coverage of the current work. For a better understanding of the remaining sections, the main concepts and assumptions of the base model are briefly reviewed in the next section.

Algorithm 1. The classical stencil algorithm pseudo-code. II, JJ, KK are the dimensions of the data set including ghost points. ℓ denotes the neighbors used for the central point contribution. $C_{Z1...Z\ell}$, $C_{X1...X\ell}$, $C_{Y1...Y\ell}$ are the spatial discretization coefficients for each direction and C_0 for the self-contribution. Notice that the coefficients are considered symmetric and constant for each axis.

1: **for** $t = 0$ to $timesteps$ **do**   ▷ Iterate in time
2:     **for** $k = \ell$ to $KK - \ell$ **do**   ▷ Y axis
3:         **for** $j = \ell$ to $JJ - \ell$ **do**   ▷ X axis
4:             **for** $i = \ell$ to $II - \ell$ **do**   ▷ Z axis
5:                 $\mathcal{X}_{i,j,k}^{t} = C_0 * \mathcal{X}_{i,j,k}^{t-1}$

$$+ C_{Z1} * (\mathcal{X}_{i-1,j,k}^{t-1} + \mathcal{X}_{i+1,j,k}^{t-1}) + \ldots + C_{Z\ell} * (\mathcal{X}_{i-\ell,j,k}^{t-1} + \mathcal{X}_{i+\ell,j,k}^{t-1})$$
$$+ C_{X1} * (\mathcal{X}_{i,j-1,k}^{t-1} + \mathcal{X}_{i,j+1,k}^{t-1}) + \ldots + C_{X\ell} * (\mathcal{X}_{i,j-\ell,k}^{t-1} + \mathcal{X}_{i,j+\ell,k}^{t-1})$$
$$+ C_{Y1} * (\mathcal{X}_{i,j,k-1}^{t-1} + \mathcal{X}_{i,j,k+1}^{t-1}) + \ldots + C_{Y\ell} * (\mathcal{X}_{i,j,k-\ell}^{t-1} + \mathcal{X}_{i,j,k+\ell}^{t-1})$$

3.1 Base Model

Considering a problem size of $I \times J \times K$ points of order ℓ, where I is the unit-stride (Z axis) and J and K the least-stride dimensions (X and Y axes), an amount of P_{read} ($2 \times \ell + 1$) and P_{write} (1) Z-X planes of $\mathcal{X}^{t-1}$ is required to compute a single $\mathcal{X}^t$ plane (see Algorithm 1). Thus, the total data to be held is $S_{total} = P_{read} \times S_{read} + P_{write} \times S_{write}$, being $S_{read} = II \times JJ$ and $S_{write} = I \times J$ their size in words. Note that II and JJ include ghost points.

Likewise, the whole execution time (T_{total}) on an architecture with n levels of cache is estimated based on the aggregated cost of transferring data on three memory hierarchy groups: *first* (T_{L1}), *intermediate* (T_{L2} to T_{Ln}) and *last* (T_{Memory}). Each transferring cost depends on their hits and misses and is computed differently. In general, the transferring cost ($T_{Li} = Hits_{Li}^{data} \times T_{Li}^{data}$) is based on the latency of bringing as much data (word or cacheline) as required ($Hits_{Li}^{data} = Misses_{Li-1}^{data} - Misses_{Li}^{data}$) from the cache level to the CPU ($T_{Li}^{data} = data/Bw_{Li}^{read}$) in order to compute the stencil. Finally, the amount of misses issued at each cache level is estimated as

$$Misses_{Li} = \lceil II/W \rceil \times JJ \times KK \times nplanes_{Li} , \tag{1}$$

where $W = cacheline/word$ is the number of words per cacheline and $nplanes_{Li}$ is the number of $II \times JJ$ planes read from the next cache level ($Li + 1$) for each k iteration due to possible compulsory, conflict or capacity misses. The cache miss calculations are described in the following section.

3.2   Cache Miss Cases and Rules

The correct estimation of $nplanes_{Li}$ is crucial for the model accuracy. To do so, four miss cases (C_1, C_2, C_3 and C_4, ordered from lower to higher penalty) and four rules (R_1, R_2, R_3 and R_4) are devised. Each of these rules triggers the transition from one miss case scenario to the next one. In this model, the rules are linked and therefore triggered in sequential order, thus exposing different levels of miss penalty.

Rule 1 (R_1): The best possible scenario (lower bound) is likely to happen when all the required Z-X planes (S_{total}) to compute one k iteration fit loosely (R_{col} factor) into the cache level ($size_{Li}$). This yields to only compulsory misses and to the following rule, $R_1 : ((size_{Li}/w) \times R_{col} \geq S_{total})$.

Rule 2 (R_2): Conversely to R_1, when all the required planes do not fit loosely in cache except the k-central plane with a higher temporal reuse (less chance to be evicted from cache), conflict misses are produced among planes. This scenario is likely to happen when the following rule is true, $R_2 : ((size_{Li}/w) > S_{total})$.

Rule 3 (R_3): On a third possible scenario, it is assumed that despite the whole data set does not fit in cache (S_{total}), the k-central plane does not overwhelm a significant part of the cache (R_{col} factor). Therefore, the possibility of temporal reuse is reduced compared to R_2 but not canceled completely. This scenario can occur when, $R_3 : ((size_{Li}/w) \times R_{col} > S_{read})$.

Rule 4 (R_4): The worst scenario (upper bound) appears when neither the planes nor the columns of the k-central plane fit loosely in the cache level. Then, capacity and conflict misses arise frequently, resulting as well in fetching the k-central plane at each j iteration of the loop. This scenario gives the following rule, $R_4 : ((size_{Li}/w) \times R_{col} < P_{read} \times II)$.

w is the word size (in single or double precision), and R_{col} is a factor proportional to the required data by the k-central plane with respect to the whole dataset ($P_{read}/2P_{read} - 1$). Putting all the ingredients together, the computation of $nplanes_{Li}$ is yielded by the following conditional equations:

$$nplanes_{Li}(II, JJ) = \begin{cases} C_1 : 1, & \text{if } R_1 \\ C_1 \sqcup C_2 : (1, P_{read} - 1], & \text{if } \neg R_1 \wedge R_2 \\ C_2 \sqcup C_3 : (P_{read} - 1, P_{read}], & \text{if } \neg R_2 \wedge R_3 \\ C_3 \sqcup C_4 : (P_{read}, 2P_{read} - 1], & \text{if } \neg R_3 \wedge \neg R_4 \\ C_4 : 2P_{read} - 1, & \text{if } R_4 , \end{cases} \tag{2}$$

which only depends on II and JJ parameters for a given architecture and a stencil order (ℓ). Figure 1 shows an example of how $nplanes_{Li}$ evolves with respect to $II \times JJ$ parameter.

Large discontinuities can appear in Eq. 2 when transitioning from one case to the next case ($C_1 \sqcup C_2$, $C_2 \sqcup C_3$ and $C_3 \sqcup C_4$). This effect can be partially smoothed by using interpolation methods. Apart from the discrete transitioning, three types of interpolations have been added in our model: linear, exponential and logarithmic. An interpolation function ($f(x, x_0, x_1, y_0, y_1)$) requires

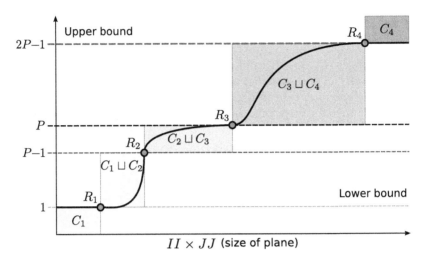

Fig. 1. The different rules (R_1, R_2, R_3 and R_4) bound the size of the problem (abscissa: $II \times JJ$) with the miss case penalties (ordinate: 1, $P_{read} - 1$, P_{read} and $2P_{read} - 1$).

five input parameters, the X-axis bounds (x_0 and x_1), the Y-axis bounds (y_0 and y_1) and the point in the X-axis (x) to be mapped into the Y-axis (y). In our problem domain, the X-axis represents the $II \times JJ$ parameters whereas the Y-axis is the unknown $nplanes_{Li}$. For instance, for $C_1 \sqcup C_2$ transition, isolating II from R_1 and R_2 rules, II_{min} (x_0) and II_{max} (x_1) are respectively obtained, bounding the interpolation. By using their respective rules and isolating the required variable for X-axis, the same procedure is also applied to the remaining transitions of Eq. 2. In this way, an easy methodology is presented to avoid unrealistic discontinuities for the model.

3.3   Cache Interference Phenomena: II × JJ Effect

As stated before, three types of cache misses (3C) can be distinguished: compulsory (*cold-start*), capacity and conflict (*interference*) misses. Compulsory and capacity misses are relatively easily predicted and estimated [23]. Contrarily, conflict misses are hard to evaluate because it must be known where data are mapped in cache and when it will be referenced. In addition, conflict misses disrupt data reuse, spatial or temporal. For instance, a high frequency of cache interferences can lead to the rare *ping-pong* phenomena, where two or more memory references fall into the same cache location, therefore competing for cache-lines. Cache associativity can alleviate this issue to a certain extent by increasing the cache locations for the same address.

The cache miss model presented in Subsect. 3.2 sets the upper bound for each of the four cases in terms of number of planes read for each plane written ($nplanes_{Li}$), thus establishing a discrete model. Nevertheless, this discrete scenario is unlikely to happen for cases C_2, C_3 and mainly C_4, due to their dependency on capacity and especially on conflict misses. There are two factors that clearly affect conflict misses: the reuse distance for a given datum [23] and the intersection of two data sets [9], giving consequently a continuum scenario. The former depends on temporal locality; the more data is loaded, the higher the probability that a given datum may be flushed from cache before its reuse. On the other hand, the latter depends on two parameters: the array base address and its leading dimensions.

In stencil computations the Z-X plane ($II \times JJ$ size) and the order of the stencil ($P_{read} = 2 \times \ell + 1$) are the critical parameters that exacerbate conflict misses. The conflict misses to estimate are related with the probability of interference, $P(i)$, and the column reuse of the central k-plane. $P(i)$ is proportional to the size in words of the columns to be reused ($II \times (P_{read} - 1)$) after reading the first central column with respect to the whole size of the central k-plane to be held in cache ($II \times JJ$),

$$P(i) = \frac{II \times JJ - II \times (P_{read} - 1)}{II \times JJ} = 1 - \frac{P_{read} - 1}{JJ} \in [0, 1] , \qquad (3)$$

which yields to a logarithmic function depending on P_{read}, II and JJ parameters. A zero value means no conflict misses at all, whereas a probability of one means disruption of temporal reuse (high ratio of interferences) for columns of the central k-plane. Therefore, the $P(i)$ probability can be added as

$$nplanes_{Li\prime} = nplanes_{Li} \times P(i) , \qquad (4)$$

tailoring the read misses case boundary to their right value depending on the conflict misses issued. Thus, the larger the data to be used to compute one output plane ($I \times J$), the higher the probability of having capacity and conflict misses. Figure 2 shows the accuracy difference between the model with and without cache interference effect.

3.4 Additional Time Overheads

During the execution of HPC stencil codes, some additional overheads may arise. In this subsection, we explain how these overheads are weighed when modeling the stencil computation performance. The overheads are categorized into three groups: parallelism, memory interferences and computational bottlenecks.

- Intra-node parallelism (OpenMP and Posix threads): small overheads may appear due to the thread initialization and synchronization tasks whether data is disjoint among threads. This overhead usually has a clear impact only on small dataset problems. In order to characterize its effect on the stencil model, a small (order of milliseconds) and constant ϵ (T_{OMP}) is included.
- Memory contention: TLB misses, ECC memories (error checking & corruption) and cache coherence policies between cores (e.g. MESI protocol) affect noticeably the memory performance. Nevertheless, all these effects are already taken into account in the memory characterization through our STREAM2 tool (see Sect. 4 for further details).

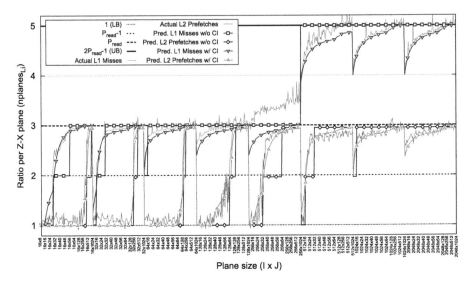

Fig. 2. Cache interference effect as a function of problem size. Whilst Eq. 4 is not applied, a discrete model is obtained (straight lines with squares and diamonds). Conversely, its use leads to a continuum model (inverted and non-inverted triangles).

– Computational bottlenecks: stencil computations are mainly considered memory bound instead of compute bound (the OI is low) [6, 25]. Therefore, for the sake of simplicity, the tampering effect of floating-point operations is expected to be negligible, and thus not considered.

4   From Single-core to Multi-core and Many-core

Current HPC platforms are suboptimal for scientific codes unless they take fully advantage of simultaneous threads running on multi- and many-cores chips. Some clear examples of such architectures are Intel Xeon family, IBM POWER7 or GPGPUs. All of them with tens of cores and their ability to run in SMT mode. So, the parallel nature of the current stencil computation deployments leads us to extend our model accordingly. To that end, the parallel memory management is a main concern, and this section is fully devoted to sort it out.

In order to characterize the memory management of multi-core architectures, the bandwidth measurement is critical. The bandwidth metrics are captured for different configurations using a bandwidth profiler such as STREAM2 benchmark [15]. Our STREAM2 version [5] has been significantly extended by adding new features such as vectorization (SSE, AVX and Xeon Phi ISAs), aligned and unaligned memory access, non-temporal writes (through Intel pragmas), prefetching and non-prefetching bandwidths, thread-level execution (OpenMP) and hardware counters instrumentation (PAPI) in order to validate results.

The process to obtain bandwidth measurements is straightforward. First, the thread number is set through the OMP_NUM_THREADS environment variable.

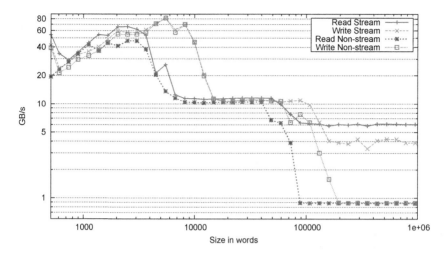

Fig. 3. STREAM2 results for Intel Xeon Phi architecture (4 threads, 2 per core). Each plateaux represents the sustainable bandwidth of a cache level.

Then, each thread is pinned to a specific core of the platform (e.g. using *numactl* or KMP_AFFINITY variable in Xeon Phi architecture). Finally, the results obtained for DOT (16 bytes/read) and FILL (8 bytes/write) kernels are respectively used as read and write bandwidths for the different cache hierarchies of the model. Figure 3 shows an example of the bandwidths used for a particular case in the Intel Xeon Phi platform. The importance of mimicking the environment conditions is crucial, in particular the execution time accuracy of the model is very sensitive to the real execution conditions. This means that the characterization of the memory bandwidth must be similarly performed in terms of: number of threads, threads per core, memory access alignment, temporal or non-temporal writes and SISD or SIMD instruction set.

Additionally, there are some memory resources that might be shared among different threads running in the same core or die. In order to model the behaviour in such cases, the memory resources are equally split among all threads. This is, if we have a cache size ($size_{Li}$ in rules $R_{1,2,3,4}$) of N KBytes, then each thread would turn out to have a cache size of $size_{Li} = N/nthreads_{core}$.

5   Modeling Prefetching

5.1   Hardware Prefetching

Modern computer architectures incorporate prefetching engines in their cache hierarchy. Its aim is to reduce the memory latency by eagerly fetching data that is expected to be required in the near future.

The prefetching mechanism modeled in our previous work [5] lacked accuracy when several threads were triggering the prefetching engine concurrently.

As stated in [5], the modeling of the prefetching mechanism is not straight-forward. In that work, a simple approach was devised. The miss model was divided into two groups, prefetched and non-prefetched misses, depending on the concurrent streams that the prefetching engine supported. Next, two different bandwidths were used for each cache miss group in order to compute their time penalty.

Recent works [14,16] have characterized the impact of prefetching mechanism on scientific application performance. They establish a new metric called *prefetching effectiveness*, which computes the fraction of data accesses to the next memory level that are initiated by the hardware prefetcher. Therefore, for a given data cache level (DC), its prefetching effectiveness is computed as

$$DC_{effectiveness} = DC\_Req\_PF/DC\_Req\_All \in [0,1] \; , \tag{5}$$

where DC_Req_PF refers to the number of cache-lines requests initiated by the prefetching engine, and DC_Req_All represents the total number of cache-lines requests initiated at the DC level (including demanding and non-demanding loads). This approach has been adopted in our model as the way to accurately capture the prefetching behaviour.

In order to be able to characterize the prefetching effectiveness in our test-bed platform, a new micro-benchmark was developed from scratch. This benchmark traverses a chunk of memory simultaneously by different threads and changes the number of stream accesses in a round-robin fashion. Then, to compute their effectiveness, a set of hardware performance counters were gathered through PAPI. For instance, on Intel Xeon Phi architecture, two native events were instrumented to compute the *prefetching effectiveness*: HWP_L2MISS and L2_DATA_READ_MISS_MEM_FILL. Figure 4 shows the results obtained for this platform over the L2 hardware prefetcher.

The *prefetching effectiveness* ($DC_{effectiveness}$) is then used to compute the total number of cache-line misses that are fetched using streaming bandwidths ($nplanes_{Li}^{S}$) and those that are fetched using a regular bandwidth ($nplanes_{Li}^{NS}$):

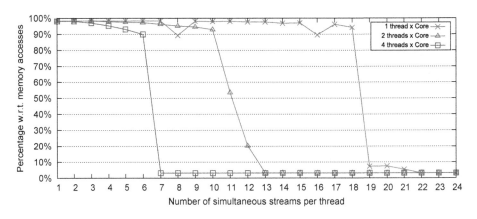

Fig. 4. L2 prefetching efficiency for Intel Xeon Phi architecture. The efficiency has been computed using one core and varying the SMT configuration from 1 to 4 threads.

$$nplanes_{Li}^{S} = nplanes_{Li} \times DC_{effectiveness},$$
$$nplanes_{Li}^{NS} = nplanes_{Li} \times (1 - DC_{effectiveness}) \,. \tag{6}$$

Similarly to the memory resources, prefetching engines might be shared among threads running on the same core. In such scenarios, the *prefetching effectiveness* is computed with our prefetching tool varying the number of threads per core (for instance, 2 and 4 threads results can be observed in Fig. 4). In fact, these results are insightful and help to understand when the core performance might be degraded due to excessive simultaneous streams, thus adversely affecting the parallel scaling of stencil computations.

5.2   Software Prefetching

Software prefetching is a technique where compilers, and also programmers, explicitly insert prefetching operations similar to load instructions into the code. Predicting the performance of software prefetching is challenging. Compilers use proprietary heuristics in order to decide where (code location), which (data array) and how much in advance (look-ahead in bytes) start prefetching data. Furthermore, programmers can even harden this task by adding special hints in the code to help the compiler make some of these decisions [17]. As software prefetching produces regular loads on the cache hierarchy, it also prevents hardware prefetcher to be triggered when it performs properly [7]. Thus, the failure or success of software prefetching affects collaterally the hardware prefetching behaviour.

Due to all above commented issues, software prefetching has not been taken into account in the present work. The software prefetching can be disabled in Intel compilers by using the `-opt-prefetch=0` flag during the compilation.

6   Stencil Optimizations

The state-of-the-art in stencil computation is constantly being extended with the publication of several optimization techniques in recent years. Under specific circumstances, some of those techniques improve the execution performance. For instance, space blocking is a tiling strategy widely used in multi-level cache hierarchy architectures. It promotes data reuse by traversing the entire domain into small blocks of size $TI \times TJ$ which must fit into the cache [12,21]. Therefore, space blocking is especially useful when the dataset structure does not fit into the memory hierarchy. This traversal order reduces capacity and conflict misses in least-stride dimensions increasing data locality and overall performance. Note that a search of the best block size parameter ($TI \times TJ$) must be performed for each problem size and architecture.

A second example of stencil optimization is the Semi-stencil algorithm [6]. This algorithm changes the way in which the spatial operator is calculated and how data is accessed in the most inner loop. Actually, the inner loop involves two phases called *forward* and *backward* where several grid points are updated simultaneously. By doing so, the dataset requirements of the internal loop is reduced, while keeping the same number of floating-point operations. Thereby, increasing data reuse and thus the OI. Conversely to read operations, the number of writes are slightly increased because the additional point updates. Due to this issue, this algorithm only improves performance on medium-large stencil orders ($\ell > 2$).

These two stencil optimizations have been included into our model. The motivation of modeling them is two-fold. First, to reveal insights of where and why an algorithm may perform inadequately for a given architecture and environment. Second, to analytically guide the search for good algorithmic parameter candidates without the necessity of obtaining them empirically (brute force).

6.1   Spatial Blocking

Space blocking is implemented in our model by including similar general ideas as [4], but adapting them in order to suit the advantages of our cost model. Basically, the problem domain is traversed in $TI \times TJ \times TK$ blocks. Then, first the blocks on each direction are computed as $NBI = I/TI$, $NBJ = J/TJ$, and $NBK = K/TK$. Therefore, the total number of tiling iterations to perform are $NB = NBI \times NBJ \times NBK$. Blocking may be performed in the unit-stride dimension as well. Given that data is brought to cache in multiples of the cache-line, additional transfer overhead may arise when TI size is not multiple of cache-line. This is considered into the model by reassigning I, J, K and their extended dimensions as follows:

$$
\begin{aligned}
I &= \lceil TI/W \rceil \times W, & J &= TJ, & K &= TK, \\
II &= \lceil (TI + 2 \times \ell)/W \rceil \times W, & JJ &= TJ + 2 \times \ell, & KK &= TK + 2 \times \ell .
\end{aligned}
\tag{7}
$$

The new II and JJ parameters are then used for rules $R_{1,2,3,4}$ to estimate $nplanes_{Li}$ based on the blocking size. Finally, Eq. 1 shall be rewritten as

$$
Misses_{Li}^{[S,NS]} = \lceil II/W \rceil \times JJ \times KK \times nplanes_{Li}^{[S,NS]} \times NB ,
\tag{8}
$$

where NB factor is considered to adjust streamed ($_{Li}^{S}$) and non-streamed ($_{Li}^{NS}$) misses depending on the total number of blocking iterations.

Architectures with prefetching features may present performance degradation when $TI \neq I$ [11]. Blocking on the unit-stride dimension may tamper streaming performance due to the interference caused to the memory access pattern detection of the prefetching engine. The triggering of the prefetching engine involves a *warm-up* phase, where a number of cache-lines must be previously read (TP). Additionally, prefetching engines keep a look-ahead distance (LAP) of how many cache-lines in advance to prefetch. Disrupting a regular memory access will produce LAP additional fetches to the next cache level if the prefetching engine was triggered. Considering all these penalties, the cache misses are updated with:

$$
\begin{aligned}
Misses_{Li}^{NS} &\overset{\pm}{=} TP \times JJ \times KK \times nplanes_{Li}^{NS} \times NB, & \text{if } II/W \geq TP, \\
Misses_{Li}^{S} &\overset{\pm}{=} LAP \times JJ \times KK \times nplanes_{Li}^{S} \times NB, & \text{if } II/W \geq TP .
\end{aligned}
\tag{9}
$$

TP and LAP parameters can be obtained from processor manufacturer's manuals or empirically through our prefetching benchmark. To deduce such parameters, the prefetching benchmark was modified to traverse arrays in a blocked fashion whilst TI parameter was slowly increased along different executions. Then, the prefetching hardware counter was monitored in order to flag at what precise point ($TP = \lceil TI/W \rceil$) the prefetching metric soared significantly. Likewise, LAP parameter was estimated by counting the extra prefetching loads (apart from the TP) that were issued.

6.2   Semi-stencil Algorithm

Adapt the model for the Semi-stencil algorithm is equally straightforward. Indeed, this can be achieved by setting P_{read} and P_{write} parameters correctly. By default, in a partial Semi-stencil implementation (*forward* and *backward* phases on X and Y axes), $\ell + 1$ Z-X planes from $\mathcal{X}^t$ and one $\mathcal{X}^{t+1}$ plane (k-central plane update) are read for each k iteration. As output, two planes are written back as partial ($\mathcal{X}^{t+1}_{i,j,k+\ell}$) and final ($\mathcal{X}^{t+1}_{i,j,k}$) results. However, these values can slightly increase when no room is left for the k-central columns; thus yielding

$$P_{read} = \ell + 2, \quad P_{write} = 2, \quad \text{if } \neg R_4$$
$$P_{read} = \ell + 3, \quad P_{write} = 3, \quad \text{if } R_4 \tag{10}$$

as the new data requirements to compute one output plane. This adaptability reveals the model resilience, where an absolutely different stencil algorithm can be modeled by simply tuning a couple of parameters.

7   Experimental Results

This section estimates through experimental results how accurate the model is when exposed to: prefetching, thread parallelism and code optimizations techniques. All experimental results in this section were validated using the StencilProbe [12], a synthetic benchmark that we have extended. The new StencilProbe features [6] include: different stencil orders (ℓ), thread support (OpenMP), SIMD code, instrumentation and new optimization techniques (e.g. spatial blocking and Semi-stencil). This benchmark implements the stencil scheme shown in Algorithm 1, where star-like stencils with symetric and constant coefficients are computed using 1st order in time and different orders in space (see Table 1).

A large number of different problem sizes were explored in order to validate the model accuracy for a wide parametrical space. Recall that the two first dimensions (on Z and X axes) are the critical parameters that increase the cache miss ratio ($nplanes_{Li}$) for a given stencil order (ℓ) and architecture. Therefore, the last dimension K was set to a fixed number, and the I and J dimensions were widely varied covering a large spectrum of grid sizes. All the experiments were conducted using double-precision, and the domain decomposition across threads was conducted by cutting in the least-stride dimension (Y axis) with static scheduling. Table 1 summarizes the different parameters used.

Table 1. List of parameters used for the model and the StencilProbe benchmark.

Parameters	Range of values
Naive sizes ($I \times J \times K$)	$8 \times 8 \times 128 \ldots 2048 \times 1024 \times 128$
Rivera sizes ($I \times J \times K$)	$512 \times 2048 \times 128$
Stencil sizes (ℓ)	1, 2, 4 and 7 (7, 13, 25 and 43-point respectively)
Algorithms	{Naive, Rivera} $\times$ {Classical, *Semi-stencil*}
Block sizes (TI and TJ)	$\{8, 16, 24, 32, 64, 128, 256, 512, 1024, 1536, 2048\}$

The testbed platform for all experiments is based on Intel Xeon Phi. The 22 nm Xeon Phi processor include 61 cores with 4-way SMT capabilities running at 1.1 GHz. Each core is in-order and contains a 512-bit vector unit (VPU). Additionally, each core has a 32 KB L1D cache, a 32 KB L1I cache and a private 512 KB L2 cache. This cache includes a hardware prefetcher able to prefetch 16 forward or backward sequential streams into 4 KB page-size boundaries. All cores are connected together via a bi-directional ring with the standard MESI coherency protocol for maintaining the shared state among cores.

Hardware counters were gathered for all experiments in order to validate the model results against actual executions. Table 2 shows the hardware performance counters instrumented. The stencil code generated by StencilProbe is vectorized, and therefore only vector reads were fetched (VPU_DATA_READ) during executions. Additionally, the L2 prefetcher in Xeon Phi can also prefetch reads for a miss in a write-back operation (L2_WRITE_HIT) when it has the opportunity. Then, in order to fairly compare the prefetched read misses of the model with actual metrics, the L2 prefetches (HWP_L2MISS) were normalized. This normalization was performed by subtracting reads due to a miss in a write operation scaled by the *prefetching efficiency*. Likewise, some writes were considered prefetched (L2_WRITE_HIT $\times DC_{effectiveness}$) and others not (L2_WRITE_HIT $\times (1 - DC_{effectiveness})$) due to contention of the L2 prefetching engine. Finally, the remaining miss counters (VPU_DATA_READ_MISS and L2_DATA_READ_MISS_MEM_FILL) only consider demanding reads, initiated by explicit reads, and therefore were directly used as non-prefetched read misses. It is important to mention that, in our previous model [5], several complex formulas were derived to estimate the number of reads issued to the first level cache ($Hits_{L1}^{word}$). This estimation was not straightforward and lacked accuracy. However, we realized that this parameter kept constant per loop iteration and could be precisely estimated by performing static analysis of the inner stencil loop only once (counting the numbers of reads in the object file).

An aim of this research is to prove that stencil computations can be accurately modeled on SMT architectures. Therefore, all possible SMT combinations for a single core were sampled. Our tests were conducted using 4 threads varying their pinning to cores. KMP_AFFINITY environment variable was accordingly set to bind threads to the desired cores. The SMT configurations tried for each test

Table 2. Hardware counters and the formulas used to compute the projected time.

Description	Intel Xeon Phi Events	Time Cost Formulas
Cycles	CPU_CLK_UNHALTED	$T_{L1} = $ (L1 Hits - L1 Misses) $\times Bw_{L1}^{cline}$
L1 Hits	VPU_DATA_READ	$T_{L2} = Bw_{L2}^{cline} \times$ (L1 Misses - L2 Misses -
L1 Misses	VPU_DATA_READ_MISS	(L2 Prefetches - L2 Writes $\times$ Pref Eff))
L2 Misses	L2_DATA_READ_MISS_	$T_{Mem} = $ L2 Misses $\times Bw_{Mem}^{NS} + Bw_{Mem}^{S} \times$
	MEM_FILL	(L2 Prefetches - L2 Writes $\times$ Pref Eff)
L2 Prefetches	HWP_L2MISS	$T_{Writes} = $ L2 Writes $\times$ Pref Eff $\times Bw_{Write}^{S}$
L2 Writes	L2_WRITE_HIT	+ L2 Writes $\times$ (1 - Pref Eff) $\times Bw_{Write}^{NS}$

were: 1 core in full usage (4 threads per core), 2 cores in half usage (2 threads per core) and 4 cores in fourth usage (1 thread per core).

Due to the sheer number of combinations sampled, only the most representative and interesting results are shown. Results have been categorized as a function of core occupancy (1, 2 and 4 threads per core) in order to explicitly visualize the effect of resource contention on the actual metrics and test the predicted results.

Figure 5 shows the actual and the predicted misses with our model (prefetched and non-prefetched for L2) on all three SMT configurations using a Naive stencil order of $\ell = 4$. In this case 680 different problem sizes (X axis in figures) were tested per configuration. Recall that software prefetching was disabled and therefore L1 or L2 cache levels do not exhibit collateral effects due to compiler-assisted prefetch. This figure is very insightful because the empirical results clearly corroborate our thoughts regarding the different bounds applied in the stencil model. Indeed, in a $\ell = 4$ stencil the read miss bounds for the model are: 1, 8 ($P_{read} - 1$), 9 (P_{read}) and 17 ($2P_{read} - 1$) per each $I \times J$ plane computed. Actual L1 and L2 misses tend to these bounds when a specific problem size is reached, never reaching beyond the upper bound ($2P_{read} - 1$) which is showed as a solid coarse horizontal line in all plots. Cache levels with prefetched and non-prefetched misses are a special case due to their direct relation with $DC_{effectiveness}$ ratio, and therefore they might be under the lower bound (1). Additionally, as the threads per core are increased, the inflection points (transitions) between bounds ($C_1 \sqcup C_2$, $C_2 \sqcup C_3$ and $C_3 \sqcup C_4$) are triggered earlier in terms of plane size ($I \times J$). The larger the number of threads running concurrently on the same core, the more contention and struggle for shared resources occurs. Likewise, some spikes appear on account of *ping-pong* effect, where different planes and columns addresses fall in the same cache set. This effect is also exacerbated as more threads are pinned to the same core. However, this effect is not captured by our model because it would require a multi-level set-associative cache model, which is not covered yet in our model.

Comparing the empirical (hardware counters) versus the analytical results (model), it can be observed that the model accurately predicts the number of misses on both levels of cache hierarchies, including those reads that are

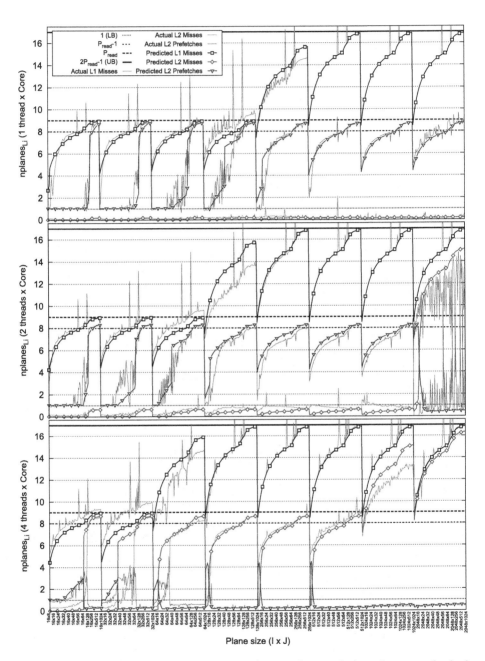

Fig. 5. Actual and predicted prefetched (inverted triangles) and non-prefetched (squares and diamonds) cache-lines for the three SMT configurations. These results are for the Naive implementation of a medium-high order ($\ell = 4$) stencil.

prefetched. However, some slight mispredictions appear on specific sizes when the transition between miss cases is triggered. Deciding a discrete point $(I \times J)$ for transitions is difficult, and it might depend on other parameters apart from those considered in this work. Nevertheless, we think that our rules $(R_{1,2,3,4})$ have approximated these transitions fairly well. It is also important to mention the prediction of the L2 prefetching engine, especially in the late executions for 2 threads and in the early ones for 4 threads per core configurations. As hardware metrics show, on these cases the prefetching effect starts disrupting the results due to contention. Nonetheless, the predicted results follow the trend of both type of misses properly as a result of the $DC_{effectiveness}$ parameter.

The model accuracy is verified in Fig. 6, which shows a summary of three types of execution times: actual, projected and predicted. The actual times were obtained using the CPU clock cycles metric (CPU_CLK_UNHALTED). On the other hand, the projected times were computed with the aggregated time of T_{L1}, T_{L2}, T_{Mem} and T_{Write} by using actual hardware counters of reads, writes and misses with their respective bandwidth parameters (STREAM2 characterization). Finally, the predicted times follow the same idea than the projected but using the estimations of our model instead of the instrumented ones. The purpose of the projected time is that it verifies the aggregated equation and calibrates the bandwidth parameters at each cache level. Therefore, it plays an important role ensuring that predicted times are a faithful representation of an actual execution.

Comparing the execution times shown in Fig. 6, we observe that the predicted relative error (right axis) is very low on most of the cases. However, as the results reveal, some predictions have a high error (2 threads per core). Reviewing the cache miss predictions (not shown here), this is due to a late deactivation of the L2 prefetching engine, misleading the aggregated predicted time. Once the prefetching efficiency is again correctly predicted, the relative error drops considerably under 10 %. Equally, some actual executions also present peaks due to the *ping-pong* effect. Projected times clearly follow this instabilities because their mirroring on cache misses. On the contrary, our model can not mimic such situations, and therefore the relative error increases considerably on those cases.

Results considering stencil optimizations such as Semi-stencil and spatial blocking are shown in Fig. 7. In this test, 88 different tiling sizes were compared. The *TP* and *LAP* parameters used for the model were set to 3 and 5 cache-lines respectively. These values were obtained empirically using the prefetching benchmark as explained in Sect. 6. As shown in Fig. 7, the model clearly estimates the different valleys (local minima) that appear when searching for the best tiling parameters due to the disruption of prefetched data and the increase of cache-line misses. The model is even able to suggest some good parameter candidates. For instance, taking a look to the *Naive+Blocking* results, the model successfully predicts the best tiling parameter for 1 and 2 threads per core configurations (512×16 and 512×8 respectively). This is not the case when running 4 threads per core. However, in this latter case, the actual best parameter is given as third candidate (512×8). On the other hand, reviewing the *Semi+Blocking* results,

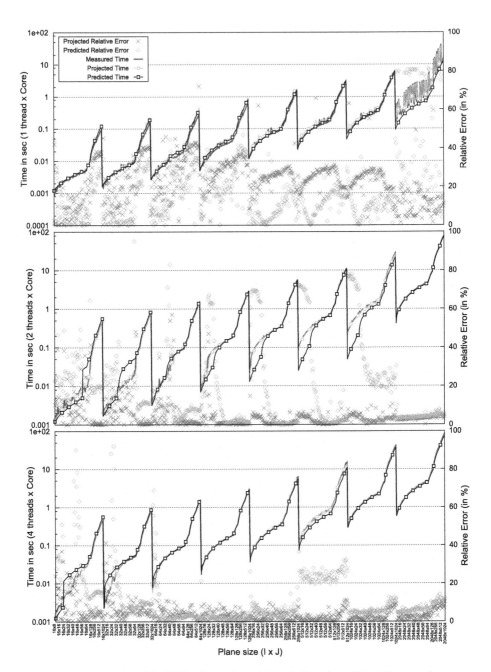

Fig. 6. Left axis: actual (solid line), projected (circles) and predicted (squares) execution times for the three SMT configurations. Right axis: relative errors compared with actual times. These results are for a high order ($\ell = 7$) Naive stencil.

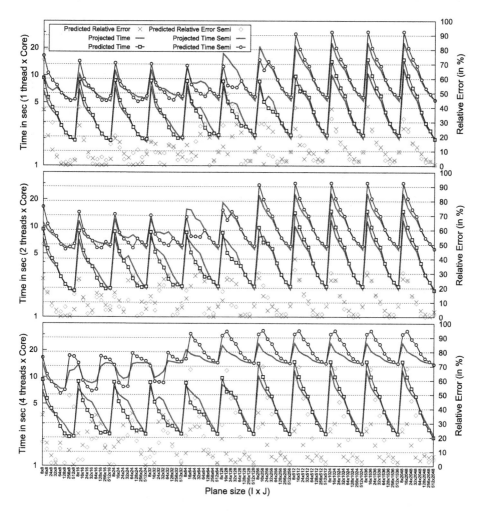

Fig. 7. Left axis: projected (solid line) and predicted (squares and circles) execution times for spatial blocking results. Right axis: relative errors compared with projected times. Results shown are for Naive ($\ell = 1$) and for Semi-stencil ($\ell = 4$).

despite of some mispredictions especially for 4 threads per core, most of the local minima areas are well predicted.

Additionally, the model can reveal other insightful hints regarding the efficiency in SMT executions. It can help to decide the best SMT configuration to be conducted in terms of core efficiency. Let τ^{SMT_i} be the execution time for a SMT_i configuration of n different combinations, we define the *core efficiency* as

$$Core_{efficiency}^{SMT_i} = \frac{\min(\tau^{SMT_1}, \ldots, \tau^{SMT_n})}{\tau^{SMT_i}} \in [0, 1] , \qquad (11)$$

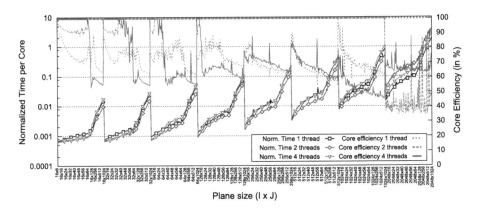

Fig. 8. Core efficiency for all three SMT combinations using a Naive stencil ($\ell = 4$).

where a *core efficiency* of 1 represents the best performance-wise SMT configuration for a set of specific stencil parameters (ℓ, $I \times J$ plane size, spatial blocking, Semi-stencil, etc.) and a given architecture. Therefore, the desirable decision would be to run the stencil code using the SMT_i configuration that maximizes the *core efficiency*. Normalizing our experiments for all three SMT combinations on a Naive stencil ($\ell = 4$) the Fig. 8 is obtained. Note that depending on the problem size, the best SMT configuration ranges from 4 threads for small sizes to 2 threads for medium sizes and just only 1 thread per core for very large problems. The factor leading to this behavior is the contention of shared resources, especially the prefetching engine.

8   Conclusions and Analysis

This paper presents a thorough methodology to evaluate and predict stencil codes performance on complex HPC architectures. We have included several new features in our model such as: multi- many-core support, better hardware prefetching modeling, cache interference due to conflict and capacity misses and other optimization techniques such as spatial blocking and Semi-stencil. The aim of this work was to develop a performance model with minimal architectural parameter dependency (flexible) and at the same time reporting accurate results (reliable). In this regard, we have obtained fairly good prediction results, where the average error for most relevant cases floats between 5–15 %. All these results factored in cache's associativities, TLB page size or complex prefetching engine specifications, but are not explicitly modeled.

Our proposed methodology also helps to unveil insights about how stencil codes might be built or executed in order to leverage prefetching efficiency. The prefetching modeling is not straightforward, especially when too many arrays are accessed concurrently, which overwhelm the hardware prefetching system and hamper the bandwidth performance. Furthermore, an aggressive prefetching intervention may also cause eviction of data that could have been reused later (temporal reuse), polluting the cache and affecting adversely the bandwidth performance. Loop fission and data layout transformations can occasionally improve the performance in these cases. Nevertheless, they must be applied carefully because some side effects may appear. In order to effectively capture the stream engine behavior in all above mentioned cases, the *prefetching effectiveness* approach has been adopted. As shown in the experiments, this approach can be successfully used in SMT context, where the prefetching efficiency is substantially reduced due to contention of the shared resources.

The proposed model could be included as static analysis in auto-tuning frameworks to guide making decisions about algorithmic parameters for stencil codes. Likewise, our model might be useful in expert systems, not only for compilers or auto-tuning tools, but also in run-time optimizations for dynamic analysis. For instance, the model might decide the SMT configuration and the number of threads to spawn per processor that outperforms the remaining combinations based on the prefetching engines, the problem size ($I \times J$) and the stencil order (ℓ).

To our knowledge, this is the first stencil model that takes into account two important phenomena: the cache interference (due to $II \times JJ$ and P_{read} parameters) and the prefetching effectiveness when concurrent threads are running in the same core. Despite the current work has been only conducted for 1st order in time and constant coefficient stencils, the model could be adapted to higher orders in time and variable coefficients (anisotropic medium) by adjusting the cost of cache miss cases ($C_{1,2,3,4}$) and their rules ($R_{1,2,3,4}$) through $P_{read,write}$ and $S_{read,write}$ variables.

Future work will include temporal blocking as optimization method, and different thread domain decomposition strategies apart from the static scheduling. Nonetheless, addition of software prefetching behavior into the model is unattainable since it depends on the internal compiler heuristics and the pragmas inserted by the user.

References

1. Araya-Polo, M., Rubio, F., Hanzich, M., de la Cruz, R., Cela, J.M., Scarpazza, D.P.: 3D seismic imaging through reverse-time migration on homogeneous and heterogeneous multi-core processors. Sci. Program. Spec. Issue Cell Processor **17**, 185–198 (2008)
2. Brandenburg, A.: Computational Aspects of Astrophysical MHD and Turbulence, vol. 9. Taylor and Francis, London (2003)
3. Christen, M., Schenk, O., Burkhart, H.: PATUS: A code generation and autotuning framework for parallel iterative stencil computations on modern microarchitectures. In: Proceedings of the 2011 IEEE International Parallel and Distributed Processing Symposium, IPDPS 2011, pp. 676–687. IEEE Computer Society, Washington, DC (2011)
4. Datta, K., Kamil, S., Williams, S., Oliker, L., Shalf, J., Yelick, K.: Optimization and performance modeling of stencil computations on modern microprocessors. SIAM Rev. **51**(1), 129–159 (2009)

5. de la Cruz, R., Araya-Polo, M.: Towards a multi-level cache performance model for 3D stencil computation. In: Proceedings of the International Conference on Computational Science, ICCS 2011. Procedia Computer Science, Singapore, vol. 4, pp. 2146–2155. Elsevier (2011)
6. de la Cruz, R., Araya-Polo, M.: Algorithm 942: semi-stencil. ACM Trans. Math. Softw. **40**(3), 23:1–23:39 (2014)
7. Fang, J., Varbanescu, A.L., Sips, H.J., Zhang, L., Che, Y., Xu, C.: An empirical study of intel xeon phi. CoRR, abs/1310.5842 (2013)
8. De Groot-Hedlin, C.: A finite difference solution to the Helmholtz equation in a radially symmetric waveguide: application to near-source scattering in ocean acoustics. J. Comput. Acoust. **16**, 447–464 (2008)
9. Harper, J.S., Kerbyson, D.J., Nudd, G.R.: Efficient analytical modelling of multi-level set-associative caches. In: Sloot, P.M.A., Hoekstra, A.G., Bubak, M., Hertzberger, B. (eds.) HPCN-Europe 1999. LNCS, vol. 1593, pp. 473–482. Springer, Heidelberg (1999)
10. Kamil, S., Chan, C., Oliker, L., Shalf, J., Williams, S.: An auto-tuning framework for parallel multicore stencil computations. In: Proceedings of the International Parallel and Distributed Processing Symposium (IPDPS), pp. 1–12, April 2010
11. Kamil, S., Datta, K., Williams, S., Oliker, L., Shalf, J., Yelick, K.: Implicit and explicit optimizations for stencil computations. In: MSPC 2006: Proceedings of the 2006 workshop on Memory System Performance and Correctness, pp. 51–60. ACM, New York (2006)
12. Kamil, S., Husbands, P., Oliker, L., Shalf, J., Yelick, K.: Impact of modern memory subsystems on cache optimizations for stencil computations. In: MSP 2005: Proceedings of the 2005 workshop on Memory System Performance, pp. 36–43. ACM Press, New York (2005)
13. Kormann, J., Cobo, P., Prieto, A.: Perfectly matched layers for modelling seismic oceanography experiments. J. Sound Vib. **317**(1–2), 354–365 (2008)
14. Marin, G., McCurdy, C., Vetter, J.S.: Diagnosis and optimization of application prefetching performance. In: Proceedings of the 27th International ACM Conference on International Conference on Supercomputing, ICS 2013, pp. 303–312. ACM, New York (2013)
15. McCalpin, J.D.: Stream: Sustainable memory bandwidth in high performance computers. Technical report, University of Virginia, Charlottesville, Virginia, 1991–2007. A continually updated technical report. http://www.cs.virginia.edu/stream/
16. McCurdy, C., Marin, G., Vetter, J.S.: Characterizing the impact of prefetching on scientific application performance. In: International Workshop on Performance Modeling, Benchmarking and Simulation of HPC Systems (PMBS13), Denver, CO (2013)
17. Mehta, S., Fang, Z., Zhai, A., Yew, P.-C.: Multi-stage coordinated prefetching for present-day processors. In: Proceedings of the 28th ACM International Conference on Supercomputing, ICS 2014, pp. 73–82. ACM, New York (2014)
18. Nishtala, R., Vuduc, R.W., Demmel, J.W., Yelick, K.A.: Performance modeling and analysis of cache blocking in sparse matrix vector multiply. Technical report UCB/CSD-04-1335, EECS Department, University of California, Berkeley (2004)
19. Faizur Rahman, S.M., Yi, Q., Qasem, A.: Understanding stencil code performance on multicore architectures. In: Proceedings of the 8th ACM International Conference on Computing Frontiers, CF 2011, pp. 30:1–30:10. ACM, New York (2011)
20. Ray, A., Kondayya, G., Menon, S.V.G.: Developing a finite difference time domain parallel code for nuclear electromagnetic field simulation. IEEE Trans. Antennas Propag. **54**, 1192–1199 (2006)

21. Rivera, G., Tseng, C.W.: Tiling optimizations for 3D scientific computations. In: Proceedings of the ACM/IEEE Supercomputing Conference (SC 2000), p. 32. IEEE Computer Society, Washington, DC, November 2000
22. Strzodka, R., Shaheen, M., Pajak, D.: Impact of system and cache bandwidth on stencil computation across multiple processor generations. In: Proceedings of the Workshop on Applications for Multi- and Many-Core Processors (A4MMC) at ISCA 2011, June 2011
23. Temam, O., Fricker, C., Jalby, W.: Cache interference phenomena. In: Proceedings of the 1994 ACM SIGMETRICS Conference on Measurement and Modeling of Computer Systems, SIGMETRICS 1994, pp. 261–271. ACM, New York (1994)
24. Treibig, J., Hager, G.: Introducing a performance model for bandwidth-limited loop kernels. In: Wyrzykowski, R., Dongarra, J., Karczewski, K., Wasniewski, J. (eds.) PPAM 2009, Part I. LNCS, vol. 6067, pp. 615–624. Springer, Heidelberg (2010)
25. Williams, S.W., Waterman, A., Patterson, D.A.: Roofline: An insightful visual performance model for floating-point programs and multicore architectures. Technical report UCB/EECS-2008-134, EECS Department, University of California, Berkeley, October 2008

Performance Modeling of the HPCG Benchmark

Vladimir Marjanović[✉], José Gracia, and Colin W. Glass

High Performance Computing Center Stuttgart (HLRS),
University of Stuttgart, Stuttgart, Germany
`marjanovic@hlrs.de`

Abstract. The TOP 500 list is the most widely regarded ranking of modern supercomputers, based on Gflop/s measured for High Performance LINPACK (HPL). Ranking the most powerful supercomputers is important: Hardware producers hone their products towards maximum benchmark performance, while nations fund huge installations, aiming at a place on the pedestal. However, the relevance of HPL for real-world applications is declining rapidly, as the available compute cycles are heavily overrated. While relevant comparisons foster healthy competition, skewed comparisons foster developments aimed at distorted goals. Thus, in recent years, discussions on introducing a new benchmark, better aligned with real-world applications and therefore the needs of real users, have increased, culminating in a highly regarded candidate: High Performance Conjugate Gradients (HPCG).

In this paper we present an in-depth analysis of this new benchmark. Furthermore, we present a model, capable of predicting the performance of HPCG on a given architecture, based solely on two inputs: the effective bandwidth between the main memory and the CPU and the highest occuring network latency between two compute units.

Finally, we argue that within the scope of modern supercomputers with a decent network, only the first input is required for a highly accurate prediction, effectively reducing the information content of HPCG results to that of a stream benchmark executed on one single node.

We conclude with a series of suggestions to move HPCG closer to its intended goal: a new benchmark for modern supercomputers, capable of capturing a well-balanced mixture of relevant hardware properties.

1 Introduction

High Performance Computing (HPC) has emerged as a powerful tool in research and industry. Thus, comparing the power of supercomputers has become a central topic. The HPC community selected the High Performance LINPACK benchmark (HPL) as the central metric, reporting the corresponding Gflop/s for the TOP500 ranking. HPL is an example of a highly scalable MPI program, heavily optimized to squeeze the utmost performance out of parallel machines. Combined with a compute heavy kernel, HPL almost reaches the theoretical Gflop/s peak performance of machines. However, the majority of real-world applications feature kernels which are memory-bound on modern hardware and usually reach

© Springer International Publishing Switzerland 2015
S.A. Jarvis et al. (Eds.): PMBS 2014, LNCS 8966, pp. 172–192, 2015.
DOI: 10.1007/978-3-319-17248-4_9

less than 20 % of the theoretical peak performance [19]. Thus, the current ranking relies purely on a heavily optimized, compute-bound application, arguably very untypical for real-world HPC applications.

The discrepancy in performance between HPL and real-world applications has grown larger over the years, mainly due to a developing trend in computer architectures: the available computing power increases a lot faster than memory speed. The latter therefore limits the data throughput of an increasing number of computational kernels. In HPL this is irrelevant, as the amount of data required per computation (Byte/Flop) is very small. Discussions on HPL's lack of representativity have become more frequent in recent years and a new benchmark was proposed to address the above mentioned issues: High Performance Conjugate Gradients (HPCG). The most expensive kernel of HPCG is dominated by a matrix-vector multiplication. With a Byte/Flop ratio bigger than 4 [10], this kernel shows memory-bound behavior for all current hardware.

In this paper, we present a model capable of predicting the performance of HPCG for a given architecture within 3 % of the real value, based on two simple hardware metrics: effective memory bandwidth from main memory and IC latency. The good predictive power of the model indicates, that only these two hardware metrics are relevant for HPCG performance. Furthermore, the model allows us to extrapolate HPCG's performance to future systems.

The paper is organized as follows: In Sect. 2 on overview of related work is presented. Section 3 describes hardware platforms and software enviroments used in this work. Section 4 explains the transition from the HPL to the HPCG benchmark and analyzes the implementation of HPCG. In Sect. 5 we introduce the performance model. Section 6 evaluates the performance model and predicts the performance of HPCG on future systems. Finally, in Sect. 7 we draw conclusions and discuss future work.

2   Related Work

In this section we give a short overview on related work, in particular alternative benchmarks to quantify the performance of HPC systems and performance models for these benchmarks where available.

While HPCG and HPL both consist of a single application which is dominated by a single kernel, the NAS parallel benchmark [4,5] is a collection of small applications or kernels from the fields of computational fluid dynamics, linear algebra, etc. A MPI + OpenMP version has been presented and analyzed in [9]. Similarly, the SPEC MPI2007 benchmark suite [17] is a collection of MPI-parallel compute-intensive applications which has been analyzed in [21]. While the type of applications used in both of these benchmark suites make up a significant part of the workload in most supercomputing centers, the resulting number is in both cases a somewhat arbitrarily weighted total execution time. Further, these benchmarks do not explicitly target scalability of very large machines.

The HPC Challenge benchmark [16] in contrast consists of very low-level kernels (including HPL, Stream, FFT, Random Access, etc.), but does not try to produce a single aggregated metric out of these. Instead the individual benchmarks can be used to measure specific characteristics of a systems. For instance, this paper uses a Stream benchmark to quantify the effective memory bandwidth. Similarly, Random Access can be used to measure the latency of remote memory accesses, and FFT to quantify the quality of all-to-all communication capabilities.

The most widely used benchmark to characterize the performance of supercomputers is still HPL [18]. Discussions on shortcomings of HPL can be found in [11,13].

The proposed new benchmark HPCG investigated here is based on a iterative sparse-matrix Conjugate Gradient kernel. The initial version of HPCG, i.e. v1.0, used a simple additive Schwarz pre-conditioner and symmetric Gauss-Seidel sweep for each sub-domain [11]. The pre-conditioner was replaced in version 2.0 with a multi-grid approach using 3 levels of coarsening. Effectively, this is a kind of tiling of the algorithm and allows to use the caches more effectively. Performance analysis of pre-conditioners is a vast field of research. Here we mention only [3], discussing a multi-grid approach similar to the one used in HPCG, and [6] for a survey of various other techniques. Most pre-conditioners use sparse-matrix vector multiplication which was modelled and optimized for instance in [7,8]. An other important part of the benchmark is network communication, were related work includes [20] on simulators for network interconnects, [14,15] on modeling of collective MPI operations and [22] on MPI communication overhead analysis.

3   Platform

In this section we describe the hardware and explain the software stack used in this work. Real performance data on HPCG (version 2.4) was collected on three different platforms, which shall be referred to as A, B and C. Furthermore, as will be described in Sect. 6, large validation runs were performed on a further platform not included in the process of modelling.

- The *platform A* is based on the XC30 architecture. It contains 64 nodes with 2 chips of the Intel SandyBridge 2,6 GHz E5-2670 per node. Each chip has 8 cores (16 HT) with 20 MB of shared L3 cache per chip and 4 memory channels connected with DDR3 1600 MHz, which makes the maximum memory bandwidth 51.2 GB/s. The cores use "Turbo Boost" technology that allows to increase the frequency to 3.3 GHz as long as the thermal budget is not exceeded. All of the cores can execute 8 Flop per cycle. Peak performance per socket is 166.4 Gflop/s. The interconnection network is an Aries [1] with a Dragonfly topology, a bandwidth of up to 117 GB/s per node and a latency between the closest nodes of less than 2 μs.
- The *platform B* is based on AMD Opteron Interlagos 6276 processors (2 chips per node). Each chip has 16 cores and 16 MB of shared L3 cache. The Interlagos with DDR3 PC3-12800 gives a memory bandwidth of 51.2 GB/s. Each core

runs at 2.3 GHz (up to 3.2 GHz with TurboCore) and can execute 4 Flop per cycle. Peak performance per socket is 147.2 Gflop/s. The interconnect is of the type Gemini [2] with a 3D torus topology, 160 GB/s bandwidth per node and the lowest latency of 2 μs.

On platforms A and B, we use the GNU Programming Environment: C/C++ GNU Compiler 4.8, MPICH-6.2 Cray MPI library that uses the MPICH2 distribution from Argonne.

– The *platform C* is based on Intel Xeon X5560 chips (Nehalem), it contains 2 chips per node. The chip contains 4 cores (8 HT) and works at 2.80 GHz (3.20 GHz maximum for Turbo Boost). The L3 cache size is 8 MB, 3 channels with 1333 MHz memory interface which delivers 32 GB/s. Peak performance per socket is 44.8 Gflop/s.

The Infiniband interconnect of platform C uses Voltaire Grid Director 4036 switches with 36 QDR (40Gbps) ports (6 backbone switches). We use C/C++ GNU Compiler 4.8 and the OpenMPI library 1.6.5.

4   From the HPL to the HPCG Benchmark

In this section, we review the HPCG benchmark. First we comment on the importance and relevance of a new benchmark for comparing the most powerful supercomputers in the world, then we describe the structure and routines of the implementation.

4.1   Transition

Two times per year, the TOP500 project publishes a ranking of the worlds most powerful supercomputers. The ranking is based on performance achieved for HPL, measured in Gflop/s. HPL implements a LU decomposition with partial pivoting.

The TOP500 measurement rules allows modifying the internal functions and tuning input parameters for an optimal result. This modification freedom has lead to significant restructuring of the code and redesigns of the input. Meanwhile, HPL is a highly optimized software package. Furthermore, the arbitrary problem size, combined with the compute complexity $\mathcal{O}(N^3)$ of the matrix multiplication, implies selecting the largest problem size that fits to the main memory. This straight forward choice leads to such enormous costs of the main kernel, that everything else becomes effectively irrelevant. Furthermore, due to the nature of the kernel, the Byte/Flop ratio is small and it is therefore purely compute-bound. HPL is a non-trivial code with complex communication patterns. However, for the reasons explained above the performance-optimized HPL runs display an almost identical behaviour to a pure matrix multiplication and reach around 90 % of the theoretical peak performance.

Real-world applications usually do not have such an increadibly expensive compute-bound kernel, but a more diverse set of kernels, which do not dwarf communication costs. Furthermore, many kernels have large Byte/Flop ratios, rendering them memory-bound. Thus, with real applications 20 % of theoretical peak is considered very good. Finally, the trend in hardware development points towards decreasing ratios of available Bytes per Flop, which will decrease the achievable percentage of theoretical peak even further.

The lacking representativity of HPL is increasingly a matter of general discussion. HPCG has been developed with these discussions in mind, aiming at a far superior representativity. HPCG is not intended to replace HPL, but rather to complement it.

HPCG features the same freedom regarding modification of routines and problem size as HPL and retains Gflop/s as the unique evaluation metric. The crucial difference between HPL and HPCG is the respective main computational kernel. While in HPL it is a matrix multiplication, in HPCG it is a matrix vector multiplication. As we will show, the higher Byte/Flop of the matrix vector multiplication renders it memory-bound on current and most likely future hardware, leading to a better representativity for real-world applications.

4.2 HPCG Structure and Routines

In this paper, we used the HPCG version 2.4 without any further modification. The code is written in C/C++ and for parallelization the user can select MPI and/or OpenMP at compile time. The problem size and minimum execution time is specified in the input file. In order to produce official results, the execution time has to be at least 1 h. The authors of HPCG suggested to increase the minimal problem size to achieve a memory footprint beyond L3 cache sizes [12], but this is currently not contained in the requirements for the benchmark (currently the minimal size is 16,16,16).

Comparing MPI with hybrid MPI/OpenMP on homogeneous clusters, we decide to model only pure MPI execution, as the performance is much higher than for hybrid execution. There are two main reasons for it: First, the HPCG algorithm is well balanced on MPI level, and the OpenMP dynamic balancing feature cannot deliver any performance improvement, and second, OpenMP threads are idle during communication operation due to the fork/join model which lead to performance drop.

The HPCG benchmark (version 2.4) is based on a conjugate gradient solver, where the pre-conditioner is a three-level hierarchical multi-grid method (MG) with Gauss-Seidel relaxation. The number of iterations is fixed at 50 per set, which is sufficient for the residual to drop below 1^{-6}. The structure of the main loop is shown in Fig. 1.

The algorithm starts with MG that contains symmetric Gauss-Seidel (SYMGS) and sparse matrix-vector multiplication(SpMV) for each depth level. Data is distributed across nodes, thus SYMGS and SpMV require data from their neighbors. Their predecessor, an exchange halos(ExchangeHalos) routine, provides data for SYMGS and SpMV, therefore performing communication with neighbors. An iteration within the main loop also calls the SpMV/ExchangeHalos pair. Dot product (DDOT) locally computes the residual, while MPI_Allreduce

```
for ( i = 0; i<50 && normr>err; i++ ){
  MG(A,r,z);
  DDOT( r ,t ,rtz );
  Allreduce ( rtz );                    /*MG routine*/

  if( i > 1 )                           if( depth <3){
    beta = rtz/rtzold;                    ExchangeHalos( );
    WAXPBY( z, beta, p );                 SYMGS( );
                                          ExchangeHalos( );
  ExchangeHalos( A, p);                   SpMV( );
  SpMV( A, p, Ap );                       MG( depth++ )
  DDOT ( p, Ap, pAp );                    ExchangeHalos( );
  Allreduce ( pAp);                       SYMGS( );
  alpha =rtz/pAp;                       }else{
  WAXPBY( x, alpha, p);                   ExchangeHalos( );
  WAXPBY( r, -alpha, Ap);                 SYMGS( );
  DDOT( r, r, normr );                  }
  Allreduce (normr);

  normr = sqrt( normr);
}
```

Fig. 1. Pseudocode of the HPCG main loop and the Multi-Grid routine. Modeled routines are basic blocks for the HPCG pseudocode.

follows DDOT and completes a global dot product operation. WAXPBY updates a vector with the sum of two scaled vectors.

The routines SYMGS, SpMV, WAXPBY, DDOT are the basic computational blocks of HPCG, while the routines MPI_Allreduce and ExchangeHalos are the basic communication blocks. In the next section we discuss internals of these routines and how they are modelled.

5   Model

In this section, we describe basic considerations for modelling the performance of HPCG. From these considerations, the executing time of every routine is derived. In combination with an estimation of the number of Flop, this results in a model for predicting the Gflop/s which can be achieved with HPCG on a given hardware (Fig. 2).

5.1   Basic Considerations

Estimating execution time of a routine requires the following information: type and number of operations of the routine, the size of memory used by the routine and technical information on the machine (system description).

Large HPC machines in essence consist of two parts: shared memory nodes for computation and the interconnection network responsible for communication between nodes.

We discuss and model two distinct classes of routines: computational and communication. Communication depends on the interconnection characteristics, while computation depends on the characteristics of the compute nodes.

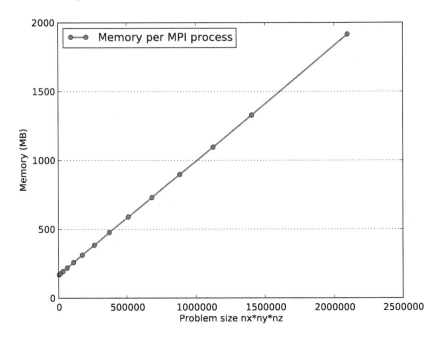

Fig. 2. Required memory per MPI process for different problem sizes of HPCG.

Memory vs. Compute Bound. The execution of a computational kernel contains two phases:

– Memory operations, *i.e.* fetching data from memory and writing results back
– Execution of arithmetic and logic operations

The memory speed and the amount of data determine the execution time of memory operations, while the CPU clock speed, Flop per cycle, amount and type of operations define the execution time of computation. The more expensive of the two, memory operations vs. computation, limits the performance and thus renders the overall kernel memory- or compute-bound.

The metric Byte/Flop quantifies the amount of data a kernel requires to perform one Flop. When used for hardware, it quantifies the maximum amount of data which can be delivered per available Flop.

HPCG mainly performs a matrix-vector operation on sparse matrices. The number of Flop to be performed is $2 * nnz$, where nnz is the total number of non-zero elements. The size of one float (double) is 8 Bytes and the required memory is $(nnz + 2 * n) * 8$ Bytes, where n is the matrix dimension. For large problem sizes $nnz \approx 27 * n$. The Byte/Flop requirement of HPCG is therefore $\approx (28/27 * nnz * 8 Bytes)/(2 * nnz Flop) > 4$ Byte/Flop.

In order to check the limitation of HPCG we compare the Byte/Flop demand of HPCG with the respective values for the used hardware, as shown in Table 1.

Clearly, HPCG is memory-bound, as the amount of Flop that can be executed is limited by the maximum data throughput of the respective platform.

Table 1. Performance for platforms A-C in terms of Byte/Flop and the Byte/Flop requirement for HPCG.

	HPCG	Platform A	Platform B	Platform C
Byte/Flop	> 4	0.3077	0.3478	0.7142

Furthermore, none of the TOP500 machines offers anywhere near 4 Byte/Flop. A vector processor delivers up to 1 Byte/Flop, while a scalar processor usually delivers less than 0.5 Byte/Flop.

Thus, knowing the effective bandwidth and the required data for a given routine directly allows us to model the execution time. The theoretical peak of memory bandwidth is not reachable due to the internal implementation of the processor architecture and its resources. Further, there is no reliable way to estimate the effective memory bandwidth from the theoretical one. Therefore, measuring the effective bandwidth is an unavoidable step and in this work we use the Triad stream benchmark kernel. Usually one core cannot exploit the whole memory bandwidth of a socket, so we occupy all cores with a stream kernel, measuring the total effective memory bandwidth of the socket. From this, we compute the average effective memory bandwidth per core and use it for the performance model.

Communication. In HPCG there is collective communication (MPI_Allreduce) and the routine HaloExchange, performing a set of point-to-point communication.

The amount of data in the MPI_Allreduce is independent of the problem size. However, the cost of the collective routine increases with number of MPI processes (N) and therefore becomes relevant for very large supercomputers.

The amount of data communicated in HaloExchange depends on the problem size. However, the cost is independent of N.

Problem Size. We evaluated HPCG on the node level for different problem sizes. Figure 3 shows performance results in terms of Gflop/s for different problem sizes, running on three different platforms. Minimum problem size corresponds to the minimal size allowed for the benchmark, 16x16x16 3D sparse matrix per MPI process. We distinguish three different phases: problem size that fits to the L3 cache, a transition phase and a constant performance regime. The smallest possible problem size requires 2.1 MB per core and only fits to the L3 cache of the platform A (2.5 MB/core). In the transition phase the problem is only slightly larger than L3 cache and the performance depends strongly on the cache properties. For larger problem sizes the performance asymptotically approaches a constant value and depends on the effective memory bandwidth to main memory only.

If the memory footprint fits to the L3 cache, the kernels still are memory bound, however, the effective bandwidth of interest is to L3 cache instead of to main memory. The difference in these bandwidths is large. We argue that, while

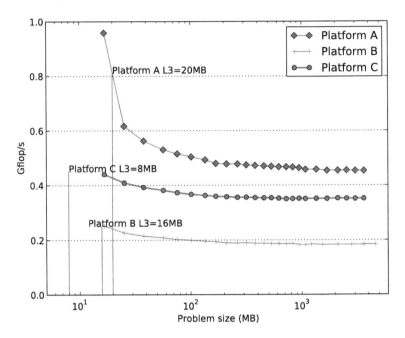

Fig. 3. Gflop/s of computational routines for different problem sizes.

the bandwidth to main memory is a relevant metric regarding the suitability of a given hardware for real-world applications, the size of the L3 cache is less relevant. It therefore makes little sense that the size of the L3 cache has a large impact on the measured performance. We suggest therefore to increase the minimal problem size, in order to avoid this scenario, which is in line with the opinion of the authors [12]. In the following we will assume this limitation is in place.

5.2   Modelling Computational Routines

The execution time of all computational kernels depend on the size of the 3D sparse matrix and the number of non-zero elements per local row. The number of local rows is equal to $nx * ny * nz$, while the number of non-zero elements in a row is 27 or fewer. The number 27 is hardcoded within the benchmark. The limit is shown below:

$$\lim_{nx*ny*nz \to \infty} numberOfNonzerosPerRow = 27$$

For a large problem size we consider the number of non-zeros as equal to 27. Instances of computational routines called directly from the main loop work on the whole domain, while the MG routine calls recursively a set of computational routines, reducing the resolution per depth. We will discuss the MG routine further down.

The number of outer iterations (LNI) appears in all computational kernels and sub-kernels:

$$LNI = \frac{nx * ny * nz}{2^{3*d}}$$

SYMGS. The Symmetric Gauss-Seidel Method is the most expensive routine in the benchmark (except for MG, which is a combination of routines). It performs two steps: forward and backward sweeps. Regarding the memory footprint and number and type of operations, the two steps are identical. Each step performs a two dimensional loop, the outer number of iterations being LNI and the inner number 27. Pseudo code is shown below:

```
Loop j=1..LNI(depth)
  Loop i=1..27
    c[i]+=a[j]*b[index[j]
  endloop
  c[i]+=d[i]*b[i]
  b[i]=c[i]/d[i]
endloop
```

The kernel is based on a Flop with double precision, where one factor has indirect addressing. The two dimensional loop fetches two doubles and one integer in each iteration which makes 20 Bytes in total (arrays a and b in pseudo code). The process unit also fetches arrays c and d in the outer loop and a number of non-zero elements, which increases the total size of data in memory. We model the execution time by dividing the required data by the effective bandwidth from main memory($BWeff$):

$$executionSYMGS(sec) = 2 * \frac{LNI * (20 + 20 * 27)(Bytes)}{BWeff(Bytes/sec)}$$

SpMV. The SpMV routine is very similar to SYMGS, but performs only one step. The pseudo code is:

```
Loop j=1..LNI(depth)
  Loop i=1..27
    c[i]+=a[j]*b[index[j]
  endloop
  d[i]=c[i]
endloop
```

The number of iterations, memory accesses and main computational operations are the same for both routines. The model is therefore analoguous to above (Fig. 4):

$$executionSpMV(sec) = \frac{LNI * (20 + 20 * 27)(Bytes)}{BWeff(Bytes/sec)}$$

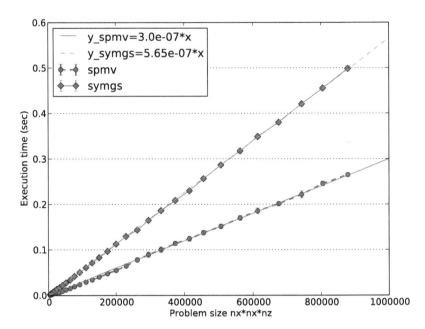

Fig. 4. Modeled and measured execution time of the two most expensive computational routines.

WAXPB. The WAXPB routine behaves like a triad vector kernel, which is the most complex scenario of all stream vector kernels. The update of two scaled vectors is shown below.

```
Loop i=1..LNI(depth=0)
  c[i]=alfa*a[i]+beta*b[i]
endloop
```

Vectors a, b and c contain elements of size double. So, 24 Bytes from memory are required for every iteration. The number of iterations is always the same for a given input set as only the main loop calls the WAXPB routine directly. The execution time is modelled as:

$$executionWAXPB(sec) = \frac{LNI * 24(Bytes)}{BWeff(Bytes/sec)}$$

DDOT. First the DDOT routine computes locally a dot product before performing a global sum operation across the system. The multiplication of vector elements and accumulation of the results into a single variable in pseudo code:

```
Loop i=1..LNI(depth=0)
  c+=a[i]*b[i]
endloop
```

While computationally WAXPB and DDOT are different, their memory footprint is very similar. However, the DDOT routine only requires 16 Bytes per iteration. The execution time without communication is modelled as:

$$executionDDOT(sec) = \frac{LNI * 16(Bytes)}{BWeff(Bytes/sec)}$$

5.3   Modelling Communication

We execute HPCG in parallel using MPI, which requires static data distribution across processes with separated address spaces. Naturally, the data decomposition is 3-dimensional due to the 3D sparse matrix. Each process receives the same input size and the algorithm is almost perfectly load balanced. Communication between processes uses the MPI interface and there are two communication routines: MPI_Allreduce that finalizes the DDOT routine and a halo exchange between neighbouring MPI processes.

Both routines use the MPI_COMM_WORLD communicator. There is no interleaving of communication between different communicators, which makes routing in the IC network easy. Both routines use blocking MPI calls and the nature of the algorithm holds no potential for overlapping communication and computation. The communication behaves as synchronization points for all processes.

Collective. The MPI_Allreduce is the only collective communication used in the algorithm. The operation reduces a single variable of size double over all processes. As with all collective operations, the MPI_Allreduce implementation relies on point-to-point communication and the optimal implementation depends on the topology of the IC network itself. The hypercube algorithm performs reduce among N processes in $log(N)$ steps. The algorithm reduces the information in the least number of steps necessary and shows the highest efficiency for regular topologies. The amount of data per communication step is 8 Bytes, thus we consider the latency between processes as the only relevant IC parameter and disregard the bandwidth in the model (Fig. 5).

For N MPI processes and a given latency l between processes, we predict the execution time of a MPI_Allreduce operation as

$$executionAllreduce(sec) = \sum_{i=1}^{M} l_i(log(M_i) - log(M_{i-1}))$$

Each index refers to a group of processes with the same latency. E.g. l_0 refers to the latency between MPIs within a socket, l_1 refers to the latency between MPIs within a node that are located on different sockets, l_2 refers to the latency between MPIs within a blade that are located on different nodes etc. M_i is the maximum number of MPI processes in a group with the same latency time.

Point to Point. The halo exchange is a nearest-neighbor data exchange. It is a common communication pattern for MPI-HPC applications. The number of neighbors of a given MPI process depends on the location in the decomposition

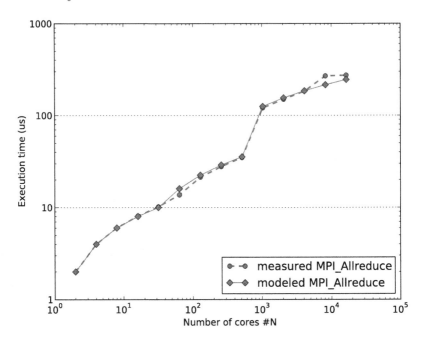

Fig. 5. Modeled and measured execution time of the MPI_Allreduce operation (8 Byte)

grid, the maximum being 26 neighbors. If HPCG is run on 27 or more MPI processes at least one process has 26 neighbors in the halo exchange phase. The maximum data size that one process receives or sends during a single halo exchange instance is:

$$maxHaloSize(Bytes) = (2(nx * ny + nx * nz + ny * nz) + \\ 4(nx + ny + nz) + 8) * 8Bytes$$

The MG routine calls the halo exchange from different depths, reducing the halo size by a factor of $2^{2*depth}$. Figure 6 shows the execution time of the ExchangeHalos routine for different problem sizes. Rendezvous protocol introduces a significant performance drop which should be part of the model.

We assume the minimal effective bandwidth for data movement across the IC in the halo exchange (IC_BW_{eff}). As even for large workloads maxHaloSize is relatively small for modern IC networks, the overhead of the MPI call plays an important role. Halo exchange is achieved through a sequence of MPI_Irecv, MPI_Send and MPI_Wait. The overall model is:

$$executionHaloEx(sec) = \frac{maxHaloSize}{IC\_BW_{eff}} + 26(overhead(Irecv, Send, Wait)) + \\ overhead(Rendezvousprotocol)$$

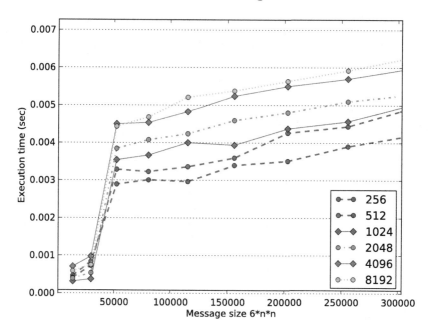

Fig. 6. Measured execution time of halo exchange for platform B with increasing message size. The impact of the rendezvous protocol is clearly visible as a jump in execution time.

The overheads for Irecv, Send and Wait can be directly determined from the latency, the overhead of the rendezvous protocol is determined from the MPI pingpong benchmark. The latter can be easily avoided by adjusting the corresponding parameter, however, as it barely impacts the model, we did not do so.

5.4 Modelling the Whole Benchmark

MG – A Combination of Routines. The MG routine combines multiple routines and calls them from different depths. The multi-grid level decreases the problem size by $2^{3*depth}$.

Thus, larger depth indicates smaller problem size and shorter execution time. In the forward recursion phase, the MG calls the sequence HaloEx-SYMGS-HaloEx-SpMV up to depth 2, while depth 3 performs only HaloEx-SYMGS. The backward recursion phase calls HaloEx-SYMGS. The following sum gives the execution time of the MG routine.

$$execution MG = HaloEx(depth = 3) + SYMGS(depth = 3) +$$
$$\sum_{depth=0}^{2} (2 * SYMGS(depth) + SpMV(depth) + 3 * HaloEx(depth))$$

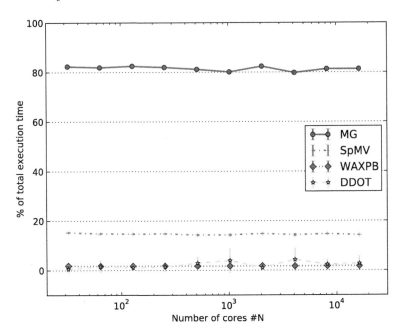

Fig. 7. Percentage of HPCG total execution time per routine. Measured on platform B.

Table 2. Effective memory bandwidth measured by using the Triad stream kernel and minimal/maximal IC latency measured by the osu mpi benchmark.

	Platform A	Platform B	Platform C
BWeff(MB/s) per core	4705	1700	3430
IC latency(μs) (min, max)	2 4	2 90	4 240

Total Execution Time. The main loop does 50 iterations, calling the sequence MG-DDOT-WAXPB-SpMV-DDOT-WAXPB-WAXPB-DDOT. The first iteration calls one instance of WAXPB less, we forgo considering this in the model. Thus, the execution time of one iteration is modelled as:

$$totalTime = MG + SpMV(depth = 0) + 3(DDOT + WAXPB)$$

Predicting Gflop/s. In order to calculate the Gflop/s, HPCG predicts the number of floating point operations necessary per routine and measures the execution time. Input data set and the total number of non-zeros define the total number of floating point operations. If we assume 27 non-zero elements per row for a large problem size, the total number of non-zero elements is:

$$nnz = N * nx * ny * nz * 27$$

The resulting total number of floating point operation is:

$$MG_{flop} = 10 * (nnz + nnz/8 + nnz/64) + 4 * (nnz/128)$$

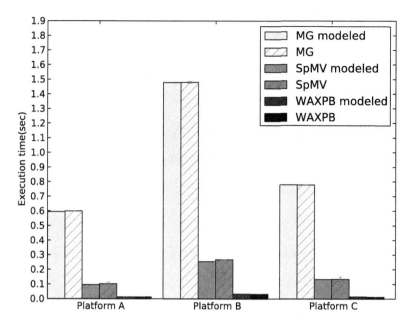

Fig. 8. Predicted vs. measured execution time per computational routine for platforms A-C.

$$SMPV_{flop} = 2 * nnz$$
$$DDOT_{flop} = 6 * N * nx * ny * nz$$
$$WAXPB_{flop} = 6 * N * nx * ny * nz$$

Combined with the prediction of the execution time, this allows us to predict the achieved Gflop/s and thus completes the performance model of HPCG. The model is suitable for large problem sizes (per MPI process) and is viable even for very large systems, which matches the HPCG target as a new benchmark for the TOP500 list.

6   Results

We have validated the proposed performance model by comparing predicted performance values to measured results. The model shows excellent predictability of HPCG performance. Based on the model we then predicted the performance on envisioned future systems.

6.1   Validating the Model

The essential part of the HPCG model is a prediction of computational routines which have almost constant execution time for different numbers of cores.

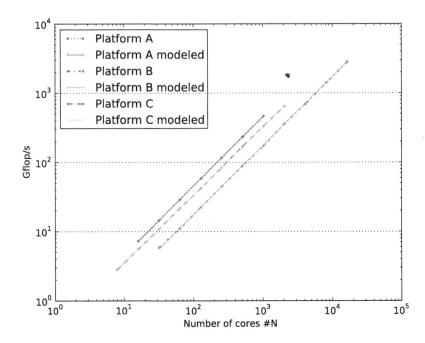

Fig. 9. Measured performance results vs. the prediction for HPCG on platforms A-C.

We analyze the HPCG routines for a large problem size and different number of cores. For all data shown, large refers to the size (96x96x96) per core. Figure 7 compares percentages of execution time per routine, measured on platform B. The MG pre-conditioner clearly is the most expensive routine, taking more than 80 % of the total execution time and very slowly become less important for larger numbers of cores, while the MPI_Allreduce slowly becomes more important. The computational routines take more than 98 % of the total execution time.

In order to determine the effective bandwidth to main memory and the latency of the IC, we obtained results by using the Triad stream benchmark kernel and a MPI pingpong benchmark respectively. Table 2 shows results for the different platforms.

Figure 8 compares the measured and modeled HPCG computational routines per node for platforms A-C.

Figure 9 shows the measured performance results vs. the predicted performance for the whole benchmark. As can be seen, HPCG scales approximately linearly with N and the performance predictions from our model are very accurate (deviations of less than 2 %).

Finally, we tested our model by predicting the performance for a full HPC system, of which we had no performance data during model creation, and subsequently comparing to the real performance results. This supercomputer is based on XC40 nodes and an Aries interconnection network. Each node contains two Intel Haswell E5-2680v3 2,5 GHz, 12 cores per socket with 128 GB of DDR4-2133 RAM memory. Each socket has 30 MB of L3 cache. Having determined the

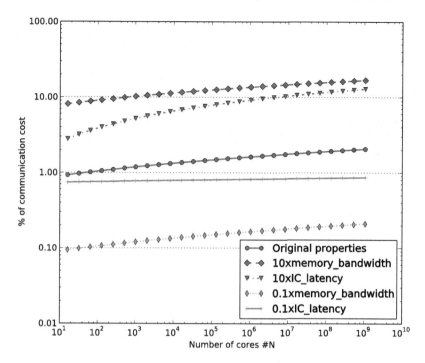

Fig. 10. Extrapolating the relative importance of communication cost in HPCG to huge HPC systems. Original properties reflect the platform B, the other lines are predictions for systems differing in IC latency or effective memory bandwidth, respectively, by one order of magnitude.

effective memory bandwidth (3740 MB/s per core) and the maximum IC latency (3 μs), we predicted the performance and then ran HPCG across all 3900 nodes (93600 cores) with a problem size of (nx,ny,nz)=(144,144,144) per MPI process. Our model predicts the overall performance to within 1 % of the real value.

6.2   Extrapolating HPCG Performance to Future Systems

High requirements for Byte/Flops renders the computational kernels of HPCG memory-bound for all modern machines. In order to predict HPCG benchmarking potential for future exascale systems, we consider that all computational kernels will remain memory-bound, which is to be expected.

Further, communication obviously costs time without producing Flop/s. Therefore, it is to be expected that the benchmark will be run with the largest problem size which fits to the main memory in order to increase the computation to communication ratio. This is analoguous to what can be observed for the HPL benchmark. Machines featured in the TOP500 currently have 2 GB of main memory or more per physical core. According to the memory usage formula from Sect. 4 the largest problem size which fits to main memory is (128,128,128) per MPI process and we assume future systems will have similar amounts of main memory per core.

Communication cost grows with N due to the MPI_Allreduce. In Fig. 10 we show an extrapolation to very large numbers of cores for platform B, the problem size is taken as (128,128,128). We have evaluated for the current hardware properties, and furthermore changed one property at a time by one order of magnitude. For the current setting, the communication cost stays below 1,2 % of the entire execution time for machines with up to one million cores. Furthermore, for one billion cores, the communication still costs below 3 %. As can be seen in Fig. 10, unless the available Byte/Flop ratio or the IC latency increase significantly for future systems, the communication cost will remain irrelevant even at the exascale.

7   Conclusion

The TOP500 list relies on HPL, a benchmark increasingly unrepresentative for the performance issues real-world applications face today. Thus, as hardware vendour try to boost HPL results, hardware development is subtly steered towards increasing overall compute cycles and frequencies, which cannot be exploited and even introduce overheads in energy consumption. HPCG, a prominent candidate for the next step in supercomputer benchmarks, moves into the right direction: by featuring memory-bound kernels, it reflects the bottlenecks of real-world applications more realistically.

As we have demonstrated in this paper, it is possible to predict the performance of HPCG with accuracy, relying only on two numbers: effective memory bandwidth from main memory and highest occurring IC latency. Obviously, the logical conclusion is, that the performance of HPCG only depends on these two numbers. The effective memory bandwidth determines the necessary time to execute the computational kernels, as the limiting factor is the availability of data to perform computations on. The IC latency determines the time to perform the MPI_Allreduce, as the amount of data (per process) being communicated is only 8 bytes and therefore IC bandwidth is irrelevant. The MPI_Allreduce is the only relevant communication, as it's time requirement increases with $\log(N)$, while the point-to-point communication is constant in N.

Furthermore, as shown in the paper, the problem size is extremely relevant. Especially, the smallest hitherto allowed problem size can fit into the L3 cache on certain hardware. In this case, the effective bandwidth of interest of course is to the L3 cache, which is a lot higher then to the main memory, speeding up the benchmark accordingly. We argue that this is a problem: Hardware with sufficiently large L3 cache get a huge competitive edge, which is not sensible. We argue the problem size should have a much more restrictive lower limit, to ensure it does not fit to L3 cache, as discussed in [12]. Given that small problem sizes will be restricted, the obvious choice will be to increase the problem size to the limit of main memory, thereby diminishing the relative cost of communication. We have shown that for a representative current supercomputer architecture, this strategy effectively dwarves communication cost. Keeping the hardware specifications and extrapolating to a system with one billion cores, the communication cost is less than 3 %. Thus, even the IC latency can be effectively ignored, rendering the overall performance approximately proportional to the effective memory bandwidth of one single node.

Thus, HPCG is in danger of encountering the same problems as HPL: by allowing arbitrary problem sizes only one system property is relevant for the final result, while the performance of real-world applications depends on a much more diverse set of properties. We suggest this approach be reconsidered. Even simple changes to the execution protocol could drastically improve on this. For example, running a suite of short simulations with varying, predefined system sizes and reporting the (weighted) average performance.

Our model targets performance prediction for the official, unmodified HPCG benchmark (version 2.4) run on homogeneous clusters. In the future, we plan to extend our model to heterogeneous architectures, *e.g.* featuring GPGPU and Xeon Phi accelerators.

Acknowledgements. The authors would like to thank Mandes Schönherr for valuable contributions. This research is partly supported by EU project POLCA (FP7-ICT-2013-10, grant agreement no. 610686).

References

1. Alverson, B., Froese, E., Kaplan, L., Roweth, D.: Cray xc® series network
2. Alverson, R., Roweth, D., Kaplan, L.: The gemini system interconnect. In: 2010 IEEE 18th Annual Symposium on High Performance Interconnects (HOTI), pp. 83–87. IEEE (2010)
3. Ashby, S.F., Falgout, R.D.: A parallel multigrid preconditioned conjugate gradient algorithm for groundwater flow simulations. Nucl. Sci. Eng. **124**(1), 145–159 (1996)
4. Bailey, D.H., Barszcz, E. Barton, J.T., Browning, D.S., Carter, R.L., Dagum, L., Fatoohi, R.A., Frederickson, P.O., Lasinski, T.A., Schreiber, R.S., Simon, H.D., Venkatakrishnan, V., Weeratunga, S.K.: The NAS parallel benchmarks—summary and preliminary results. In: Proceedings of the 1991 ACM/IEEE Conference on Supercomputing, Supercomputing 1991, pp. 158–165, ACM, New York (1991)
5. Bailey, D.H., Barszcz, E., Barton, J.T., Browning, D.S., Carter, R.L., Fatoohi, R.A., Frederickson, P.O., Lasinski, T.A., Simon, H.D., Venkatakrishnan, V., Weeratunga, S.K.: The NAS parallel benchmarks. Technical report, The International Journal of Supercomputer Applications (1991)
6. Benzi, M.: Preconditioning techniques for large linear systems: a survey. J. Comput. Phys. **182**(2), 418–477 (2002)
7. Bolz, J., Farmer, I., Grinspun, E., Schröoder, P.: Sparse matrix solvers on the GPU: conjugate gradients and multigrid. In: ACM Transactions on Graphics (TOG), vol. 22, pp. 917–924. ACM, New York (2003)
8. Buluc, A., Williams, S., Oliker, L., Demmel, J.: Reduced-bandwidth multithreaded algorithms for sparse matrix-vector multiplication. In: 2011 IEEE International on Parallel and Distributed Processing Symposium (IPDPS), pp. 721–733. IEEE (2011)
9. Cappello, F., Etiemble, D.: MPI versus MPI+OpenMP on the IBM SP for the NAS benchmarks. In: ACM/IEEE 2000 Conference Supercomputing, p. 12. IEEE (2000)

10. Demmel, J., Hoemmen, M., Mohiyuddin, M., Yelick, K.: Avoiding communication in sparse matrix computations. In: IEEE International Symposium on Parallel and Distributed Processing, IPDPS 2008, pp. 1–12. IEEE (2008)
11. Dongarra, J., Heroux, M.A.: Toward a new metric for ranking high performance computing systems. Sandia report, SAND2013-4744, 312 (2013)
12. Dongarra, J., Luszczek, P.: HPCG: one year later. In: ISC 2014 (2014)
13. Heroux, M.A., Dongarra, J., Luszczek, P.: HPCG benchmark technical specification. Technical report, October 2013
14. Hoefler, T., Gropp, W., Thakur, R., Träff, J.L.: Toward performance models of MPI implementations for understanding application scaling issues. In: Keller, R., Gabriel, E., Resch, M., Dongarra, J. (eds.) EuroMPI 2010. LNCS, vol. 6305, pp. 21–30. Springer, Heidelberg (2010)
15. Hoefler, T., Lumsdaine, A., Rehm, W.: Implementation and performance analysis of non-blocking collective operations for MPI. In: Proceedings of the 2007 ACM/IEEE Conference on Supercomputing, SC 2007, pp. 1–10. IEEE (2007)
16. Luszczek, P., Dongarra, J.J., Koester, D., Rabenseifner, R., Lucas, B., Kepner, J., McCalpin, J., Bailey, D., Takahashi, D.: Introduction to the HPC Challenge Benchmark Suite. Lawrence Berkeley National Laboratory (2005)
17. Muller, M.S., van Waveren, M., Lieberman, R., Whitney, B., Saito, H., Kumaran, K., Baron, J., Brantley, W.C., Parrott, C., Elken, T., et al.: SPEC MPI2007an application benchmark suite for parallel systems using MPI. Concurr. Comput.: Prac. Exp. **22**(2), 191–205 (2010)
18. Petitet, A.: HPL-A portable implementation of the high-performance linpack benchmark for distributed-memory computers (2004). http://www.netlib.org/benchmark/hpl/
19. Shalf, J., Dosanjh, S., Morrison, J.: Exascale computing technology challenges. In: Palma, J.M.L.M., Daydé, M., Marques, O., Lopes, J.C. (eds.) VECPAR 2010. LNCS, vol. 6449, pp. 1–25. Springer, Heidelberg (2011)
20. Smith, J.E., Taylor, W.R.: Accurate modelling of interconnection networks in vector supercomputers. In: Proceedings of the 5th International Conference on Supercomputing, pp. 264–273. ACM, New York (1991)
21. Szebenyi, Z., Wylie, B.J.N., Wolf, F.: SCALASCA parallel performance analyses of SPEC MPI2007 applications. In: Kounev, S., Gorton, I., Sachs, K. (eds.) SIPEW 2008. LNCS, vol. 5119, pp. 99–123. Springer, Heidelberg (2008)
22. Xu, Z., Hwang, K.: Modeling communication overhead: MPI and MPL performance on the IBM SP2. IEEE Parallel Distrib. Technol.: Syst. Appl. **4**(1), 9–24 (1996)

On the Performance Prediction of BLAS-based Tensor Contractions

Elmar Peise$^{(\boxtimes)}$, Diego Fabregat-Traver, and Paolo Bientinesi

AICES, RWTH Aachen, Aachen, Germany
{peise,fabregat,pauldj}@aices.rwth-aachen.de

Abstract. Tensor operations are surging as the computational building blocks for a variety of scientific simulations and the development of high-performance kernels for such operations is known to be a challenging task. While for operations on one- and two-dimensional tensors there exist standardized interfaces and highly-optimized libraries (BLAS), for higher dimensional tensors neither standards nor highly-tuned implementations exist yet. In this paper, we consider contractions between two tensors of arbitrary dimensionality and take on the challenge of generating high-performance implementations by resorting to sequences of BLAS kernels. The approach consists in breaking the contraction down into operations that only involve matrices or vectors. Since in general there are many alternative ways of decomposing a contraction, we are able to methodically derive a large family of algorithms. The main contribution of this paper is a systematic methodology to accurately identify the fastest algorithms in the bunch, *without executing them*. The goal is instead accomplished with the help of a set of cache-aware micro-benchmarks for the underlying BLAS kernels. The predictions we construct from such benchmarks allow us to reliably single out the best-performing algorithms in a tiny fraction of the time taken by the direct execution of the algorithms.

1 Introduction

Tensor contractions play an increasingly important role in various scientific computations such as general relativity [1,2] and electronic structure calculations in quantum chemistry [3–5]. Computationally, contractions are generalizations of matrix-vector and matrix-matrix products that involve operands of higher dimensionality. While there are several highly-tuned implementations of the Basic Linear Algebra Subprograms (BLAS) [6–8] for operands with up to 2 dimensions, there are no equivalently standardized high-performance libraries for general tensor contractions. Fortunately, just as matrix-matrix products can computationally be decomposed into a sequence of matrix-vector products, most higher dimensional tensor contractions can be cast in terms of matrix-matrix or matrix-vector BLAS kernels. However, each tensor contraction can be computed via BLAS kernels in many, even hundreds, of different ways, each with its own performance signature. This work addresses the problem of accurately predicting the performance of BLAS-based algorithms for tensor contractions.

© Springer International Publishing Switzerland 2015
S.A. Jarvis et al. (Eds.): PMBS 2014, LNCS 8966, pp. 193–212, 2015.
DOI: 10.1007/978-3-319-17248-4_10

One could argue that only algorithms that use the **gemm** kernel[1] are real candidates to achieve the best performance; while for the most part this observation is true, due to the fact that in practical contractions it is often the case that one or more dimensions are very small (while BLAS is mostly optimized for large dimensions), the difference in performance between two **gemm**-based algorithms can be dramatic. At any rate, with this work we aim at the accurate prediction of any BLAS-based contraction, irrespective of which kernel is used. Our approach, which never resorts to timing a full algorithm, makes use of what we call micro-benchmarks. These benchmarks execute only one BLAS operation in a prescribed memory environment. The idea is to analyze the structure of the code, and determine the state of the cache (precondition) prior to the execution of the kernel; we carefully recreate this state within the micro-benchmark so that the specific kernel can be timed in conditions analogous to those experienced in the actual algorithm. Based on these timings, we extrapolate the total algorithm execution times with sufficient accuracy to single out the fastest algorithms. This micro-benchmark-based prediction proves to be several orders of magnitude faster than executions of the actual algorithms.

Tensor Notation. In the following, we denote tensor contractions by means of the Einstein notation;[2] let us briefly explain said notation by means of an example. In the contraction $C_{abc} := A_{ai}B_{ibc}$, the entries C[a,b,c] of the resulting three-dimensional tensor $C \in \mathbb{R}^{a \times b \times c}$ are computed as

$$\forall \mathtt{a} \forall \mathtt{b} \forall \mathtt{c}. C\mathtt{[a,b,c]} := \sum_\mathtt{i} A\mathtt{[a,i]}\, B\mathtt{[i,b,c]}.$$

(In this notation, a matrix-matrix product is denoted by $C_{ab} := A_{ai}B_{ib}$.) The indices that appear in both tensors A and B — the summation indices $i, j, \ldots$ — are called *contracted*, while those that only appear in either A or B (and thus in C) — $a, b, c, \ldots$ — are called *free* or *uncontracted*. W.l.o.g., we assume that tensors are stored as Fortran-style contiguous multidimensional double precision arrays: vectors (1D tensors) are stored contiguously, matrices (2D tensors) are stored as sequence of column vectors, 3D tensors (visualized as cubes) are stored as a sequence of matrices (planes of the cube), and so on.

Related Work. The most prominent project targeting the efficient computation of tensor contractions is probably the Tensor Contraction Engine, a compiler built specifically for multi-tensor multi-index contractions to be executed within memory constraints [9]; in light of the wide diffusion and nearly optimal efficiency of the BLAS library, an extension to TCE was proposed to compute

---

[1] **gemm** is the BLAS-3 routine for matrix-matrix multiplication, which on many systems is optimized within a few percent of peak performance.

[2] For the sake of simplicity and without any loss of generality, we ignore any distinction between covariant and contravariant vectors; this means we treat any index as a subscript.

contractions via BLAS operations [10]. In the same spirit, we provided simple rules to build a taxonomy for all contractions between two tensors, identifying which BLAS routines are usable and how to best exploit them [11].

There also exists a variety of work in the field of performance prediction in the context of dense linear algebra. A notable example is Iakymchuk et al. [12,13], where the authors model the performance of dense linear algebra algorithms analytically based on very detailed models of the occurring cache-misses. Also, in [14], we use measurement-based performance models to predict the behavior of blocked algorithms. However, none of these works target or address high-performance tensor contractions and their peculiarities, i.e., very regular patterns in routine invocation and memory access, but highly skewed dimensionality (tiny sizes for at least one of the dimensions).

Structure of the Paper. The rest of this paper is structured as follows. The systematic generation of BLAS-based algorithms for tensor contractions is discussed in Sect. 2. Our performance prediction framework is introduced in Sect. 3, and experimental results for a range of contractions are presented Sect. 4.

2   Algorithm Generation

In this section, we briefly explain how we systematically generate a family of BLAS-based algorithms for a tensor contraction. For a detailed discussion of the topic, we refer the reader to [11].

Aware of the extreme level of efficiency inherent to the best BLAS implementations, our approach for computing a contraction consists in reducing it to a sequence of calls to one of the BLAS kernels. Since BLAS operates on scalars, vectors and matrices (zero-, one- and two-dimensional objects), tensors must be expressed in terms of a collection of such objects. To this end, we introduce the concept of *slicing*: With the help of Matlab's ":" notation,[3] slicing a d-dimensional operand $\mathcal{O}p \in \mathbb{R}^{n_1 \times n_2 \times \cdots \times n_d}$ along the i-th index (or dimension) means creating the n_i $(d{-}1)$-dimensional slices $\mathcal{O}p[\underbrace{:,\ldots,:}_{i-1},\mathtt{k},\underbrace{:,\ldots,:}_{d-i}]$, where $\mathtt{k} = 1,\ldots,n_i$.

Example 1. Consider the matrix-matrix product $C_{ab} := A_{ai}B_{ib}$. Slicing the matrix B along dimension b reduces the matrix to a collection of column vectors; accordingly, the matrix-matrix product is reduced to a sequence of matrix-vector operations:[4]

---

[3] In the Matlab-like notation used in this paper, $\mathtt{1:}b$ are the numbers from 1 to b, while an index : in a tensor refers to all elements along that dimension, e.g., $C[\mathtt{:,b}]$ is the b-th column of C.

[4] The pictogram next to the algorithm visualizes the slicing of the tensors that originates the algorithm's sequence of gemvs. The red objects represent the operands of the BLAS kernel.

```
for b = 1:b                                    b-gemv
    C[:,b] += A[:,:] B[:,b]                     (gemv)
```

Similarly, a multi-dimensional tensor contraction can be reduced to operations involving solely matrices and vectors.

Depending on the slicing choices, a contraction is reduced to a number of nested loops with one of the following kernels at the innermost loop's body:

– BLAS-1:
  • dot (vector-vector inner product: $\alpha := x^T y$),
  • axpy (vector scaling and addition: $y := \alpha x + y$),
– BLAS-2:
  • gemv (matrix-vector product: $y := Ax + y$),
  • ger (vector-vector outer product: $A := xy^T + A$), and
– BLAS-3:
  • gemm (matrix-matrix product: $C := AB + C$).

Notice that to comply with the BLAS interface, the elements in one of the two dimensions of a matrix must be contiguous. Therefore, algorithms that rely on gemv, ger, or gemm as their computational kernel may require a temporary copy of slices before and/or after the invocation of the corresponding BLAS routine.

As a case study, let us consider the contraction

$$C_{abc} := A_{ai} B_{ibc}, \tag{1}$$

which is visualized as follows:

Instead of a blind search for appropriate slicings, we generate algorithms by following a goal-oriented approach: For each of the five kernels of interest, we know the dimensionality required for each operand; accordingly, we deduce how many slices are needed and which combination of free/contracted indices to slice. Table 1 (left) exhibits, for each kernel, the conditions necessary for a contraction to be computed in terms of that kernel. In particular, the second and the third columns indicate how many contracted and free indices, respectively, appear in each kernel. A and B refer to the first and the second input operand of the kernel; in a contraction between tensors of arbitrary dimension, all indices beyond those indicated in these columns must be sliced.

Example 2. Since gemm involves one free index in each of its operands A and B, and one contracted index (common to both A and B), in order to reduce a contraction to a sequence of gemm calls, one must slice all free indices of A but one, all free indices of B but one, and all contracted indices but one. With reference to (1), this is achieved by slicing either dimension b or c, resulting in the two algorithms (b-gemm and c-gemm)[5] shown in the last two examples of Algorithm 1[6].

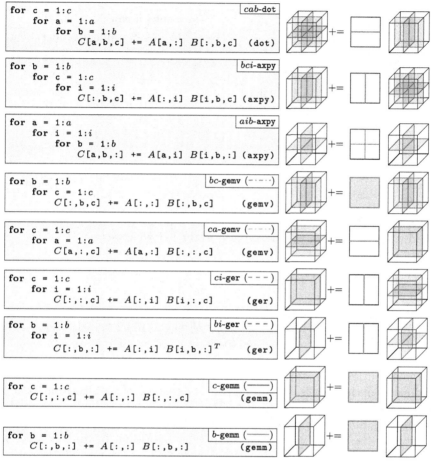

```
for c = 1:c                          cab-dot
    for a = 1:a
        for b = 1:b
            C[a,b,c] += A[a,:] B[:,b,c]  (dot)
```

```
for b = 1:b                          bci-axpy
    for c = 1:c
        for i = 1:i
            C[:,b,c] += A[:,i] B[i,b,c] (axpy)
```

```
for a = 1:a                          aib-axpy
    for i = 1:i
        for b = 1:b
            C[a,b,:] += A[a,i] B[i,b,:] (axpy)
```

```
for b = 1:b                    bc-gemv (-·-··)
    for c = 1:c
        C[:,b,c] += A[:,:] B[:,b,c]
                                      (gemv)
```

```
for c = 1:c                    ca-gemv (-·-··)
    for a = 1:a
        C[a,:,c] += A[a,:] B[:,:,c]
                                      (gemv)
```

```
for c = 1:c                      ci-ger (- - -)
    for i = 1:i
        C[:,:,c] += A[:,i] B[i,:,c]
                                       (ger)
```

```
for b = 1:b                      bi-ger (- - -)
    for i = 1:i
        C[:,b,:] += A[:,i] B[i,b,:]^T
                                       (ger)
```

```
for c = 1:c                     c-gemm (——)
    C[:,:,c] += A[:,:] B[:,:,c]
                                      (gemm)
```

```
for b = 1:b                     b-gemm (——)
    C[:,b,:] += A[:,:] B[:,b,:]
                                      (gemm)
```

Algs. 1: $C_{abc} := A_{ai}B_{ibc}$: 9 exemplary algorithms out of 36.

As already mentioned, given a contraction, there is no obvious a-priori choice of kernel and slicings to attain the highest performance. We therefore generate all possible combinations. Moreover, due to their impact on performance and to further stress our modeling tool, we generate all possible permutations of the loops.

We developed a small algorithm and code generator that produces all such algorithms, constructs for each of them a C-implementation, as well as an abstract

---

[5] The algorithm names are composed of two parts: The first part is the list of sliced tensor indices iterated over by the algorithm's loops including an apostrophe ' for each copy-kernel; the second part is the BLAS-kernel at the algorithm's core.

[6] For algorithms with more than 1 for-loop, all slicings are visualized in blue and only the kernel operands (the slicings' intersections) are in red.

Table 1. Rules for tensor slicing to obtain a given BLAS kernel. Left: how many contracted and free indices appear in a kernel. Right: different slicings make it possible to express one contraction in terms of different kernels. The names in the rightmost column refer to Algorithm 1.

Kernel	Number of indices		Examples from $C_{abc} := A_{ai}B_{ibc}$		
	Contracted	Free	Kernel indices	Sliced indices	Resulting algorithm
dot	1	0	i	c, a, b	cab-dot
axpy	0	(1 in A ∧ 0 in B) ∨	a	b, c, i	bci-axpy
		(0 in A ∧ 1 in B)	c	a, i, b	aib-axpy
gemv	1	(1 in A ∧ 0 in B) ∨	i, a	b, c	bc-gemv
		(0 in A ∧ 1 in B)	i, b	c, a	ca-gemv
ger	0	1 in A ∧ 1 in B	a, c	i, b	ib-ger
gemm	1	1 in A ∧ 1 in B	i, a, b	c	c-gemm

syntax tree (AST) representing its loop-based structure. The ASTs are then passed to the prediction tool introduced in the following section.

3   Performance Prediction

In this section, we present how to accurately model the performance of algorithms that compute tensor contractions through BLAS kernels. These algorithms consist of one or more nested loops and cast all computation in terms of one single BLAS kernel. Taking advantage of this structure, we aim at estimating the execution time of a target algorithm with the help of only few micro-benchmarks of the kernels, i.e., with no direct execution of the algorithm itself. In order to obtain reliable estimates, the micro-benchmarks need to be executed in a setup that mirrors as closely as possible the computing environment (most importantly the cache) within the contraction algorithm. In the following, we incrementally go through the steps required to build a meaningful "replica" of the computing environment.

Throughout this section, we track the changes in the performance prediction by considering the exemplary contraction $C_{abc} := A_{ai}B_{ibc}$. We chose the tensors $A \in \mathbb{R}^{a \times i}$ and $B \in \mathbb{R}^{i \times b \times c}$ of size $i = 8$ and $a = b = c = 8, \ldots, 1{,}000$ — a deliberately challenging scenario due to the thin tensor dimension i, for which BLAS kernels are generally not optimized. Our generator produces 36 algorithms for the considered contraction, some of which are shown in Algs. 1:

- 6 dot-based,
- 18 axpy-based,
- 6 gemv-based: bc-gemv (–·–·), cb-gemv (– – –), ac-gemv (– – –), ca-gemv (·· ··), ab-gemv (–·–·), ba-gemv (–·–·),

– 4 ger-based: ci-ger (- - -), ic-ger (- - -), bi-ger (- - -), ib-ger (- - -), and
– 2 gemm-based: c-gemm (——), b-gemm (——).

In this section, to focus our attention, we will only consider the BLAS-2 and BLAS-3 based algorithms (i.e., with kernels gemv, ger, and gemm).

We execute these algorithms on 1 core of an Intel Penryn E5450 (Harpertown) CPU[7] linking with the OPENBLAS library [15]. Figure 1a displays the performance, in terms of computed floating point operations per clock cycle (flops/cycle), measured for each algorithm; our goal is to accurately reproduce, without executing the algorithms, such performance profiles. While it is evident that only two of the algorithms — the gemm-based c-gemm (——) and b-gemm (——) — are competitive, we aim at predicting the behavior of all algorithms to develop and demonstrate the broad applicability of our methodology.

3.1   Repeated Execution

The first, most intuitive, attempt to predict the performance of an algorithm relies on the isolated and repeated measurement of its BLAS kernel's performance. We implemented this approach by executing each kernel ten times and extracting the median execution time; the corresponding estimate is then obtained by multiplying the median by the number of kernel invocations within the algorithm. In our example, this boils down to multiplying the kernel execution time with the product of all loop lengths.

The performance profiles predicted by this first, rough approach are shown in Fig. 1b. By comparing this figure with the reference Fig. 1a, it becomes apparent that while the two top algorithms are already correctly identified, the performance of almost all algorithms is consistently overestimated — the average absolute error with respect to the measured performance is 154 %. In other words, when executed as part of the algorithms, the BLAS kernels take longer to complete than in the isolated micro-benchmarks. The reason for this discrepancy is that the micro-benchmarks invoke the kernels repeatedly with the same memory regions as operands, i.e., they operate on warm data (the operands remain in the CPU's cache). Within the algorithm, by contrast, at least one, and potentially even all of the operands, vary from one invocation to the next, i.e., the kernels operate at least partially on cold data.

3.2   Operand Access Distance

In order to improve the accuracy of the predictions, the idea is to first identify the state of the cache in the algorithm prior to the invocation of the BLAS kernel ("precondition"), and to then replicate this status in the micro-benchmark. For this purpose, each algorithm is symbolically analyzed to reconstruct the order of memory accesses involving the kernel's operands. For each operand, we determine the set of memory regions M that were loaded into cache since its last access, and define the *access distance* as the sum of the size of these regions M.

---

[7] 2 GHz, 4 cores, 4 double precision flops/cycle/core, 6 MB L2 cache/2 cores.

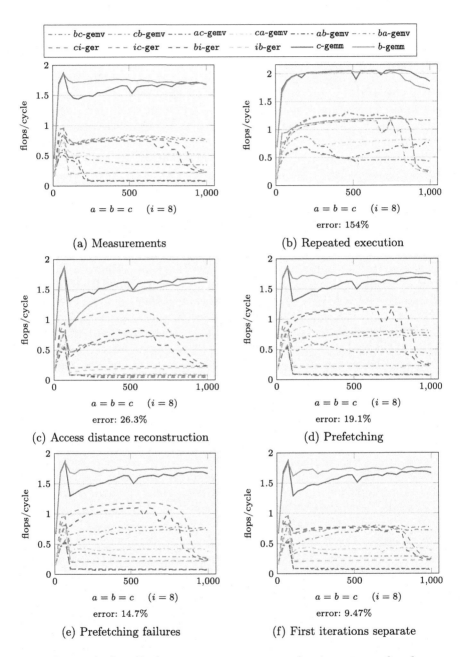

Fig. 1. $C_{abc} := A_{ai}B_{ibc}$: Performance measurements and various stages of performance predictions (BLAS-2 and BLAS-3). The presented errors for the predictions (b) – (f) are the average absolute difference with respect to the measurements (a).

Once the access distances for all operands of a kernel are determined, we can create an artificial sequence of memory accesses to reconstruct the cache precondition. Based on this cache setup, the BLAS kernels are timed in a micro-benchmark that closely resembles the actual execution of the algorithm. As before, these micro-benchmarks are repeated and timed ten times to yield a stable median. From the median, the performance of the algorithm is again obtained based on the number of kernel invocations per algorithm execution.

To predict which memory regions are in cache, we assume a fully associative Least Recently Used (LRU) cache replacement policy[8] and sum up the size of all memory regions accessed since an operand's last use, yielding the access distance. In first instance, we also assume that all loops surrounding the kernel are somewhere in the middle of their traversal (i.e., not in their first iteration); this assumption will be lifted later.

We now describe how to obtain the access distance for each operand. The presented method is general and allows for any combinations of loops and multiple kernels within the abstract syntax tree (AST), however for the sake of clarity, we limit the discussion to ASTs that only consist of a series of loops with a single call to a BLAS kernel at their core.

For each operand $\mathcal{O}p$, we examine the algorithm's AST (see Sect. 2) with the kernel of interest as a starting point. The AST is traversed backwards until the previous access to $\mathcal{O}p$ (or the AST's root) is found, thereby collecting all other operands involved in kernels in the initially empty set M. Going up the AST, three different cases can be encountered.

1. **$\mathcal{O}p$ does not vary across the surrounding loop.**
   Example 3. In algorithm ca-gemv ($--\,-$), repeated below, the operand $b[:,:,c]$ does not depend on the surrounding loop's iterator a. Hence, $M = \emptyset$ and $b[:,:,c]$'s access distance is 0.

```
for c = 1:c                    ca-gemv (- - - -)
    for a = 1:a
        C[a,:,c] += A[a,:] B[:,:,c]    (gemv)
```

$\mathcal{O}p$ refers to the same memory region as in the previous iteration of the surrounding loop. The back-traversal therefore terminates and the memory regions collected in M so far determine the access distance.

2. **$\mathcal{O}p$ varies across the surrounding loop.**
   Example 4. In algorithm ca-gemv ($-\,-$), the operand $A[a,:]$ depends on the surrounding loop's iterator a.
   $\mathcal{O}p$ referred to a different memory region in the previous iteration of the loop. As a result, it is safe to assume that at least all memory regions covered by all kernel operands throughout this loop's iterations were accessed since the last access to $\mathcal{O}p$. Hence, all operands are added to M and the memory regions are symbolically joined along the dimensions the loop iterates over.

---

[8] Due to the regular storage format and memory access strides of dense linear algebra operations such as the considered tensor contractions, this simplifying assumption does not affect the reliability of the results.

Example 4 (continued). The algorithm's kernel operates on $A[\texttt{a},:]$, $B[:,:,\texttt{c}]$, and $C[\texttt{a},:,\texttt{c}]$. Joining these operands across the index $\texttt{a}$ yields the memory regions $M = \{A[:,:], B[:,:,\texttt{c}], C[:,:,\texttt{c}]\}$.

Since a previous access to $\mathcal{O}p$ was not yet detected, the traversal proceeds by going up one level in the AST, and applying the method recursively: the surrounding loop now takes the role of the starting node and we look for a previous access to $\mathcal{O}p$ joined across this loop.

Example 4 (continued). The back-traversal now looks for a previous access to $A[:,:]$ ($A[\texttt{a},:]$ joint across $\texttt{a}$) on the second-innermost loop. This time, the region is independent of the surrounding loop's iterator $\texttt{c}$; therefore, in this second step, case 1. above applies and the access distance is computed from the previously collected set $M = \{A[:,:], B[:,:,\texttt{c}], C[:,:,\texttt{c}]\}$.

3. **The parent node is the AST's root.**

   Example 5. In algorithm *ca*-gemv (- - -), the operand $C[\texttt{a},:,\texttt{c}]$ depends on both of the surrounding loops' iterators $\texttt{a}$ and $\texttt{c}$. Therefore, the back-traversal encounters case 2. above in both its first and second step, joining the kernel's operands $A[\texttt{a},:]$, $B[:,:,\texttt{c}]$, and $C[\texttt{a},:,\texttt{c}]$ across first $\texttt{a}$ and then $\texttt{c}$, yielding $M = \{A[:,:], B[:,:,:], C[:,:,:]\}$. In the third step of the back-traversal, the outermost loop is already the starting point — the algorithm's root is reached.

   In this case, the considered region is accessed only once (and for the first time). Since we do not know how the contraction is used (within a surrounding program), we can generally not make any assertions on the access distance. For the purpose of this paper, in which we execute the contraction repeatedly to measure its performance, however, we assume that no further memory regions were loaded since the last invocation of the contraction — i.e., we compute the access distance from the previously collected memory regions in M.

Based on the such obtained access distance for each operand of an algorithm's kernel, we now construct a list of memory accesses that emulates the accesses within the algorithm prior to the kernel's execution. This list consists of accesses to the kernel's operands, interleaved with accesses to remote memory regions, in order to flush portions of the cache corresponding to the access distances: First, we access the operand with the largest access distance, then a remote region that accounts for the difference to the next smaller access distance, followed by the next operand, and so on until the operands with the smallest access distance followed by a remote access of this size. If the access distances to the first operands in this list are larger than $\frac{5}{4}$ times the cache size, the list is truncated down to this limit at the front.

Example 6. For algorithm *ca*-gemv (- - -), the following table summarizes the operands $\mathcal{O}p$, their sizes s, the corresponding collections M and the implicated access distances d for contraction sizes $a = b = c = 400$ and $i = 8$ (all sizes in doubles $= 8$ bytes):

$\mathcal{O}p$	s	M	d
$B[:,:,c]$	3,200	$\emptyset$	0
$A[a,:]$	8	$\{A[:,:], B[:,:,c], C[:,:,c]\}$	166,400
$C[a,:,c]$	400	$\{A[:,:], B[:,:,:], C[:,:,:]\}$	65,283,200

From these distances, we get the following list of memory accesses as a setup for the gemv-kernel, where $[s]$ correspond to remote memory accesses of size s:

$$C[a,:,c], [65{,}116{,}792], A[a,:], [163{,}200], B[:,:,c].$$

Note, that the remote accesses do not directly correspond to the access distances; instead, this size is reached for each operand as the sum of the sizes of all accesses to its right in this list. (e.g., the access distances of $A[a,:]$ is reached as $163{,}200 + \text{sizeof}(B[:,:,c]) = 166{,}400$).

Now, the largest access distance is at $65{,}283{,}200$ considerably larger than $983{,}040$ ($\frac{5}{4}$ times the cache size of $\frac{6\,\text{MB}}{8} = 786{,}432$ doubles). Hence, the list is cut at this size, yielding the final setup for this algorithm's micro-benchmark:

$$[816{,}632], A[a,:], [163{,}200], B[:,:,c].$$

The thus obtained benchmark, consisting of the setup followed by the kernel invocation, is once more executed ten times. The median of the kernel run-times of these ten benchmarks is then used to compute our second execution time estimate.

In Fig. 1c, we present the flops/cycle performance of our new estimates. These predictions are much closer to the measured performance (Fig. 1a) than the first rough estimates (Fig. 1b): the average error is reduced to 26.3 %. For several algorithms (such as *ic*-ger $(---)$, Algs. 1), the error is already within a few percent; for many others instead, the predictions are still off. In particular, the performance of some algorithms — for instance, *bi*-ger $(---)$ (see Algs. 1) — is now underestimated; this is due to the fact that based on the access distance, certain operands are placed out of cache, while in practice they are (partially) brought into cache through either prefetching or because they share cache-lines across the innermost loop's iterations. We address this discrepancy by further refining our micro-benchmarks.

3.3   Cache Prefetching

In the considered type of tensor contraction algorithms, prefetching of operands or sharing of cache lines across loop iterations occur frequently.

Example 7. In algorithm *bi*-ger $(---)$, the operand $A[:,i]$ points to a different memory location in each iteration of the inner loop across i. However, these vectors-operands are consecutive in memory; thus, when reaching the end of $A[:,i]$, the prefetcher will likely already load the next memory elements, which constitute $A[:,i]$ in the next iteration. Likewise, operand $B[i,b,:]$ varies across inner loop iterations; however, since this loop iterates over the region's first dimension i, 8 consecutive operands[9] $B[i,b,:]$ will occupy the same cache-line.

Such prefetching situations occur when a certain set of conditions are met, namely:

1. the operand varies across the directly surrounding loop, and
2. the iterator of this loop indexes
   - either the first dimension of the operand,
   - or its second dimension, while the first is accessed entirely, or fits in a single cache-line.

As part of our AST-based algorithm analysis, these conditions are tested; when both of them are met, we can use a slight modification of the previously introduced method to compute the *prefetch distance*, i.e., how long ago the prefetching occurred. These prefetch distances are then integrated into the micro-benchmark's setup list just like the access distances, only that for prefetch accesses the access is limited to one cache-line along an operand's first dimension.

Example 8. In algorithm ca-gemv (————), for which we explicitly constructed the setup list in the previous section, both operands $A[a,:]$ and $C[a,:,b]$ meet both prefetching conditions: 1. they vary across the surrounding loop iterator a and 2. a indexes their first dimensions (sharing of cache-lines). As a result, their prefetch distances are 0 and the prefetching access will load the entire operands since their extension along the first, contiguously stored dimension is 1. Since the remaining operand $B[:,:,c]$ has an access distance of 0, all operands are now accessed immediately before the kernel invocation; the setup list is reduced to

$$C[a,:,c], A[a,:], B[:,:,c].$$

(Since this setup consists only of accesses to the operands, it becomes redundant in our micro-benchmarks, because each of the ten repetitions will already touch all operands for the next repetition; hence, in such a case, we omit the setup altogether.)

Now accounting for prefetching, we obtain the performance estimates shown in Fig. 1d. Here, several algorithms, such as ba-gemv (—————), are estimated closer to their measured performance, leading to an improved average error of 19.1 %. However, several other algorithms, including ca-gemv (————), are overestimated in performance (i.e., underestimated in execution time). There are two separate causes for this discrepancy.

- In several algorithms, such as ca-gemv (————), where prefetching implicitly happens due to sharing of cache-lines, the prefetcher fails once a new cache-line is reached.

---

[9] The cache-line size is 64 B = 8 doubles.

– In other algorithms, such as *bi-*ger (- - -), the innermost loop is so short (here: 8 iterations) that each first iteration of the loop significantly impacts performance.

These two causes are treated separately in the following sections.

3.4 Prefetching Failures

For those algorithms in which certain operands are identified as prefetched because they share cache lines across iterations (i.e., the surrounding loop indexes their first dimension), the CPU would need to prefetch the next cache-line every 8 iterations (1 cache-line = 8 doubles). However, as a detailed analysis of hand-instrumented algorithms has shown, it fails to do so. As a result, in every 8th iteration of the innermost loop, the operand is not available and the kernel may take significantly longer.

We account for this prefetching-artifact by performing two separate micro-benchmarks: one simulating the 7 iterations in which the operand is available in cache as before, and one for the 8th iteration, where we account for the failure to prefetch and eliminate the emulated prefetching from our setup-list. The prediction for the total execution time is now obtained from weighting these two benchmark timings according to their number of occurrences in the algorithm and summing them up.

Example 9. In algorithm *ca-*gemv (- - -), the memory regions of both $A[$a$,:]$ and $C[$a$,:,$c$]$, respectively, share cache-lines across iterations of the innermost loops over a. Hence, affecting not one but two of the kernel's operands, in every 8th iteration the kernel execution time increases drastically by a factor of about 4.5. To account for these "prefetching failures", we introduce a second set of micro-benchmarks, where the prefetching emulating accesses are removed from the setup list, resulting for $a = b = c = 400$ and $i = 8$, as without prefetching, in:

$$[816,632], A[\text{a},:], [163,200], B[:,:,\text{c}].$$

Fig. 1e shows the predictions obtained after this improvement: the error is further reduced to 14.7%. Most apparent in *ca-*gemv (- - -), the overestimation of algorithms where iterations share cache-lines are now corrected.

3.5 First Loop Iterations

The predictions for several algorithms, such as *ci-*ger (- - -), are still severely off, because the innermost loop of these algorithms is very short (in our example 8 iterations long). In such a case, the predictions are very accurate for all but the first iteration. Due to vastly different cache preconditions for this first iteration, however, its performance can be significantly different (in our case, up to 10× slower). Combined with the low total iteration count, this results in predictions that are off by a factor of up to 2.

To treat such situations, we introduce separate benchmarks to predict the performance of the first iteration of the innermost loop (and further loops if their first iterations account for more than 1 % of the total kernel invocations). For this purpose, the access distance evaluation method is slightly modified: instead of the kernel itself, the starting point is now the loop whose first iteration is considered, and the set M already contains all of the kernel's memory regions joined across this loop.

Example 10. In algorithm *ci*-ger (- - -), the innermost loop over i is in our example only 8 iterations long. For all but the first iteration, the operand $C[:,:,c]$ stays the same, while $A[:,i]$ and $B[i,:,c]$ are prefetched, leading to optimal conditions for performance. In the first iteration (i.e., the next c iteration) however, $C[:,:,c]$ refers to a different memory location and prefetching fails for both $A[:,i]$ and $B[i,:,c]$, leading to severely lower performance.

From these improved access distances, the cache setup and micro-benchmark are performed just as before. As for the "prefetching failures", the prediction for the total execution time is now obtained from weighting of all relevant benchmark timings with the corresponding number of occurrences within the algorithm.

In Fig. 1f, we present the improved performance predictions obtained from this modification. The performance of all algorithms is now predicted with satisfying accuracy — the average absolute error is 9.47 %.

4   Results

In order to showcase its applicability and effectiveness, in this section we apply our technique for performance prediction to a range of contractions. We consider three test cases: In Sect. 4.1, we use different hard- and software, as well as changing the problem sizes. In Sect. 4.2, we consider a contraction that only allows the use of BLAS-1 and BLAS-2. Finally, in Sect. 4.3, we consider a more complex contraction with numerous alternative algorithms and multithreading.

4.1   Test 1: $C_{abc} := A_{ai}B_{ibc}$, Different Setup

We commence with the same contraction used as a case study in the previous section, yet with an entirely different setup: the sizes a, b, and c are now fixed to 128, while i ranges from 8 to 1,000. As experimental environment, we use a 10-core Intel Ivy Bridge-EP E5-2680 v2 processor running at 3.6 GHz (Turbo Boost) and 25 MB of L3 cache. Each core can execute 8 double precision flops/cycle. The routines for both the actual measurements and the micro-benchmarks were linked to the BLAS implementation of Intel's Math Kernel Library (MKL, version 11.0). Figure 2 contains the performance measurements and corresponding predictions for all 36 algorithms (see Algs. 1). Although everything, ranging from the problem size to the machine and BLAS library was changed in this setup, the predictions are of equivalent quality and our tool correclty determines that the gemm-based algorithms (*c*-gemm (——) and *b*-gemm (——)) perform best and equally well.

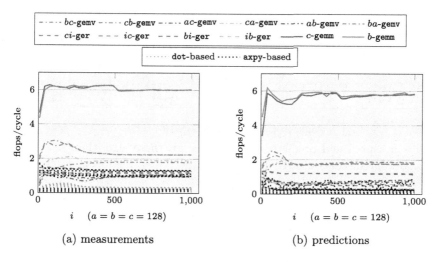

Fig. 2. $C_{abc} := A_{ai}B_{ibc}$, different setup: Performance measurements and predictions.

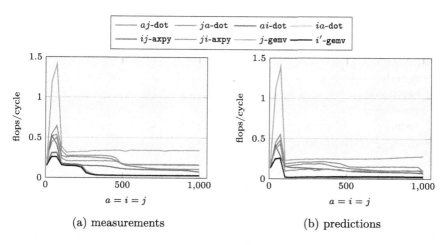

Fig. 3. $C_a := A_{iaj}B_{ji}$: Performance measurements and predictions.

4.2 Test 2: $C_a := A_{iaj}B_{ji}$, only BLAS-1 and BLAS-2

For certain contractions (e.g., those involving 1D tensors), **gemm** cannot be used as a compute kernel, and only algorithms based on BLAS-2 or BLAS-1 are possible. One such scenario is encontered in the contraction $C_a := A_{iaj}B_{ji}$, for which our generator yields 8 algorithms:

- 4 dot-based: aj-dot (———), ja-dot (———), ai-dot (———), ia-dot (———),
- 2 axpy-based: ij-axpy (———), ji-axpy (———), and
- 2 gemv-based (see Algs. 2): j-gemv (———), i'-gemv (———).

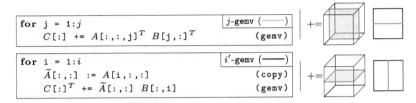

Algs. 2: $C_a := A_{iaj}B_{ji}$, **gemv**-based.

The measured and predicted performance for these algorithms is shown in Fig. 3. Our predictions clearly discriminate the fastest algorithm j-gemv (———) across the board. Furthermore, the next group of four algorithms is also correctly identified and the low performance of the second **gemv**-based algorithm i'-gemv (———) (due to the overhead of the involved matrix-copy operation) is predicted too.

4.3   Test 3: $C_{abc} := A_{ija}B_{jbic}$, Challenging Contraction

We now turn to a more complex example inspired by space-time continuum computations in the field general relativity [1]: $C_{abc} := A_{ija}B_{jbic}$. For this contraction, we generated a total of 176 different algorithms:

– 48 **dot**-based (⋯⋯),
– 72 **axpy**-based (⋯⋯),
– 36 **gemv**-based (⋯⋯),
– 12 **ger**-based (   ), and
– 8 **gemm**-based:
  cj'-gemm (———), jc'-gemm (———), ci'-gemm (———), $i'c$-gemm (   ), bj'-gemm (———),
  jb'-gemm (———), bi'-gemm (———), $i'b$-gemm (———).

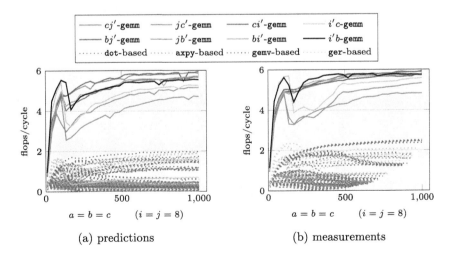

Fig. 4. $C_{abc} := A_{ija}B_{jbic}$: Performance prediction and measurements.

All gemm-based (see Algs. 3) and several of the gemv-based algorithms involve copy operations to ensure that each matrix has a contiguously stored dimension, as required by the BLAS interface. Once again, we consider a very challenging scenario where both contracted indices are of size $i = j = 8$ and the free indices $a = b = c$ vary together.

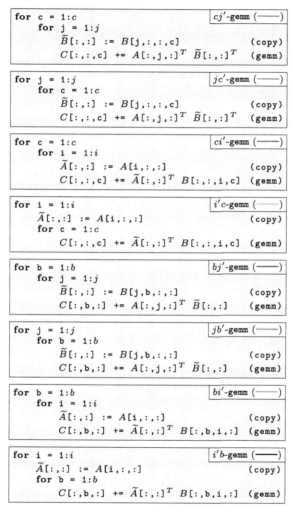

Algs. 3: $C_{abc} := A_{ija}B_{jbic}$, gemm-based.

Starting with the predictions, in Fig. 4a, we present the expected performance in flops/cycle of the 176 algorithms, where BLAS-1 and BLAS-2 algorithms are grouped by kernel. Even with the copy operations, the gemm-based algorithms are the fastest. However, within these 8 algorithms, the performance differs by more than 20 %. Focusing on the gemm-algorithms, we compare with corresponding

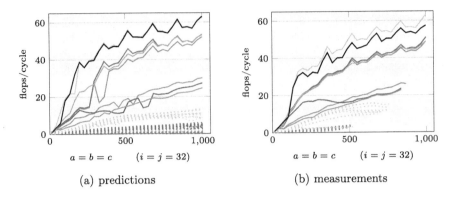

(a) predictions   (b) measurements

Fig. 5. $C_{abc} := A_{ija}B_{jbic}$: Performance prediction and measurements with 10 threads.

performance measurements[10] in Fig. 4b. The comparison shows that our predictions clearly separate the bulk of fast algorithms from the slightly less efficient ones.

Multithreading. The algorithms considered here can make use of shared memory parallelism by employing multithreaded BLAS kernels. To focus on the impact of parallelism, we increase the contracted tensor dimension sizes to $i = j = 32$ and use all 10 cores of the Ivy Bridge-EP CPU with OPENBLAS.

Performance predictions and measurements for this setup are presented in Fig. 5. Our predictions correctly separate the three groups of **gemm**-based implementations; moreover, algorithms $i'c$-**gemm** (———) and $i'b$-**gemm** (——) (see Algs. 3), which reach 60 flops/cycle,[11] are identified as the fastest. The slowest algorithm (jb'-**gemm** (——)) on the other hand merely reaches 20 flops/per cycle. This 3× difference in performance among **gemm**-based algorithms emphasizes the importance of selecting the right algorithm.

4.4 Efficiency Study

The ultimate goal of this work is to automatically and quickly select the fastest algorithm for a given tensor contraction. The experiments presented so far provide evidence that our automated approach successfully identifies the fastest algorithm(s). In this last study, we investigate the efficiency of our micro-benchmark-based approach. For this purpose, we once more consider the contraction $C_{abc} := A_{ai}B_{ibc}$, with $i = 8$ and varying $a = b = c$. Figure 6 displays the ratio of how much faster our micro-benchmark is compared to executing the corresponding algorithm. In general, our prediction proves to be several orders of magnitude faster than the algorithm itself. At $a = b = c = 1,000$, this relative improvement is smallest for the **gemm**-based algorithms (——) at $10^3×$, since

---

[10] Slow tensor contraction algorithms were stopped before reaching the largest test-cases by limiting the total measurement time per algorithm to 15 minutes.

[11] Using 10 cores, the theoretical peak performance is 80 flops/cycle.

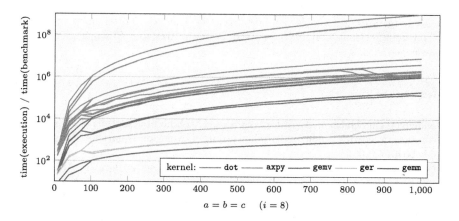

Fig. 6. $C_{abc} := A_{ai}B_{ibc}$: Prediction efficiency.

each **gemm** performs a significant portion of the computation; for the **ger**-based algorithms (——), it lies between $6 \cdot 10^3$ and $10^4 \times$ and for the **gemv**-based algorithms (——) the gain is $5 \cdot 10^5$ to $10^6 \times$; finally, the gain for both BLAS-1-based algorithms (——,——), where each BLAS-call only performs a tiny fraction of the contraction, our prediction is between 6 and 9 orders of magnitude faster than the execution.

5   Conclusion

In this paper, we focused on the performance prediction of BLAS-based algorithms for tensors contractions. First, based on previous work, we developed an algorithm and code generator that given the mathematical description of a tensor contraction, casts the computation in terms of five different BLAS kernels; since, in general, a tensor contraction may be decomposed in terms of matrix and vector products in many different ways, the generator often returns dozens of alternative algorithms.

Then, we tackled the problem of selecting the fastest algorithms without ever executing them. Instead of executing the full algorithms, our approach is based on timing the BLAS kernels in a small set of micro-benchmarks. These micro-benchmarks are run in a context that emulates that of the actual computation; thanks to careful treatment of cache-locality and a model of the cache prefetcher's behavior, our performance prediction tool is capable of identifying the best-performing algorithms in a tiny fraction of the time required to actually run and time all of them.

The quality of the predictions was showcased for a number of challenging scenarios, including contractions among tensors with small dimensions, contractions that can only be cast in terms of BLAS 1 and BLAS 2 kernels, and multi-threaded computations.

Acknowledgments. Financial support from the Deutsche Forschungsgemeinschaft (DFG) through Grant GSC 111 and the Deutsche Telekom Stiftung is gratefully acknowledged.

References

1. Kidder, L.E., Scheel, M.A., Teukolsky, S.A.: Extending the lifetime of 3d black hole computations with a new hyperbolic system of evolution equations. Phys. Rev. D **64**, 064017 (2001)
2. Lehner, L.: Numerical relativity: a review. Class. Quantum Gravity **18**(17), R25 (2001)
3. Helgaker, T., Jorgensen, P., Olsen, J.: Molecular Electronic-Structure Theory. Wiley, Chichester (2000)
4. Čížek, J.: On the correlation problem in atomic and molecular systems calculation of wavefunction components in ursell type expansion using quantum-field theoretical methods. J. Chem. Phys. **45**(11), 4256–4266 (1966)
5. Bartlett, R.J., Musiał, M.: Coupled-cluster theory in quantum chemistry. Rev. Mod. Phys. **79**, 291–352 (2007)
6. Lawson, C.L., Hanson, R.J., Kincaid, D.R., Krogh, F.T.: Basic linear algebra subprograms for fortran usage. ACM Trans. Math. Softw. **5**(3), 308–323 (1979)
7. Dongarra, J.J., Du Croz, J., Hammarling, S., Hanson, R.J.: An extended set of fortran basic linear algebra subprograms. ACM Trans. Math. Softw. **14**(1), 1–17 (1988)
8. Dongarra, J.J., Du Croz, J., Hammarling, S., Duff, I.S.: A set of level 3 basic linear algebra subprograms. ACM Trans. Math. Softw. **16**(1), 1–17 (1990)
9. Baumgartner, G., Auer, A., Bernholdt, D., Bibireata, A., Choppella, V., Cociorva, D., Gao, X., Harrison, R., Hirata, S., Krishnamoorthy, S., Krishnan, S., Lam, C., Lu, Q., Nooijen, M., Pitzer, R., Ramanujam, J., Sadayappan, P., Sibiryakov, A.: Synthesis of high-performance parallel programs for a class of ab initio quantum chemistry models. Proc. IEEE **93**(2), 276–292 (2005)
10. Lu, Q., Gao, X., Krishnamoorthy, S., Baumgartner, G., Ramanujam, J., Sadayappan, P.: Empirical performance model-driven data layout optimization and library call selection for tensor contraction expressions. J. Parallel Distrib. Comput. **72**(3), 338–352 (2012)
11. Di Napoli, E., Fabregat-Traver, D., Quintana-Orti, G., Bientinesi, P.: Towards an efficient use of the blas library for multilinear tensor contractions. Appl. Math. Comput. **235**, 454–468 (2014)
12. Iakymchuk, R., Bientinesi, P.: Modeling performance through memory-stalls. SIGMETRICS Perform. Eval. Rev. **40**(2), 86–91 (2012)
13. Iakymchuk, R., Bientinesi, P.: Execution-less performance modeling. In: Proceedings of the Second International Workshop on Performance Modeling, Benchmarking and Simulation of High-Performance Computing Systems (PMBS 2011) held as part of the Supercomputing Conference (SC 2011), Seattle, USA, November 2011
14. Peise, E., Bientinesi, P.: Performance modeling for dense linear algebra. In: Proceedings of the 2012 SC Companion: High Performance Computing, Networking Storage and Analysis. SCC 2012, pp. 406–416. IEEE Computer Society, Washington, DC, USA (2012)
15. OpenBLAS. http://xianyi.github.com/OpenBLAS

Section C: Power, Energy and Checkpointing

Assessing General-Purpose Algorithms to Cope with Fail-Stop and Silent Errors

Anne Benoit[1], Aurélien Cavelan[1]([⊠]), Yves Robert[1,2], and Hongyang Sun[1]

[1] CNRS and INRIA, École Normale Supérieure de Lyon, Lyon, France
aurelien.cavelan@ens-lyon.fr
[2] University of Tennessee Knoxville, Knoxville, USA

Abstract. In this paper, we combine the traditional checkpointing and rollback recovery strategies with verification mechanisms to address both fail-stop and silent errors. The objective is to minimize either makespan or energy consumption. While DVFS is a popular approach for reducing the energy consumption, using lower speeds/voltages can increase the number of errors, thereby complicating the problem. We consider an application workflow whose dependence graph is a chain of tasks, and we study three execution scenarios: (i) a single speed is used during the whole execution; (ii) a second, possibly higher speed is used for any potential re-execution; (iii) different pairs of speeds can be used throughout the execution. For each scenario, we determine the optimal checkpointing and verification locations (and the optimal speeds for the third scenario) to minimize either objective. The different execution scenarios are then assessed and compared through an extensive set of experiments.

1 Introduction

For HPC applications, scale is a major opportunity. Massive parallelism with 100,000+ nodes is the most viable path to achieving sustained petascale performance. Future platforms will enrol even more computing resources to enter the exascale era. Unfortunately, scale is also a major threat. Resilience is the first challenge. Even if each node provides an individual MTBF (Mean Time Between Failures) of, say, one century, a machine with 100,000 such nodes will encounter a failure every 9 h in average, which is larger than the execution time of many HPC applications. Furthermore, a one-century MTBF per node is an optimistic figure, given that each node is composed of several hundreds of cores. Worse, several types of errors need to be considered when computing at scale. In addition to classical fail-stop errors (such as hardware failures), silent errors (a.k.a silent data corruptions) cannot be ignored any longer.

Another challenge is energy consumption. The power requirement of current petascale platforms is that of a small town, hence measures must be taken to reduce the energy consumption of future platforms. A widely-used strategy is to use DVFS techniques: modern processors can run at different speeds, and lower speeds induce big savings in energy consumption. In a nutshell, this is because the dynamic power consumed when computing at speed s is proportional

© Springer International Publishing Switzerland 2015
S.A. Jarvis et al. (Eds.): PMBS 2014, LNCS 8966, pp. 215–236, 2015.
DOI: 10.1007/978-3-319-17248-4_11

to s^3, while execution time is proportional to $1/s$. As a result, computing energy (which is time times power) is proportional to s^2, and using lower speeds reduces global energy consumption in most practical settings, where static power is not too high. To further complicate the picture, energy savings have an impact on resilience. Obviously, the longer the execution, the higher the expected number of errors, hence using a lower speed to save energy may well induce extra time and overhead to cope with more errors throughout execution. Even worse (again!), lower speeds are usually obtained via lower voltages, which themselves induce higher error rates and further increase the latter overhead.

In this paper, we introduce a model that addresses both challenges: resilience and energy consumption. In addition, we address both fail-stop and silent errors, which, to the best of our knowledge, has never been achieved before. While checkpoint and rollback recovery is the de-facto standard for dealing with fail-stop errors, there is no widely adopted general-purpose technique to cope with silent errors. The problem with silent errors is *detection latency*: contrarily to a fail-stop error whose detection is immediate, a silent error is identified only when the corrupted data is activated and/or leads to an unusual application behavior. However, checkpoint and rollback recovery assumes instantaneous error detection, and this raises a new difficulty: if the error stroke before the last checkpoint, and is detected after that checkpoint, then the checkpoint is corrupted and cannot be used to restore the application. To solve this problem, one may envision to keep several checkpoints in memory, and to restore the application from the last *valid* checkpoint [23]. This multiple-checkpoint approach has three major drawbacks. First, it is very demanding in terms of stable storage. The second drawback is the possibility of fatal failures. Indeed, if we keep k checkpoints in memory, the approach assumes that the error that is currently detected did not strike before all the checkpoints still kept in memory, which would be fatal: in that latter case, all live checkpoints are corrupted, and one would have to re-execute the entire application from scratch. The third drawback of the approach is the most serious, and applies even without memory constraints, i.e., if we could store an infinite number of checkpoints in storage. The critical question is to determine which checkpoint is the last valid one. We need this information to safely recover from that point on. However, because of the detection latency, we do not know when the silent error has indeed occurred, hence we cannot identify the last valid checkpoint, unless some verification system is enforced.

We introduce such a verification system in this paper. This approach is agnostic of the nature of this verification mechanism (checksum, error correcting code, coherence tests, etc.). It is also fully general-purpose, although application-specific information, if available, can always be used to decrease the cost of verification: see the overview of related work in Sect. 2 for examples. In this context, the simplest protocol is to take only verified checkpoint (VC). This corresponds to performing a verification just before taking each checkpoint. If the verification succeeds, then one can safely store the checkpoint. If the verification fails, then a silent error has struck since the last checkpoint, which was duly verified, and one can safely recover from that checkpoint to resume the execution of the application. Of course, if a fail-stop error strikes, we also safely recover from the last checkpoint, just as in the classical checkpoint and rollback recovery method. This VC-ONLY protocol basically amounts to replacing the cost C of a checkpoint by the cost $V+C$ of a verification followed by a checkpoint. However, because we deal with two sources of errors, one detected immediately and the other only when we reach the verification, the analysis of the optimal strategy is more involved. We extend both the classical bound by Young [33] or Daly [11], and the dynamic programming algorithm of Toueg and Babaoglu [31], to deal with these error sources.

While taking checkpoints without verifications seems a bad idea (because of the memory cost, and of the risk of saving corrupted data), taking a verification without checkpointing may be interesting. Indeed, if silent errors are frequent enough, it is worth verifying the data in between two (verified) checkpoints, so as to detect a possible silent error earlier in the execution, and thereby re-executing less work. We refer to VC+V as the protocol that allows for both verified checkpoints and isolated verifications. One major objective of this paper is to study VC+V algorithms coupling verification and checkpointing, and to analytically determine the best balance of verifications between checkpoints so as to minimize either makespan (total execution time) or energy consumption. To achieve this ambitious goal, we restrict to a simplified, yet realistic, application framework. We consider application workflows that consist of a number of parallel tasks that execute on the platform, and that exchange data at the end of their executions. In other words, the task graph is a linear chain, and each task (except maybe the first one and the last one) reads data from its predecessor and produces data for its successor. This scenario corresponds to a high-performance computing application whose workflow is partitioned into a succession of (typically large) tightly-coupled computational kernels, each of them being identified as a task by the model. At the end of each task, we can either perform a verification on the task's output, or perform a verification followed by a checkpoint.

In addition, we have to select a speed for each execution of each task. We envision three different execution scenarios. In the simple SINGLESPEED scenario, a unique speed s is available throughout execution. In the intermediate REEXECSPEED scenario, the same speed s is used for the first execution of each task, but another speed σ is available for re-execution after a fail-stop or silent error. Here the first speed s can be seen as the regular speed, while the second speed σ corresponds to an adjusted speed to either speed up or to slow down the re-execution after an error strikes, depending on the optimization objective. Finally, in the advanced MULTISPEED scenario, two different speeds s_i and σ_i can be used to execute the tasks in between two consecutive checkpoints (which we call a task segment). Each speed s_i or σ_i can be freely chosen from a set of K discrete speeds. Note that these speeds may well vary from one segment to another. For each execution scenario, we provide a dynamic programming algorithm to determine the optimal locations of checkpoints and verifications (and for the MULTISPEED scenario we also provide the corresponding optimal pair of speeds for each segment).

The main contributions of this paper are the following:

- We introduce a general-purpose model to deal with both fail-stop and silent errors, combining checkpoints with a verification mechanism.
- We consider several execution scenarios, first with a single speed, then in case of re-execution, and finally with several discrete speeds that can freely change after each checkpoint.
- For all scenarios and for both makespan and energy objectives, we consider two approaches, one using verified checkpoints only, and the other using additional isolated verifications. We provide a dynamic programming algorithm that determines the best locations of checkpoints and verifications across application tasks for each scenario/approach/objective combination.
- We provide an extensive set of simulations to support the theory and which enables us to assess the usefulness of each algorithm.

The rest of the paper is organized as follows. Section 2 provides an overview of related work. Section 3 is devoted to formally defining the framework and all model parameters. Section 4 deals with the main algorithmic contributions: for all three execution scenarios, we design optimal algorithms for the VC-ONLY approach, and then for the VC+V approach, targeting either time or energy minimization. Then in Sect. 5, we report on a comprehensive set of experiments to assess the impact of each scenario and approach. Finally, we outline main conclusions and directions for future work in Sect. 6.

2   Related Work

2.1   Fail-Stop Errors

The de-facto general-purpose error recovery technique in high performance computing is checkpoint and rollback recovery [9,16]. Such protocols employ checkpoints to periodically save the state of a parallel application, so that when an error strikes some process, the application can be restored back to one of its former states. There are several families of checkpointing protocols, but they share a common feature: each checkpoint forms a consistent recovery line, i.e., when an error is detected, one can rollback to the last checkpoint and resume execution, after a downtime and a recovery time.

Many models are available to understand the behavior of checkpoint and restart [7,11,25,33]. For a divisible load application where checkpoints can be inserted at any point in execution for a nominal cost C, there exist well-known formulas due to Young [33] and Daly [11] to determine the optimal checkpointing period. For an application composed of a chain of tasks, which is also the subject of this paper, the problem of finding the optimal checkpoint strategy, i.e., of determining which tasks to checkpoint, in order to minimize the expected execution time, has been solved by Toueg and Babaoglu [31], using a dynamic programming algorithm. One major contribution of this paper is to extend both the Young/Daly formulas and the result of Toueg and Babaoglu to deal with silent errors in addition to fail-stop errors, and with several discrete speeds instead of a single one.

2.2   Silent Errors

Most traditional approaches maintain a single checkpoint. If the checkpoint file includes errors, the application faces an irrecoverable failure and must restart from scratch. This is because error detection latency is ignored in traditional roll-back and recovery schemes, which assume instantaneous error detection (therefore mainly targeting fail-stop failures) and are unable to accommodate silent errors. We focus in this section on related work about silent errors. A comprehensive list of techniques and references is provided by Lu, Zheng and Chien [23].

Considerable efforts have been directed at error-checking to reveal silent errors. Error detection is usually very costly. Hardware mechanisms, such as ECC memory, can detect and even correct a fraction of errors, but in practice they are complemented with software techniques. The simplest technique is triple modular redundancy and voting [24], which induces a highly costly verification. For high-performance scientific applications, process replication (each process is equipped with a replica, and messages are quadruplicated) is proposed in the RedMPI library [18]. Elliot et al. [15] combine partial redundancy and check-pointing, and confirm the benefit of dual and triple redundancy. The drawback is that twice the number of processing resources is required (for dual redundancy).

Application-specific information can be very useful to enable ad-hoc solutions, which dramatically decrease the cost of detection. Many techniques have been advocated. They include memory scrubbing [22] and ABFT techniques [6, 21, 30], such as coding for sparse-matrix vector multiplication kernels [30] and coupling a higher-order with a lower-order scheme for PDEs [5]. These methods can only detect an error but do not correct it. Self-stabilizing corrections after error detection in the conjugate gradient method are investigated by Sao and Vuduc [28]. Heroux and Hoemmen [19] design a fault-tolerant GMRES capable of converging despite silent errors. Bronevetsky and de Supinski [8] provide a comparative study of detection costs for iterative methods.

A nice instantiation of the checkpoint and verification mechanism that we study in this paper is provided by Chen [10], who deals with sparse iterative solvers. Consider a simple method such as the PCG, the Preconditioned Conjugate Gradient method: Chen's approach performs a periodic verification every d iterations, and a periodic checkpoint every $d \times c$ iterations, which is a particular case of the VC+V approach with equi-distance verifications. For PCG, the verification amounts to checking the orthogonality of two vectors and to recomputing and checking the residual. The cost of the verification is small in front of the cost of an iteration, especially when the preconditioner requires much more flops than a sparse matrix-vector product.

As already mentioned, our work is agnostic of the underlying error-detection technique and takes the cost of verification as an input parameter to the model.

2.3   Energy Model and Error Rate

Modern processors are equipped with *dynamic voltage and frequency scaling* (DVFS) capability. The total power consumption is the sum of the static/idle power and the dynamic power, which is proportional to the cube of the processing speed s [3,32], i.e., $P(s) = P_{idle} + \beta \cdot s^3$, where $\beta > 0$. A widely used reliability model assumes that radiation-induced transient faults (soft errors) follow a Poisson process with an average arrival rate λ. The impact of DVFS on the error rate is, however, not completely clear.

On the one hand, lowering the voltage/frequency is believed to have an adverse effect on the system reliability [13,35]. In particular, many papers (e.g., [2,12,34,35]) have assumed the following exponential error rate model: $\lambda(s) = \lambda_0 \cdot 10^{\frac{d(s_{max} - s)}{s_{max} - s_{min}}}$, where λ_0 denotes the average error rate at the maximum speed s_{max}, $d > 0$ is a constant indicating the sensitivity of error rate to voltage/frequency scaling, and s_{min} is the minimum speed. This model suggests that the error rate increases exponentially with decreased processing speed, which is a result of decreasing the voltage/frequency and hence lowering the circuit's critical charge (i.e., the minimum charge required to cause an error in the circuit).

On the other hand, the failure rates of computing nodes have also been observed to increase with temperature [17,20,26,29], which generally increases together with the processing speed (voltage/frequency). As a rule of thumb, Arrenhius' equation when applied to microelectronic devices suggests that the error rate doubles for every 10°C increase in the temperature [17]. In general, the mean time between failure (MTBF) of a processor, which is the reciprocal of failure rate, can be expressed as [29]: $MTBF = \frac{1}{\lambda} = A \cdot e^{-b \cdot T}$, where A and b are thermal constants, and T denotes the temperature of the processor. Under the reasonable assumption that higher operating voltage/frequency leads to higher temperature, this model suggests that the error rate increases with increased processing speed. Clearly, the two models above draw contradictory conclusions on the impact of DVFS on error rates. In practice, the impact of the first model may be more evident, as the temperature dependency in some systems has been observed to be linear (or even not exist) instead of being exponential [14]. Generally speaking, the processing speed should have a composite effect on the average error rate by taking both voltage level and temperature into account. In the experimental section of this paper (Sect. 5), we adopt a tradeoff model to include the impact of temperature.

3   Framework

In this section we introduce all model parameters. We start with a description of the application workflows. Then we present parameters related to energy consumption. Next we detail the resilient model to deal with fail-stop and silent errors. We conclude by presenting the various execution scenarios.

Application Workflows. We consider application workflows whose task graph is a linear chain $T_1 \to T_2 \cdots \to T_n$. Here n is the number of tasks, and each task T_i is weighted by its computational cost w_i. We target a platform with p identical processors. Each task is a parallel task that is executed on the whole platform. A fundamental characteristic of the application model is that it allows to view the platform as a single (albeit very powerful) *macro-processor*, thereby providing a tractable abstraction of the problem.

Energy Consumption. When computing (including verification), we use DVFS to change the speed of the processors, and assume a set $S = \{s_1, s_2, \ldots, s_K\}$ of K discrete computing speeds. During checkpointing and recovery, we assume a dedicated (constant) power consumption. Altogether, the total power consumption of the macro-processor is p times the power consumption of each individual resource. It is decomposed into three different components:

- P_{idle}, the static power dissipated when the platform is on (even idle);
- $P_{cpu}(s)$, the dynamic power spent by operating the CPU at speed s;
- P_{io}, the dynamic power spent by I/O transfers (checkpoints and recoveries).

Assume w.l.o.g. that there is no overlap between CPU operations and I/O transfers. Then the total energy consumed during the execution of the application can be expressed as: $Energy = P_{idle}(T_{cpu} + T_{io}) + \sum_{i=1}^{K} P_{cpu}(s_i)T_{cpu}(s_i) + P_{io}T_{io}$, where $T_{cpu}(s_i)$ is the time spent on computing at speed s_i, $T_{cpu} = \sum_{i=1}^{K} T_{cpu}(s_i)$ is the total time spent on computing, and T_{io} is the total time spent on I/O transfers. The time to compute tasks T_i to T_j at speed s is $T_{i,j}(s) = \frac{1}{s}\sum_{k=i}^{j} w_i$ and the corresponding energy is $E_{i,j}(s) = T_{i,j}(s)(P_{idle} + P_{cpu}(s))$.

Resilience. We assume that errors only strike during computations, and not during I/O transfers (checkpoints and recoveries) nor verifications. We consider two types of errors: *fail-stop* and *silent*.

To cope with fail-stop errors, we use checkpointing, and to cope with silent errors, an additional verification mechanism is used. The time to checkpoint (the output of) task T_i is C_i, the time to recover from (the checkpoint of) task T_i is R_i, and the time to verify (the output of) task T_i at speed s is $V_i(s)$. We assume that both fail-stop errors and silent errors follow an exponential distribution with average rates $\lambda^F(s)$ and $\lambda^S(s)$, respectively, where s denotes the current computing speed. Given an error rate λ, let $p(\lambda, L) = 1 - e^{-\lambda L}$ denote the probability that a error strikes during an execution of length L. For convenience, we define $p_{i,j}^F(s) = p(\lambda^F(s), T_{i,j}(s))$ to be the probability that a fail-stop error strikes when executing from T_i to T_j, and define $p_{i,j}^S(s) = p(\lambda^S(s), T_{i,j}(s))$ similarly for silent errors.

Resilience also has a cost in terms of energy consumption. Specifically, the energy to checkpoint task T_i is $E_i^C = C_i(P_{idle} + P_{io})$, to recover from task T_i is $E_i^R = R_i(P_{idle} + P_{io})$, and to verify task T_i at speed s is $E_i^V(s) = V_i(s)(P_{idle} + P_{cpu}(s))$.

Execution Scenarios. We consider three different execution scenarios: (i) SINGLESPEED: a single speed s is used during the whole execution ($K = 1$); (ii) REEXECSPEED: there are two speeds, s for the first execution of each task, and σ for any potential re-execution ($K = 2$); (iii) MULTISPEED: we are given K discrete speeds, where K is arbitrary. The workflow chain is cut into subchains called segments, which are delimited by checkpoints. For each segment, we can freely choose a speed for the first execution, and a (possibly different) speed for any ulterior execution, among the K speeds.

Optimization Problems. For each execution scenario, we deal with four problems: (i) TIME-VC: minimize the makespan using the VC-ONLY approach; (ii) TIME-VC+V: minimize the makespan using the VC+V approach; (iii) ENERGY-VC: minimize the total energy consumption using the VC-ONLY approach; (iv) ENERGY-VC+V: minimize the total energy consumption using the VC+V approach. For the SINGLESPEED and REEXECSPEED scenarios, we have to decide for the optimal locations of the checkpoints (VC-ONLY) and of the verifications (VC+V). For the MULTISPEED scenario, we further have to select a pair of speeds (first execution and re-execution) for each segment.

4   Optimal Algorithms

In this section, we present optimal algorithms for the three execution scenarios. For each scenario, we have four combinations: two approaches—VC-ONLY and VC+V, and two objectives—makespan and energy. Due to the lack of space, we include only two (representative) proofs here, namely those of the TIME-VC and TIME-VC+V algorithms for the SINGLESPEED scenario. The other proofs can be found in the companion research report [4] of this paper.

4.1   SingleSpeed Scenario

In this scenario, we are given a single processing speed, and we investigate the VC-ONLY and VC+V approaches. For each approach, we present an optimal polynomial-time dynamic programming algorithm. As only one speed is present, the speed parameter s is omitted in all expressions for notational convenience.

VC-Only: Using Verified Checkpoints Only. In this approach, we aim at finding the best checkpointing positions in order to minimize the total execution time (TIME-VC) or the total energy consumption (ENERGY-VC).

Theorem 1. *For the* SINGLESPEED *scenario, the* TIME-VC *and* ENERGY-VC *problems can be solved by a dynamic programming algorithm in* $O(n^2)$ *time.*

Proof. Due to the lack of space, we only present the optimal algorithm to compute the expected makespan for the TIME-VC problem. The optimal solution for the ENERGY-VC problem can be similarly derived.

We define $Time_C(j)$ to be the optimal expected time to successfully execute tasks $T_1, \ldots, T_j$, where T_j has a verified checkpoint, and there are possibly other verified checkpoints from T_1 to T_{j-1}. We always verify and checkpoint the last task T_n to save the final result. Therefore, the goal is to find $Time_C(n)$. To compute $Time_C(j)$, we formulate the following dynamic program by trying all possible locations for the last checkpoint before T_j:

$$Time_C(j) = \min_{0 \le i < j} \{Time_C(i) + T_C(i+1, j)\} + C_j,$$

where $T_C(i,j)$ denotes the expected time to successfully execute tasks T_i to T_j, provided that T_{i-1} and T_j are both verified and checkpointed while no other task in between is verified nor checkpointed. Note that we also account for the checkpointing cost C_j for task T_j, which is not included in the definition of T_C. To initialize the dynamic program, we define $Time_C(0) = 0$.

In the following, we show how to compute $T_C(i,j)$ for each (i,j) pair with $i \le j$. We start by considering only *silent errors* and use the notation $T_C^S(i,j)$ for that purpose. Silent errors can occur at any time during the computation but we can only detect them after all tasks have been executed. Thus, we always have to pay $T_{i,j} + V_j$, the time to execute from task T_i to T_j and then to verify T_j. If the verification fails, which happens with probability $p_{i,j}^S$, a silent error has occurred and we have to recover from T_{i-1} and start anew. For convenience, we assume that there is a virtual task T_0 that is always verified and checkpointed, with a recovery cost $R_0 = 0$. Mathematically, we can express $T_C^S(i,j)$ as

$$T_C^S(i,j) = T_{i,j} + V_j + p_{i,j}^S \left(R_{i-1} + T_C^S(i,j) \right),$$
$$\Rightarrow T_C^S(i,j) = e^{\lambda^S T_{i,j}} (T_{i,j} + V_j) + (e^{\lambda^S T_{i,j}} - 1) R_{i-1}.$$

Things are different when accounting for *fail-stop errors*, because the application will stop immediately when a fail-stop error occurs, even in the middle of the computation. Let $T_{lost_{i,j}}$ denote the expected time lost during the execution from T_i to T_j if a fail-stop error strikes, and it can be expressed as

$$T_{lost_{i,j}} = \int_0^\infty x\mathbb{P}(X = x | X < T_{i,j}) dx = \frac{1}{\mathbb{P}(X < T_{i,j})} \int_0^{T_{i,j}} x\lambda^F e^{-\lambda^F x} dx,$$

where $\mathbb{P}(X = x)$ denotes the probability that a fail-stop error strikes at time x. By definition, we have $\mathbb{P}(X < T_{i,j}) = 1 - e^{-\lambda^F T_{i,j}}$. Integrating by parts, we get

$$T_{lost_{i,j}} = \frac{1}{\lambda^F} - \frac{T_{i,j}}{e^{\lambda^F T_{i,j}} - 1}.$$

Therefore, the expected execution time $T_C^F(i,j)$ when considering only fail-stop errors is given by

$$T_C^F(i,j) = p_{i,j}^F \left(T_{lost_{i,j}} + R_{i-1} + T_C^F(i,j) \right) + \left(1 - p_{i,j}^F\right) T_{i,j},$$
$$\Rightarrow T_C^F(i,j) = (e^{\lambda^F T_{i,j}} - 1) \left(\frac{1}{\lambda^F} + R_{i-1} \right).$$

We now account for both *fail-stop and silent errors*, and use the notation $T_C^{SF}(i,j)$ for that purpose. To this end, we consider fail-stop errors first. If the application stops, then we do not need to perform verification since we must do a recovery anyway. If no fail-stop error stroke during the execution, we can then proceed with the verification and check for silent errors. Therefore,

$$
\begin{aligned}
T_C^{SF}(i,j) = {}& p_{i,j}^F \left(T_{lost_{i,j}} + R_{i-1} + T_C^{SF}(i,j) \right) \\
& + \left(1 - p_{i,j}^F \right) \left(T_{i,j} + V_j + p_{i,j}^S \left(R_{i-1} + T_C^{SF}(i,j) \right) \right).
\end{aligned}
$$

When plugging $p_{i,j}^F$, $p_{i,j}^S$ and $T_{lost_{i,j}}$ into the above equation, we get

$$
T_C^{SF}(i,j) = e^{\lambda^S T_{i,j}} \left(\frac{e^{\lambda^F T_{i,j}} - 1}{\lambda^F} + V_j \right) + \left(e^{(\lambda^F + \lambda^S) T_{i,j}} - 1 \right) R_{i-1}.
$$

By setting $T_C(i,j) = T_C^{SF}(i,j)$, we can now compute $Time_C(j)$ for all $j = 1, \cdots, n$. For the complexity, the computation of $T_C^{SF}(i,j)$ for all (i,j) pairs with $i \leq j$ takes $O(n^2)$ time. The computation of the dynamic programming table for $Time_C(j)$ also takes $O(n^2)$ time, as $Time_C(j)$ depends on at most j other entries in the same table, which are already computed. Therefore, the overall complexity is $O(n^2)$, and this concludes the proof.   □

Theorem 1 nicely extends the result of Toueg and Babaoglu [31] to a linear chain of tasks subject to both fail-stop and silent errors. For the sake of comparing with the case of a divisible load application, we can extend Young/Daly's formula [11,33] in the following. Again, the proof can be found in [4].

Proposition 1. *For a divisible load application subject to both fail-stop and silent errors, a first-order approximation of the optimal checkpointing period is*

$$
T_{opt}(s) = \sqrt{\frac{2(V + C)}{\lambda^F + 2\lambda^S}},
$$

where C is the checkpointing cost, V is the verification cost, λ^F is the rate of fail-stop errors and λ^S is the rate of silent errors.

VC+V: Using Verified Checkpoints and Single Verifications. In this approach, we can place additional verifications between two checkpoints, which allows to detect (silent) errors before reaching the next checkpoint, and hence to avoid wasted execution by performing early recoveries. We aim at finding the best positions for checkpoints and verifications in order to minimize the total execution time (TIME-VC+V) or the total energy consumption (ENERGY-VC+V). For both objectives, adding extra verifications between two checkpoints adds an extra step in the algorithm, which results in a higher complexity.

Theorem 2. *For the* SINGLESPEED *scenario, the* TIME-VC+V *and* ENERGY-VC+V *problems can be solved by a dynamic programming algorithm in $O(n^3)$ time.*

Proof. Due to the lack of space, we only deal with the TIME-VC+V problem, while the solution for ENERGY-VC+V can be similarly derived.

The main idea is to replace T_C in the dynamic program of Theorem 1 by another expression $Time_V(i, j)$, which denotes the optimal expected time to successfully execute from task T_i to task T_j (and to verify it), provided that T_{i-1} has a verified checkpoint and only single verifications are allowed from task T_i to task T_{j-1}. Furthermore, we use $Time_{VC}(j)$ to denote the optimal expected time to successfully execute the first j tasks, where T_j has a verified checkpoint, and there are possibly other verified checkpoints and single verifications before T_j. The goal is to find $Time_{VC}(n)$. The dynamic program can then be formulated as:

$$Time_{VC}(j) = \min_{0 \le i < j} \{Time_{VC}(i) + Time_V(i+1, j)\} + C_j.$$

In particular, we try all possible locations for the last checkpoint before T_j, and for each location T_i, we compute the optimal expected time $Time_V(i+1, j)$ to executed tasks T_{i+1} to T_{j-1} with only single verifications in between. We also account for the checkpointing time C_j, which is not included in the definition of $Time_V$. By initializing the dynamic program with $Time_{VC}(0) = 0$, we can then compute the optimal solution as in the TIME-VC problem.

It remains to compute $Time_V(i, j)$ for each (i, j) pair with $i \le j$. To this end, we formulate another dynamic program by trying all possible locations for the last single verification before T_j:

$$Time_V(i, j) = \min_{i-1 \le l < j} \{Time_V(i, l) + T_V(l+1, j, i-1)\},$$

where $T_V(i, j, l_c)$ is the expected time to successfully execute all the tasks from T_i to T_j (and to verify T_j), knowing that if an error strikes, we can recover from T_{l_c}, the last task before T_i to have a verified checkpoint.

First, we show how to compute $T_V(i, j, l_c)$. When accounting for only *silent errors* (with notation T_V^S), we always execute from task T_i to task T_j and then verify T_j. In case of failure, we recover from T_{l_c} and redo the entire computation from T_{l_c+1} to T_j, which contains a single verification after T_{i-1} and possibly other single verifications between T_{l_c+1} and T_{i-2}. Hence, we have

$$T_V^S(i, j, l_c) = T_{i,j} + V_j + p_{i,j}^S \left(R_{l_c} + Time_V(l_c+1, i-1) + T_V^S(i, j, l_c)\right),$$
$$\Rightarrow T_V^S(i, j, l_c) = e^{\lambda^S T_{i,j}} (T_{i,j} + V_j) + (e^{\lambda^S T_{i,j}} - 1) (R_{l_c} + Time_V(l_c+1, i-1)).$$

When there are only *fail-stop errors*, we do not need to perform any single verification, and hence the problem becomes simply the TIME-VC problem. When accounting for both *silent and fail-stop errors* (with notation T_V^{SF}), we apply the same method as in the previous proof. Specifically, if a fail-stop error strikes between two verifications, we directly perform a recovery; otherwise we check for silent errors:

$$T_V^{SF}(i,j,l_c) = p_{i,j}^F \left(T_{lost_{i,j}} + R_{l_c} + Time_V(l_c+1,i-1) + T_V^{SF}(i,j,l_c)\right)$$
$$+ \left(1 - p_{i,j}^F\right)\left(T_{i,j} + V_j + p_{i,j}^S \left(R_{l_c} + Time_V(l_c+1,i-1) + T_V^{SF}(i,j,l_c)\right)\right),$$
$$\Rightarrow T_V^{SF}(i,j,l_c) = e^{\lambda^S T_{i,j}} \left(\frac{e^{\lambda^F T_{i,j}} - 1}{\lambda^F} + V_j\right)$$
$$+ \left(e^{(\lambda^F + \lambda^S)T_{i,j}} - 1\right)\left(R_{l_c} + Time_V(l_c+1,i-1)\right).$$

Notice that $Time_V(i,j,l_c)$ depends on the value of $Time_V(l_c+1,i-1)$, except when $l_c + 1 = i$, in which case we initialize $Time_V(i,i-1) = 0$. Hence, in the dynamic program, $Time_V(i,j)$ can be expressed as a function of $Time_V(i,l)$ for all $l = i-1, \cdots, j-1$.

Finally, the complexity is dominated by the computation of the second dynamic programming table for $Time_V(i,j)$, which contains $O(n^2)$ entries and each entry depends on at most n other entries that are already computed. Hence, the overall complexity of the algorithm is $O(n^3)$, and this concludes the proof.

4.2 ReExecSpeed Scenario

Despite the additional speed, the REEXECSPEED scenario turns out to have the same complexity as the SINGLESPEED scenario.

Theorem 3. *For the* REEXECSPEED *scenario:*

- *The* TIME-VC *and* ENERGY-VC *problems can be solved by a dynamic programming algorithm in* $O(n^2)$ *time.*
- *The* TIME-VC+V *and* ENERGY-VC+V *problems can be solved by a dynamic programming algorithm in* $O(n^3)$ *time.*

4.3 MultiSpeed Scenario

Optimal algorithms for the MULTISPEED scenario are more intricate and have higher complexity than the other scenarios.

Theorem 4. *For the* MULTISPEED *scenario:*

- *The* TIME-VC *and* ENERGY-VC *problems can be solved by a dynamic programming algorithm in* $O(n^2 K^2)$ *time.*
- *The* TIME-VC+V *and* ENERGY-VC+V *problems can be solved by a dynamic programming algorithm in* $O(n^3 K^2)$ *time.*

5 Experiments

We conduct simulations to evaluate the performance of the dynamic programming algorithms under different execution scenarios and parameter settings. We instantiate the model parameters with realistic values taken from the literature, and we point out that the code for all algorithms and simulations is publicly available at http://graal.ens-lyon.fr/~yrobert/failstop-silent, so that interested readers can build relevant scenarios of their choice.

5.1   Simulation Settings

We generate linear chains with different number n of tasks while keeping the total computational cost at $W = 5 \times 10^4$ s ≈ 14 h. The total amount of computation is distributed among the tasks in three different patterns: (1) *Uniform*, all tasks share the same cost W/n, as in matrix multiplication or in some iterative stencil kernels; (2) *Decrease*, task T_i has cost $\alpha \cdot (n + 1 - i)^2$, where $\alpha \approx 3W/n^3$. This quadratically decreasing function resembles some dense matrix solvers, e.g., using LU or QR factorization. (3) *HighLow*, a set of identical tasks with large cost is followed by tasks with small cost. This distribution is created to distinguish the performance of different execution scenarios. In this case, we fix the number of large tasks to be 10 % of the total number n of tasks while varying the computational cost dedicated to them.

We adopt the set of speeds from the Intel Xscale processor. Following [27], the normalized speeds are $\{0.15, 0.4, 0.6, 0.8, 1\}$ and the fitted power function is given by $P(s) = 1550s^3 + 60$. From the discussion in Sect. 2.3, we assume the following model for the average error rate of fail-stop errors:

$$\lambda^F(s) = \lambda^F_{\text{ref}} \cdot 10^{\frac{d \cdot |s_{\text{ref}} - s|}{s_{\max} - s_{\min}}}, \tag{1}$$

where $s_{\text{ref}} \in [s_{\min}, s_{\max}]$ denotes the reference speed with the lowest error rate λ^F_{ref} among all possible speeds in the range. The above equation allows us to account for higher fail-stop error rates when the CPU speed is either too low or too high. In the simulations, the reference speed is set to be $s_{\text{ref}} = 0.6$ with an error rate of $\lambda^F_{\text{ref}} = 10^{-5}$ for fail-stop errors, and the sensitivity parameter is set to be $d = 3$. These parameters represent realistic settings reported in the literature [1,2,34], and they correspond to 0.83 $\sim$ 129 errors over the entire chain of computation depending on the processing speed chosen.

For silent errors, we assume that its error rate is related to that of the fail-stop errors by $\lambda^S(s) = \eta \cdot \lambda^F(s)$, where $\eta > 0$ is constant parameter. To achieve realistic scenarios, we try to vary η to assess the impact of both error sources on the performance. However, we point out that our approach is completely independent of the evolution of the error rates as a function of the speed. In a practical setting, we are given a set of discrete speeds and two error rates for each speed, one for fail-stop errors and one for silent errors. This is enough to instantiate our model.

In addition, we define cr to be the ratio between the checkpointing/recovery cost and the computational cost for the tasks, and define vr to be the ratio between the verification cost and the computational cost. By default, we execute the tasks using the reference speed s_{ref}, and set $\eta = 1$, $cr = 1$ and $vr = 0.01$. This initial setting corresponds to tasks with costly checkpoints (same order of magnitude as the costs of the tasks) and lightweight verifications (average cost 1 % of task cost); examples of such tasks are data-oriented kernels processing large files and checksumming for verification. We will vary these parameters to study their impacts on the performance.

5.2   Results

SingleSpeed Scenario for Makespan. The first set of experiments is devoted to the evaluation of the time-optimal algorithms in the SINGLESPEED scenario.

Impact of n and cost distribution. Figure 1(a) shows the expected makespan (normalized by the ideal execution time at the default speed, i.e., $W/0.6$) with different n and cost distributions. For the *HighLow* distribution, the large tasks are configured to contain 60 % of the total computational cost. The results show that having more tasks reduces the expected makespan, since it enables the algorithms to place more checkpoints and verifications, as can be seen in Fig. 1(b). The distribution that renders a larger variation in task sizes create more difficulty in the placement of checkpoints/verfications, thus resulting in worse makespan. The figure also compares the performance of the TIME-VC algorithm with that of TIME-VC+V. The latter algorithm, being more flexible, naturally leads to improved makespan under all cost distributions. Because of the additionally placed verifications, it also reduces the number of verified checkpoints in the optimal solution.

Comparison with a divisible load application. Figure 2(a) compares the makespan of the TIME-VC algorithm under *Uniform* cost distribution with the makespan of a divisible load application, whose total load is W and whose checkpointing cost is the same as the corresponding discrete tasks. For the divisible load application, we use Proposition 1 to compute the optimal period, the waste and then derive the makespan. In addition, Fig. 2(b) compares the number of verified checkpoints in the two cases. We see that the makespan for divisible load is worse for large cr and becomes better as cr decreases. Furthermore, the makespans in both cases get closer when the number of tasks increases. This is because the checkpointing cost decreases with cr and as n increases, which makes the first order approximation used in Proposition 1 more accurate. Moreover, as divisible

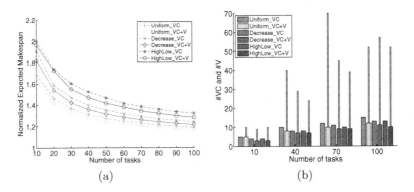

Fig. 1. Impact of n and cost distribution on the performance of the TIME-VC and TIME-VC+V algorithms. In (b), the thick bars represent the verified checkpoints and the yellow thin bars represent the total number of verifications.

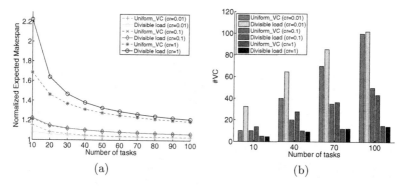

Fig. 2. Performance comparison of the TIME-VC algorithm for tasks with *Uniform* cost distribution and the optimal checkpointing algorithm for divisible load application.

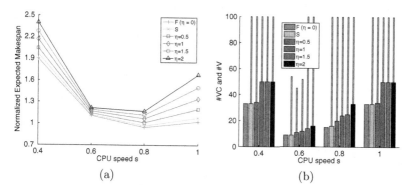

Fig. 3. Impact of η and speed s on the performance. F denotes fail-stop error only and S denotes silent error only. Speed $s = 0.15$ leads to extremely large makespan, which is omitted in the figure.

load does not impose restrictions in the checkpointing positions, it tends to place more checkpoints than the case with discrete tasks.

We could think of the following greedy algorithm as an alternative to the TIME-VC algorithm for a linear chain of tasks: position the next checkpoint as soon as the time spent on computing since the last checkpoint plus the checkpointing cost of the current task exceeds the optimal period given by Proposition 1. Figure 2 suggests that this linear-time algorithm (with cost $O(n)$) would give a good approximation of the optimal solution (returned by the TIME-VC algorithm with cost $O(n^2)$), at least for uniform distribution of task costs.

In the rest of this section, we will focus on the TIME-VC+V algorithm and $n = 100$ tasks with *Uniform* cost distribution.

Impact of η and error mode. Figure 3(a) compares the performance under different error modes, namely, fail-stop (F) only, silent (S) only, and fail-stop plus silent with different values of η. As silent errors are harder to detect and hence to deal with, the S-only case leads to larger makespan than the F-only case.

In the presence of both types of errors, the makespan becomes worse with larger η, i.e., with increased rate for silent errors, despite the algorithm's effort to place more checkpoints as shown in Fig. 3(b). Moreover, the performance degrades significantly as the CPU speed is set below the reference speed s_{ref} for the error rate increases exponentially. A higher CPU speed, on the other hand, first improves the makespan by executing the tasks faster and then causes degradation due to a larger increase in the error rate.

Impact of cr and vr. Figure 4(a) presents the impact of checkpointing/recovery ratio (cr) and verification ratio (vr) on the performance. Clearly, a smaller cr (or vr) enables the algorithm to place more checkpoints (or verifications), which leads to better makespan. Having more checkpoints also allows the algorithm to use faster speeds to complete the tasks. Finally, if checkpointing cost is on par with verification cost (e.g., $cr = 0.1$), reducing the verification cost can additionally increase the number of checkpoints (e.g., at $s = 0.6$), since each checkpoint also has a verification cost associated with it. For high checkpointing cost, however, reducing the verification cost could no longer influence the algorithm's checkpointing decisions.

SingleSpeed Scenario for Energy. This set of experiments focuses on the evaluation of the ENERGY-VC+V algorithm in the SINGLESPEED scenario. The default power parameters are set to be $P_{idle} = 60$ and $P_{cpu}(s) = 1550s^3$ according to [27]. The dynamic power consumption due to I/O is equal to the dynamic power of the CPU at the lowest discrete speed 0.15. We will also vary these parameters to study their impacts.

Impact of CPU speed s. Figure 5 compares the performance of the ENERGY-VC+V algorithm in comparison with its makespan counterpart TIME-VC+V for $n = 100$ tasks. At speed 0.15, the power consumed by the CPU is identical to that of I/O. This yields the same number of checkpoints placed by the two algorithms, which in turn leads to the same performance for both makespan and energy. As the CPU speed increases, the I/O power consumption becomes much smaller, so the energy algorithm tends to place more checkpoints to improve the energy consumption at the expense of makespan. From Fig. 3, we know that the makespan of TIME-VC+V degrades at speed $s = 1$. This diminishes its makespan advantage at the highest discrete speed. Figure 5 also suggests that the TIME-VC+V algorithm running at speed $s = 0.8$ offers a good energy-makespan tradeoff. Compared to the ENERGY-VC+V algorithm, it provides more than 25 % improvement in makespan with only 10 % degradation in energy under the default parameter settings.

Impact of P_{idle} and P_{io}. Figure 6 shows the relative performance of the two algorithms by varying P_{idle} and P_{io} separately according to the dynamic power function $1550s^3$, while keeping the other one at the smallest CPU power, i.e., $1550 \cdot 0.15^3$. The CPU speed is fixed at $s = 0.6$. Figure 6 further shows the number of checkpoints in the ENERGY-VC+V algorithm at different P_{idle} and P_{io} values. (The TIME-VC+V algorithm is apparently not affected by these

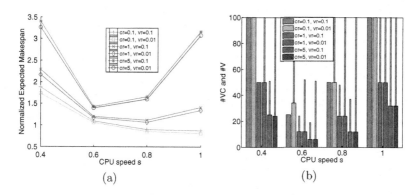

Fig. 4. Impact of cr and vr on the performance with different CPU speeds.

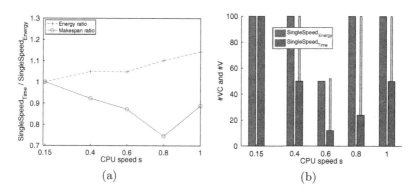

Fig. 5. Relative performance of the ENERGY-VC+V and TIME-VC+V algorithms with different CPU speeds.

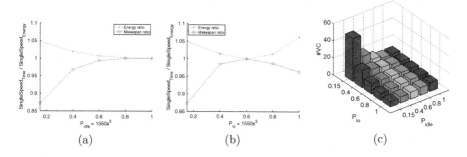

Fig. 6. (a) and (b): Impact of P_{idle} and P_{io} on the relative performance of the ENERGY-VC+V and TIME-VC+V algorithms at $s = 0.6$. (c): Number of checkpoints placed by the ENERGY-VC+V algorithm with different P_{io}, P_{idle} values ($= 1550s^3$) at $s = 0.6$.

two parameters and always places 11 checkpoints in this experiment.) First, setting the smallest value for both parameters creates a big gap between the CPU and I/O power consumptions. This leads to a large number of checkpoints placed by the ENERGY-VC+V algorithm. Increasing P_{idle} closes this gap and hence reduces the number of checkpoints, which leads to the performance convergence of the two algorithms. While increasing P_{io} has the same effect, a larger value than $P_{cpu} = 1550 \cdot 0.6^3$ further reduces the number of checkpoints below 11, since checkpointing is now less power-efficient. This again gives the ENERGY-VC+V algorithm advantage in terms of energy.

ReExecSpeed and MultiSpeed Scenarios. This set of experiments evaluates the REEXECSPEED and MULTISPEED scenarios for both makespan and energy. To distinguish them from the SINGLESPEED model, we consider the *HighLow* distribution, which yields a larger variance among the computational costs of the tasks. In the simulation, we again focus on the VC+V algorithms for $n = 100$ tasks, and vary the *cost ratio*, which is the percentage of computational cost in the large tasks compared to the total computational cost.

Figure 7(a) compares the makespan of the TIME-VC+V algorithms under the three scenarios. For the SINGLESPEED and REEXECSPEED scenarios, only $s = 0.6$ and $s = 0.8$ are drawn, since the other speeds lead to much larger makespans. For a small cost ratio, no task has a very large computational cost, so the faster speed $s = 0.8$, despite its higher error rate, appears to give the best performance as we have already seen in Fig. 3(a). When the cost ratio increases, tasks with large cost start to emerge. With the high error rate of $s = 0.8$, these tasks will experience many re-executions, thus degrading the makespan. Here, $s = 0.6$ becomes the best speed due to its smaller error rate. In the REEXECSPEED scenario, regardless of the initial speed s, the best re-execution speed σ is always 0.6 or 0.8 depending on the cost ratio, and it improves upon the respective SINGLESPEED scenario with the same initial speed, as we can see in Fig. 7(b) for cost ratio of 0.6. However, the improvement is marginal compared to the best performance achievable in the SINGLESPEED scenario. The MULTISPEED scenario, with its flexibility to choose different speeds depending on the costs of the tasks, always provides the best performance. The advantage is especially evident at medium cost ratios with up to 6 % improvement, as this situation contains a good mix of large and small tasks, which is hard to deal with by using fixed speed(s). Figure 8 shows similar results for the energy consumption of the ENERGY-VC+V algorithms under the three scenarios, with more than 7 % improvement in the MULTISPEED scenario. In this case, speed $s = 0.4$ consumes less energy at small cost ratio due to its better power efficiency.

Finally, Fig. 9 shows the relative performance of the ENERGY-VC+V and TIME-VC+V algorithms under the MULTISPEED scenario. As small cost ratio favors speed 0.4 for the energy algorithm and 0.8 for the time algorithm, it distinguishes the two algorithms in terms of their respective optimization objectives, by up to 100 % in makespan and even more in energy consumption. Increasing the cost ratio creates more computationally demanding tasks, which need to be executed at speed 0.6 for both makespan and energy efficiency as it incurs fewer

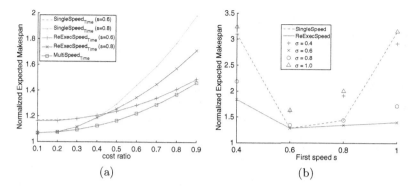

(a)   (b)

Fig. 7. Performance comparison of the TIME-VC+V algorithms in MULTISPEED, REEXECSPEED and SINGLESPEED scenarios for $n = 100$ tasks with *HighLow* cost distribution. In (b), the cost ratio is 0.6.

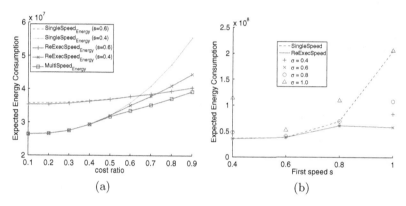

(a)   (b)

Fig. 8. Performance comparison of the ENERGY-VC+V algorithms in MULTISPEED, REEXECSPEED and SINGLESPEED scenarios for $n = 100$ tasks with *HighLow* cost distribution. In (b), the cost ratio is 0.6.

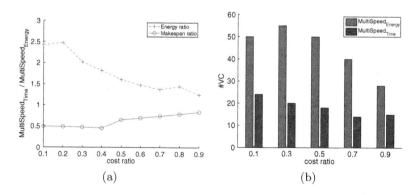

(a)   (b)

Fig. 9. Impact of cost ratio on the relative performance of the ENERGY-VC+V and TIME-VC+V algorithms under the MULTISPEED scenario.

errors. This closes the performance gap of the two algorithms as well as the number of checkpoints placed by them. In either case, the number of checkpoints also reduces with the cost ratio, because the total computational cost in the small tasks shrinks, thus fewer checkpoints are needed among them.

Summary. To summarize, we have evaluated and compared various algorithms under different execution scenarios. The algorithms under the most flexible VC+V and MULTISPEED scenario generally provide better performance, which in practice would translate to shorter makespan or lower energy consumption.

For tasks with similar computational costs as in the *Uniform* distribution, we observe that the SINGLESPEED algorithm, or the greedy approximation in the context of divisible load application, could in fact provide comparable solutions with lower computational complexity. The REEXECSPEED algorithms show only marginal benefit compared to SINGLESPEED, but clear performance improvements are observed from the MULTISPEED algorithms, especially for tasks with very different costs. The results also show that the optimal solutions are often achieved by processing around the reference speed that yields the least number of failures.

In terms of computation time, the most advanced VC+V algorithms in the MULTISPEED scenario take less than a second to find the optimal solution for $n = 100$ tasks. As application workflows rarely exceed a few tens of tasks, these algorithms could be efficiently applied in many practical contexts to determine the optimal checkpointing and verification locations.

6   Conclusion

In this paper, we have presented a general-purpose solution that combines checkpointing and verification mechanisms to cope with both fail-stop errors and silent data corruptions. By using dynamic programming, we have devised polynomial-time algorithms that decide the optimal checkpointing and verification positions on a linear chain of tasks. The algorithms can be applied to several execution scenarios to minimize the expected execution time (makespan) or energy consumption. In addition, we have extended the classical bound of Young/Daly for divisible load applications to handle both fail-stop and silent errors. The results are supported by a set of extensive simulations, which demonstrate the quality and tradeoff of our optimal algorithms under a wide range of parameter settings. One useful future direction is to extend our study from linear chains to other application workflows, such as tree graphs, fork-join graphs, series-parallel graphs, or even general DAGs.

References

1. Assayad, I., Girault, A., Kalla, H.: Tradeoff exploration between reliability, power consumption, and execution time for embedded systems. Int. J. Softw. Tools Technol. Transf. **15**(3), 229–245 (2013)

2. Aupy, G., Benoit, A., Robert, Y.: Energy-aware scheduling under reliability and makespan constraints. In: Proceedings of the International Conference on High Performance Computing (HiPC), pp. 1–10 (2012)

3. Bansal, N., Kimbrel, T., Pruhs, K.: Speed scaling to manage energy and temperature. J. ACM **54**(1), 3:1–3:39 (2007)

4. Benoit, A., Cavelan, A., Robert, Y., Sun, H.: Assessing general-purpose algorithms to cope with fail-stop and silent errors. Research report RR-8599, INRIA, September 2014

5. Benson, A.R., Schmit, S., Schreiber, R.: Silent error detection in numerical timestepping schemes. CoRR, abs/1312.2674 (2013)

6. Bosilca, G., Delmas, R., Dongarra, J., Langou, J.: Algorithm-based fault tolerance applied to high performance computing. J. Parallel Distrib. Comput. **69**(4), 410–416 (2009)

7. Bougeret, M., Casanova, H., Rabie, M., Robert, Y., Vivien, F.: Checkpointing strategies for parallel jobs. In: 2011 International Conference for High Performance Computing, Networking, Storage and Analysis (SC), pp. 1–11 (2011)

8. Bronevetsky, G., de Supinski, B.: Soft error vulnerability of iterative linear algebra methods. In: Proceedings 22nd International Conference on Supercomputing, ICS 2008, pp. 155–164. ACM (2008)

9. Chandy, K.M., Lamport, L.: Distributed snapshots: determining global states of distributed systems. ACM Trans. Comput. Syst. **3**(1), 63–75 (1985)

10. Chen, Z., Online-ABFT: an online algorithm based fault tolerance scheme for soft error detection in iterative methods. In: Proceedings of the 18th ACM SIGPLAN Symposium on Principles and Practice of Parallel Programming, PPoPP 2013, pp. 167–176. ACM (2013)

11. Daly, J.T.: A higher order estimate of the optimum checkpoint interval for restart dumps. FGCS **22**(3), 303–312 (2004)

12. Das, A., Kumar, A., Veeravalli, B., Bolchini, C., Miele, A.: Combined DVFS and mapping exploration for lifetime and soft-error susceptibility improvement in MPSoCs. In: Proceedings of the Conference on Design, Automation and Test in Europe (DATE), pp. 1–6 (2014)

13. Dixit, A., Wood, A.: The impact of new technology on soft error rates. In: IEEE International on Reliability Physics Symposium (IRPS), pp. 5B.4.1–5B.4.7 (2011)

14. El-Sayed, N., Stefanovici, I.A., Amvrosiadis, G., Hwang, A.A., Schroeder, B.: Temperature management in data centers: why some (might) like it hot. SIGMETRICS Perform. Eval. Rev. **40**(1), 163–174 (2012)

15. Elliott, J., Kharbas, K., Fiala, D., Mueller, F., Ferreira, K., Engelmann, C.: Combining partial redundancy and checkpointing for HPC. In: Proceedings of the ICDCS 2012. IEEE Computer Society (2012)

16. Elnozahy, E.N.M., Alvisi, L., Wang, Y.-M., Johnson, D.B.: A survey of rollbackrecovery protocols in message-passing systems. ACM Comput. Surv. **34**, 375–408 (2002)

17. Feng, W.-C.: Making a case for efficient supercomputing. Queue **1**(7), 54–64 (2003)

18. Fiala, D., Mueller, F., Engelmann, C., Riesen, R., Ferreira, K., Brightwell, R.: Detection and correction of silent data corruption for large-scale high-performance computing. In: Proceedings of the ACM/IEEE SC International Conference SC 2012. IEEE Computer Society Press (2012)

19. Heroux, M., Hoemmen, M.: Fault-tolerant iterative methods via selective reliability. Research report SAND2011-3915 C, Sandia National Laboratories (2011)

20. Hsu, C.-H., Chun Feng, W.: A power-aware run-time system for high-performance computing. In: Proceedings of the ACM/IEEE Supercomputing Conference, pp. 1–9 (2005)
21. Huang, K.-H., Abraham, J.A.: Algorithm-based fault tolerance for matrix operations. IEEE Trans. Comput. $33(6)$, 518–528 (1984)
22. Hwang, A.A., Stefanovici, I.A., Schroeder, B.: Cosmic rays don't strike twice: understanding the nature of dram errors and the implications for system design. SIGARCH Comput. Archit. News $40(1)$, 111–122 (2012)
23. Lu, G., Zheng, Z., Chien, A.A.: When is multi-version checkpointing needed. In: 3rd Workshop for Fault-Tolerance at Extreme Scale (FTXS). ACM Press (2013). https://sites.google.com/site/uchicagolssg/lssg/research/gvr
24. Lyons, R.E., Vanderkulk, W.: The use of triple-modular redundancy to improve computer reliability. IBM J. Res. Dev. $6(2)$, 200–209 (1962)
25. Ozaki, T., Dohi, T., Okamura, H., Kaio, N.: Distribution-free checkpoint placement algorithms based on min-max principle. IEEE TDSC 3, 130–140 (2006)
26. Patterson, M.: The effect of data center temperature on energy efficiency. In: Proceedings of 11th Intersociety Conference on Thermal and Thermomechanical Phenomena in Electronic Systems, pp. 1167–1174 (2008)
27. Rizvandi, N.B., Zomaya, A.Y., Lee, Y.C., Boloori, A.J., Taheri, J.: Multiple frequency selection in DVFS-enabled processors to minimize energy consumption. In: Zomaya, A.Y., Lee, Y.C. (eds.) Energy-Efficient Distributed Computing Systems. Wiley, Hoboken (2012)
28. Sao, P., Vuduc, R.:Self-stabilizing iterative solvers. In: Proceedings ScalA 2013. ACM (2013)
29. Sarood, O., Meneses, E., Kale, L. V.: A 'cool' way of improving the reliability of HPC machines. In: Proceedings of the International Conference on High Performance Computing, Networking, Storage and Analysis, pp. 58:1–58:12 (2013)
30. Shantharam, M., Srinivasmurthy, S., Raghavan, P.: Fault tolerant preconditioned conjugate gradient for sparse linear system solution. In: Proceedings of the ICS 2012. ACM (2012)
31. Toueg, S., Babaoglu, Ö.: On the optimum checkpoint selection problem. SIAM J. Comput. $13(3)$, 630–649 (1984)
32. Yao, F., Demers, A., Shenker, S.: A scheduling model for reduced CPU energy. In: Proceedings of the 36th Annual Symposium on Foundations of Computer Science (FOCS), p. 374 (1995)
33. Young, J.W.: A first order approximation to the optimum checkpoint interval. Comm. ACM $17(9)$, 530–531 (1974)
34. Zhao, B., Aydin, H., Zhu, D.: Reliability-aware dynamic voltage scaling for energy-constrained real-time embedded systems. In: Proceedings of the IEEE International Conference on Computer Design (ICCD), pp. 633–639 (2008)
35. Zhu, D., Melhem, R., Mosse, D.: The effects of energy management on reliability in real-time embedded systems. In: Proceedings of the IEEE/ACM International Conference on Computer-Aided Design (ICCAD), pp. 35–40 (2004)

A Case for Epidemic Fault Detection and Group Membership in HPC Storage Systems

Shane Snyder[1]([⊠]), Philip Carns[1], Jonathan Jenkins[1], Kevin Harms[1],
Robert Ross[1], Misbah Mubarak[2], and Christopher Carothers[2]

[1] Argonne National Laboratory, Argonne, IL, USA
{ssnyder,carns,jenkins,rross}@mcs.anl.gov, harms@alcf.anl.gov
[2] Rensselaer Polytechnic Institute, Troy, NY, USA
{mubarm,chrisc}@cs.rpi.edu

Abstract. Fault response strategies are crucial to maintaining performance and availability in HPC storage systems, and the first responsibility of a successful fault response strategy is to detect failures and maintain an accurate view of group membership. This is a nontrivial problem given the unreliable nature of communication networks and other system components. As with many engineering problems, trade-offs must be made to account for the competing goals of fault detection efficiency and accuracy.

Today's production HPC services typically rely on distributed consensus algorithms and heartbeat monitoring for group membership. In this work, we investigate epidemic protocols to determine whether they would be a viable alternative. Epidemic protocols have been proposed in previous work for use in peer-to-peer systems, but they have the potential to increase scalability and decrease fault response time for HPC systems as well. We focus our analysis on the Scalable Weakly-consistent Infection-style Process Group Membership (SWIM) protocol.

We begin by exploring how the semantics of this protocol differ from those of typical HPC group membership protocols, and we discuss how storage systems might need to adapt as a result. We use existing analytical models to choose appropriate SWIM parameters for an HPC use case. We then develop a new, high-resolution parallel discrete event simulation of the protocol to confirm existing analytical models and explore protocol behavior that cannot be readily observed with analytical models. Our preliminary results indicate that the SWIM protocol is a promising alternative for group membership in HPC storage systems, offering rapid convergence, tolerance to transient network failures, and minimal network load.

1 Introduction

As the scale of modern distributed systems continues to grow, so too does the frequency of system component failures. Ensuring efficient and correct behavior in the presence of such failures requires both a reliable fault detection mechanism and a suitable strategy for fault recovery. Example distributed services that rely on efficient and accurate fault detection include distributed storage

© Springer International Publishing Switzerland 2015
S.A. Jarvis et al. (Eds.): PMBS 2014, LNCS 8966, pp. 237–248, 2015.
DOI: 10.1007/978-3-319-17248-4_12

systems [16,21] and reliable multicast protocols [6,7]. Fault detection is one component of broader group membership protocols [6,11,19] that are used to maintain a global view of available participants as they enter or leave the system. An HPC storage system might use this view to determine the set of available servers for data placement, and changes to the group membership can be used to trigger the re-replication of data in order to maintain resilience. An inefficient failure detector (i.e., one that takes too long to disseminate failure notifications to the group) could lead to data loss if data is not re-replicated before additional failures occur, while an inaccurate failure detector could lead to costly, unnecessary rebuilds of the storage system.

Group membership protocols often use heartbeat mechanisms to detect faults [1,8,15,20]: each participant sends out periodic "heartbeat" messages to inform other participants that it is alive. If no new heartbeat messages are received for some prescribed duration, the participant is declared faulty and removed from the group. Unfortunately, the scalability of heartbeat protocols has proven unacceptable for group sizes exceeding more than a few hundred participants [7]. This limitation arises from the network load imposed by group membership protocols in order to provide complete and efficient detection of failures [13]. In practice, failure detector implementations usually divide systems into smaller groups with independent failure domains (introducing artificial limitations on the range of failures the system can tolerate) or delegate group membership maintenance to a specialized subset of participants (increasing engineering complexity and failing to leverage the full network capacity of the system).

In this work, we analyze the efficiency and scalability of the SWIM (Scalable Weakly-consistent Infection-style Process Group Membership) protocol. Previous work [11] proposed the SWIM protocol and evaluated it using both analytical models and a prototype implementation, but to the best of our knowledge it is not used in production on any present-day system. SWIM achieves scalability through the use of a randomized, probe-based failure detection mechanism coupled with an epidemic-style (also known as infection-style or gossip-style) failure dissemination component. As a result, neither the expected network load per participant nor the expected time to first detect a failed participant will depend directly on the size of the group. While much of the analysis given in [11] assumes a distributed peer-to-peer environment, we instead explore how to adapt SWIM to a horizontally scalable data center storage environment as would be used for HPC or big data applications. This environment is characterized by lower network latency and lower churn rate but also higher expectations of consistency and responsiveness. Although failure modes such as silent data corruption are important considerations in HPC storage system design, in this work we focus on total server failures and assume that additional mechanisms will be used to detect silent errors.

The rest of this paper is organized as follows. In Sect. 2, we summarize the SWIM group membership protocol. Section 3 explores the implications of using the SWIM protocol in an HPC storage system, while Sect. 4 analyzes how to tune its parameters for that environment. In Sect. 5 we provide initial simulation results to confirm its performance and to explore its behavior in lossy network environments. In Sect. 6 we summarize our findings and propose avenues for future research.

2 Background: SWIM

As defined in [11], the SWIM group membership protocol can be functionally decomposed into two primary components: a failure detector and a mechanism for disseminating group membership updates. The failure detection mechanism is based on the periodic probing of random group participants, while the failure dissemination component is implemented by using an epidemic protocol.

To provide a high-level overview of the SWIM failure detector, we outline its operation at an arbitrary participant P_i. The failure detection protocol is governed by two key parameters: protocol period length T' and size of failure detection subgroups k. At the beginning of each of its protocol periods, P_i will select a random participant (which we refer to as P_j) from its local group membership view and probe it using a direct ping request. P_i then waits a prespecified timeout duration to receive an ack from P_j. If no ack is received, the protocol selects k more participants at random and sends an indirect ping request to each of them. Each participant in this subgroup will then ping P_j on behalf of P_i, forwarding any received acks back to P_i to inform that P_j is alive. The indirect ping requests are used to circumvent potential congestion on the network path between P_i and P_j and other phenomena that may have caused the loss of the original direct ping request or response. At the end of the protocol period (of duration T'), if no ack has been received by P_i (whether from direct or indirect probes), then a subprotocol is triggered that marks P_j as *suspected*, and this update is passed to the SWIM dissemination component to be communicated to the rest of the group.

After a participant is declared as *suspected* by the SWIM failure detector, the protocol continues normal operation—the *suspected* participant may still be selected as a probe target in future iterations of the protocol. However, if a participant P_j remains *suspected* for more than s iterations (i.e., the *suspicion timeout*) of the protocol on P_i, then P_i will mark P_j as *failed* and disseminate that information to other participants. If a *suspected* participant becomes responsive again before the suspicion timeout expires, it will be marked as *alive* with a corresponding update disseminated to rejuvenate it in other participants' membership views.

While it seems natural to disseminate membership updates throughout the group by using traditional multicast primitives (e.g., hardware, IP), this approach is unlikely to work at larger scales because of the cost of implementing multicast portably in unreliable networks. For this reason, SWIM disseminates membership information using a gossip-style strategy [20], where information propagates similarly to the way that gossip propagates through society. Compared with typical multicast protocols, gossip-style protocols offer higher efficiency and robustness to failures, although at the cost of a higher dissemination latency. In the SWIM protocol, group membership updates are disseminated by piggybacking this data on the ping and ack messages already generated by the failure detection protocol. This dissemination therefore introduces no extra packets and imposes minimal additional network load. The information then spreads through the group as participants randomly ping (and ack) each other, ultimately resulting in complete dissemination of the update.

3   Implications of Using SWIM in HPC Storage Systems

Current production HPC storage systems typically use distributed consensus algorithms on subsets of servers to maintain a coherent view of group membership; examples include the Totem single-ring protocol [3] in Corosync [10] (used by a variety of distributed services) and the PAXOS protocol [17] in Ceph [21]. The SWIM protocol semantics differ from such protocols in two notable ways with respect to storage system design. First, SWIM does not provide a strongly consistent view of membership among all participants. At any given time, two participants may have different views of the system. Second, it does not guarantee that updates are disseminated in a consistent order.

SWIM *does* guarantee, however, that all participants will converge to agreement on the state of a failed participant. SWIM also guarantees time-bounded strong completeness when using a randomized round-robin ping strategy [11]. We can therefore calculate both an upper bound and an expected amount of time needed to disseminate a membership update.

Based on these properties, we propose the following design recommendations for fault recovery in storage systems using SWIM for group membership. Note that we leave fault detection and group membership entirely to storage system servers; storage clients are excluded as participants in order to simplify the fault recovery process.

- Avoid the use of fault response protocols that require strict ordering of group updates across servers.
- Allow each server to initiate its own fault response (e.g., generating replicas or recalculating parity) once it has confirmed a fault.
- Validate state agreement between pairs of servers that coordinate during recovery by piggybacking state information on recovery messages. This approach ensures consistency while limiting synchronization overhead.

In general, we observe that the SWIM protocol is not a drop-in replacement for existing fault detection mechanisms in today's storage systems. We will contrast with conventional approaches and explore their impact on storage system design in future work based on the outcome of this preliminary study.

4   SWIM Parameter Selection

Before evaluating SWIM's performance in the context of a large-scale HPC storage system, we must select appropriate protocol parameters. As we vary the number of storage servers (n), we focus on two key input parameters: the protocol period length (T') and the suspicion timeout in periods (s). These parameters can be used in conjunction with existing analytical models for SWIM to calculate the expected time before a fault is detected by a single server (t_{detect}) as well as the expected time for a given status update to be disseminated to all alive servers (t_{dissem}). We define t_{detect} (derived entirely from analytical models in [13]) as follows, where q_f is the probability that a server is not faulty.

$$t_{detect} = T' \times \frac{1}{1 - e^{-q_f}}$$

We obtain t_{dissem} using the following equation from [11], where x is the number of infected servers (initially 1), n is the group size, and t is time (in protocol periods): $x = \frac{n}{1+(n-1)e^{-(2-\frac{1}{n})t}}$. Then, t_{dissem} may be given as follows, where p_{dissem} is the number of complete protocol periods t from above that results in total dissemination to all alive storage servers.

$$t_{dissem} = T' \times p_{dissem}$$

We further define the total time elapsed from the occurrence of a fault to all servers being aware of the confirmed failure as follows.

$$t_{total} = t_{detect} + (T' \times s) + t_{dissem}$$

We observe the following constraints in order to select SWIM parameters (particularly s and T') that are appropriate for HPC storage systems:

- **Network RTT:** According to the original SWIM protocol definition [11], a participant must wait at least three round-trip times for a ping response from a remote peer. This produces the constraint that $T' > 3 \times RTT$.
- **Network Load:** The minimum value of T' is further bounded by the network capacity of the system. If the period length is too short, then the SWIM network traffic (defined by analytical models in [13] in terms of average number of messages per time unit per participant) may perturb the I/O performance. The acceptable network traffic load threshold depends on the available network capacity.
- **Fault Response Time:** The ultimate value of t_{total} should be complementary to the time needed by the storage system to assess a fault and plan a fault response. Otherwise the fault detection may become a bottleneck to system availability. In this study we propose a goal of $t_{total} \leq 30$ s. For comparison, popular moderate-scale group membership implementations such as Pacemaker [5] are often deployed with a 30-s monitoring interval, which does not include time to reach consensus.
- **Transient Failure Sensitivity:** If the suspicion time in seconds ($T' \times s$) is too short, then the protocol may be susceptible to false positives due to congestion or transient network card errors. We propose a goal of $(T' \times s) \geq 10$ s, which is long enough to account for the default network driver transmission timeout of 5 s as of Linux 3.15.

Table 1. Effect of SWIM group size, period length, and suspect timeout on expected performance. †

n	T' (ms)	s	Network Load (avg. messages/s per server)	t_{detect} (ms)	$T' \times s$ (ms)	t_{dissem} (ms)	t_{total} (ms)
1024						.70	15000.86
2048	.10	150000	20976.0	.16	15000.00	.80	15000.96
4096						.90	15001.06
1024						70.00	15085.91
2048	10.00	1500	209.8	15.91	15000.00	80.00	15095.91
4096						90.00	15105.91
1024						7000.00	23591.28
2048	1000.00	15	2.1	1591.28	15000.00	8000.00	24591.28
4096						9000.00	25591.28
2048	200.00	75	10.5	318.26	15000.00	1600.00	16918.26

† Note: The analytical results here are calculated by assuming a 1% chance of a node being faulty, a 1% chance of packet loss, and a subgroup size (k) of 1.

Table 1 shows the impact of protocol period length (T') for storage system sizes (n) ranging from 1,024 to 4,096 servers, given a constant suspicion time $(T' \times s)$. Smaller values of T' lead to faster failure detection and dissemination times at the cost of a higher network load. For a given value of T', tolerance to transient failures can be tuned by setting s such that $T' \times s$ is larger than the expected transient failure duration. We can therefore use these parameters to balance performance, network load, and transient failure tolerance.

We selected the example system size (2,048 servers) and parameters $(T' = 200$ ms, $s = 75)$ highlighted in gray for in-depth analysis via parallel discrete event simulation. The period length of 200 ms allows us to detect faults and disseminate notifications rapidly in 318 ms and 1.6 s, respectively. Further, the average network load imposed by this configuration is still negligible compared with the bandwidth of typical network interconnects in high-performance data centers. A suspicion timeout of 75 protocol period lengths allows the protocol to be resilient to transient failures of up to 15 s, depending on how fast subsequent *alive* updates are disseminated to the group. This greatly reduces the probability of unnecessary recovery actions, such as rebuilding storage system data. Note that Das et al. [11] recommend a shorter s value of $(3\lceil\log(n + 1)\rceil)$, but we extend it in this context to account for shorter period intervals (T') while still remaining tolerant of transient failures. The total time expected for the protocol to reach global consensus on a failed server is approximately 17 s. This combination of parameters readily meets the constraints described at the beginning of this section. We believe these constraints to be a reasonable starting point for configuring SWIM for use in a large-scale data center, although in-depth characterization of data center failure scenarios could warrant further parameter tuning.

One detail of the SWIM protocol that has been neglected thus far is the number of membership updates to piggyback on each ping and ack message. This piggyback buffer must be large enough to effectively disseminate (potentially numerous) membership updates throughout the system. This requirement is particularly important in groups where membership is continually changing or in systems with high message loss rates, since the dissemination component may become overwhelmed by the volume of membership updates. However, it is also important to bound the size of this piggyback buffer as part of minimizing the network load imposed by the protocol. For our simulation model, we use a piggyback buffer size of 12, which yields a total message size of 256 bytes if we assume a 64-byte base message and 16 bytes per membership update. This message size in conjunction with the selected configuration parameters in Table 1 produces an expected network consumption of roughly 2.5 KiB/s per server.

5 Simulation Analysis

We developed a parallel discrete event model of the protocol in order to perform an in-depth analysis of an example configuration with the following goals: validation of the analytical model results from Sect. 4 and analysis of the protocol's performance in failure scenarios that are not captured by the analytical model. This simulation will also enable integration with complete storage system models in future work. We constructed our model using the CODES [9,18] storage simulation framework. CODES is built on top of ROSS [4], a high-performance parallel discrete event simulator capable of processing billions of events per second. To our knowledge this is the first discrete event simulation of the SWIM protocol.

Our simulator uses a LogGP network model [2] to calculate network delays. The model assumes full-duplex network cards with independent send and receive queues and infinite buffering in the switch complex. The parameters for our LogGP model were obtained by using the `netgauge` utility [14] on the Tukey Linux cluster at the Argonne Leadership Computing Facility. Each Tukey node uses a single-port Mellanox ConnectX 2 QDR InfiniBand NIC. The `netgauge` utility assumes that the overhead parameter (o) (representing the CPU time consumed during transmission) overlaps with network fabric transmission costs, so we do not apply the o parameter to the communication time calculation. We also take advantage of the fact that `netgauge` calculates LogGP parameters independently for a range of message sizes, creating a lookup table to reflect varying protocol characteristics.

Figure 1 compares the empirically measured point-to-point bandwidth on the Linux cluster (measured by using `mpptest` [12]) with a simulation of the point-to-point performance using our simulation framework. We see that the simulated performance closely matches the performance trends on the example system, including protocol crossover points.

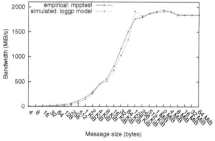

Fig. 1. Point-to-point empirical and simulated bandwidth on QDR InfiniBand network with MPI.

5.1   Sensitivity to Message Loss

We executed a collection of 30-min., 2,048-server simulations of the SWIM protocol in order to evaluate the protocol's sensitivity to message loss. The simulation
was configured such that no server failed completely, but the probability of packet
loss was varied between 0.2 %, 1 %, and 5 %. A 5 % message loss rate would be
an extraordinary occurrence in a data center environment, but we include it as
a demonstration of SWIM behavior in extreme conditions. Figure 2 illustrates
several performance and accuracy metrics as the SWIM subgroup size k is varied from 1 to 6. The first two figures are accuracy metrics: the number of false
positives (i.e., the number of servers falsely confirmed as failed) and the number
of servers falsely suspected as failed. The last two are performance metrics: the
message rate for each server and the average number of membership updates
piggybacked on each message. We gathered the performance metrics from the
beginning of the simulation (the first 15 to 30 s) before any false positives were
generated that would reduce the number of alive servers.

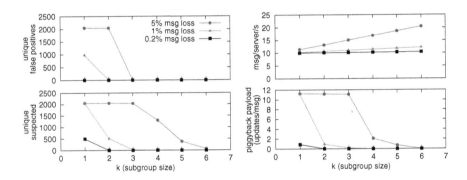

Fig. 2. Accuracy and network load metrics over a 30 min interval with 2,048 servers,
a piggyback buffer size of 12, and varying message loss rates.

Protocol accuracy is particularly poor at k values of 1 or 2 for high message
loss rates. With a 5 % message loss rate almost all servers are falsely confirmed
as failed. In this configuration, the probability of failed direct and indirect pings
generates a large volume of failure suspicions that overwhelms the capacity of
the dissemination component to correct them. With a subgroup size of 3 there is
only a single false positive at a message loss rate of 5 %, although we still observe
that nearly all servers are suspected at some point. The piggyback buffer size is
near capacity (as evidenced by the piggyback/message metric) but the increased
subgroup size allows the dissemination component to more effectively propagate
membership updates. We further observe that the protocol can easily manage the
1 % message loss rate at this subgroup size. At a subgroup size of 4, the number
of suspect servers declines and the protocol no longer produces any false positives
at any message loss rate. With subgroup sizes of 5 or 6 the number of suspected
servers diminishes because of the decreased likelihood of all direct and indirect

pings failing for a given target. We observe that the network load imposed by the protocol (measured in the average number of messages per server per second) scales linearly with k, while the accuracy of the protocol increases exponentially with k.

5.2   Validation

Based on our findings from the previous section, we set $k = 6$ to make the protocol more robust against message loss. Using this configuration, in conjunction with the parameters derived in Sect. 4, we performed a set of simulation experiments to measure the response time to single server failures (with no message loss) as we varied the storage system size. We configured our simulation to choose a random server to fail at a random time. We also configured each server in the model to begin its period at a random point within the first T' seconds of the simulation, in order to prevent the SWIM algorithm from producing synchronized bursts of ping traffic. Figure 3 compares the performance measured by simulation with expected values based on the existing analytical models. To be concise, we consider only the time taken to detect a fault (t_{detect}) and the time to disseminate updates to all servers (t_{dissem}). The overall time from fault occurrence to global convergence (t_{total}) is dominated by the suspicion time $T' \times s$, which is a fixed value. We observe that, on average, t_{detect} remains roughly constant regardless of scale and tracks closely with the expected detection time calculated by using the analytical models. In some instances, however, the measured time to detect a server failure is significantly slower (multiple protocol period lengths) than expected. The analytical model includes simplifying assumptions (e.g., it assumes immediate delivery of all pings and acks) that we believe accounts for some of this deviation. The time taken to first detect a failure also depends on when the failure occurs relative to the start of the next protocol period. The t_{dissem} shown in Fig. 3 exhibits $O(\log(n))$ scaling as expected but is consistently faster than predicted by the analytical model. One factor contributing to this discrepancy is that we deliberately desynchronized the

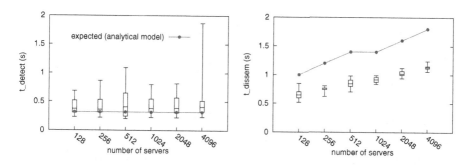

Fig. 3. t_{detect} and t_{dissem} as measured via simulation using highlighted parameters from Table 1. Each box plot shows the minimum, median, maximum, and Q1 and Q3 quartiles for 15 simulation samples. The predicted values according to analytical models are also shown for comparison.

period start times for each server by a random amount, meaning that it typically does not take a full $T' = 200$ ms for a given update to be relayed between two servers. We are also using a more efficient round-robin probing strategy (as suggested by Das et al. [11]) that is not accounted for in the analytical dissemination time calculation. This round-robin probing causes wider dispersal on average than does purely random selection of ping targets in each interval.

These results confirm that both t_{detect} and t_{dissem} are relatively minor components of performance and that they scale well with system size. The largest factor influencing overall performance will be the suspicion timeout s. This SWIM configuration with 4,096 servers would reliably propagate fault notifications to all servers in roughly 17 s while still remaining resilient to transient faults of up to 15 s and imposing negligible network load (still about 2.5 KiB/s, since the load does not scale with the group size). In addition, the constraints from Sect. 4 could readily be modified to accommodate other use cases.

6   Conclusion

In this work we explored the feasibility of adapting peer-to-peer style epidemic fault detection and group membership protocols for use in large-scale HPC storage systems. We identified a set of characteristics necessary for using eventually consistent group membership protocols such as SWIM in HPC storage systems. We used a combination of analytical models and simulation to select appropriate SWIM parameters for an HPC environment while still being tolerant of extraordinary message loss rates. We also studied the SWIM protocol response time as we varied the number of storage servers from 128 to 4,096, and we confirmed that the protocol scales well for basic failure cases. We found that the SWIM protocol could be configured to detect and fully disseminate failure notifications in an exemplar 4,096-server storage system in roughly 17 s, while remaining resilient to transient failures of up to 15 s and imposing a negligible network load. These results suggest that the SWIM protocol is a promising solution for fault detection and group membership in future HPC storage architectures.

We intend to analyze more complex, statistically generated failure scenarios across extended time spans in future work. We also plan to develop models for more traditional group membership protocols, such as those based on the PAXOS family of distributed consensus protocols, in order to perform head-to-head comparisons.

Acknowledgments. This research was supported by the U.S. Department of Defense. This material also was based on work supported by the U.S. Department of Energy, Office of Science, Advanced Scientific Computer Research Program under contract DE-AC02-06CH11357. The research used resources of the Argonne Leadership Computing Facility at Argonne National Laboratory, which is a DOE Office of Science User Facility.

References

1. Aguilera, M.K., Chen, W., Toueg, S.: Heartbeat: A timeout-free failure detector for quiescent reliable communication. In: Mavronicolas, Marios (ed.) WDAG 1997. LNCS, vol. 1320, pp. 126–140. Springer, Heidelberg (1997)
2. Alexandrov, A., Ionescu, M.F., Schauser, K.E., Scheiman, C.: LogGP: Incorporating long messages into the LogP model – one step closer towards a realistic model for parallel computation. In: Proceedings of the Seventh Annual ACM Symposium on Parallel Algorithms and Architectures, SPAA 1995, pp. 95–105. ACM, New York (1995). http://doi.acm.org/10.1145/215399.215427
3. Amir, Y., Moser, L.E., Melliar-Smith, P.M., Agarwal, D.A., Ciarfella, P.: The totem single-ring ordering and membership protocol. ACM Trans. Comput. Syst. **13**(4), 311–342 (1995)
4. Barnes, Jr., P.D., Carothers, C.D., Jefferson, D.R., LaPre, J.M.: Warp speed: Executing time warp on 1,966,080 cores. In: Proceedings of the 2013 ACM SIGSIM Conference on Principles of Advanced Discrete Simulation, SIGSIM-PADS 2013, pp. 327–336. ACM, New York (2013). http://doi.acm.org/10.1145/2486092.2486134
5. Beekhof, A.: Pacemaker: a scalable high availability cluster resource manager. http://clusterlabs.org/. Retrieved July 2014
6. Birman, K.P.: The process group approach to reliable distributed computing. Commun. ACM **36**(12), 37–53 (1993). http://doi.acm.org/10.1145/163298.163303
7. Birman, K.P., Hayden, M., Ozkasap, O., Xiao, Z., Budiu, M., Minsky, Y.: Bimodal multicast. ACM Trans. Comput. Syst. **17**(2), 41–88 (1999). http://doi.acm.org/10.1145/312203.312207
8. Chen, W., Toueg, S., Aguilera, M.K.: On the quality of service of failure detectors. IEEE Trans. Comput. **51**(5), 561–580 (2002)
9. Cope, J., Liu, N., Lang, S., Carns, P., Carothers, C., Ross, R.: Codes: Enabling co-design of multilayer exascale storage architectures. In: Proceedings of the Workshop on Emerging Supercomputing Technologies (2011)
10. Dake, S.C., Caulfield, C., Beekhof, A.: The Corosync cluster engine. In: Linux Symposium, vol. 85 (2008)
11. Das, A., Gupta, I., Motivala, A.: Swim: Scalable weakly-consistent infection-style process group membership protocol. In: Proceedings of the 2002 International Conference on Dependable Systems and Networks, DSN 2002, pp. 303–312. IEEE Computer Society Press, Washington, DC (2002). http://ieeexplore.ieee.org/xpls/abs_all.jsp?arnumber=1028914
12. Gropp, W., Lusk, E.: Reproducible measurements of MPI performance characteristics. In: Margalef, T., Dongarra, J., Luque, E. (eds.) PVM/MPI 1999. LNCS, vol. 1697, pp. 11–18. Springer, Heidelberg (1999)
13. Gupta, I., Chandra, T.D., Goldszmidt, G.S.: On scalable and efficient distributed failure detectors. In: Proceedings of the Twentieth Annual ACM Symposium on Principles of Distributed Computing, PODC 2001, pp. 170–179. ACM Press, New York (2001). http://doi.acm.org/10.1145/383962.384010
14. Hoefler, T., Mehlan, T., Lumsdaine, A., Rehm, W.: Netgauge: a network performance measurement framework. In: Perrott, R., Chapman, B.M., Subhlok, J., de Mello, R.F., Yang, L.T. (eds.) HPCC 2007. LNCS, vol. 4782, pp. 659–671. Springer, Heidelberg (2007)

15. Jahanian, F., Fakhouri, S., Rajkumar, R.: Processor group membership protocols: specification, design and implementation. In: Proceedings of the 12th Symposium on Reliable Distributed Systems, pp. 2–11, October 1993

16. Lakshman, A., Malik, P.: Cassandra: A decentralized structured storage system. SIGOPS Operating Sys. Rev. **44**(2), 35–40 (2010). http://doi.acm.org/10.1145/1773912.1773922

17. Lamport, L.: The part-time parliament. ACM Trans. Comput. Syst. (TOCS) **16**(2), 133–169 (1998)

18. Liu, N., Cope, J., Carns, P., Carothers, C., Ross, R., Grider, G., Crume, A., Maltzahn, C.: On the role of burst buffers in leadership-class storage systems. In: 2012 IEEE 28th Symposium on Mass Storage Systems and Technologies (MSST), pp. 1–11. IEEE (2012)

19. Reiter, M.K.: A secure group membership protocol. IEEE Trans. Softw. Eng. **22**(1), 31–42 (1996)

20. van Renesse, R., Minsky, Y., Hayden, M.: A gossip-style failure detection service. In: Davies, N., Jochen, S., Raymond, K. (eds.) Middleware 1998, pp. 55–70. Springer, London (1998). http://dx.doi.org/10.1007/978-1-4471-1283-9_4

21. Weil, S.A., Brandt, S.A., Miller, E.L., Long, D.D.E., Maltzahn, C.: Ceph: A scalable, high-performance distributed file system. In: Proceedings of the 7th Symposium on Operating Systems Design and Implementation, OSDI 2006, pp. 307–320. USENIX Association, Berkeley (2006). http://dl.acm.org/citation.cfm?id=1298485

Analysis of the Tradeoffs Between Energy and Run Time for Multilevel Checkpointing

Prasanna Balaprakash[1,2]([✉]), Leonardo A. Bautista Gomez[1],
Mohamed-Slim Bouguerra[1], Stefan M. Wild[1], Franck Cappello[1,3],
and Paul D. Hovland[1]

[1] Mathematics and Computer Science Division,
Argonne National Laboratory, Argonne, IL, USA
{pbalapra,leobago,medslim,wild,cappello,hovland}@anl.gov
[2] Leadership Computing Facility, Argonne National Laboratory,
Argonne, IL, USA
[3] University of Illinois at Urbana-Champaign,
Champaign, IL, USA

Abstract. In high-performance computing, there is a perpetual hunt for performance and scalability. Supercomputers grow larger offering improved computational science throughput. Nevertheless, with an increase in the number of systems' components and their interactions, the number of failures and the power consumption will increase rapidly. Energy and reliability are among the most challenging issues that need to be addressed for extreme scale computing. We develop analytical models for run time and energy usage for multilevel fault-tolerance schemes. We use these models to study the tradeoff between run time and energy in FTI, a recently developed multilevel checkpoint library, on an IBM Blue Gene/Q. Our results show that energy consumed by FTI is low and the tradeoff between the run time and energy is small. Using the analytical models, we explore the impact of various system-level parameters on run time and energy tradeoffs.

1 Introduction

Large-scale scientific simulations require larger supercomputers to produce more accurate results. In high-performance computing (HPC) researchers and engineers are pushing the envelops to increase scalability and performance. As systems scale, new challenges appear, in particular, two major challenges for next generation supercomputers consists of minimizing power/energy consumption and maximizing reliability. However, these two objectives are in conflict which each other because increased reliability comes at the expense of power and energy usage.

Researchers in the HPC community have developed various fault tolerance techniques to improve the reliability of current and future machines. Nevertheless, all these techniques involve overheads in terms of storage space, computation and their respective energy consumption, hinting at the existence of a tradeoff

© Springer International Publishing Switzerland 2015
S.A. Jarvis et al. (Eds.): PMBS 2014, LNCS 8966, pp. 249–263, 2015.
DOI: 10.1007/978-3-319-17248-4_13

between execution run time and energy efficiency. Multilevel checkpointing is a promising approach to deal with reliability at extreme scale. The key idea of this approach consists in using layers of checkpointing, each one of them offering different levels of resilience and overheads. Low-cost levels offer limited fault tolerance while highly resilient levels involve large overheads. Consequently, the correct usage of the multiple levels should lead to substantial gains in performance, resilience, and energy consumption.

In this paper, we study the impact of optimal multilevel checkpointing intervals on the tradeoffs between run time and energy consumption. Our experimental study with FTI, a multilevel checkpointing library on an IBM Blue Gene/Q supercomputer shows that performance-energy tradeoffs are minimal, but may be significantly larger under certain future exascale HPC scenarios. The contributions of this paper are as follows:

- We derive analytical models for expected run time and energy consumption for multilevel checkpointing.
- We characterize the Pareto-optimal solution set and investigate the tradeoffs between time and energy consumption.
- We perform power consumption measurements of large-scale executions on an IBM Blue Gene/Q with several applications.
- We present an experimental study to analyze several system-level parameters for multilevel checkpointing that can potentially impact the tradeoffs.

The rest of the paper is organized as follows. Section 2 describes the main concepts used by multilevel checkpointing. Section 3 introduces models for time and energy for multilevel checkpointing strategies. We introduce the notion of Pareto optimality in Sect. 4. Section 5 presents the results of our empirical evaluation and several future tradeoff projections. Section 6 reviews related work, and Sect. 7 presents conclusions and a brief look at future work.

2   Multilevel Checkpointing

Long-running scientific simulations executed on large supercomputers are checkpointed periodically to stable storage in order to avoid having to restart from the beginning in case of failure. Traditionally, applications will stop, write all the required data to the parallel file system (PFS), and then continue. Checkpoint sizes have been constantly increasing with the exponential growth of supercomputers. Unfortunately, the speed at which one can write to the PFS has been increasing only linearly, leading to long checkpointing times and causing large overhead to the application.

To minimize the impact of checkpointing on run time, researchers have proposed multilevel checkpointing [4,13] which leverages multiple storage layers and limits the load on the PFS. This is achieved by using local storage in the compute nodes. However, local storage is not resilient against node crashes, even for persistent storage devices, as access to those devices might be lost after a failure. Therefore, local storage is usually coupled with data replication or erasure codes to guarantee that any unaccessible data can be reconstructed. We used the multilevel checkpointing library FTI [4] that provides four checkpoint levels, namely, Local checkpoint, Local checkpoint + Partner-copy, Local checkpoint + Reed-Solomon coding, and PFS-based checkpoint. Note that the model developed proposed in this paper can be used to analyze other multilevel checkpoint libraries.

Applications using FTI can perform checkpoints of different levels at different frequencies. Those frequencies can be easily configured through a configuration file. When a checkpoint of level i is done, FTI automatically removes all previous checkpoints of level j for $j \leq i$ because i is more recent and offers more reliability. Previous checkpoints of level k for $k > i$ are kept however, so that if a failure cannot be recovered by using level i, it can try to recover from a higher level. In addition to these four checkpointing levels, FTI offers features such as having dedicated processes that perform fault-tolerance tasks in the background, which speeds the checkpoints and limits the overhead imposed on the application's run. Dedicated processes could, for instance, copy a local checkpoint to the PFS in the background at the same time the application is running. In this way, applications are blocked only to perform the local checkpoint; all the rest of the work associated with addressing fault tolerance is hidden.

3 Energy and Checkpoint Models

A multilevel checkpoint strategy is defined by the intervals between checkpoints. We denote these intervals by the vector $\tau \in \mathbb{R}_+^L$, where L is number of different levels of checkpointing and the ith component, τ_i, of the vector τ denotes the amount of time between checkpoints at level i. The checkpoint cost (in terms of time) at level i is denoted by c_i.

After a failure, the application uses the most recent checkpoint to restart the application. Suppose we have a failure at level i, the restart time is r_i and the down time is d_i. For a failure model we consider μ_i as the rate of failures affecting only level i. Hence, μ_1 corresponds to the rate of transient failures; μ_2 is the rate of permanent failures that affect many nodes but not two buddies at the same time; μ_3 represents the rate of failures affecting at least one partner node at the same time; and μ_4 is the rate of failures that occur at the same time and affect at least one group at the same time. Several derivations of μ_i are provided in [7,13]. Also, we note that $1/\mu_i$ can be interpreted as the mean time between failures at level i. The basic model notation is summarized in Table 1, with all times and powers taken in expectation.

3.1 Model for Run Time

We express the expected overall completion time as the sum of two times: the time for a failure-free execution of an application without checkpointing and the expected time wasted because of failures and/or checkpointing, $T_{\text{overall}} = T_a + T_{\text{wasted}} = T_a + \mathbb{W}T_{\text{overall}}$. The amount of waste per unit of time, $\mathbb{W}$, comprises

Table 1. Summary of model notation.

	Description
τ_i	Time between level i checkpoints
c_i	Time for a level i checkpoint
r_i	Time for a restart from level i
T_a	Time for a failure-free computation without checkpointing
d_i	Downtime after a failure affecting level i
L	Number of levels
μ_i	Expected rate for failure affecting level i
$\mathcal{P}_i^c$	Power for a level i checkpoint
$\mathcal{P}_i^r$	Power for a restart from level i
$\mathcal{P}^a$	Power for a failure-free computation without checkpointing

the time to perform checkpointing, rework, and restart, as well as the downtime. We now examine the contributors to the wasted time: the checkpoint overhead per unit of time $\mathfrak{W}^{ch}$, the rework overhead per unit of time $\mathfrak{W}^{rew}$, and the restart per unit of time $\mathfrak{W}^{down}$.

Checkpoint overhead. We have two sources of overhead because of checkpointing. The first is based on the number of checkpoints performed in one unit of time. The number of checkpoints can be approximated by $\frac{1}{\tau_i}$. A tighter approximation is given by $\frac{1}{\tau_i + c_i}$, but $\frac{1}{\tau_i}$ is a good upper bound. The second term, $\mu_i \tau_i \sum_{j=1}^{i-1} \frac{c_j}{2\tau_j}$, represents the expected lost time due to extra checkpoints at levels $1, \ldots, i-1$ if a failure occurs at level i. The overall fraction of time spent in checkpointing is thus given by

$$\mathfrak{W}^{ch} = \sum_{i=1}^{L} \left(\frac{c_i}{\tau_i} + \mu_i \tau_i \sum_{j=1}^{i-1} \frac{c_j}{2\tau_j} \right).$$

Rework time. We follow the classical first-order approximation and assume that a failure occurs at the half of the interval. The expected lost time due to re-execution (rework) is thus

$$\mathfrak{W}^{rew} = \sum_{i=1}^{L} \frac{\mu_i \tau_i}{2}.$$

Downtime and restart. The expected wasted time because of downtime and restart is

$$\mathfrak{W}^{down} = \sum_{i=1}^{L} \mu_i (r_i + d_i).$$

The total waste per unit time, $\mathbb{W}$, is thus given by

$$\sum_{i=1}^{L} \left(\frac{c_i}{\tau_i} + \frac{\mu_i \tau_i}{2} \left(1 + \sum_{j=1}^{i-1} \frac{c_j}{2\tau_j} \right) + \mu_i (r_i + d_i) \right). \tag{1}$$

3.2 Model for Energy

We now develop a model for the expected wasted energy per unit of time. We let $\mathcal{P}^a$, $\mathcal{P}_i^c$, and $\mathcal{P}_i^r$ denote respectively the amount of power (e.g., in watts) used by the user application to perform computation, checkpoint at level i, and restart from level i. Note that $\mathcal{P}^a$, $\mathcal{P}_i^c$, and $\mathcal{P}_i^r$ include the idle power as well.

We have the three sources of wasted energy:

$$\mathcal{E}^{ch} = \sum_{i=1}^{L} \left(\mathcal{P}_i^c \frac{c_i}{\tau_i} + \mu_i \tau_i \sum_{j=1}^{i-1} \frac{\mathcal{P}_j^c c_j}{2\tau_j} \right),$$

$$\mathcal{E}^{rew} = \sum_{i=1}^{L} \mathcal{P}^a \frac{\mu_i \tau_i}{2},$$

$$\mathcal{E}^{down} = \sum_{i=1}^{L} \mathcal{P}_i^r \mu_i (r_i + d_i),$$

corresponding to the checkpoint energy, the energy for rework because of failures, and the energy for restart, respectively.

3.3 Optimal Checkpoint Intervals

The optimal checkpoint intervals with respect to run time are obtained by minimizing (1) as a function of $\tau \in \mathbb{R}_+^L$. Similarly, the optimal intervals with respect to energy are obtained by minimizing the wasted energy during one unit of time,

$$\mathbb{E} = \sum_{i=1}^{L} \left(\frac{\mathcal{P}_i^c c_i}{\tau_i} + \mu_i \tau_i \left(\frac{\mathcal{P}^a}{2} + \sum_{j=1}^{i-1} \frac{\mathcal{P}_j^c c_j}{2\tau_j} \right) \right)$$
$$+ \sum_{i=1}^{L} \mathcal{P}_i^r \mu_i (r_i + d_i), \tag{2}$$

as a function of τ.

Under reasonable restrictions on the checkpoint intervals (based only on the failure rates μ; see the Appendix), one can show that $\mathbb{W}$ and $\mathbb{E}$ are both convex over this restricted domain. Thus each has a unique optimal solution, which we can obtain, for example, using an iterative method such as Newton's method.

The first derivatives of Eqs. (1) and (2) with respect to τ_i are given by

$$\frac{\partial \mathbb{W}}{\partial \tau_i} = \frac{\mu_i}{2} \left(1 + \sum_{j=1}^{i-1} \frac{c_j}{\tau_j} \right) - \frac{c_i}{\tau_i^2} \left(1 + \sum_{j=i+1}^{L} \frac{\mu_j \tau_j}{2} \right) \tag{3}$$

$$\frac{\partial \mathbb{E}}{\partial \tau_i} = \frac{\mu_i}{2} \left(\mathcal{P}^a + \sum_{j=1}^{i-1} \frac{\mathcal{P}_j^c c_j}{\tau_j} \right) - \frac{\mathcal{P}_i^c c_i}{\tau_i^2} \left(1 + \sum_{j=i+1}^{L} \frac{\mu_j \tau_j}{2} \right). \tag{4}$$

Setting these derivatives to zero, we note that the solutions for time and energy satisfy

$$\tau_i^{\mathrm{W}} = \sqrt{\frac{c_i(2 + \sum_{j=i+1}^{L} \mu_j \tau_j^{\mathrm{W}})}{\mu_i(1 + \sum_{j=1}^{i-1} \frac{c_j}{\tau_j^{\mathrm{W}}})}}$$

$$\tau_i^{\mathrm{E}} = \sqrt{\frac{\rho_i c_i(2 + \sum_{j=i+1}^{L} \mu_j \tau_j^{\mathrm{E}})}{\mu_i(1 + \sum_{j=1}^{i-1} \frac{\rho_j c_j}{\tau_j^{\mathrm{E}}})}},$$

respectively, with $\rho_i = \mathcal{P}_i^c / \mathcal{P}^a$.

When there is only a single level, the interval that minimizes run time is $\tau^{\mathrm{W}} = \sqrt{2c/\mu}$, while the interval that minimizes energy is $\tau^{\mathrm{E}} = \tau^{\mathrm{W}}\sqrt{\mathcal{P}^c/\mathcal{P}^a}$. Whenever $\mathcal{P}^c \neq \mathcal{P}^a$, we have that $\tau^{\mathrm{W}} \neq \tau^{\mathrm{E}}$, and hence the two objectives are conflicting, a subject we formalize next.

4 Tradeoffs Between Time and Energy

We now turn to the checkpoint-scheduling problem of minimizing *both* time and energy. Sometimes such *bi-objective optimization problems* have a single solution: there is a single decision that minimizes both objectives simultaneously. In other cases (such as seen at the end of Sect. 3), the objectives are conflicting, and many solutions may be "optimal" in the bi-objective sense.

The concept of two conflicting objectives is best illustrated by an example. Figure 1 shows the wasted time and energy per unit of time for a single-level

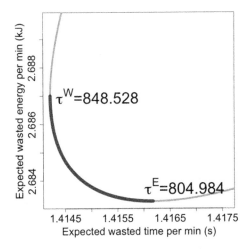

Fig. 1. Pareto front for single-level checkpointing for LAMMPS on BG/Q. The power for computing and checkpointing are 2 kW and 1.8 kW, respectively; μ=1/36000 Hz and the cost of a checkpoint is 10 s. The thin line shows the strategies dominated by the Pareto front (thick line).

checkpointing scheme (see Sect. 5 for details). The thinner curve illustrates the behavior of the objective pairs $(\mathbb{W}(\tau), \mathbb{E}(\tau))$. If the objective $\mathbb{W}$ [$\mathbb{E}$] is minimized in isolation, then we obtain the solution τ^W [τ^E] and the corresponding point $(\mathbb{W}(\tau^W), \mathbb{E}(\tau^W))$ $[(\mathbb{W}(\tau^E), \mathbb{E}(\tau^E))]$ in Fig. 1. From a bi-objective perspective however, τ^W and τ^E provide only the boundary of the solution set: for any τ between the values τ^W and τ^E, we obtain time and energy quantities that cannot both be improved upon. Formally, a point τ^j is dominated by a point τ^i when $\mathbb{W}(\tau^i) \leq \mathbb{W}(\tau^j)$ and $\mathbb{E}(\tau^i) \leq \mathbb{E}(\tau^j)$ (with at least one of these inequalities being strict). A point τ^i is said to be *Pareto-optimal* if it is not dominated by any other τ^j. The set of $(\mathbb{W}, \mathbb{E})$ values from all Pareto-optimal points is called the *Pareto front* (illustrated by the bold portion of the curve in Fig. 1); see [3,8] for further details.

In general, Pareto fronts can be nonconvex, and finding Pareto-optimal points can be a task significantly more challenging than optimizing a single objective. When the Pareto front is convex, any point on the front can be obtained by minimizing a linear combination of the objectives. This corresponds to minimizing the single objective

$$f_\lambda(\tau) = \lambda \mathbb{W}(\tau) + (1 - \lambda)\mathbb{E}(\tau), \tag{5}$$

where $\lambda \in [0, 1]$ represents the weight placed on $\mathbb{W}(\tau)$. For convex Pareto fronts, solving (5) for all $\lambda \in [0, 1]$ yields the Pareto-optimal solutions, with the extreme case $\lambda = 1$ ($\lambda = 0$) corresponding to minimizing time (energy) in isolation.

Because $\mathbb{W}$ and $\mathbb{E}$ are convex, it follows that the function f_λ is convex for every $\lambda \in [0, 1]$ and thus has a unique minimizer $\tau^*(\lambda)$. Using the derivatives in (3) and (4), one can easily show that the optimal $\tau_i^*(\lambda)$ satisfies

$$\tau_i^*(\lambda) = \sqrt{\frac{c_i(\lambda + (1-\lambda)\mathcal{P}_i^c)\left(2 + \sum_{j=i+1}^{L} \mu_j \tau_j^*\right)}{\mu_i \left(\lambda + (1-\lambda)\mathcal{P}^a + \sum_{j=1}^{i-1}(\lambda + (1-\lambda)\mathcal{P}_j^c)\frac{c_j}{\tau_j^*}\right)}}, \tag{6}$$

where each $\tau_j^* = \tau_j^*(\lambda)$ depends on λ. For example, in the single-level case, we have that

$$\tau^*(\lambda) = \tau^W \sqrt{\frac{\lambda + (1-\lambda)\mathcal{P}^c}{\lambda + (1-\lambda)\mathcal{P}^a}}. \tag{7}$$

Equation (7) reiterates that tradeoffs are present in the single-level case whenever $\mathcal{P}^c \neq \mathcal{P}^a$. When $L > 1$, the situation is more complex; in the next section we investigate the behavior for specific values of the multilevel parameters.

5   Experiments

Our evaluation was performed on MIRA, a 10-petaflops IBM Blue Gene/Q (BG/Q) system and Vesta, a developmental platform for Mira, at the Argonne Leadership Computing Facility. Mira has 48 racks with a total of 49,152 nodes, each one with 16 cores of 1.6 GHz PowerPC A2 and 16 GB of DDR3 memory.

The compute nodes run on CNK, a proprietary, lightweight kernel that minimizes OS noise. A proprietary 5-D torus network connects all the compute nodes and the PFS. The machine is water-cooled for thermal efficiency. Vesta's architecture is the same as Mira's but with 2,048 nodes. For measuring power on BG/Q, we use MonEQ, a low overhead power-profiling library [16] that samples power readings at a frequency of 560 ms. The power measurements include the overall node consumption as well as core, DRAM and network. Further details on the power profiling used can be found in [16]. Because of control system limitations, MonEQ can collect power data only at the node-card level which includes 32 compute nodes. In addition, MonEQ only measures power consumption on the compute nodes, and does not provide data for the I/O power consumption. We revisit this issue in Sect. 5.2.

5.1   FTI on BG/Q

Our first set of experiments was done with LAMMPS, a production-level molecular dynamics application [14]. First, we measured the performance of LAMMPS on Mira to confirm that our setup was correct. We next ported LAMMPS to perform checkpoints with FTI and confirmed that the performance overhead imposed by FTI was low. We then added the MonEQ library to our setup and ran several tests to verify that the power measurements were being correctly logged. With this configuration, we ran a Lennard-Jones simulation of 1.3 billion atoms using 512 nodes and launching 64 MPI processes per node (32,678 ranks in total). Molecular dynamics applications such as LAMMPS are known to have a low memory footprint. Each rank used 16.2 MB of memory and checkpointed 2.9 MB of data. Thus, the checkpoint size per node is about 187 MB, and the total checkpoint size for the whole execution is roughly 93 GB. The checkpoint intervals for levels 1, 2, 3, and 4 were set to 4, 8, 16, and 32 min, respectively, producing the checkpoint order {1, 2, 1, 3, 1, 2, 1, 4}. This first experiment was done without using dedicated processes for fault tolerance. Thus, every process participated in the application, and the execution was blocked during the checkpoints.

Figure 2a shows the power consumption of LAMMPS checkpointing with FTI in a synchronous fashion. During normal execution, LAMMPS consumes about 32 kW on 512 nodes (32,678 processes). We introduce one minute idle phase (i.e. sleep) before the application starts, to measure the idle power consumption of the nodes. We observe that the idle phase consumes roughly 25 kW. The periodic drop (every four minutes) in power consumption is due to checkpointing. We can identify the checkpoint levels by measuring the time that nodes spend in different power consumption regimes. Short drops in DRAM corresponds to the checkpoint level 1. Checkpoints level 2 and 3 expose two parts of checkpoint: DRAM power drop when the checkpoint data is being copied locally and core power drop where the checkpoint is either being transferred to a partner copy or a encoded with Reed-Solomon encoding, for level 2 and 3 respectively. Finally, PFS-based checkpoint is visible as a long drop in power consumption due to the time that it takes to transfer the checkpoint data to the PFS via I/O nodes and erase the previous local checkpoints. Since MonEQ provides only the power consumption of the participating compute

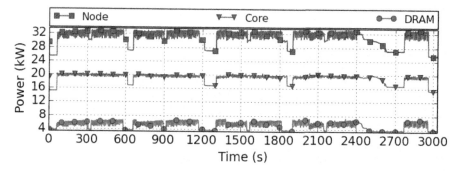

(a) Synchronous multilevel checkpointing

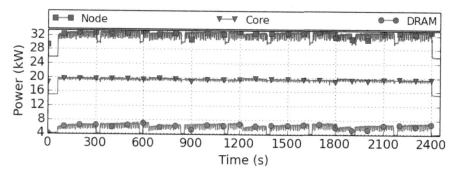

(b) Asynchronous multilevel checkpointing

Fig. 2. Power profile of LAMMPS running a 1.3 billion-atom Lennard-Jones simulation and checkpointing with FTI on BG/Q. Execution on 512 nodes running 64 MPI ranks per node (32,678 proc.). The power consumption of node is a sum of all power consumptions of the components.

nodes, the experiments do not allow us to accurately quantify the energy usage for level 4 PFS-based checkpointing. The power consumption of all other checkpoint levels vary between 27 kW and 30 kW. We note that although they have relatively similar power costs, their run times vary significantly. We verified that all node cards (set of 32 nodes) consume the same power, roughly 1.6 kW, 1.8 kW, and 2 kW during idle time, checkpointing, and execution, respectively.

The next experiment aims to test the asynchronous feature of FTI to speed the checkpoints. LAMMPS is a good candidate for this type of optimization because it does not require a particular number of MPI ranks. Therefore, one can easily dedicate one MPI process per node (out of 64) for fault tolerance. The same checkpoint frequencies are kept, producing the same checkpointing pattern as in the previous configuration. The results in Fig. 2b illustrate that the drops in power consumption are much shorter because the application is blocked only during the local copy; the rest of the work is done in the background by the dedicated processes (one per node), and does not involve a significant extra power cost. As a result of this optimization, the application runs about 20 % faster than in the previous configuration.

We also study the power profile of four mini-applications from the CORAL benchmark suite developed for the procurement of pre-exascale systems [1]. Qbox is a first-principles molecular dynamics code used to compute the properties of materials from the underlying physics equations. AMG is a parallel algebraic multigrid solver for linear systems arising from problems on unstructured grids. LULESH performs hydrodynamics stencil calculations, and miniFE is a finite-element code.

We ran the four applications on a single-node board of 32 nodes of Vesta with 512 MPI ranks (16 MPI ranks per node). Figure 3 shows the power profile of the fault-free computations, $\mathcal{P}^a$, on a node card. Except for Qbox, on average, the observed $\mathcal{P}^a$ values are similar to those of LAMMPS; for Qbox, $\mathcal{P}^a$ reaches up to 2.2 kW.

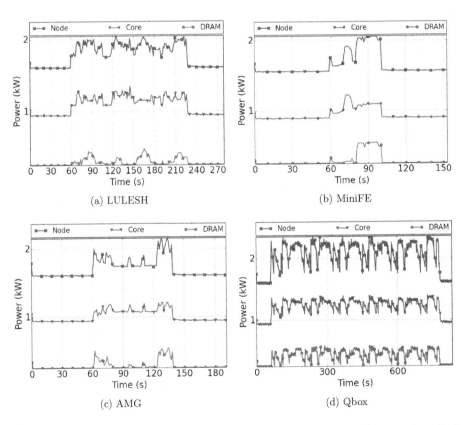

Fig. 3. Power profile of CORAL benchmark applications on a BG/Q node board of 32 nodes. Each application is run with a configuration of 16 MPI ranks per node (512 processes).

5.2 Tradeoff Analysis

We now revisit the energy-performance models from Sect. 3 and use the power consumption and checkpointing cost observed on BG/Q and presented in Sect. 5.1. In particular, we examine several system-level parameters that can affect the energy-performance tradeoffs.

For this analysis, we consider values at a node-board level and applications with similar checkpoint sizes as the ones observed for LAMMPS. As a default, we use the configuration $c = [10, 30, 50, 150]$ s; $\mu = [1, 0.5, 0.25, 0.05]/36000$ Hz; $\mathcal{P}^a = 2$ kW; $\mathcal{P}_1^c = \mathcal{P}_2^c = \mathcal{P}_3^c = 1.8$ kW; and, since there is no power monitoring infrastructure to measure the I/O power involved in level 4 checkpointing, we take $\mathcal{P}_4^c = 2 \times \mathcal{P}_3^c$. We note that the default failure rates are those commonly used for petascale HPC systems [4,7,13]. Note that, given a fixed checkpoint size, the wasted time and energy consumption per unit time during checkpointing will be the same for different applications, because FTI performs the same amount of work (e.g., transfer) independently of the content of the checkpoint data. In what follows we report the *expected waste in time and energy per minute*.

With all other values held fixed, we first vary the number of levels considered for checkpointing (and at which failures can occur). Table 2 illustrates that the optimal checkpoint intervals depend on what is happening at *all* other levels. Despite the overall time between any failure (the final column) decreasing, the checkpoint intervals at a level actually increase because of the increases in the number of levels. Furthermore, differences in wasted time and energy between the two single-objective solutions τ^W and τ^E increase as the number of levels grows. Nevertheless, for a given number of levels, these differences are small.

Table 2. Optimal multilevel checkpoint intervals (s) for schemes with 1, 2, 3, and 4 levels.

Level	1	2	3	4	$\mathbb{W}(\tau), \mathbb{E}(\tau)$	$(\sum\limits_{j=1}^{L} \mu_j)^{-1}$
τ^W	848.5	n/a	n/a	n/a	(1.41, 2.69)	36000 (s)
τ^E	805.0	n/a	n/a	n/a	(1.42, 2.68)	
τ^W	854.6	2066	n/a	n/a	(3.16, 6.00)	108000 (s)
τ^E	810.5	1961	n/a	n/a	(3.16, 5.99)	
τ^W	860.1	2080	3746	n/a	(4.76, 9.04)	252000 (s)
τ^E	815.4	1973	3556	n/a	(4.76, 9.02)	
τ^W	864.3	2090	3765	14417	(6.01, 12.53)	972000 (s)
τ^E	820.8	1986	3580	19362	(6.07, 12.37)	

Since we cannot measure I/O-intensive level 4 power consumption, we analyze the tradeoffs under various $\mathcal{P}_4^c$ scenarios. We consider $\mathcal{P}_4^c = \alpha \mathcal{P}_3^c$, where $\alpha \in [1, 2, 4, 6, 8, 10]$ and the default $\mathcal{P}_3^c$. Figure 4a shows that increasing $\mathcal{P}_4^c$ relative to other levels has a significant impact on the observed tradeoff between

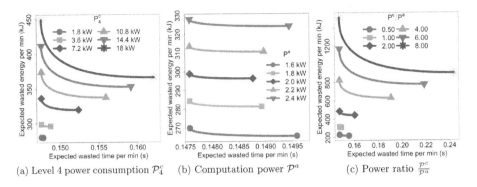

Fig. 4. Time-energy Pareto fronts for multilevel schemes as different parameters are varied. The two end points represent only the boundary of the solution set: all values between them correspond to non-dominated points.

$\mathbb{W}$ and $\mathbb{E}$. In particular, richer tradeoff is observed for $\alpha = 10$ (18 kW). We also analyze the impact of different $\mathcal{P}^a$ values on time and energy. Figure 4b shows that varying $\mathcal{P}^a$ increases energy, but the tradeoffs are insignificant.

The projected low power consumption and high failure rate for next-generation systems can have a significant impact on energy-performance tradeoffs. Here, we characterize power consumption by the ratio $\frac{\mathcal{P}^c}{\mathcal{P}^a}$. We set the $\mathcal{P}^a$ and $\mathcal{P}^c_1$ values to obtain $\frac{\mathcal{P}^c}{\mathcal{P}^a} \in \{0.5, 1.0, 2.0, 4.0, 6.0, 8.0\}$, with all other default values unchanged. Recall that $\mathcal{P}^c_1 = \mathcal{P}^c_2 = \mathcal{P}^c_3$ and $\mathcal{P}^c_4 = 2\mathcal{P}^c_3$. In Fig. 4c, we see that $\frac{\mathcal{P}^c}{\mathcal{P}^a}$ has a significant impact on the tradeoffs between $\mathbb{W}$ and $\mathbb{E}$, with these tradeoffs increasing as ρ increases. This suggests that power for computation should be significantly less than that for checkpointing in order for richer tradeoffs to exist. This situation could happen for several reasons. For instance, applications could be significantly more aware of data locality than what multilevel checkpointing techniques could achieve, because resilience can be achieved only through data dispersion across space, which requires communication. We also analyzed the tradeoffs by increasing μ values, but we did not observe significant tradeoffs.

6   Related Work

A rich body of literature exists for computing an optimal checkpoint period with respect to run time for various checkpoint protocols [5–7]. However, energy models and analysis of tradeoffs in current and future HPC systems are still in their infancy. Diouri et al. [9] modeled and evaluated the energy consumption of checkpointing, task coordination, and message logging components of a fault tolerance protocol. They showed that neither of these tasks significantly increases the power draw of a node and that minimizing execution time will minimize energy consumption. Later, they developed the ECOFIT framework [10] using component power models, and studied energy consumption of an application using coordinated, uncoordinated, and hierarchical protocols. Meneses et al. [12] developed models for expected run time and energy consumption for global recovery, message logging, and parallel recovery protocols. They observed tradeoffs in message logging due to significant run time overhead but faster recovery. They applied these models in an exascale scenario and showed that parallel recovery is more effective than a checkpointing protocol since parallel recovery reduces the rework time. A limitation of the model is that it considers failures at a single node level. Moreover, the RAPL API used to report the power consumption measures only the energy consumption at a processor-level and does not cover the I/O, or the communication [11]. Aupy et al. [2] developed performance and energy models and applied them to analyze the minimizers of each objective in isolation. Under an expensive I/O scenario with a low idle power of 10 mW/node, the authors showed different tradeoffs. However, the proposed models do not take into account multilevel checkpointing and are not used to assess the tradeoffs more generally. The authors considered the power consumption values from elsewhere [15]: the checkpointing power consumption was set to 10 times the computer power, a primary reason for the significant differences in time and energy.

7   Conclusions

We developed analytical models of performance and energy for multilevel checkpoint schemes. We went beyond minimizing the two corresponding objectives in isolation and examined them simultaneously. We proved that both models—and hence their shared Pareto front—are convex and used this result to analyze the performance-energy tradeoffs for the FTI multilevel checkpoint library on BG/Q. We ran a well-known molecular dynamics application (LAMMPS) over 32,000 ranks as well as other CORAL applications and performed detailed power measurements on them. The empirical results and analysis showed that the relative energy overhead due to the adoption of FTI is small on the studied applications and thus the tradeoffs between the run time and the energy consumption is not significant. This is due to the fact that the difference between power consumption during computation and multilevel checkpointing is minor. The exploratory analysis showed the existence of richer tradeoffs where the power consumption of checkpointing is significantly higher than that of the computation such a situation can be observed when using I/O-intensive and/or data-intensive checkpoint strategies.

Our future work includes analyzing power profile of different fault tolerance protocols such as full/partial replication and message logging. We plan to develop performance and energy models for replication and checkpointing in order to assess the viability of both protocols with respect to the power cap of future exascale platforms.

Acknowledgment. This work was supported by the SciDAC and X-Stack activities within the U.S. Department of Energy, Office of Science, Advanced Scientific Computing Research program under contract number DE-AC02-06CH11357.

Appendix

We first formalize our assumption on the checkpoint intervals of interest.

Assumption (A1). *We consider checkpoint intervals* $\tau \in \mathbb{R}_+^L$ *that satisfy (for* $i = 1, \ldots, L$*): (i)* $\tau_i > 0$*; (ii)* $\tau_j > \tau_i/2$ *whenever* $j > i$*; and (iii)* $\tau_i < 4/\sum_{j=1}^{i-1} \mu_j$*.*

The second condition says that the checkpoint at level j cannot be that frequent relative to checkpoints at lower levels. The third condition says that the time between checkpoints needs to be sufficiently smaller than the expected time between *any* failure at a lower level.

Theorem 1. *If (A1) holds, then the time* $\mathbb{W}$ *and energy* $\mathbb{E}$ *are convex functions of* $\tau \in \mathbb{R}^L$*.*

Proof. Following (3) and (4), the second-order derivatives of $\mathbb{W}$ are given by

$$\frac{\partial^2 \mathbb{W}}{\partial \tau_i^2} = \frac{c_i}{\tau_i^3} \left(2 + \sum_{j=i+1}^{L} \mu_j \tau_j \right)$$

$$\frac{\partial^2 \mathbb{W}}{\partial \tau_i \partial \tau_j} = -\frac{c_i \mu_j}{2\tau_i^2}, \qquad j \neq i.$$

We then have

$$\frac{\partial^2 \mathbb{W}}{\partial \tau_i^2} - \sum_{j \neq i} \left| \frac{\partial^2 \mathbb{W}}{\partial \tau_i \partial \tau_j} \right|$$
$$= \frac{c_i}{\tau_i^2} \left(\sum_{j=i+1}^{L} \mu_j \left(\frac{\tau_j}{\tau_i} - \frac{1}{2} \right) + \frac{2}{\tau_i} - \sum_{j=1}^{i-1} \frac{\mu_j}{2} \right), \tag{8}$$

which is positive by (A1). Equation (8) being positive for all i means that the Hessian $\nabla_{\tau\tau}^2 \mathbb{W}(\tau)$ is diagonally dominant, and thus $\mathbb{W}$ is a convex function of τ over the domain prescribed by (A1).

The convexity of $\mathbb{E}$ follows by a similar argument, with the derivatives of $\mathbb{E}$ given by

$$\frac{\partial^2 \mathbb{E}}{\partial \tau_i^2} = \frac{\mathcal{P}_i^c c_i}{\tau_i^3} \left(2 + \sum_{j=i+1}^{L} \mu_j \tau_j \right)$$

$$\frac{\partial^2 \mathbb{E}}{\partial \tau_i \partial \tau_j} = -\frac{\mathcal{P}_i^c c_i \mu_j}{2\tau_i^2}, \qquad j \neq i.$$

As a result, there are unique minimizers $\tau^{\mathbb{W}}$ and $\tau^{\mathbb{E}}$ over the domain prescribed by (A1).

References

1. CORAL. http://asc.llnl.gov/CORAL-benchmarks/
2. Aupy, G., Benoit, A., Hérault, T., Robert, Y., Dongarra, J.: Optimal checkpointing period: time vs. energy. In: Jarvis, S.A., Wright, S.A., Hammond, S.D. (eds.) PMBS 2013. LNCS, vol. 8551, pp. 203–214. Springer, Heidelberg (2014)
3. Balaprakash, P., Tiwari, A., Wild, S.M.: Multi objective optimization of HPC kernels for performance, power, and energy. In: Jarvis, S.A., Wright, S.A., Hammond, S.D. (eds.) PMBS 2013. LNCS, vol. 8551, pp. 239–260. Springer, Heidelberg (2014)
4. Bautista-Gomez, L., Tsuboi, S., Komatitsch, D., Cappello, F., Maruyama, N., Matsuoka, S.: FTI: high performance fault tolerance interface for hybrid systems. In: Proceedings 2011 International Conference on High Performance Computing, Networking, Storage and Analysis (SC11), pp. 32:1–32:32. ACM (2011)
5. Bouguerra, M.-S., Trystram, D., Wagner, F.: Complexity analysis of checkpoint scheduling with variable costs. IEEE Trans. Comput. 62(6), 1269–1275 (2013)
6. Daly, J.T.: A higher order estimate of the optimum checkpoint interval for restart dumps. Future Gener. Comput. Syst. 22(3), 303–312 (2006)
7. Di, S., Bouguerra, M.S., Bautista-Gomez, L., Cappello, F.: Optimization of multi-level checkpoint model for large-scale HPC applications. In: International Parallel and Distributed Processing Symposium (2014, to appear)
8. Ehrgott, M.: Multicriteria Optimization. Springer-Verlag, Heidelberg (2005)
9. el Mehdi Diouri, M., Gluck, O., Lefèvre, L., Cappello, F.: Energy considerations in checkpointing and fault tolerance protocols. In: 2012 IEEE/IFIP 42nd International Conference on Dependable Systems and Networks Workshops (DSN-W), pp. 1–6 (2012)
10. el Mehdi Diouri, M., Gluck, O., Lefevre, L., Cappello, F.: ECOFIT: A framework to estimate energy consumption of fault tolerance protocols for HPC applications. In: 13th IEEE/ACM International Symposium on Cluster, Cloud and Grid Computing (CCGrid13), pp. 522–529 (2013)
11. Hackenberg, D., Ilsche, T., Schone, R., Molka, D., Schmidt, M., Nagel, W.E.: Power measurement techniques on standard compute nodes: A quantitative comparison. In: 2013 IEEE International Symposium on Performance Analysis of Systems and Software (ISPASS13), pp. 194–204 (2013)
12. Meneses, E., Sarood, O., Kalé, L.V.: Energy profile of rollback-recovery strategies in high performance computing. Parallel Comput. 40(9), 536–547 (2014)
13. Moody, A., Bronevetsky, G., Mohror, K., de Supinski, B.R.: Design, modeling, and evaluation of a scalable multi-level checkpointing system. In: Proceedings 2010 International Conference on High Performance Computing, Networking, Storage and Analysis (SC10), pp. 1–11 (2010)
14. Plimpton, S., Crozier, P., Thompson, A.: LAMMPS: Large-scale Atomic/Molecular Massively Parallel Simulator. Sandia National Laboratories, Albuquerque (2007)
15. Shalf, J., Dosanjh, S., Morrison, J.: Exascale computing technology challenges. In: Palma, J.M.L.M., Daydé, M., Marques, O., Lopes, J.C. (eds.) VECPAR 2010. LNCS, vol. 6449, pp. 1–25. Springer, Heidelberg (2011)
16. Wallace, S., Vishwanath, V., Coghlan, S., Tramm, J., Lan, Z., Papka, M.E.: Application power profiling on IBM Blue Gene/Q. In: 2013 IEEE International Conference on Cluster Computing (CLUSTER13), pp. 1–8 (2013)

On the Energy Proportionality of Distributed NoSQL Data Stores

Balaji Subramaniam[(✉)] and Wu-chun Feng

Department of Computer Science, Virginia Tech, Blacksburg, USA
{balaji,feng}@cs.vt.edu

Abstract. The computing community is facing several *big data* challenges due to the unprecedented growth in the volume and variety of data. Many large-scale Internet companies use distributed NoSQL data stores to mitigate these challenges. These NoSQL data-store installations require massive computing infrastructure, which consume significant amount of energy and contribute to operational costs. This cost is further aggravated by the lack of energy proportionality in servers.

Therefore, in this paper, we study the energy proportionality of servers in the context of a distributed NoSQL data store, namely Apache Cassandra. Towards this goal, we measure the power consumption and performance of a Cassandra cluster. We then use *power and resource provisioning* techniques to improve the energy proportionality of the cluster and study the feasibility of achieving an energy-proportional data store. Our results show that a *hybrid (i.e., power and resource) provisioning* technique provides the best power savings — as much as 55 %.

1 Introduction

The computing community is facing a data deluge. Software developers have to deal with large volumes and variety of data (a.k.a. *big data*). NoSQL data stores, such as Cassandra [11], Bigtable [5] and DynamoDB [17], have emerged as a viable alternative to the traditional relational databases to handle *big data*. They provide fast and scalable storage with unconventional storage schemas. The entire set of data is partitioned and stored in many different servers, and a key-value store is used to respond to queries from clients. In order to meet service-level objectives (SLOs), these distributed data stores can span several hundred servers (or a cluster) to provide efficient access to huge volumes of data. For example, Netflix uses Cassandra installations that span 2500 servers and stores 300 terabytes of data.

Such cluster installations consume a significant amount of energy, and in turn, contribute to their operational costs. Moreover, the operational cost is exacerbated by the lack of energy proportionality in servers. To address these issues, *power provisioning* techniques [7,9,18,19] have been shown to improve the energy proportionality of such servers. These techniques take advantage of low utilization periods or short idle periods to assign low-power states to subsystems, such as the CPU and memory, using mechanisms such as dynamic voltage-frequency

© Springer International Publishing Switzerland 2015
S.A. Jarvis et al. (Eds.): PMBS 2014, LNCS 8966, pp. 264–274, 2015.
DOI: 10.1007/978-3-319-17248-4_14

scaling (DVFS) or Intel's running average power limit (RAPL). Other researchers have provided solutions to improve the energy proportionality by using *resource provisioning* techniques. These techniques use workload consolidation to minimize the number of servers required to sustain a desired throughput and reduce energy consumption by turning off the servers not in use [22].

With the volume of data growing at a rapid pace and the variety of data continuing to evolve and change, distributed NoSQL systems will need increasingly larger cluster installations. Improvements in the energy proportionality of such installations will need to come from both hardware- and software-controlled power management. Thus, our aim in this paper is to study the energy proportionality of clusters in the context of distributed NoSQL data stores. Specifically, we analyze the effectiveness of different software-controlled power management techniques, such as *power and resource provisioning*, to improve the energy proportionality of NoSQL data store installations. Using Cassandra as our distributed NoSQL data store, we make the following contributions:

- *A detailed study of the power consumption and energy proportionality of a Cassandra cluster, including power measurements of individual components within the cluster.* In short, we find that the idle power consumption is very high in such distributed NoSQL installations and that the CPU contributes most to the dynamic power range of the cluster.
- *An investigation into the effects of different power management techniques on the energy proportionality of a Cassandra cluster.* Our results show that significant power savings (upto 55 %), and in turn, improvements in energy proportionality can be achieved at low load-levels by taking advantage of the difference between measured latency and SLO. We also find that a hybrid (i.e., power and resource) provisioning technique provides the best power savings, closely followed by resource provisioning.

The rest of the paper is structured as follows. A brief overview of the workload generator, Cassandra, the power management interface and the experimental setup is described in Sect. 2. We present the baseline power and performance measurements in Sect. 3. The trade-offs between latency, power savings and energy proportionality using different power management techniques is described in Sect. 4. A discussion of the related work is presented in Sect. 5. Section 6 concludes the paper.

2 Background

In this section, we present the following background information to provide context for our work: (1) the workload generator, (2) the distributed NoSQL data store, (3) the power management interface and (4) the experimental set-up.

2.1 Workload Generator: YCSB

To generate the workload for our experiments, we use the Yahoo! Cloud Serving Benchmark (YCSB) [3]. YCSB is a benchmarking framework to evaluate the performance of cloud data-serving systems. The framework consists of a load-generating client and a set of standard workloads, such as read-heavy or write-heavy workloads, which helps in stressing important performance aspects of a data-serving system. YCSB also allows the user to configure benchmarking parameters such as number of client threads and the number of record counts.

2.2 NoSQL Data Store: Apache Cassandra

We use Cassandra [1, 11] as our distributed NoSQL data store. Cassandra aims to manage large amounts of data distributed across many commodity servers. It provides a reliable, high-availability service using a peer-to-peer architecture. The data is split across each node in the cluster using consistent hashing. Specifically, a random value within the range of the hash-function output is assigned to each node in the system and represents its position in the ring. Each data item identified by a key is assigned to a node by hashing the data item's key to yield its position on the ring and then walking the ring clockwise to find the first node with a position larger than the item's position.

To improve availability, each data item can be replicated at N different hosts, where N is the replication factor. Cassandra uses a gossip protocol to locally determine whether any other nodes in the cluster have failed. A Cassandra cluster can be provisioned with extra resources easily by providing the newly added node with information about the *seed* node (initial contact points) in the already existing cluster. All of the above features make Cassandra not only tolerant against single points of failure but also scalable. To evaluate Cassandra, we use the aforementioned YCSB workload generator.

2.3 Power Management Interface

To study energy proportionality in the context of a distributed NoSQL data store, namely Cassandra, we use Intel's Running Average Power Limit (RAPL) [2, 6] interfaces for power management. RAPL, which debuted in Intel Sandy Bridge processors, provides interfaces to mechanisms that can measure the energy consumption of specific subsystems and enforce power consumption limits on them. The RAPL interfaces can be programmed using the model-specific registers (MSRs).

2.4 Experimental Setup

With respect to hardware, we use a four-node cluster as our evaluation testbed. Each node consists of an Intel Xeon E5-2620 processor, 16 GB of memory, and a 256-GB hard disk. A separate server runs the YCSB client, which sends data serving requests to the Cassandra cluster.

For configuration, we load 10-million records into the data store with a replication of three so that the Cassandra cluster can sustain multiple node failures. For the workloads, we evaluate with a read-only workload and an update-only workload. The requests follow a Zipfian distribution.

For data collection, the YCSB client reports the performance achieved in terms of throughput and latency, specifically average latency and latencies at the 95th and 99th percentile. To collect power numbers, a *Watts Up* power meter recorded full-system power measurements while the RAPL interfaces collected subsystem-level power measurements.

3   Baseline Measurements for Power and Latency

Here we measure the performance and corresponding power consumption of the Cassandra cluster. The goals are two-fold: (1) to improve our understanding of the relationship between power and performance for a distributed NoSQL data store and (2) to identify any potential for power savings.

Figure 1 shows the power distribution for the read-only workload and the update-only workload across the entire cluster. The values reported in Fig. 1 are based on the sum of the power consumption from each node in the cluster and averaged over multiple runs. System components other than the processor and memory are represented as *"Others"*[1] in legend of the figure.

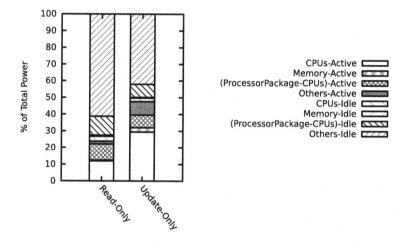

Fig. 1. Component-level power distribution.

The other components of the system consumed a significant portion of the power when idling (i.e., 61 % and 42 % of the total power for the read-only and update-only workloads, respectively). However, they only add 2 % and 8 % more to the power consumption when the system is under load for the two work-load cases, respectively. In contrast, the processor package adds another 22 % and 37 % to the power consumption distribution for the workloads under evaluation. This shows that the processor contributes significantly to the dynamic

---

[1] The other components, denoted by "Others," also include the power consumption of the hard disk.

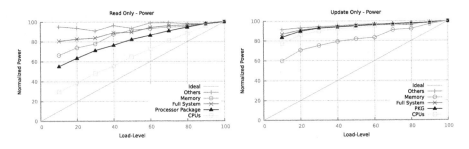

Fig. 2. Energy proportionality

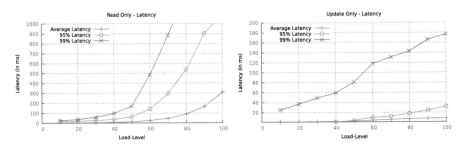

Fig. 3. Latency profile

power range of the cluster under test. The plot shows only the distribution of power consumption at the highest load on the system (i.e., 100 % load-level). However, we are also interested in analyzing the energy proportionality (i.e., the power consumption at different load-levels) of the system, which leads us to Fig. 2.

Figure 2 shows the normalized power consumed by the system at different load-levels. We normalize power relative to the power consumed at 100 % load-level by that component. For example, each value in the CPU power trend is normalized to the power consumed by the CPU at 100 % load-level. We also show the ideal energy proportional case for comparison purposes. Several insights can be gleaned from these figures. As evident from the figure, the system exhibits poor energy proportionality for both the workloads as it varies between 80 % and 100 % of normalized power. The read-only workload, however, exhibits better energy proportionality on the cluster than the update-only workload. For example, the CPUs have a linear increase in power consumption and varies between 30 % and 100 % for the read-only workload. However, the power consumption of the CPU varies only between 75 % and 100 % for the update-only workload even though the CPUs consume a higher percentage of the overall power, as shown in Fig. 1. Later in this paper, we analyze whether existing power-management techniques can help to improve the energy proportionality of the cluster system.

Figure 3 shows the latency profile for the two workloads. We present the average latency as well as the latencies at the 95th and 99th percentile at different load-levels for each workload. The performance targets (or SLOs) are typically based on either the 95th or 99th percentile rather than by the average. These SLOs are fixed at a particular value by the service provider and do not depend on the load-level of the system. SLOs provide us with the opportunity to trade latency for power under certain load-levels.

If the cluster achieves lower latencies at low load-levels, power-management techniques can be used to improve the efficiency of the cluster by provisioning power or provisioning server resources. For example, if the SLO is set as 160 ms on the 99th-percentile latency for the update-only workload, there exists headroom between the measured latency and the SLO for any load-level less than 90 %. We can use this headroom to improve the power consumption of the cluster, thus improving energy proportionality. In rest of the paper, we examine this power versus latency trade-off using different power-management techniques.

4 Evaluation of Power-Management Techniques for NoSQL Data Store

In this section, we evaluate the effect of different power-management techniques on the power consumption and energy proportionality of the Cassandra cluster. In this paper, we evaluate three different techniques: *power, resource, and hybrid (i.e., power and resource) provisioning*. The power-management techniques are applied while meeting the SLOs. Two different SLOs on latency, one on the 95th percentile and the other on the 99th percentile, are evaluated for each of the workload. For the read-only workload, we fix the SLOs at 600 ms for the 95th-percentile latency and 1000 ms for the 99th-percentile latency. For the update-only workload, the SLOs are fixed at 2 ms for the 95th-percentile latency and 160 ms for the 99th-percentile latency.

For power provisioning, we use the power-limiting interface of RAPL. RAPL maintains an average power limit over a sliding window instead of enforcing strict limits on the instantaneous power. The advantage of having an average power limit is that if the average performance requirement is within the specified power limits, the workload will not incur any performance degradation even if the performance requirement surpasses the power limit over short bursts of time. (The user has to provide a power bound and a time window in which the limit has to be maintained.)

In this paper, we use only CPU power limiting as we have shown that it contributes most to the dynamic power range of the system (see Fig. 1). We run the workload at a particular load-level and manually change the CPU power limit in order to find the best power limit for the CPU which satisfies the SLOs. The evaluation of resource provisioning is done by manually hibernating nodes in the cluster. Hibernating nodes saves approximately 40 watts per node. We manually find the optimal number of nodes to run Cassandra to satisfy SLOs at a given load-level. We also evaluate a hybrid version of power and resource provisioning. First, we run the workload on the optimal number of nodes and then find the best possible CPU power limit on those nodes that satisfy the SLOs.

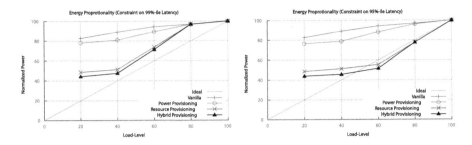

Fig. 4. Read only workload - full system energy proportionality

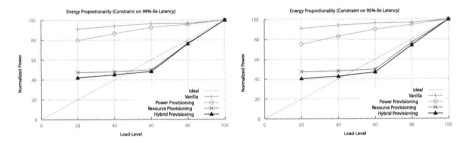

Fig. 5. Update only workload - full system energy proportionality

4.1   Energy Proportionality

Our main goal in this section is to understand the effects of the different power-management techniques on the energy proportionality of the system. Figures 4 and 5 show the effects of different power-management techniques on the energy proportionality of the read-only and update-only workloads, respectively, under different SLO targets. Energy proportionality is improved in every case.

Power provisioning is the least effective technique. However, it still saves power even at low load-levels. Resource provisioning and hybrid provisioning achieve better than energy-proportional operation at certain load-levels for both the workloads. Resource provisioning in certain cases provides higher energy-proportionality improvements when the SLO target is relaxed. For example at 80 % load-level in the read-only workload case, better energy proportionality is achieved when the SLO is changed from the 99th percentile to the 95th. In this case, we achieve better energy proportionality because the 95th-percentile SLO can be maintained with only three nodes when compared to the four nodes used for satisfying the SLO for the 99th percentile.

We quantify energy proportionality using the energy-proportionality (EP) metric [15]. The EP metric is calculated, as shown in Eq. (1), where $Area_{System}$ and $Area_{Ideal}$ represent the area under the system and ideal power curve, respectively. A value of 1 for the metric represents an ideal energy-proportional system. A value of 0 represents a system that consumes a constant amount of power irrespective of the load-level. A value greater than 1 represents a system which is better than energy proportional.

$$EP = 1 - \frac{Area_{System} - Area_{Ideal}}{Area_{Ideal}} \tag{1}$$

Figure 6 shows the EP metric for the power-management techniques under different SLOs. In general, the power management techniques under evaluation improve the energy proportionality of the update-only workload better than the read-only workload. In certain cases for the update-only workload, EP > 1 is achieved.

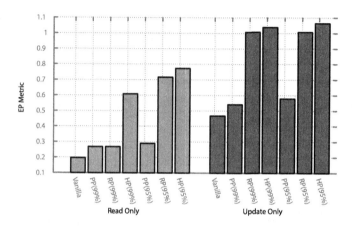

Fig. 6. EP Metric (PP = Power Provisioning, RP = Resource Provisioning, HP = Hybrid Provisoning)

4.2 Power Savings

Figure 7 shows the power savings resulting from the different power-management techniques. The savings range from 5 % to 45 % for the read-only workload and 15 % to 55 % for the update-only workload. In each case, hybrid provisioning provides the most power savings, but it is only marginal power savings over resource provisioning. We also observe that if the same number of nodes are used, relaxing the SLO target only provides marginal power savings. For example, power savings in the case of power provisioning under both the SLOs for the workloads provide similar power savings.

5   Related Work

Dimitris et al. [20] provide a comprehensive study of component-level power consumption of relational databases on a single node. They analyze the energy efficiency of database servers using different hardware and software knobs such

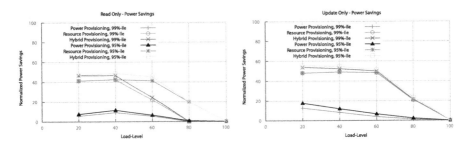

Fig. 7. Power savings

as CPU frequency, scheduling policy and inter-query parallelism. They conclude that the most energy-efficient operating point is also the highest performing configuration. Willis et al. [12] study the trade-offs between performance scalability and energy efficiency for relational databases. They identify hardware and software bottlenecks that affect performance scalability and energy efficiency. In addition, they provide guidelines for energy-efficient cluster design in the context of parallel database software. Our research complements theirs by addressing with the energy proportionality of non-relational (a.k.a. NoSQL) databases.

In our previous work [18,19], we studied the effects of RAPL power limiting on the performance, energy proportionality and energy efficiency of enterprise applications. We also designed a runtime system to decrease the energy proportionality gap. To design this runtime system, we used a load-detection model and optimization framework that uses statistical models for capturing the performance of an application under power limit. Wong et al. [21,22] provide an infrastructure for improving the energy proportionality using server-level heterogeneity. They combine a high-power compute node with a low-power processor essentially creating two different power-performance operation regions. They save power by redirecting requests to the low-power processor at low request rates thereby improving energy proportionality. In addition, they compare cluster-level packing techniques (resource provisioning) and server-level low power modes to identify if one of these technique is better with current generation of processors. Fan et al. [10] study the improvements to peak power consumption of a group of servers due to the improvements in non-peak power efficiency using their power model. They provide analytical evidence that shows energy-proportional systems will enable improved power capping at the data-center level. In this paper, we complement the existing literature by studying the effects of power and resource provisioning on the energy proportionality of a NoSQL cluster installation. Our paper is also the first step towards a runtime system for power management of such installations.

Deng et al. [7–9] propose the CoScale framework, which dynamically adapts the frequency of the CPU and memory while respecting a certain application performance degradation target. They also take per-core frequency settings into account. Li et al. [13] study the CPU microarchitectural adaptation and memory low-power states to reduce energy consumption of applications bounding the performance loss by using a slack allocation algorithm. Sarood et al. [16] present an interpolation scheme to optimally allocate power for CPU and memory subsystems in an over-provisioned high-performance computing cluster for scientific workloads. This paper deals with improving energy efficiency of the compute nodes across different levels of utilization (and not just at the peak utilization levels) as data centers running even well-tuned applications spend a significant fraction of their time below peak utilization levels [4, 10, 14].

6 Conclusion

In this paper, we analyze the power distribution and energy proportionality of a distributed NoSQL data store. We find that the idle power in such an installation is significant, and most of the power is consumed by the CPUs when the system is under load. We apply different power-management techniques to the cluster supporting the distributed NoSQL data store in order to investigate whether we can trade latency for power at low utilization of the cluster by taking advantage of the difference between the measured latency and SLO. Our results show that our hybrid-provisioning technique delivers the most power savings (upto 55 %), followed by resource provisioning.

References

1. Apache Cassandra. http://cassandra.apache.org/
2. Intel 64 and IA-32 Software Developer Manuals - Volume 3. www.intel.com/content/www/us/en/processors/architectures-software-developer-manuals.html
3. Yahoo Cloud Serving Benchmark (YCSB). https://github.com/brianfrankcooper/YCSB/wiki
4. Barroso, L.A., Hölzle, U.: The case for energy-proportional computing. IEEE Comput. **40**(12), 33–37 (2007)
5. Chang, F., Dean, J., Ghemawat, S., Hsieh, W.C., Wallach, D.A., Burrows, M., Chandra, T., Fikes, A., Fikes, R.E.: A distributed storage system for structured data. ACM Trans. Comput. Syst. **26**(2), 26 (2008)
6. David, H., Gorbatov, E., Hanebutte, U.R., Khanna, R., Le, C.: RAPL: memory power estimation and capping. In: International Symposium on Low Power Electronics and Design, ISLPED (2010)
7. Deng, Q., Meisner, D., Bhattacharjee, A., Wenisch, T.F., Bianchini, R.: CoScale: coordinating CPU and memory system DVFS in server systems. In: International Symposium on Microarchitecture, MICRO (2012)
8. Deng, Q., Meisner, D., Bhattacharjee, A., Wenisch, T.F., Bianchini, R.: Multiscale: memory system DVFS with multiple memory controllers. In: International Symposium on Low Power Electronics and Design, ISLPED (2012)
9. Deng, Q., Meisner, D., Ramos, L., Wenisch, T. F., Bianchini, R.: Memscale: Active low-power modes for main memory (2011)
10. Fan, X., Weber, W.-D., Barroso, L.A.: Power provisioning for a warehouse-sized computer. In: International Symposium on Computer Architecture, ISCA (2007)
11. Lakshman, A., Malik, P.: Cassandra: a decentralized structured storage system. SIGOPS Operating Syst. Rev. **44**(2), 35–40 (2010)

12. Lang, W., Harizopoulos, S., Patel, J.M., Shah, M.A., Tsirogiannis, D.: Towards energy-efficient database cluster design. arXiv:1208.1933 [cs], August 2012

13. Li, X., Gupta, R., Adve, S.V., Zhou, Y.: Cross-component energy management: joint adaptation of processor and memory. ACM Trans. Archit. Code Optim. **4**(3), 14 (2007)

14. Mars, J., Tang, L., Hundt, R., Skadron, K., Soffa, M.L.: Bubble-up: increasing utilization in modern warehouse scale computers via sensible co-locations. In: International Symposium on Microarchitecture, MICRO (2011)

15. Ryckbosch, F., Polfliet, S., Eeckhout, L.: Trends in server energy proportionality. IEEE Comput. **9**, 69–72 (2011)

16. Sarood, O., Langer, A., Kale, L., Rountree, B., Supinski, B.: Optimizing power allocation to CPU and memory subsystems in overprovisioned HPC systems. In: Proceedings of IEEE Cluster (2013)

17. Sivasubramanian, S.: Amazon dynamoDB: a seamlessly scalable non-relational database service. In: Proceedings of the International Conference on Management of Data, SIGMOD (2012)

18. Subramaniam, B., Feng, W.: Towards energy-proportional computing for enterprise-class server workloads. In: Proceedings of the International Conference on Performance Engineering, ICPE (2013)

19. Subramaniam, B., Feng, W.: Enabling efficient power provisioning for enterprise applications. In: Proceedings of the International Symposium on Cluster, Cloud and Grid Computing, CCGRID (2014)

20. Tsirogiannis, D., Harizopoulos, S., Shah, M.A.: Analyzing the energy efficiency of a database server. In: Proceedings of the International Conference on Management of Data, SIGMOD 2010 (2010)

21. Wong, D., Annavaram, M.: KnightShift: scaling the energy proportionality wall through server-level heterogeneity. In: Proceedings of the International Symposium on Microarchitecture, MICRO (2012)

22. Wong, D., Annavaram, M.: Implications of high energy proportional servers on cluster-wide energy proportionality. In: Proceedings of the International Symposium on High Performance Computer Architecture, HPCA (2014)

Author Index

Printed in the United States
By Bookmasters